JOSHUA

Brazos Theological Commentary on the Bible

JOSHUA

PAUL R. HINLICKY

BrazosPress

a division of Baker Publishing Group
Grand Rapids, Michigan

Published by Brazos Press
a division of Baker Publishing Group
PO Box 6287, Grand Rapids, MI 49516-6287
www.brazospress.com

Printed in the United States of America

Library of Congress Cataloging-in-Publication Control Number: 2020053958

ISBN 978-1-58743-345-0

Unless otherwise indicated, Scripture quotations are from the New Revised Standard Version of the Bible, copyright © 1989 National Council of the Churches of Christ in the United States of America. Used by permission. All rights reserved.

Scripture quotations labeled AT are the author's own translation.

Quotations from L. Daniel Hawk, *Joshua*, Berit Olam (Collegeville, MN: Liturgical Press, 2000), appear courtesy of the publisher. Copyright 2000 by Order of Saint Benedict. Published by Liturgical Press, Collegeville, Minnesota. Used with permission.

21   22   23   24   25   26   27   7   6   5   4   3   2   1

To all my former students,
both in Slovakia and at Roanoke College,
who answered the call to minister
the word and sacraments of Christ

CONTENTS

Acknowledgments ix
Series Preface xi
Abbreviations xix

Introduction 1
Preliminary Considerations 5

Part 1 YHWH Usurps the Usurpers of the Earth (Joshua 1–12)

YHWH Commissions Joshua to Succeed Moses (1:1–9) 53
Preparations for the Battle of the Kingdom of YHWH (1:10–18) 60
Rahab, Confessing YHWH, Tricks Her King, Saving Joshua's Spies and
 Her Own Family (2:1–24) 64
Israel Passes Over the Jordan and Memorializes the Event (3:1–4:24) 76
Joshua Prepares the New Generation and Is Prepared by the Prince of the
 Army of YHWH (5:1–15) 91
The War Procession of the Throne of YHWH (6:1–27) 102
Achan Covets (7:1–26) 120
Ḥerem Consumes Ai and Its King (8:1–29) 134
Covenant Renewal in the Promised Land (8:30–35) 144
The Paradox of the Gibeonites (9:1–27) 149
The Messianic Paradox (10:1–15) 158
The Campaign against the Southern Kings (10:16–43) 166
The Alliance of the Northern Kings against Israel and Their Defeat
 (11:1–15) 172
The Hardening of the Hearts of the Canaanite Kings (11:16–20) 179
Defeat of the Anakim and the End of Battle (11:21–23) 182
The End of Canaanite Sovereignty (12:1–24) 183

Part 2 To Inherit the Earth (Joshua 13–21)

Unconquered Canaan (13:1–7)   191
The Transjordan (13:8–33)   196
The Cisjordan (14:1–5)   199
The Kenite's Inheritance (14:6–15)   202
The Territory of Judah and Its Satellites (15:1–17:18)   204
Casting Lots at Shiloh for the Seven Remaining Tribes (18:1–19:51)   215
Sanctuary (20:1–9)   223
Cities Assigned to the Levites (21:1–42)   229
Conclusion to Israel's Initial Land Reform (21:43–45)   232

Part 3 An Inconclusive Conclusion (Joshua 22–24)

The True Unity of the Israel of God (22:1–34)   237
The Aged Joshua Bids Israel Farewell, Not Once but Twice
    (23:1–24:33)   250

Epilogue   273
Scripture Index   286
Author Index   290
Subject Index   293

ACKNOWLEDGMENTS

This book has been more than five years in the making. I was excited when I received the assignment because I had long wanted to test my life's work in systematic theology (which I prefer to call "critical dogmatics") with a sustained exercise in biblical exegesis and theological commentary. Moreover, I have had an abiding theological interest in reaping a harvest from the postwar Jewish-Christian dialogue and the reassessment in Christian theology of traditional anti-Judaism. This interest began under the sponsorship of the late Richard John Neuhaus, who invited me to consultations he organized with Jewish theologians including David Novak, Peter Ochs, Leon Klenicki, and, on one memorable occasion, Michael Wyschogrod. Thus, I undertook the book of Joshua as a fitting challenge—this particularly *problematic* book of the Bible. In historical fact, the problem of Joshua was already felt in the Greek translation of the Hebrew known as the Septuagint, and the problem became acute in face of the objections to its violence in gnostic circles, both Jewish and Christian. But the problem of the book of Joshua has become inescapable for us today after the twentieth century's barbaric descent into "total" war—a paradigm of utter destruction, divinely sanctioned no less, on display in the book of Joshua.

Full of enthusiasm, I plunged in. After a year or more of intensive research in the literature on Joshua, however, I was unexpectedly felled by a stroke. A steady but slow recovery further delayed the work until this past year when I was finally able to concentrate fully on the composition of the commentary. In hindsight, I am glad about the delay because the long simmering of the multiple ingredients composing Joshua has made for a more savory stew—at least to the taste of the chef. Taste for yourselves and see!

I am grateful to Ellen, my wife of forty-six years, who has cheerfully and faithfully supported me in this challenging time, and also to our son, Will, who has likewise taken up many tasks on our St. Gall Farm in the mountains of Virginia—farmer tasks, which my stroke-injured left hand can no longer perform. To any others suffering with such a disability, I would like to mention here that this entire book has been composed through voice recognition technology. When I lost the ability to type, I feared for the future of my work as an author. But this technology has wonderfully provided the means to continue, and I heartily recommend it to others who need this kind of help.

I am also indebted to a number of theological friends and colleagues who have read all or part of this work in its various stages and provided feedback. Initially, biblical scholars Dr. Wesley Hill and Dr. Kathryn Schifferdecker commented on the chapter below called "Preliminary Considerations," which works out the interpretive framework for the commentary that follows. When the full commentary was drafted, I greatly benefited from the scholarly feedback provided by literary critic Dr. Fritz Oehlschlaeger and from the Rev. Dr. Dave Delaney, Hebraist, colleague, pastor, and adjunct faculty at Roanoke College. For this project I also sought out readers who are working pastors. I am thus most happily indebted for reactions and reflections to the Rev. Gregory Fryer, who scrupulously proofread; the Rev. David C. Drebes, my pastor, who read the text as a journalist demanding clarity; and the Rev. Canon Natalie L. G. Hall, who deeply engaged the draft. Hall brought to bear her own multiple identities as child of a Jewish mother and a Lutheran father, and an ordained Lutheran serving an Episcopal diocese, offering numerous comments and suggestions and in the process saving the author from many a cultural faux pas. Both Drebes and Hall are Roanoke College alums, thus former students who have matured to become contemporary colleagues in ordained ministry. Finally, thanks are owed to my partner in podcast adventures (see our tongue-in-cheek-titled *Queen of the Sciences*), the Rev. Dr. Sarah Hinlicky Wilson. Sarah, who is a pastor of Tokyo Lutheran Church in Japan (and this author's daughter), also provided rich reflection on the draft of the commentary, for which among many other things I am deeply grateful. The book everywhere reflects the criticism and appreciation provided by these readers, and the faults that remain are solely the author's. *Soli Deo gloria!*

Paul R. Hinlicky

Easter 2020

SERIES PREFACE

Near the beginning of his treatise against gnostic interpretations of the Bible, *Against Heresies*, Irenaeus observes that scripture is like a great mosaic depicting a handsome king. It is as if we were owners of a villa in Gaul who had ordered a mosaic from Rome. It arrives, and the beautifully colored tiles need to be taken out of their packaging and put into proper order according to the plan of the artist. The difficulty, of course, is that scripture provides us with the individual pieces, but the order and sequence of various elements are not obvious. The Bible does not come with instructions that would allow interpreters to simply place verses, episodes, images, and parables in order as a worker might follow a schematic drawing in assembling the pieces to depict the handsome king. The mosaic must be puzzled out. This is precisely the work of scriptural interpretation.

Origen has his own image to express the difficulty of working out the proper approach to reading the Bible. When preparing to offer a commentary on the Psalms he tells of a tradition handed down to him by his Hebrew teacher:

> The Hebrew said that the whole divinely inspired scripture may be likened, because of its obscurity, to many locked rooms in our house. By each room is placed a key, but not the one that corresponds to it, so that the keys are scattered about beside the rooms, none of them matching the room by which it is placed. It is a difficult task to find the keys and match them to the rooms that they can open. We therefore know the scriptures that are obscure only by taking the points of departure for understanding them from another place because they have their interpretive principle scattered among them.[1]

---

1. Fragment from the preface to *Commentary on Psalms 1–25*, preserved in the *Philokalia*, in *Origen*, trans. Joseph W. Trigg (London: Routledge, 1998), 70–71.

As is the case for Irenaeus, scriptural interpretation is not purely local. The key in Genesis may best fit the door of Isaiah, which in turn opens up the meaning of Matthew. The mosaic must be put together with an eye toward the overall plan.

Irenaeus, Origen, and the great cloud of premodern biblical interpreters assumed that puzzling out the mosaic of scripture must be a communal project. The Bible is vast, heterogeneous, full of confusing passages and obscure words, and difficult to understand. Only a fool would imagine that he or she could work out solutions alone. The way forward must rely upon a tradition of reading that Irenaeus reports has been passed on as the rule or canon of truth that functions as a confession of faith. "Anyone," he says, "who keeps unchangeable in himself the rule of truth received through baptism will recognize the names and sayings and parables of the scriptures."[2] Modern scholars debate the content of the rule on which Irenaeus relies and commends, not the least because the terms and formulations Irenaeus himself uses shift and slide. Nonetheless, Irenaeus assumes that there is a body of apostolic doctrine sustained by a tradition of teaching in the church. This doctrine provides the clarifying principles that guide exegetical judgment toward a coherent overall reading of scripture as a unified witness. Doctrine, then, is the schematic drawing that will allow the reader to organize the vast heterogeneity of the words, images, and stories of the Bible into a readable, coherent whole. It is the rule that guides us toward the proper matching of keys to doors.

If self-consciousness about the role of history in shaping human consciousness makes modern historical-critical study actually critical, then what makes modern study of the Bible actually modern is the consensus that classical Christian doctrine distorts interpretive understanding. Benjamin Jowett, the influential nineteenth-century English classical scholar, is representative. In his programmatic essay "On the Interpretation of Scripture," he exhorts the biblical reader to disengage from doctrine and break its hold over the interpretive imagination. "The simple words of that book," writes Jowett of the modern reader, "he tries to preserve absolutely pure from the refinements or distinctions of later times." The modern interpreter wishes to "clear away the remains of dogmas, systems, controversies, which are encrusted upon" the words of scripture. The disciplines of close philological analysis "would enable us to separate the elements of doctrine and tradition with which the meaning of scripture is encumbered in our own

2. *Against Heresies* 9.4.

day."[3] The lens of understanding must be wiped clear of the hazy and distorting film of doctrine.

Postmodernity, in turn, has encouraged us to criticize the critics. Jowett imagined that when he wiped away doctrine he would encounter the biblical text in its purity and uncover what he called "the original spirit and intention of the authors."[4] We are not now so sanguine, and the postmodern mind thinks interpretive frameworks inevitable. Nonetheless, we tend to remain modern in at least one sense. We read Athanasius and think of him stage-managing the diversity of scripture to support his positions against the Arians. We read Bernard of Clairvaux and assume that his monastic ideals structure his reading of the Song of Songs. In the wake of the Reformation, we can see how the doctrinal divisions of the time shaped biblical interpretation. Luther famously described the Epistle of James as an "epistle of straw," for, as he said, "it has nothing of the nature of the gospel about it."[5] In these and many other instances, often written in the heat of ecclesiastical controversy or out of the passion of ascetic commitment, we tend to think Jowett correct: doctrine is a distorting film on the lens of understanding.

However, is what we commonly think actually the case? Are readers naturally perceptive? Do we have an unblemished, reliable aptitude for the divine? Have we no need for disciplines of vision? Do our attention and judgment need to be trained, especially as we seek to read scripture as the living word of God? According to Augustine, we all struggle to journey toward God, who is our rest and peace. Yet our vision is darkened and the fetters of worldly habit corrupt our judgment. We need training and instruction in order to cleanse our minds so that we might find our way toward God.[6] To this end, "the whole temporal dispensation was made by divine Providence for our salvation."[7] The covenant with Israel, the coming of Christ, the gathering of the nations into the church—all these things are gathered up into the rule of faith, and they guide the vision and form of the soul toward the end of fellowship with God. In Augustine's view, the reading of scripture both contributes to and benefits from this divine pedagogy. With countless variations in both exegetical conclusions and theological frameworks, the same pedagogy of a doctrinally ruled reading of scripture characterizes the

---

3. Benjamin Jowett, "On the Interpretation of Scripture," in *Essays and Reviews* (London: Parker, 1860), 338–39.

4. Jowett, "On the Interpretation of Scripture," 340.

5. *Luther's Works*, vol. 35, ed. E. Theodore Bachmann (Philadelphia: Fortress, 1959), 362.

6. *On Christian Doctrine* 1.10.

7. *On Christian Doctrine* 1.35.

broad sweep of the Christian tradition from Gregory the Great through Bernard and Bonaventure, continuing across Reformation differences in both John Calvin and Cornelius à Lapide, Patrick Henry and Bishop Bossuet, and on to more recent figures such as Karl Barth and Hans Urs von Balthasar.

Is doctrine, then, not a moldering scrim of antique prejudice obscuring the Bible, but instead a clarifying agent, an enduring tradition of theological judgments that amplifies the living voice of scripture? And what of the scholarly dispassion advocated by Jowett? Is a noncommitted reading—an interpretation unprejudiced—the way toward objectivity, or does it simply invite the languid intellectual apathy that stands aside to make room for the false truism and easy answers of the age?

This series of biblical commentaries was born out of the conviction that dogma clarifies rather than obscures. The Brazos Theological Commentary on the Bible advances upon the assumption that the Nicene tradition, in all its diversity and controversy, provides the proper basis for the interpretation of the Bible as Christian scripture. God the Father Almighty, who sends his only begotten Son to die for us and for our salvation and who raises the crucified Son in the power of the Holy Spirit so that the baptized may be joined in one body—faith in *this* God with *this* vocation of love for the world is the lens through which to view the heterogeneity and particularity of the biblical texts. Doctrine, then, is not a moldering scrim of antique prejudice obscuring the meaning of the Bible. It is a crucial aspect of the divine pedagogy, a clarifying agent for our minds fogged by self-deceptions, a challenge to our languid intellectual apathy that will too often rest in false truisms and the easy spiritual nostrums of the present age rather than search more deeply and widely for the dispersed keys to the many doors of scripture.

For this reason, the commentators in this series have not been chosen because of their historical or philological expertise. In the main, they are not biblical scholars in the conventional, modern sense of the term. Instead, the commentators were chosen because of their knowledge of and expertise in using the Christian doctrinal tradition. They are qualified by virtue of the doctrinal formation of their mental habits, for it is the conceit of this series of biblical commentaries that theological training in the Nicene tradition prepares one for biblical interpretation, and thus it is to theologians and not biblical scholars that we have turned. "War is too important," it has been said, "to leave to the generals."

We do hope, however, that readers do not draw the wrong impression. The Nicene tradition does not provide a set formula for the solution of exegetical problems. The great tradition of Christian doctrine was not transcribed, bound in folio, and issued in an official, critical edition. We have the Niceno-Constantinopolitan Creed, used for centuries in many traditions of Christian worship. We have ancient baptismal affirmations of faith. The Chalcedonian Definition and the creeds and canons of other church councils have their places in official church documents. Yet the rule of faith cannot be limited to a specific set of words, sentences, and creeds. It is instead a pervasive habit of thought, the animating culture of the church in its intellectual aspect. As Augustine observed, commenting on Jeremiah 31:33, "The creed is learned by listening; it is written, not on stone tablets nor on any material, but on the heart."[8] This is why Irenaeus is able to appeal to the rule of faith more than a century before the first ecumenical council, and this is why we need not itemize the contents of the Nicene tradition in order to appeal to its potency and role in the work of interpretation.

Because doctrine is intrinsically fluid on the margins and most powerful as a habit of mind rather than a list of propositions, this commentary series cannot settle difficult questions of method and content at the outset. The editors of the series impose no particular method of doctrinal interpretation. We cannot say in advance how doctrine helps the Christian reader assemble the mosaic of scripture. We have no clear answer to the question of whether exegesis guided by doctrine is antithetical to or compatible with the now-old modern methods of historical-critical inquiry. Truth—historical, mathematical, or doctrinal—knows no contradiction. But method is a discipline of vision and judgment, and we cannot know in advance what aspects of historical-critical inquiry are functions of modernism that shape the soul to be at odds with Christian discipline. Still further, the editors do not hold the commentators to any particular hermeneutical theory that specifies how to define the plain sense of scripture—or the role this plain sense should play in interpretation. Here the commentary series is tentative and exploratory.

Can we proceed in any other way? European and North American intellectual culture has been de-Christianized. The effect has not been a cessation of Christian activity. Theological work continues. Sermons are preached. Biblical scholars produce monographs. Church leaders have meetings. But each dimension of a formerly unified Christian practice now tends to function independently. It is as if a weakened army has been fragmented, and various corps have retreated to isolated fortresses in order to survive. Theology has lost its competence in exegesis.

---

8. *Sermon* 212.2.

Scripture scholars function with minimal theological training. Each decade finds new theories of preaching to cover the nakedness of seminary training that provides theology without exegesis and exegesis without theology.

Not the least of the causes of the fragmentation of Christian intellectual practice has been the divisions of the church. Since the Reformation, the role of the rule of faith in interpretation has been obscured by polemics and counterpolemics about *sola scriptura* and the necessity of a magisterial teaching authority. The Brazos Theological Commentary on the Bible series is deliberately ecumenical in scope because the editors are convinced that early church fathers were correct: church doctrine does not compete with scripture in a limited economy of epistemic authority. We wish to encourage unashamedly dogmatic interpretation of scripture, confident that the concrete consequences of such a reading will cast far more light on the great divisive questions of the Reformation than either reengaging in old theological polemics or chasing the fantasy of a pure exegesis that will somehow adjudicate between competing theological positions. You shall know the truth of doctrine by its interpretive fruits, and therefore in hopes of contributing to the unity of the church, we have deliberately chosen a wide range of theologians whose commitment to doctrine will allow readers to see real interpretive consequences rather than the shadowboxing of theological concepts.

The Brazos Theological Commentary on the Bible endorses a textual ecumenism that parallels our diversity of ecclesial backgrounds. We do not impose the thankfully modest inclusive-language agenda of the New Revised Standard Version, nor do we insist upon the glories of the Authorized Version, nor do we require our commentators to create a new translation. In our communal worship, in our private devotions, and in our theological scholarship, we use a range of scriptural translations. Precisely as scripture—a living, functioning text in the present life of faith—the Bible is not semantically fixed. Only a modernist, literalist hermeneutic could imagine that this modest fluidity is a liability. Philological precision and stability is a consequence of, not a basis for, exegesis. Judgments about the meaning of a text fix its literal sense, not the other way around. As a result, readers should expect an eclectic use of biblical translations, both across the different volumes of the series and within individual commentaries.

We cannot speak for contemporary biblical scholars, but as theologians we know that we have long been trained to defend our fortresses of theological concepts and formulations. And we have forgotten the skills of interpretation. Like stroke victims, we must rehabilitate our exegetical imaginations, and there are likely to be different strategies of recovery. Readers should expect this reconstructive—not reactionary—series to provide them with experiments in postcritical doctrinal interpretation, not commentaries written according to the settled principles of a well-functioning tradition. Some commentators will follow classical typological and allegorical readings from the premodern tradition; others will draw on contemporary historical study. Some will comment verse by verse; others will highlight passages, even single words that trigger theological analysis of scripture. No reading strategies are proscribed, no interpretive methods foresworn. The central premise in this commentary series is that doctrine provides structure and cogency to scriptural interpretation. We trust in this premise with the hope that the Nicene tradition can guide us, however imperfectly, diversely, and haltingly, toward a reading of scripture in which the right keys open the right doors.

R. R. Reno

ABBREVIATIONS

General

LXX — Septuagint   MT — Masoretic Text

Old Testament

Gen.	Genesis	Song	Song of Songs
Exod.	Exodus	Isa.	Isaiah
Lev.	Leviticus	Jer.	Jeremiah
Num.	Numbers	Lam.	Lamentations
Deut.	Deuteronomy	Ezek.	Ezekiel
Josh.	Joshua	Dan.	Daniel
Judg.	Judges	Hos.	Hosea
Ruth	Ruth	Joel	Joel
1–2 Sam.	1–2 Samuel	Amos	Amos
1–2 Kgs.	1–2 Kings	Obad.	Obadiah
1–2 Chr.	1–2 Chronicles	Jonah	Jonah
Ezra	Ezra	Mic.	Micah
Neh.	Nehemiah	Nah.	Nahum
Esth.	Esther	Hab.	Habakkuk
Job	Job	Zeph.	Zephaniah
Ps. (Pss.)	Psalm (Psalms)	Hag.	Haggai
Prov.	Proverbs	Zech.	Zechariah
Eccl.	Ecclesiastes	Mal.	Malachi

New Testament

Matt.	Matthew	John	John
Mark	Mark	Acts	Acts
Luke	Luke	Rom.	Romans

1–2 Cor.	1–2 Corinthians	Phlm.	Philemon
Gal.	Galatians	Heb.	Hebrews
Eph.	Ephesians	Jas.	James
Phil.	Philippians	1–2 Pet.	1–2 Peter
Col.	Colossians	1–3 John	1–3 John
1–2 Thess.	1–2 Thessalonians	Jude	Jude
1–2 Tim.	1–2 Timothy	Rev.	Revelation
Titus	Titus		

INTRODUCTION

"Theological exposition takes the Bible as the book of the church and interprets it as such."[1] Bonhoeffer wrote these words about the first three chapters of the Bible in the Christian Old Testament in a commentary titled *Creation and Fall*. The commentary was actually an intervention at the time of Hitler's rise to power, when Protestant Christians in Germany had developed an acute allergy to all things Hebrew. The sources of this allergy were manifold. The combination of the "higher criticism" of the Bible (accused by some of being the "higher anti-Semitism") and the rise of evolutionary biology in the nineteenth century had discredited hitherto predominantly literal readings of Genesis. The meteoric cultural ascent of Nietzsche's "philosophy of life," with its jugular attack on Judaic morality as resentment against life and on its theology as the cunning ploy of the weak to tyrannize the strong by conjuring the picture of a vengeful deity, seemed to correlate with modern Protestant Christianity's supersession of the burdensome religion of law by a liberating religion of grace. Long-standing tropes about the church as the new Israel superseding the old Israel enabled leading intellectuals like Adolf von Harnack to defend the second-century heretic Marcion as a misunderstood genius ahead of his time, and thus to take up his cause that contemporary Christians jettison Old Testament Scripture.

In some respects, and for similar reasons, the situation today is uncomfortably similar. The Old Testament is dying.[2] Hence this commentary takes up the

---

1. Dietrich Bonhoeffer, *Creation and Fall*, Dietrich Bonhoeffer Works 3 (Minneapolis: Fortress, 2004), 22.
2. Brent A. Strawn, *The Old Testament Is Dying: A Diagnosis and Recommended Treatment* (Grand Rapids: Baker Academic, 2017).

interpretive task that Bonhoeffer then announced with the intention of making an intervention in a fraught situation. In what follows, commentary will take the form of a learned paraphrase, based on this author's own review of the Hebrew text of the book of Joshua. The paraphrase follows the canonical narrative's "causal sequence"[3]—effecting a literary reading that seeks to understand the meaning of the textual narrative on its own terms, which, as we shall see, are intrinsically theological. The procedure is similar but not identical to that of literary criticism in today's academy in that it takes the horizon of the canonical book's first readers and the intention of the final author/editor within canonical scripture as an essential key to determining "what the letters say." This determination locates the canonical book of Joshua as a part within the whole, which is the panorama of the Genesis-to-Revelation story of God's history with humanity through the particular history of Israel and a particular son of Israel, the second Joshua who is Jesus Christ.

It is important, accordingly, to see from the outset that Joshua is a promissory narrative, a history that portends a promised future. Indeed, its knowledge of God consists in the identification of the God who promises the coming of his reign. What that could mean for us today who read the book of Joshua long after its original horizon of meaning has passed away is a question that must be engaged step-by-step along the way. This engagement is possible because the creation of landed Israel once upon a time, like the biblical account of the creation of the world once upon a time, is a "promise projected backward."[4] It is this promissory character of the "historical" narrative, moreover, that sharply distinguishes the knowledge of God rendered in Joshua from any kind of so-called dominion theology. Triumphalist readings of Joshua misunderstand the book categorically, as the commentary will show.

This commentary by paraphrase will thus be interlaced with observations, questions, and connections relevant for rendering its knowledge of God. Readers are advised section by section to review in advance the text of canonical Joshua in any standard and scholarly responsible English translation. As this commentary is engaged in harvesting from the biblical book its knowledge of God for us today, it will not provide its own technical contribution to numerous exegetical difficulties but only report on, and synthesize to the extent that it is useful for its theological purpose, the excellent work of experts in this connection.

3. Robert W. Jenson, *Systematic Theology* (New York: Oxford University Press, 1999), 2:282.
4. Dietrich Bonhoeffer, *Sanctorum Communio*, Dietrich Bonhoeffer Works 1 (Minneapolis: Fortress, 2004), 61.

Sufficient reference to this specialist work of biblical scholars is provided in the notes for those readers who wish to descend into labyrinthine rabbit holes. For the literary-theological purpose of this commentary, however, overly technical discussion of such problems would be little more than a distraction. Indeed, the book of Joshua as it came to rest in the scriptural canon is problem enough to tackle, especially for a theologically focused commentary. The narrative thrust of Joshua is sufficiently clear, and it becomes abundantly clear when read literarily to draw out its (disruptive!) knowledge of God.

Readers, especially pastors and other teachers looking for help in sermon or Bible study or to answer a thorny question or even a wholesale objection raised by a parishioner, often jump to the passage in question in a commentary. It is important, however, for readers to work through the rather lengthy first chapter, "Preliminary Considerations," in order to use this commentary intelligently. To warrant the proposed literary-theological approach to Joshua executed in the commentary, this chapter must clear in advance a path through a field chock-full of difficulties.

It must first hermeneutically justify the distinction between literary and literal readings, which are ambiguously confused in the precritical ecclesiastical tradition, and then provide validity tests for the literary yield of knowledge of God. It must then identify literarily the gospel promise in Joshua as its constantly reiterated proclamation of YHWH[5] who fights for Israel, and interpret this kerygma in light of the dreadful divine command for the utter destruction of the Canaanites. Accomplishing this theological interpretation of the celebrated—or notorious—violence of the Divine Warrior, moreover, requires the registration of a protest that will run throughout the commentary against the widespread tendency in modern theology to reduce knowledge of God to religious ideology: YHWH's warfare according to the book of Joshua is not the "holy war" common in the ancient Near East nor in the literalistic and thus inept appropriations of it by Christian Crusade or Islamic Jihad or European colonialism/imperialism or today's nationalistic "dominion" theology. Rather it belongs in the genre of apocalyptic theology's deliberate resort to what I will term "the fabulous," a classification for "tales of the gods," which Augustine borrowed from the philosopher Varro.

I use this term instead of the ambiguous "myth," a word of Greek origin that simply means "story." Consequently, confused attempts to "demythologize"

5. For the use of this transliteration of the Hebrew for the divine name, the Tetragrammaton or Hashem, see the epilogue. When citing others, I will give their English rendering of the word, usually "Yahweh."

biblical narrative to render its message intelligible and existentially compelling for modern people actually end up "denarrativizing" the text with disastrous implications for the knowledge of God. "Deliteralization," by which we decode the fabulous theologically, is to be preferred. In the words of Jewish theologian Michael Wyschogrod, "when the prophet speaks of the messianic future in which the lion will lie down with the lamb (and in which both and not only one will rise) he is indeed foreseeing the transformation of nature, but this transformation is not an evolutionary but an apocalyptic one. It is a transformation that is discontinuous with nature as it has been. It envisages a break with the autonomy of nature brought about by God's intervention and not by the working itself out of the telos of nature."[6] In tandem with this apocalyptic turn in contemporary theology, a preliminary clarification of the nature of the gift of the land—inheritance as opposed to a privately traded commodity—is needed, which in turn opens up the messianic resonances attending the figure of Joshua.

With these preliminary clarifications behind us, we will be prepared to follow the narrative step-by-step to its disruptive conclusion disclosing Israel's incapacity. Following the commentary, an epilogue is provided, speaking to what the knowledge of God from the book of Joshua means for us, specifically for Jews and Christians together, today.

---

6. Michael Wyschogrod, *The Body of Faith: God in the People Israel* (Lanham, MD: Rowman & Littlefield, 1996), 227.

PRELIMINARY CONSIDERATIONS

Joshua does little to mute the triumphalism and brutality of Israel's memories of conquest or to complete piecemeal remembrances of lands and boundaries. Yet something quite profound is accomplished in the way these memories are connected and presented. The whole of Joshua conveys a very different message than the pieces within it.

—L. Daniel Hawk, *Joshua*, xxxii

Literary, Not Literal, Reading

The whole, it is said, is greater than the sum of its parts. Reading Joshua piecemeal, picking out passages as theo-political prooftexts—whether with hostile intent to demonstrate a gruesome brutality at the core of ancient Israel's exclusive faith in YHWH, a "holy and jealous God,"[1] or with political intent to support contemporary Zionist claims on the "land of Canaan"[2] once given to the twelve tribes of

1. There are many lesser representatives of contemporary polemic against Israel's monotheism as the canonical sanction for exclusivist intolerance but perhaps the most impressive comes from the pen of Karen Armstrong in her sweeping survey *Fields of Blood*. Her reading of the book of Joshua locates its genesis in the monotheistic reform of Judah's king, Josiah, who brought ancient Israel's faith to a "wholly new intransigence" when he ruthlessly uprooted the hitherto prevailing interfaith bonhomie, as it were, of polytheistic syncretism. She correlates Deut. 7 and the book of Joshua with this new and violent fanaticism. But, as we shall see, the figure of Joshua in no way anticipates King Josiah but would rather challenge it. Karen Armstrong, *Fields of Blood: Religion and the History of Violence* (New York: Knopf, 2014), 116–17.

2. Unfortunately, this judgment must be rendered against the whole, if not all the parts, of *The New Christian Zionism: Fresh Perspectives on Israel and the Land*, ed. Gerald R. McDermott (Downers Grove, IL: IVP Academic, 2016), particularly in its theological brief for contemporary Israeli land possession. In the perspective of the postexilic dispossessed, as we shall see, the longing for the land has quite literally shrunk to Zion, the worship that it houses, and the priestly service to it. Moreover, careful literary

Israel—is a fundamental *literary* mistake. In other words, both or either of these contemporary claims may be congruent with the book of Joshua—or not. But we cannot tell until we establish the literary meaning of the Joshua narrative on its own terms.

Literary meaning is a widely proposed revision today of the classical "literal sense," which in any case has always been regarded as primary and foundational to any further senses. This revision is necessary because literary meaning differs in several important ways from the now common understanding of the *literal* sense as if replicating by a verbal picture some state of past affairs and thus presenting a critically discerned fact. In contrast, a literary reading of a scriptural text receives the text as scriptural. That entails theologically an act of faith in the biblical story's final—that is, *eschatological*—coherence; in the interim, it tests this presumption by exploring how the plot integrates parts and whole and conversely how the integration of parts and whole manifests plot that, in a feedback loop, confirms at least provisionally the literary reading as referring to the coming of the reign of God and identifying it in specific ways. Scriptural narrative is not a replication by a verbal picture of the status quo ante but is "promissory narrative,"[3] anticipating a promised future of God in creative tension with the way things are. Tension, even conflict, between the parts is what makes the achievement of theological coherence *dramatic*, and "dramatic coherence"[4] is in turn characteristic of biblical narrative read theologically. Literary meaning is thus the gateway to what had been classically called the "spiritual meaning," which is discovered as the close literary reading, following the causal sequence of the words of the text (literally, "what the letters say," the traditional literal sense), yields knowledge of God. The spiritual sense is the theological meaning of the literary sense.

As Robert Jenson explains, drawing on the work of Henri de Lubac,

> Contrary to what has often been thought, therefore, spiritual exegesis does not intend to "spiritualize" its texts; the mystery supposed to be hidden in an Old

---

reading of the distribution of the land in Josh. 12–19 cannot in any way be summoned to support contemporary Israeli territorial claims; these may rather be reasoned, and if reasoned also negotiated, in terms of Christian realism (cf. the contribution by Robert Benne, 221–47). In any case, the identification of Israel through the course of the book of Joshua does not consist in possession of territory but in the covenant of this people as vassal to its Lord.

3. Christopher Morse, *The Logic of Promise in Moltmann's Theology* (Philadelphia: Fortress, 1979); Ronald Thiemann, *Revelation and Theology: The Gospel as Narrated Promise* (South Bend, IN: University of Notre Dame Press, 1987).

4. Robert W. Jenson, *The Triune Story: Collected Essays on Scripture*, ed. Brad East (New York: Oxford University Press, 2019), 151, 160, 270–77, 304–9.

Testament event or testimony "is not . . . a timeless truth. It is . . . an action, the realization of a great plan, and is therefore . . . itself a historical reality." The "letter" is the succession of events narrated by the text and the best masters of spiritual exegesis, when reading *ad litteram*, labored like any modern exegete to trace the events in their causal sequence. The "spirit" is the meaning of those events, within the gospel's whole teleological narrative.[5]

To be explicit, then, such "literary-spiritual" reading of the book of Joshua in the Christian canon is undertaken by faith in its eschatological coherence according to the gospel that tells of another Joshua, crucified and risen from the dead to triumph for us all—when and if this reading proves to be no arbitrary imposition on the book of Joshua, even though it obviously exceeds what was the historical horizon of canonical Joshua and its first audience. Yet this excess is permitted with committing the Joshua narrative to writing and receiving it among those writings of Israel that Israel and then the church following deemed sacred. In any event, as we shall see, the canonical book tells its own gospel of *YHWH who fights for Israel* such that the gospel of Jesus Christ can and did find itself anticipated in this message. Thus there is an integral relationship between the gospel of Jesus, the *Christus victor*, and the gospel told beforehand in the book of Joshua.

In order to prevent supposedly peaceful-and-universal Christian triumphalism from lording over allegedly warlike-and-particularist Jewish Joshua, the following brutal point of continuity must be stated with candor and taken thematically: "In Israel, war was one element connected with the anger or wrath of God, a theme that runs through the prophets, the psalms, apocalyptic, the Gospels, and the Pauline writings. . . . The theme is prevalent throughout Scripture."[6] One cannot sing the "feast of victory of our God," in other words, apart from identifying also the Christian God as Divine Warrior.

This pairing of Joshuas, moreover, is to be distinguished materially from, but equally paralleled formally to, the way Judaism—also *literarily-spiritually*—reads the book: "The church reads it about Christ; the pharisaic synagogue reads it about *torah*."[7] By "pharisaic" Jenson is *not* denigrating the synagogue but historically identifying the rise of early normative or rabbinic Judaism (concomitant with the rise of early catholic Christianity) whose leadership in historical fact

---

5. Robert W. Jenson, *Systematic Theology* (New York: Oxford University Press, 1999), 2:282, citing Henri de Lubac, *Exégèse Médiévale: Les Quatre Sens de l'Écriture* (Paris: Aubier, 1959–1964), 1:504.

6. Trent C. Butler, *Joshua 1–12*, 2nd ed., Word Biblical Commentary 7A (Grand Rapids: Zondervan, 2014), 181.

7. Jenson, *Systematic Theology*, 2:284.

descended from the Pharisees of Jesus's day. This statement of difference and relation, therefore, allows us to envision coexistence, in sharp distinction from supersessionism, which does not. *Supersessionism* is the term frequently used today to capture a certain feature of Christian theologies of salvation history in which Judaism has been left behind as a dead religion. To the extent that precritical "spiritual" exegesis of Old Testament scripture in Christianity was supersessionist, it is self-critically to be repudiated today as a sinful and heterodox triumphalism that confuses a once-upon-a-time political triumph of the church over defeated Judaism with the realization of the reign of God on the earth.

To illustrate, despite its many virtues, as we shall see, we read in Origen's *Homilies on Joshua* how Jesus

> came between those Jews who accepted his presence and those who did not only not accept but killed themselves more completely than him, saying, "The blood of that one be upon us and upon our sons!" . . . Therefore, these are part of the dead people because they do not properly perform either the feast of unleavened bread or the feast days. . . . They themselves of their own accord refute the true altar and the heavenly high priest and have been brought to such a point of unhappiness that they both lost the image and did not accept the truth. Therefore it is said to them, "Behold your house is left to you deserted" [Luke 13:35] for the grace of the Holy Spirit has been transferred to the nations . . . which is "the church of the living God," and where true Israel exists, in Christ Jesus our Lord.[8]

Origen's casual invocation of the "blood curse" libel from Matt. 27:25 has echoed through the centuries as fuel for anti-Judaic rabble-rousing.

What we have learned penitently in the generations since the Nazi crime against the Jews on the soil of Christian Europe is that the church's literary readings of Hebrew scripture do not supersede Jewish readings in the way that the passage from Origen projects but coexist with them as those of separated brothers and sisters, each community differently but equally awaiting the messianic fulfillment. Triumphalist Christian supersessionism, in this light, is the precipitate of a heterodox "realized eschatology," as if the messianic future were fully present and realized in the church's political triumph (which in any case today has crumbled in Euro-American post-Christendom). One strategy for resisting this still latent danger in undertaking a Christian theological commentary on

8. Origen, *Homilies on Joshua*, trans. Barbara J. Bruce, Fathers of the Church (Washington, DC: Catholic University of America Press, 2002), 219–20.

Joshua, and indeed for doing repentance for this tradition's classical anti-Judaic "teaching of contempt" that accompanied triumphalism as its arrogant shadow side, is to leaven our present endeavor in commentary with testimony of Judaism's different reading of Joshua. Happily, this may be done by resort to a significant contemporary Jewish thinker who has somewhat controversially championed within Judaism the theological reading of scripture: Michael Wyschogrod, who explicitly draws this theological differentiation between suffering Judaism and self-triumphant Christianity.[9]

Wyschogrod registers a vital correction as well against antinomian Christianity for those with ears to hear, especially salient for this commentary's attempt to execute a literary-spiritual reading of a most volatile text within the Christian Old Testament. Christian "contempt for religion of the law can with considerable justification be dismissed as another instance of false spiritualization. . . . When we remember the teaching of contempt for Judaism inherent in much of Christianity, we are entitled to refer to the foundation of this teaching as anti-Semitic."[10] We are armed in advance by this warning against "false," antinomian "spiritualization" and will see to it that this warning accompanies our commentary each step of the way. On the other hand, there is also true "spiritualization," according to Wyschogrod, which is the need for interpretation of the Torah as the word of God according to the "intention of the divine lawgiver, who is its author."[11] Such true reading of the letter according to the Spirit is necessary over against a legalistic literalism that actually gets "God out of the law by establishing the law as an autonomous domain of human interpretation and application"[12]—a criticism Wyschogrod self-critically directs against the rabbinic tradition itself.

So the literary-spiritual reading of Joshua here undertaken critically retrieves the precritical tradition's spiritual grasp of the literary text, especially of Hebrew scripture texts, for theological purposes—a tradition that, as Jenson explained, took as primary "what the letters say." By contrast, the *literal* sense is often today taken to mean the text's representation of the reality to which it refers, in the process begging the question of what reality is in view. In fact, for various reasons in modernity, it came to be widely assumed that the reality referenced by biblical narrative was "what really happened" in past time and

---

9. Michael Wyschogrod, *The Body of Faith: God in the People Israel* (Lanham, MD: Rowman & Littlefield, 1996), 81.

10. Wyschogrod, *Body of Faith*, 187.

11. Wyschogrod, *Body of Faith*, 203.

12. Wyschogrod, *Body of Faith*, 206.

space; "historical facts" were taken in turn as providing evidence for the primary authority accorded to canonical scripture in the life of the community of faith. Consequently, historical reconstruction became the task of literal interpretation in modern theology, whether apologetically to validate the authority of scripture or deconstructively to undermine it. But, as Judaism knows by bitter experience, history is not God.

Predominantly, question-begging about the text's reference and naïveté regarding the text's representations combined to subvert theological reference by putting in its place reference to so-called commonsense constructions of reality current in the reader's time and place, though not in the text's. Consequently, modern biblical literalism cannot forthrightly concede manifest tensions and blatant contradictions between the parts of biblical narrative because intellectual honesty here threatens to collapse significance as a whole, taken as representation of historical reality that validates scripture's claim to authority. Consequently, tensions and contradictions must be ingeniously but also artificially harmonized—or if not, then piously swept under the obscurantist rug of "mystery." To his credit, conservative evangelical scholar Trent C. Butler, in his well-researched two-volume commentary on Joshua, faces this dilemma when he asks, "To what degree must the biblical narrative mirror historical events for the truth quality of the narrative to be validated?" And he acknowledges poignantly that "to raise such questions risks theological consequences."[13] In reality, what has discredited the Bible as we actually have it is the long Protestant history, especially in the modern period, of defending it falsely as an inerrant deposit of revealed propositions that cannot admit of tensions or contradictions—a stance that obliterates perception of the literary-dramatic character of biblical narrative. We may claim, therefore, in postliberal vein, that facing the dissonances integral to biblical narrative is to begin theological inquiry. Such will be the procedure in this commentary.

The Specific Problems of Joshua

The task of literary-spiritual reading is urgent with respect to a text like Joshua because its primary reference is to YHWH, the living God in heaven and on earth, holy and jealous, who fights for Israel as he advances his reign into the land of Canaan. It yields this knowledge of God. But, as I wrote several years ago after an initial immersion in Joshua and the literature about it, read otherwise as

13. Butler, *Joshua 1–12*, 152–53.

ostensible historical representation, the book is beset with baffling tensions and outright contradictions:

> Genocide and dispossession in the name of the Lord. Miraculous victories in improbable warfare along with a similarly magical taboo on booty. The equivocating "devotion" of the conquered as holy sacrifice to the LORD,[14] which categorically dooms all that is conquered to annihilation yet sometimes, without explanation of the exception, permits repossession of livestock and other spoil. Obsession with matters of identity and boundaries at the expense of "the Other," alongside frank acknowledgment of failure to establish either.[15] The failure is on display in the tricksterism of the Canaanite Gibeonites and of Rahab the foreign prostitute, although Rahab tricks the Canaanite king of Jericho and the Canaanite Gibeonites trick Joshua and the Israelites. The expansive claim to the land, the overlapping distributions of territory to the twelve tribes, the conflict thereafter between tribes east and west of the Jordan over a central worship site—all of the above indicate a book beset with unresolved questions. On top of such unsettling discontinuities within the surface narrative of canonical Joshua comes the bizarre exchange in the conclusion of the book. After recounting how the people obeyed Joshua religiously in the purportedly sweeping victory, the book culminates in reproach. Joshua avers that the people, who have just sworn their everlasting fidelity, cannot and will not keep the covenant. The Book of Joshua, it seems, cannot make up its mind about what story it is trying to tell![16]

The same set of difficulties also engages Douglas S. Earl in two of his efforts to reclaim, after considerable wrestling, the book of Joshua as Christian scripture.[17] Earl frequently points out how misleading the naïve so-called "plain sense" interpretation can be, not only for would-be believers but also for hostile critics. Both read into the text modernist assumptions about literal correspondence to what actually happened in history without due attention to the text as a part within the whole of canonical scripture or without due diligence with respect to Joshua

14. Giorgio Agamben, *Homo Sacer: Sovereign Power and Bare Life*, trans. D. Heller-Roazen (Stanford, CA: Stanford University Press, 1998).

15. This is the special focus and merit of the literary study of L. Daniel Hawk, which contends for a reading of the canonical book of Joshua in which wrestling over the identity of the people of God finally detaches from the idols of land, race, and ritual to consist in divine election. See Hawk, *Joshua*, Berit Olam (Collegeville, MN: Liturgical Press, 2000).

16. Paul R. Hinlicky, "The Theology of the Divine Warrior in the Book of Joshua," *Word and World* 37, no. 3 (Summer 2017): 271.

17. Douglas S. Earl, *The Joshua Delusion? Rethinking Genocide in the Bible* (Eugene, OR: Cascade 2010); and Earl, *Reading Joshua as Christian Scripture* (Winona Lake, IN: Eisenbrauns, 2010).

as an ancient text whose literary meaning must be established first and foremost on its own terms. All too easily for such readers, Earl argues, citing the words of Richard Dawkins, the "destruction of Jericho, and the invasion of the Promised Land in general, is morally indistinguishable from Hitler's invasion of Poland, or Saddam Hussein's massacres of the Kurds and the Marsh Arabs."[18] Begging the question, a would-be modern Christian apologist might, invoking the spirit of Calvin, reply that to human reason these massacres are morally indistinguishable but that God has his own sovereign but assuredly good reasons, albeit hidden to us, for commanding Israel to commit mass murder. Whether by hostile criticism or by obscurantist apologetics, modern readers forget that it is "the text that the church has accepted as authoritative and *not the history behind the text*."[19]

As mentioned, the authoritative text of Joshua is but part of the much larger whole that for Christians is the canonical unity of Old and New Testaments. In this regard, the message of the book of Joshua that YHWH fights for us is not to be discarded, but neither is it to be taken literally as represented by the book of Joshua. Rather, to anticipate a conclusion that must be demonstrated step-by-step in the commentary, it is to be received as written for our instruction and encouragement in anticipation of God's triumph *for* humanity against demonic usurpers and the victory *in* humanity of death to sin and resurrection to newness of life in the body of this good earth on which the cross of Christ stood, when one and all shall have rest from war. Achieving the dramatic coherence of theological reading by means of literary analysis is both an urgent need in the case of Joshua and a fitting challenge for the theological approach to the biblical text, given the distinction argued above between literary and literal senses and the hermeneutical revisions requisite to it. The explicit distinction between literary and literal senses thus proves to clarify an ambiguity in the ecclesiastical tradition necessary to advance the biblical knowledge of God in "postmodernity"—that is, after the predominantly critical attempt in modernity to reduce the theology of the scriptural text to human religious ideologies on the basis of a reconstruction of "what really happened."

Ultimately, then, our close literary-spiritual reading asks, What story is the Holy Spirit telling in the juxtaposing memories and testimonies woven together in the book of Joshua, itself woven into Israel's canonical narrative as adopted by the church of Christ? Invocation here of the Holy Spirit, of course, may seem like sneaking a joker into the deck to play in one's own favor—but this is not the case

---

18. Earl, *Joshua Delusion?*, 5, quoting Richard Dawkins, *The God Delusion* (London: Bantam, 2006), 247.
19. Earl, *Joshua Delusion?*, 5.

if the Holy Spirit refers to the external word of God provided in the text, just as in turn the word of God in the text refers ultimately to the Spirit who searches the deep things of God to know them and make them known to patient and faithful readers. There is a dialectic here, as we shall see in the commentary. But the safeguard against indiscriminate and self-serving spiritualizing of the text is the hard fact of the otherness of the text that demands to be heard in its own voice.

Thus *penultimately* we must insist on an epistemology of access. Whatever other appropriations, repudiations, or criticisms readers may make, the literary reading of the text is primary in that the text as it is conveyed by canonical scripture is "what is given to thought"—that is, prior to reflection[20]—for the sake, to be sure, of reflection (*fides quarens intellectum*), as Augustine, Anselm, and Barth have held. Indeed, appropriation of the Joshua *narrative* begins already within the tradition-canonical process of the gathering, selection, and editing of Israel's scriptures[21] so that modern critical scholarship that illuminates this redactional process contributes much to illuminate the text literarily—particularly a book like Joshua with all its baffling dissonances. Yet the literary meaning of the *book* of Joshua depends on reading it within its canonical context, where it serves as a bridge between the Pentateuch and the Deuteronomic history, the "latter prophets" as Judaism named the grand narrative from Joshua's conquest of Canaan to the rise and fall of the kingdoms of Israel and Judah. Not only the book, then, but the book as placed in this sequence is what is given to thought prior to reflection. Awareness, therefore, not only of *what* is given but *how* it is given is crucial to proper reading. Butler tells us how we gain access to canonical Joshua: "In the hands of an editor joining Joshua to the other history books

20. Paul R. Hinlicky, "Metaphorical Truth and the Language of Christian Theology," in *Indicative of Grace, Imperative of Freedom: Essays in Honor of Eberhard Jüngel in His Eightieth Year*, ed. R. David Nelson (New York: Bloomsbury T&T Clark, 2014), 89–100.

21. Many contemporary scholars believe that an *Ur-Joshua* existed prior to its incorporation and editing to conform it to the overarching purpose of the Deuteronomic history. Here its "northern" and anti-monarchical tendencies were mitigated and subsumed by a postexilic theological agenda focused on the temple in Jerusalem and Zion as the site of the promises to the Davidic dynasty. Be that as it may, readers of the book of Joshua will know from Gen. 12:1–7; 13:14–18; and 15:17–21 the promises of the land of Canaan made to Israel's forefathers. They will know the figure of Joshua the servant of Moses from Exodus and Numbers (e.g., Exod. 17:9–16; 24:13; 32:17; Num. 11; 13; 14:28–30, 36–38; 26:65; 27:18–23; 32:28; 34:17). If they read the concluding book of the Pentateuch, Deuteronomy, the "second Torah," which follows, they will know that Moses himself commissioned Joshua as his successor in Deut. 31:6–8, 23 and Deut. 34. If they continue reading beyond the conclusion of Joshua, they will find notices about the death and burial of Joshua in Judg. 1:1; 2:6–10, 21–23. And New Testament readers will also be familiar with certain passages from the book in Heb. 4:8; 11:30–31 as well as Acts 7:45; 13:19 and Matt. 1:21.

(Judges through Kings), Joshua becomes a manifesto for a life beyond the Jordan for a people who have lost the land and seek new hope. . . . In the exile, without a king, how does Israel model its leadership? How can a leader who is not a king bring hope to a punished people?"[22]

Why is knowledge of this epistemic setting crucial? This awareness requires the reader to adopt the canonical perspective of dispossessed exiles who have lost the land once given to their ancestors.[23] Embracing this cruel and perplexing irony is crucial for proper understanding of the literary meaning of the book of Joshua and thus determining its claim to truth, which is its specific knowledge of God. In Butler's blunt and painful words, "For the exilic audience, the final author of the book of Joshua sketched a picture bold with meaning. The curses had been fulfilled. Israel had lost her land. Israel had not been faithful to her pledge to the covenant law. God has been faithful to his pledge to curse an unfaithful people."[24] Blunt and painful but truthful: after the postexilic scribe Ezra recalls YHWH's saving history with Israel culminating in the possession of the land under Joshua (Neh. 9:23–25), he concludes his great oration with the lament: "Here we are, slaves to this day—slaves in the land that you gave to our ancestors to enjoy its fruit and its good gifts. Its rich yield goes to the kings whom you have set over us because of our sins; they have power also over our bodies and over our livestock at their pleasure, and we are in great distress" (Neh. 9:36–37).

This explication of Christian epistemic access to the book of Joshua in spiritual solidarity with suffering Israel (think of the Advent hymn *O Come, O Come, Emmanuel*) is essential to bear in mind as we traverse the Joshua narrative of victory upon victory. It constantly reminds us that what we're reading is something written for those who have lost political sovereignty over, and title to, the land. Adopting this perspective of those dispossessed of the land once given to their ancestors as inheritance opens up to view the messianic/eschatological hopes radiating from the narrative figure of Joshua, who is less a royal figure like Josiah than the "servant of YHWH" who enacts what Moses taught. Under the weight of such a heavy cross of exile and dispossession, the book of Joshua thus also discloses "a paradigm of hope . . . for victory once more."[25] With the emergent messianic

22. Butler, *Joshua 1–12*, 78–79.

23. Listening to a text with the ears of the first auditors is a method of historical criticism to determine an original historical sense that at the same time avoids the intentionalist fallacy. I learned it from my teacher J. Louis Martyn, who explained this approach in a semiautobiographical essay, "Listening to John and Paul on the Subject of Gospel and Scripture," *Word and World* 12, no. 1 (Winter 1992): 68–81.

24. Butler, *Joshua 1–12*, 182.

25. Butler, *Joshua 1–12*, 182.

prospect and in a "Judaism that remains true to its messianic faith," Wyschogrod writes, there can be only "provisional trust in categories of thought derived from an unredeemed world destined to pass away. If the future is decisive, reason must be prepared to see itself transcended by developments that cannot yet be dreamt of."[26] As we shall see, in the book of Joshua we may detect the birth pangs of the apocalyptic genre in the Second Temple period with its stories of fabulous warfare against the usurpers of the good earth. Having thus acknowledged that canonical placement that provides our latter-day epistemic access to the book of Joshua, "most important is that in the existing versions of the Bible Joshua is a single book, and this fact must be the basis of every inquiry."[27]

In sum, the literary meaning of the specifically problematic text that is canonical Joshua must be differentiated from its ostensible historical representation. In fact, the various historical representations of the book of Joshua are so at odds not only with critically assessed historical plausibility but above all, as mentioned, *with each other* that literary analysis alone[28] could demonstrate that the multitude of conflicting historical representations woven together in Joshua not only are impossible to harmonize historically but indeed are not intended to be harmonized. Rather, they are to be resolved by a history yet to come. What crystallizes in the text of canonical Joshua is in fact the process internal to the community of faith of taking up and reframing over time the varied memories of origins to probe for the knowledge of God. It cuts against the grain of the text that we actually possess, then, to require of it historical representation as its primary meaning—a construction that will in any case collapse like the walls of Jericho if pressed hard by historical-critical scrutiny. Rather, the primary literary meaning of the book of Joshua is ineradicably *theological*, and that in the very specific and highly problematic sense of the theology of the Divine Warrior that the narrative renders. The book purports to give knowledge of YHWH and his will for the faith and obedience of God's elect people; it accomplishes this by constructing a narrative of the conquest of the land of Canaan by the united twelve tribes headed by Joshua under the leitmotif *YHWH fights for us!* And this deliverance is key to the plot of Joshua with which the book begins and with which it ironically

26. Wyschogrod, *Body of Faith*, 69–70; cf. 168, 171.

27. Hartmut N. Rösel, *Joshua*, Historical Commentary on the Old Testament (Leuven: Peeters, 2011), 1.

28. Contra Rösel, the claim to the land is as historically problematical as the execution of the ban on the Canaanites, as the commentary will show; and in either case, the theology of the Divine Warrior in Joshua is especially significant among the books of the Old Testament.

ends when Joshua warns that YHWH will also fight *against* Israel. That *partial* resolution—*part* within the larger whole of canonical scripture—is the quintessence of dramatic coherence.

Testing Claims to Knowledge of God

The object of interpretation is given for all in the received text of canonical Joshua.[29] Success in regard to the objectivity of the text given to us thus to read, mark, learn, and inwardly digest can be measured by a twofold test. First, without resort to artificial harmonization, does the reading account for *all* the evidence of the text, especially evidence of the many dissonances within the text of Joshua?[30] Second, does this full account of the evidence enable the text to pose its own questions *to us* in the form of its claim to truth upon the contemporary reader—namely, that it is YHWH who fights *for us* but also possibly *against us*?

The first test is the ordinary one of literary competence such that this commentary may be judged on its own literary-critical merits. The literary thesis of this commentary in regard to this first test is that exposition of the book of Joshua yields this theological claim to truth: God is the Divine Warrior who fights for Israel. As Richard D. Nelson observes in corroboration of this claim, "From a literary standpoint . . . , YHWH is the most prominent character."[31] It is YHWH whose promises and purposes in history shape the plot of Joshua as these grow out of YHWH's earlier saving deeds in the promises to the fathers, the exodus from Egypt, and the instruction from Sinai for new life in the liberated land. It is YHWH who now commissions Joshua as successor of Moses his servant and directly speaks to Joshua to direct his every step. It is YHWH who fights for Israel and by the mechanism of the lot guides Israel in the division of

29. We shall follow by and large the MT in keeping with Protestant tradition to treat as primary the literary sense in its original historical context of the Hebrew language (cf. Rösel, *Joshua*, 21). "The promises of the covenant that established the Jews as a people, gave them the land of Canaan, and promised them a king who would reign forever had to be rethought in the Hellenistic period, when most of the Jews lived outside the land, did not speak one language, and were governed not by a theocratic descendent of David but by a pagan king. The cherished promises of a national leader of a united people were preserved in the Greek version, but a sensitivity to the political situation of the Jews is also evident." Karen H. Jobes and Moisés Silva, *Invitation to the Septuagint*, 2nd ed. (Grand Rapids: Baker Academic, 2015), 107.

30. For a relevant case illustrating *failure* of this test of literary objectivity, in which assertion of a Canaanite subjectivity suffocates the voice of the book of Joshua, see Cheryl Kirk-Duggan, "Inside, Outside, or In Between: Feminist/Womanist Hermeneutical Challenges for Joshua and Judges," in *Joshua and Judges*, ed. Athalya Brenner and Gale A. Yee (Minneapolis: Fortress, 2013), 69–90.

31. Richard D. Nelson, *Joshua: A Commentary* (Louisville: Westminster John Knox, 1997), 14.

the land. The book of Joshua concludes with reiteration of the threats of YHWH against covenant infidelity. If, therefore, "the primary function of the canonical narrative," as George A. Lindbeck writes quoting David Kelsey, "is 'to render a character . . . , offer an identity description of an agent,' namely God,"[32] a literary-theological reading of Joshua is as fitting as also—certainly—frightening; so the commentary will show.

Indeed, as Wyschogrod points out, so dangerous is this knowledge of God, and so tempting is it therefore to somehow neutralize it, that Judaism finds itself caught on the horns of a dilemma. "We cannot overlook a basic contradiction. The God of the Bible is a person. He is one of the characters who appears in the stories told in the Bible. He has a personality that undergoes development in the course of the story. . . . Against the simple fact, Jewish philosophy has marshaled all of its resources. The personality of God had to be demythologized. How could God have human failings such as emotions and how could his actions have unexpected results?"[33] While Wyschogrod faults the great Platonizing influence of Maimonides for this estrangement of Judaism from the God of its own Bible, he allows that "the estrangement had already begun in the rabbinic mind,"[34] to the extent that the deposit of the Torah in the scriptures supplanted the lived experience of the prophets in the immediacy of the *Deus dixit*. In many respects Wyschogrod's project is to restore to Judaism its own vital relationship to the God of the prophets.

As we shall see, however, already the book of Joshua wrestles with the conundrums of Torah as a fixed written code when one perceives contrary imperatives in the face of morally ambiguous realities. Somehow theology must capture "the spirit"—that is, the mind and intention of the divine lawgiver—in order rightly to discern the sense of the imperatives and thus the concrete shape of the obedience of faith. But this recovery of the spiritual intention of the letter depends on a return to biblical narrative and its characterization of God. Apart from this, "there is thus an immense absence of real writing about God in Judaism. This is not true of the Bible and not completely true of rabbinic literature because midrashic writing has many genuinely theological passages if by theology we mean taking seriously the reality of God as a person. But . . . the process of the

32. George A. Lindbeck, *The Nature of Doctrine: Religion and Theology in a Postliberal Age* (Philadelphia: Westminster, 1984), 121, quoting David Kelsey, *The Uses of Scripture in Recent Theology* (Philadelphia: Fortress, 1975), 48.
33. Wyschogrod, *Body of Faith*, 84.
34. Wyschogrod, *Body of Faith*, 85.

depersonalization of God begins in rabbinic Judaism . . . and it is of course completed in philosophical Judaism of the Maimonidean variety."[35] Yet recovery is possible as well as necessary because Judaism as a community of faith still listens to the Bible from which the living word of the living God may yet break forth. And we may add in rabbinic fashion: if this conundrum afflicts Judaism, how much more does it afflict Christianity!

There is a further complication here, however, concerning the mixed reality of the community of faith that cannot be avoided but begs for explicit clarification from the outset. In merely "literary readings of Joshua," Nelson writes, "it is up to the reader to hear and appraise the contradictory messages and then create from them a pattern of meaning that relates to the reader's particular situation."[36] True enough as an acknowledgment of the *double* character of theological subjectivity (e.g., the present author is *both* a baptized Christian *and* a straight, white male who is an American citizen several millennia removed from the book of Joshua and its first audience). But it is unclear here whether Nelson makes a concession to the sinful persistence of Canaanite self-understanding within the life of redeemed Israel or an agnostic recommendation to let interpretation atomize into incoherence. The concession is necessary, but a recommendation to sin that grace may abound threatens in this case to dissolve the text into the multitude of subjective appropriations in which the carnal proclivities of Canaan go unchecked and are even reasserted over against divine election and incorporation into the Israel of God, the covenanted people of God.

Such were the heresies of the pro-Nazi German Christians in the 1930s and the pro-apartheid South African churches condemned by the Lutheran World Federation in the 1980s. "For neither circumcision nor uncircumcision is anything; but a new creation is everything! As for those who will follow this *rule*— peace be upon them, and mercy, and upon the Israel of God" (Gal. 6:15–16). This Pauline *rule of faith* specifies the assembly of the new covenant as a politics of reconciliation under the lordship of Jesus Christ; it must govern theological subjectivity lest the carnal desires of Canaan revive and reassert a destructively divisive claim to finality within the assembly of God, contrary to baptismal faith (Gal. 3:26–28). Note well: the apostle here does not argue that the church supersedes Israel but that in the Israel of God neither circumcision nor uncircumcision avails. Therefore a Canaanite church that makes uncircumcision its ground of

---

35. Wyschogrod, *Body of Faith*, 92.
36. Nelson, *Joshua*, 13.

boasting is equally rejected. As we shall see, that inclusion of Canaanites alongside the circumcised reflects ultimately a well-grounded reading of the book of Joshua. Coexistence, not the either/or of circumcision or uncircumcision, manifests the beloved community of the Israel of God.

Consequent to the lordship of Jesus Christ, a second test of objectivity is not and cannot be fully in the control either of author or of reader. The knowledge of God has this peculiar character that it does not confirm the knower in his quest for mastery but brings the knower under its judgment. An objective danger thus is to be acknowledged here—namely, the ferocious holiness of YHWH, who appears as "a devouring fire" (Exod. 24:17; cf. Deut. 5:22) that incinerates indiscriminately anyone who trespasses (Num. 11:1; 16:35; 2 Kgs. 1:10, 12).[37] This danger is evident throughout the book of Joshua, notably in the Levitical themes attending the procession of the ark of the covenant borne aloft by priests but also elsewhere as the commentary will indicate. To be recalled here is the tersely narrated episode in Lev. 10:1–3 wherein Nadab and Abihu, the sons of Aaron, "offered unholy fire before the LORD" and "fire came out from the presence of the LORD and consumed them, and they died before the LORD. . . . And Aaron was silent." In explaining this fearful and fascinating episode, Jacob Milgrom explains the word of YHWH to Moses "I will show myself holy" with the paraphrase "I shall be treated as holy." Milgrom finds two ways of taking this in subsequent tradition. In one way, "Israel's chosenness implies its greater responsibility; it is more culpable for its defection precisely because of its favored status." Another way, however, emphasizes punishment: "the deaths of God's intimate priests, Nadab and Abihu, perform the function of sanctifying God—providing awe and respect for his power to all who witnessed the incident or who will subsequently learn of it."[38] Intriguingly, Milgrom also places the petition of the Lord's Prayer "Hallowed be your name" and the Johannine iteration of it in John 12:28, "Father, glorify your name," in the same train of tradition.[39] There is no need to choose here: all of these priestly resonances regarding ferocious divine holiness bear on the interpretation of the book of Joshua.

The command to ḥerem (Hebrew, meaning "to devote to God by destruction"; see below), as we shall see, manifests this burning fire of the divine otherness/holiness with its message that YHWH fights for Israel. Attending to this is manifestly risky. It demands to know whether or not we, who are theological

---

37. Jacob Milgrom, *Leviticus 1–16*, Anchor Bible 3 (New York: Doubleday, 1991), 599.
38. Milgrom, *Leviticus 1–16*, 601.
39. Milgrom, *Leviticus 1–16*, 603.

subjects and members of the community of faith that holds to the book of Joshua as scripture, are on the side of YHWH; that is, the question threatens thereby to destroy also us who faithlessly fight for ourselves and, adding blasphemy to unbelief, do so by misuse of the name of YHWH. Generations later, John the Baptist enunciated this very test-question of theological objectivity to his contemporaries within Judaism: "Do not begin to say to yourselves, 'We have Abraham as our ancestor'; for I tell you, God is able from these stones to raise up children of Abraham. Even now the ax is lying at the root of the trees" (Luke 3:8–9). Genuine theology, as objective knowledge of God, is *radical* and therefore *dangerous* in this way.

So dangerous is the question about us that YHWH the Divine Warrior puts to the interpreter/reader of Joshua that the immediate temptation is to disown it, suppress it, or debunk it, perhaps to offload it as a trope for some contemporary bogeyman (say, "fundamentalism"). Be that as it may, it is also true that once this message has been committed to writing, thus giving it a permanence independent of the intentions of its original author and the reception by its original readers, whether already in the book of Joshua or derivatively in New Testament christological appropriation, or at length in a commentary on it like this, the written Joshua passes out of the control of its human author and becomes subject to every manner of appropriation, including violent and exploitative misreadings that have turned the theology of the Divine Warrior into its opposite, an ideology of holy war/crusade and so, as we shall see, doubly deserving of the divine anathema. The equally risky safeguard against this danger of misusing Joshua for self-aggrandizement is the true and spiritual risk of being exposed to the exclusive claim of the warrior God whom the book attests. That exposure is the inescapable cost of the genuinely theological reading of the book of Joshua. The frightening message of YHWH who fights for us entails the responsible reader's vulnerability to YHWH who may also fight against her. Such exposure, however, is in the control of neither author nor reader. In regard to the second test of objectivity, we are and ever remain at the mercy of the Spirit.

There are of course many ways of reading scripture other than the postliberal-spiritual way undertaken here, as the "liberal" in "postliberal" indicates. There exists today a plentitude of scholarly, historical, and critical studies that your present author has greatly profited from and to which selectively he will refer as is helpful or relevant. That being said, the present theological commentary will not delve into complicated questions of a textual nature, including interesting divergences between the MT and the LXX, nor into speculative inquiries concerning the sources of the canonical book, the prehistory of the Joshua narrative, nor the agendas of various redactors or editors of this material; least of all will it indulge in historical reconstructions of "what really happened." The historical-critical commentaries excel in investigating such questions, generally referred to as "source criticism." Admittedly, the literary-theological hermeneutic applied in this commentary takes the risk of sounding like a merely apologetic ruse designed to protect the authority of a text that clearly does not cohere internally. But what if the literary point of the text as canonically given is to impose a certain kind of perplexity precisely in referring to the coming of the reign of God?[40] The proof is in the pudding. In any case, readers anxious about the historicity of the book of Joshua—and I stress that this anxiety can be either liberal fear that slaughter really did so happen in obedience to the questionable command of a questionable deity or conservative fear that in fact Joshua, slaughter and all, is a pious fiction—are advised to look elsewhere. Of chief interest in what follows is Joshua's gospel of *YHWH who fights for us*. Thus for the balance of this chapter on preliminary considerations we will overview this theme and its ancillaries by way of anticipation of the commentary on the text.

The Themes of Joshua

YHWH Fights for Us!

In his seminal study, Gerhard von Rad, who had belonged to the Confessing Church during the Hitler regime, articulated a substantive insight that belied the unfortunate title he gave to his book, *Holy War* [= *Der Heilige Kriege*] *in Ancient Israel*. The insight is this:

> We would be greatly misunderstanding these wars if we sought to comprehend them as religious wars in the sense that has become current for us—that is, as a conscious fighting for religion. That they were not, at least not in the sense that they would have been carrying on a war against the gods of the enemies and their cults. . . . In other words, in the holy wars Israel did not arise to protect faith in Yahweh, but Yahweh came on the scene to defend Israel, for the members of the amphictyony were sheltered under his protection; Israel was Yahweh's possession.[41]

40. Thanks to Dave Delaney for this formulation of the problem.
41. Gerhard von Rad, *Holy War in Ancient Israel*, trans. Marva J. Dawn (Grand Rapids: Eerdmans, 1991), 72.

In the same context, von Rad pointed to Israel's "sense of the discovery, a joyful surprise" as expressed in Exod. 15:3's jubilant theological exclamation at the far side of the Red Sea, *YHWH is a warrior!*[42]

This theologoumenon, admittedly, is an answer to a question that has not much been asked in Euro-American modernity, though it is reemerging in our postmodern and increasingly global situation. When John Howard Yoder raised the topic in a chapter of his influential 1972 *The Politics of Jesus*, it was with a touch of embarrassment at Israel's faith in the fabulous—for instance, Jericho's walls tumbling down or Joshua commanding sun and moon to stand still.[43] Tracing a line of "holy war" theology from the exodus event and Joshua through the Chronicler and on to Jesus, Yoder argued hermeneutically, "If, with the cultural empathy that is the elementary requisite for honestly understanding any ancient documents, we measure Jesus's meaning, not by what we can possibly conceive of as happening but by what his listeners can have understood, then we are forbidden to filter his message through our modern sense of reality, of the uniformity of nature and the inconceivability of the extraordinary. 'Miracles don't happen' is the one assumption we dare not impose from outside on Jesus or his listeners."[44] Yoder's purpose here (*not*, incidentally, well served by his adoption of von Rad's terminology of "holy war"; see further below) was to underscore how essential is the element of the fabulous in scriptural accounts of the exodus ("the LORD will fight for you, and you have only to keep still," Exod. 14:14) and the subsequent conquest: "If Israel would believe and obey, the occupants of the land would be driven out little by little (Exod. 23:29–30) by 'the angel' (23:23) or 'terror' (v. 27) or the 'hornets' (v. 28) of God."[45] Yoder's willingness to suffer modern embarrassment by insisting on the fabulous as integral to Israel's salvation confession, YHWH fights for us, may be traced to his own ancestor in faith Menno Simons, the Anabaptist who saved the movement by reinstating faith in the fabulous, repudiating Thomas Müntzer's violent interpretation of the Joshua narrative as "crusade" or "holy war" (on Müntzer, see further below).

In *True Christian Faith*, Menno offers an analysis of the faith of Joshua and Caleb according to Num. 13–14. In contrast to the cowardly spies who returned from their mission to the land of Canaan with a discouraging report about the

---

42. Von Rad, *Holy War in Ancient Israel*, 73.
43. John Howard Yoder, "God Will Fight for Us," in *The Politics of Jesus: Vicit Agnus Noster*, 2nd ed. (Grand Rapids: Eerdmans 1994), 76–89.
44. Yoder, "God Will Fight for Us," 85.
45. Yoder, "God Will Fight for Us," 79.

military superiority of the inhabitants, Joshua and Caleb rallied Israel to faith in YHWH's promise to give them the land. Menno comments, "These two faithful men believe the word and promise of God with all their hearts, as if they had already attained them and trusted firmly in his almighty power, paternal mercy, and great works. . . . They saw the awful unbelief . . . [how] it detracted from the Almighty Majesty, as if he were unable to fulfill his promises to them and as though he had deceived them by his word of promise."[46] Menno contrasts the two groups of spies as carnal Israel and spiritual Israel, a classification he carried over into "the present day" of the Christian community, though with the difference that carnal Christians "think more of the perishable things, such as home, land, gold, silver, wife, children, life and limb, than of the everlasting God in his eternal kingdom. They have a greater desire to enjoy physical peace for a year or two, the dark Egypt of this ungodly world; than to inherit the pleasant fruitful land in endless peace with God."[47] Faith in the fabulous is thus retained here in Menno's Christian appropriation of Joshua, but it is transferred eschatologically from the literal land of Canaan to the new promised land of heaven.

In the cited passage, Menno employs the eminently biblical metaphor of darkness, which indicates the state of being lost and confused under the epistemic domination of oppressive Egypt. Some contemporaries are now objecting to this metaphor on the grounds that it somehow stigmatizes and inferiorizes people of color. Not only is this critique breathtakingly stupid, but it is also a depressing signal of the decline of theology in contemporary circles of the church. It is stupid because human beings of darker pigmentation work with the same optical equipment as human beings of lighter pigmentation; as equally human, each knows well what it means to stumble in the dark, lacking light to see where one is going! And it is depressing that such stupid criticism can gain traction, for it indicates how steep is the decline in the theological vocation of pastors and preachers. Language is saturated with metaphors that communicate in innovative ways but as a result can also be ambiguous. Interpretation is an ongoing demand to clarify the proper sense and reference of metaphor. This is most fundamentally what preachers are supposed to do theologically in handling the biblical language and its metaphors. "The dark Egypt of this world" does not refer injuriously to Egyptians as dark-skinned people (what, are Hebrew slaves supposed to be light-skinned?) but to the darkness that is ignorance of the saving God of exodus and Easter.

46. *The Complete Writings of Menno Simons c. 1496–1561*, trans. Leonard Verduin, ed. J. C. Wenger (Scottdale, PA: Herald, 1984), 355.
47. *Complete Writings of Menno Simons*, 356.

Menno's persecuted Christian consequently does not expect military victory on earth by virtue of a divine miracle intervening to complete a militaristic stepping out in faith into insurrectionary violence. Rather, Menno expected cross-bearing witness of true Christians, for whom everything in the conduct of life is staked on the promise of the resurrection of the dead. The accent accordingly falls presently on the suffering witness of the true and spiritual Christian who leaves behind all earthly goods for the "inheritance" of "the spiritual promised land, the eternal rest in peace."[48] Menno's emphasis differs somewhat from the latter-day Mennonite Yoder's with the latter's stress on the this-worldliness of ancient Israel's faith. Yet Yoder remains in continuity with Menno's Christian appropriation of Joshua's theology of the Divine Warrior in urging that "Jesus' proclamation of the kingdom was unacceptable to most of his listeners not because they thought it could not happen but because they feared it might, and that it would bring down judgment upon them."[49] A major burden of his *Politics of Jesus* was to demonstrate that Jesus too holds to the gospel of Joshua: "God will fight for us"—as this chapter in his book is titled. This conviction of faith is the very reason that nonviolent resistance in Menno's "dark Egypt of this ungodly world" is possible. How is that to be understood?

Not, I fear, in the fashion of a contemporary Mennonite theologian, Gregory A. Boyd, who has published an impressive, two-volume study, *The Crucifixion of the Warrior God*. Valiant in its intention and sprawling in its discussion of issues, the heart of the argument amounts to a hermeneutically violent destruction of what the text of canonical Joshua means literarily when it affirms as gospel that YHWH fought for Israel. For Boyd, "there is, in reality, nothing particularly unique—let alone 'holy'—about the fact that ancient Israelites believed that their deity wanted them to kill and, therefore, they fought their battles under the banner of their God. . . . This view was not only common to ANE [ancient Near Eastern] nations, but it has unfortunately been an almost universally shared characteristic of tribes and nations throughout history."[50] Boyd's strategy is thus historically and critically to relativize scriptural "depictions" of the warrior God by assimilating them to the pagan militarism of savage times. Further, his strategy is theologically to marshal "counter-testimony" from other passages (hardly to be found in the book of Joshua!) to demonstrate that "far from being 'holy,' Israel's

---

48. *Complete Writings of Menno Simons*, 357.
49. Yoder, "God Will Fight for Us," 85.
50. Gregory A. Boyd, *Crucifixion of the Warrior God: Interpreting the Old Testament's Violent Portraits of God in Light of the Cross*, vol. 1, *The Cruciform Hermeneutic* (Minneapolis: Fortress, 2017), 302–3.

use of the sword must be assessed as reflecting a sinful lack of trust in Yahweh" and that "if Yahweh is in any sense a true warrior, he is 'a warrior who fights for peace.'"[51] One may surely come to this blessed conclusion in facing the sacrifice of God for his enemies on Golgotha, but not by the path Boyd would lead us, which simply begs the question of the violence of God in the cross of Jesus.[52] An alternative is the path to be trod in this commentary: that the God of love finds the costly way to overcome the *very real* wrath of his love against the sinful ruin of the creation and to gain the mercy of it through the crucifixion of that second Joshua, who wages a war of *ḥesed* by innocently bearing the sin of the world, a deliverance, moreover, by which the risen and vindicated Jesus Christ emerges as the victor who usurps the usurpers of the earth.

More consequent than Boyd's, another well-intentioned effort to neutralize the "genocidal" implications of the book of Joshua belongs to Eric A. Seibert's *The Violence of Scripture: Overcoming the Old Testament's Troubling Legacy*. In passing, Seibert discusses the literary criticism executed by L. Daniel Hawk as providing an "internal critique" of *ḥerem* warfare,[53] a method that the present commentary will draw on. Hawk's literary method of internal critique or immanent criticism[54] is preferable because it does not impose on the text a criterion external to it, which is expressly the fulcrum on which Seibert's own argument turns for reading "these texts in an ethically responsible manner." Seibert continues, "When the Bible portrays God as one who commands genocide, and the text approves of the slaughter of men, women, children, and infants, we must step up and speak out. It is imperative to confront and critique the immorality of genocide lest people think God actually wills such atrocities."[55] Seibert prefers his way of explicit, external criticism of the text by the criterion of modern notions of genocide and atrocity and consequently warns against "spiritualizing" the conquest narrative: "While I do not deny the book of Joshua can be read in [Hawk's] way, I am nervous about this approach because it never directly challenges or critiques the violence sanctioned in the text."[56] Needless to say, Seibert's approach may also be

---

51. Boyd, *Crucifixion*, 1:304.

52. Richard J. Mouw, "Violence and the Atonement," in *Must Christianity Be Violent? Reflections on History, Practice, and Theology*, ed. Kenneth R. Chase and Alan Jacobs (Grand Rapids: Brazos, 2003), 159–71.

53. Eric A. Seibert, *The Violence of Scripture: Overcoming the Old Testament's Troubling Legacy* (Minneapolis: Fortress, 2012), 178, 198–99.

54. Cf. Titus Stahl, "What Is Immanent Critique?," *Social Science Research Network*, June 3, 2014.

55. Seibert, *Violence of Scripture*, 108.

56. Seibert, *Violence of Scripture*, 111.

found to be question-begging: Just what is his self-evident "ethically responsible manner" that may serve as a foundation external to scripture and put it in the dock? As Alasdair McIntyre once asked, "Whose justice? Which rationality?"

Be that as it may, the acknowledgment of genocide and atrocity need not be evaded. Wyschogrod frankly and explicitly insists that alongside its usual "moral sensitivity, the Bible is also quite amoral. The commandment for the destruction of the previous inhabitants of Canaan is a relevant example." The book of Joshua "is a story that those who identify Judaism with the love of peace find deeply embarrassing. It is the outstanding example of a clash between the divine historic command and the ethical."[57] Such candor at what the text actually says and how consequently there are real tensions within scripture draws Wyschogrod into illuminating discussions of the categorical difference between personal and social moralities—Niebuhr's distinction between "moral man" and "immoral society." "People who lead states—as we have learned since the emergence of the state of Israel—make difficult decisions that inevitably lead to the deaths of many, including many innocent."[58] Wyschogrod remembers that it was not the sentimental preaching of toothless love that forced Nazism to its knees and ended the Shoah, but the combined might of the Soviet and Western Allied armies in whose ranks, one hastens to point out, many atrocities were committed on the way to victory.

Brent A. Strawn has argued an alternative, taken up in this commentary, to Seibert's path to the same goal of rightly relativizing literal *ḥerem* warfare so that it is clearly seen to speak no word of God for us today. The alternative is to accomplish this by scripture interpreting scripture, which is the hard hermeneutical work of theology, not the easy work of posturing and denunciation that succeeds only in telling the modern person what she already knows, as Seibert manifestly proposes to do. Against Seibert's doubts, Strawn defends figural (i.e., typological) reading—that is to say, scripture interpreting scripture. In figural reading, a connection is established between two persons or events in which the first refers not only to itself but also to the second. This is a hermeneutic necessitated by Christian reading of Hebrew scripture as its own "Old Testament," though it has antecedents in the Hebrew scriptures, a notable example being the Second Isaiah's figuring of the return to Zion from Babylonian exile as a second exodus. Thus Strawn argues: (1) Figural readings do not completely ignore the literal violence of Joshua, but on the contrary "it is *precisely* the difficulties and grittiness

57. Wyschogrod, *Body of Faith*, 218.
58. Wyschogrod, *Body of Faith*, 180–81.

that give rise to the need for subtler and defter interpretation." The literary sense, especially in its offense, is always foundational for figural readings. (2) Figural reading is not covert apologetics, attempting to salvage the Old Testament, but is a "proactive and generative strategy" that "enabled Christians to use the whole Bible as the church's book" as opposed to gnosticism new and old, which would disqualify the Old Testament and sever the New Testament from its deep roots therein. And (3) figural readings are "not, therefore, performing some sort of Herculean feat of interpretive magic by which the Old Testament is saved (and without which it is doomed), so much as they are making sense of the entire linguistic system" of canonical scripture.[59] Scripture is the matrix of faith, and to learn its language is for faith to become knowledgeable and competent in life lived before YHWH. For this commentary, scripture, including Joshua, is the very *matrix* of faith, whose originating word is the gospel that YHWH fights for us.

To begin down this path we ask, Against whom precisely does YHWH fight? A preliminary answer might be what the ill-chosen term "holy war" seems to indicate: other gods. But interestingly, as von Rad pointed out, this is not the case, at least expressly, in the book of Joshua. Pekka M. A. Pitkänen explains the historical surroundings of the Joshua narrative: "The question in the Ancient Near East was not whether one believed in a God or in the divine generally, as may be asked in the modern world, but, rather, which God or gods one believed in. Moreover, in the Ancient Near East, religion was usually national. A particular country and region had its own God or gods that it followed, and the people of that country were assumed to be under the aegis of that particular God or gods. Once wars were fought, they were seen as a battle of the gods of the warring factions on a cosmic scale."[60] But the book of Joshua, in its contention that YHWH fights for us, never pits YHWH against Canaanite gods but rather against covetous human desires that animate and objectify as idols. The historical-contextual insight here can thus be retooled theologically in equally Deuteronomic and Augustinian fashion: what is at issue is not whether there is a god in heaven, but to which god on the earth one clings with all one's heart and thus also in bodily obedience. Put theologically, what does one entrust this god to do for believers?

---

59. Brent A. Strawn, *The Old Testament Is Dying: A Diagnosis and Recommended Treatment* (Grand Rapids: Baker Academic, 2017), 120.

60. Pekka M. A. Pitkänen, *Joshua*, Apollos Old Testament Commentary 6 (Nottingham, UK: Apollos; Downers Grove, IL: InterVarsity, 2010), 32. Pitkänen provides examples of contemporaneous divine warrior ideology in the ancient Near East (47–50).

Answering these questions would be one way of identifying God and, in virtue of that identification, answering the question about what God fights against.

By contrast to the Deuteronomic-Augustinian way, for the abstract or philosophical monotheism that has dominated the now passing period of Western modernity, God does not "do" any such things, especially not something as unseemly as *fighting*, but just *is*, simply and absolutely, grounding our being. In dread, as we anxious moderns are, at the shaking of the foundations of our secular peace[61] by Huntington's prospective "clash of civilizations," the religious need is for a distant but "therapeutic" theism projecting a generic religious perspective above the fray of rival religions. This modern need can thus quickly displace rigorous and honest confrontation with Joshua's testimony to YHWH who fights for us. Joshua's testimony can be historically distanced and relativized by treating it as the relic of a primitive stage of polytheistic culture with its wars of the gods, a dispensation now happily overcome and left behind, surviving only, as it were, to congratulate us on how far we have progressed. Of course God is "one"—what else could God be, if there is a God? Biblical faith, however, poses the question of the oneness or unity of God differently: How is God the creator also God the redeemer? The God of the past also God of the future? How does God's promise prove true if fulfillment can be long delayed and the fulfillments that do come prove only to be partial or temporary? How does God "dramatically cohere"?

Joshua commentator Richard D. Nelson gave voice to our modern religious need for unity above the fray of contested history: modern readers "recoil from its chronicle of a brutal conquest.... The concept of the divine warrior who fights the battles of one nation at the expense of others seems incompatible with enlightened notions of religion."[62] Such reluctance of the "modern" person of "enlightened" religion is surely understandable after the century of Hitler, Hiroshima, and Stalin. But it is doubtful that the unprecedented bloodshed of the twentieth century can be understood or explained as a resurgence of barbaric religion such that the solution is to continue all the more stridently on the cosmopolitan project of modernity. Hitler, Stalin, and the atomic bombers were each and all happy champions of modernity, each convinced that they were driving the people to happiness (albeit with an iron fist) according to the utilitarian ethos of modernity. They were no friends of the scriptures of Israel. If in our modern religious need we keep YHWH who fights for us far away at the safe distance of the primitive past only to mark therefrom

61. Mark Lilla, *The Stillborn God: Religion, Politics, and the Modern West* (New York: Vintage Books, 2008).

62. Nelson, *Joshua*, 2.

our forward progress, we evade the testimony of Joshua that would speak to our modern world, precisely the modern world after Hitler, Hiroshima, and Stalin, the world whose formidable Canaanite defenses are now collapsing like old Jericho's. If we persist in this act of "othering" Joshua, we do not and cannot entertain the question the book would put to us in the persons of Rahab and the Gibeonites: whether we will turn from our sublime idol of escape into transcendence to confess the God of Israel on this earth and so be joined to his sometimes triumphant but usually suffering people; or again, in the person of Achan, whether we will endanger the people of God to which we belong by misusing the God of Israel's name and exclusive claim and taking for our own what belongs solely to him.

Ḥerem Warfare

To be sure, the theologoumenon "YHWH fights for us" brings with it the appalling directives but also the extraordinary limitations of "the ban"[63]—a Hebrew term with both noun and verb forms that I will transliterate as *ḥerem* in what follows because its peculiar meaning must be gathered by its usage, and the usual translations of "devoted things," "things devoted to destruction," "sacrifice," or "the ban" are each in some way inadequate. I will not therefore provide even a working definition of the term, whose meaning must be established by working through the entire drama of its deployment in the book of Joshua. What this will reveal is what I shall call a "politics of purity" unfolding to its logical extreme until it is met and transcended by the intimation of a messianic politics of reconciliation, one that restores the fallen.[64]

To grasp this usage we must see that the account of warfare in the book of Joshua has a prehistory, as Moshe Weinfeld has shown. Referring to Exod. 23:27, he writes that "instead of having the Canaanites 'turned back' the Deuteronomic author has them 'wiped out.' . . . Indeed, in the ancient sources it is God who drives out the Canaanites (Exod. 23:22, 27f.; 33:2; 34:11; Josh. 24:12; Judg. 2:3; 6:9; Amos 2:9; Ps. 44:3; 78:55; 80:9), while in the Deuteronomic sources exterminating the Canaanites is the task of the Israelites. . . . [Thus] one can discern a

---

63. A comprehensive and illuminating historical-critical discussion is found in Thomas B. Dozeman, *Joshua 1–12: A New Translation with Introduction and Commentary*, Anchor Yale Bible 6B (New Haven: Yale University Press, 2015), 54–59. See also John H. Walton and J. Harvey Walton, *The Lost World of the Israelite Conquest: Covenant, Retribution and the Fate of the Canaanites* (Downers Grove, IL: IVP Academic, 2017).

64. Giorgio Agamben, *The Time That Remains: A Commentary on the Letter to the Romans*, trans. Patricia Dailey (Stanford, CA: Stanford University Press, 2005).

development in the Pentateuch tradition concerning the removal of the Canaanites from the land of Israel."[65] Weinfeld also notes a "significant difference" in the posthistory of the book of Joshua "between the first Temple *herem* 'vow,' which involved execution, and the second Temple 'vow,' which involved separation."[66] If the teaching in Deut. 7 on *herem* was itself a development of Exod. 23, one could consequently see in the book of Joshua, as this commentary will show, a certain controversy being carried on in the postexilic community regarding the impossibility, both factual and moral, of executing the divine command for the execution of the Canaanites. To use contemporary jargon, one might say that if Deut. 7 is the construction of *herem*, the book of Joshua is its deconstruction. Perceiving this, of course, is a matter of close and careful reading of Joshua.

Herem in the book of Joshua recalls the liturgical practice of burnt offering, something dramatically taken out of all possible human usage by its destruction through fire: the smoke rising up to heaven to please the nostrils of God, leaving behind only a pile of ash, humanly useless. Such priestly themes, which suffuse the book of Joshua in its final form, moreover, will indicate how "in post-exilic times the election developed into a feeling of responsibility to serve as an example for other nations. Israel was chosen in order to bring light to the nations (Isa. 49:6–7; cf. 41:8–9; 42:2; 43:10, 44:1–2; 45:4)."[67] As the commentary will bear out, therefore, the decisive point in interpreting Joshua's use of *herem* to illuminate the sense of its gospel that YHWH fights for Israel is that its prohibition against coveting the evil goods of Canaan turns against Israel when Israel is tempted to fight for itself, let alone to use YHWH to fight for its own purposes—the unholy purposes of greed for goods that are no true goods. Fighting for oneself according to oneself in the name of one's God is more accurately termed "crusade" or "holy war" or (perhaps[68]) "jihad"[69]—precisely the religious ideology, as we shall see, that fabulous *herem* warfare forbids!

65. Moshe Weinfeld, *Deuteronomy 1–11*, Anchor Bible 5 (New York: Doubleday, 1991), 383.

66. Weinfeld, *Deuteronomy 1–11*, 364.

67. Weinfeld, *Deuteronomy 1–11*, 367.

68. One hadith tells: "The first (whose) case will be decided on the Day of Judgment will be a man who died as a martyr. He shall be brought and Allah will make him recount his blessings and say, 'What did you do in return?' He will say, 'I fought for you until I died as a martyr.' Allah will say, 'You have told a lie. You fought so that you might be called a "brave warrior" and you were called so.' (Then) orders will be passed against him and he will be dragged with his face downcast and thrown into hell." Cited in Harfiyah Haleem, "What Is Martyrdom?," *Witnesses to Faith? Martyrdom in Christianity and Islam*, ed. Brian Booker (Burlington, VT: Ashgate, 2006), 53. Thanks to Cara Anderson for this reference.

69. Failure to make this subtle distinction in the *title* (though not the content) of the book mars the otherwise seminal study by von Rad, *Holy War in Ancient Israel*.

In justified horror at the *ḥerem* requirement of the total extermination of the
enemy in the book of Joshua, we moderns might readily object that the foregoing
amounts to a distinction without a difference. What better way to justify oneself,
after all, than to say that the Lord himself fights for us and we are merely his
instruments?[70] That is a plausible objection. But understanding the good news of
the book of Joshua that YHWH fights for us requires, minimally, that we suspend
disbelief for the duration of this reading of Joshua until we have heard the book
speak in its own right about *ḥerem* warfare. If the foregoing distinction holds up
against the objection, we are then free to return to our important question at the
end of modernity about the horror of total war—our own modern denouement
captured in the phrase "Hitler, Hiroshima, and Stalin." In fact, the distinction
does make considerable literary difference, as we shall see, and this difference
may well enable a better path forward to peaceful coexistence.

This much may be said here by way of anticipation of the commentary. The
most profound challenge to taking Joshua as scripture is *not* an objection to the
thesis that a theological reading produces the knowledge of YHWH who fights
for us, but *rather* the post-Holocaust objection, not only that YHWH failed to
fight for the Jewish innocent against the Nazi slaughter, but more darkly that
Nazis learned genocide ultimately from this book of the Hebrew Bible, disseminated in the Western tradition through its status in canonical Christian scripture.
That is not as implausible as it may sound, since Nazis maintained that the Jews
were from time immemorial already at war with Aryan culture, the enemy that had
infiltrated the Aryan Canaan in a cunning act of total war. Nazi mass murder was
thus justified as retaliation in kind. Be that as it may, Jewish theologian Zachary
Braiterman captures this profounder objection well: "It is no longer evident why
people should hold to a covenant whose terms have included recurring patterns of
marginalization, vilification, persecution, exile and (in the twentieth century) systematic genocide. . . . Catastrophic suffering may not logically preclude the image
of the covenant people, but it threatens to make the very notion unbearable."[71]
(On Braiterman, see further the epilogue.) Unbearable as the yoke of the Torah
seems to have become after the Holocaust (so Braiterman), however, one may
fairly counter: Would it not be too cruel and equally unbearable to give Nazism

---

70. Thanks to Fritz Oehlschlaeger for this formulation.

71. Zachary Braiterman, *(God) after Auschwitz: Tradition and Change in Post-Holocaust Jewish
Thought* (Princeton: Princeton University Press, 1998), 28. In the conclusion of this book, Braiterman
points to Wyschogrod's work as charting a new path forward for Jewish theology, especially his "messianic maximalism" (177).

the "posthumous victory" (Fachenheim) of permitting their catastrophic crime to destroy Jewish and Christian faith in YHWH who fights for us? Clarification and vindication of this faith in God "after Auschwitz"[72] is theologically urgent, and the book of Joshua is a territory on which this battle might be fought.

Setting aside the egregious uses of Joshua in so-called dominion theology, not infrequent in the history of interpretation of Joshua is the attempt to redeem *ḥerem* warfare by making a distinction between colonial or imperial aggression on the one side and revolutionary or insurrectionary violence on the other. This is the impressive historical thesis of Thomas B. Dozeman, who writes, "The invasion is not an account of conquest. . . . Rather, it is a story about the execution of kings, the destruction of their royal cities, and the extermination of the urban population through the implementation of the ban."[73]

This agrarian-insurrectionist reading of Joshua as holy war was anticipated by the sixteenth-century agitator of the Peasants' Revolt, Thomas Müntzer. In his *Sermon to the Princes*, he spoke against passive waiting on miraculous intervention from above. Divine intervention should rather be expected as the reward of stepping out in radical faith. Müntzer preached that we should not "understand Daniel to say that the Antichrist should be destroyed without human hands when it really means that he is intimidated already like the inhabitants of the promised land when the chosen people entered it. Yet, as Joshua tells us, he did not spare them the sharp edge of the sword. . . . The sword was the means used, just as eating and drinking is a means for us to stay alive. . . . For the godless have no right to live, unless by the sufferance of the elect, as it is written in [Exod. 23]."[74]

Undoubtedly, Dozeman and Müntzer articulate a possible, if one-sided, reading of Joshua on the theological supposition (if I may stoop to a banal slogan) that "God has no hands but ours." Here God becomes an idea and theology an ideology legitimating, indeed sacralizing, the particular human-all-too-human political (and in this case bloodthirsty) activism of a fanatical politics of purity. If this characteristic modern reduction is to be avoided theologically, however, it will be necessary, as mentioned above, to give some affirmative account of the integral role of the fabulous (or miraculous) in *ḥerem* warfare according to the

72. Richard Rubenstein, *After Auschwitz: History, Theology, and Contemporary Judaism*, 2nd ed. (Baltimore: Johns Hopkins University Press, 1992).

73. Dozeman, *Joshua 1–12*, 3.

74. *The Collected Works of Thomas Müntzer*, trans. and ed. Peter Matheson (Edinburgh: T&T Clark, 1994), 250–51. See further in this connection, Paul R. Hinlicky, "Luther in Marx," in *Oxford Encyclopedia of Martin Luther*, ed. Derek R. Nelson and Paul R. Hinlicky (New York: Oxford University Press, 2017), 2:322–41.

book of Joshua. As difficult as is Joshua's testimony to the fabulous for us moderns, "Joshua's concept of historical causality is primarily theological"[75]—in other words, *fabulous*, not political, economic, or for that matter military.

To appreciate and profit from Dozeman's attempted distinction, however, it is helpful to bear in mind that the fundamental purpose of aggression in the ancient Near East was the acquisition of booty, especially the expropriation of property, including enslavement of women and children, after the military resistance of men was negated by the slaughter of the defeated forces. Biblically, this standard operating procedure in ancient warfare is familiar in the stories of the slaughter of the Hebrew baby boys in Egypt by Pharaoh and the slaughter of the baby boys in Bethlehem by King Herod. Just this assertion of dominion and acquisition of booty by the elimination of the male threat, however, and, more profoundly as the Achan story shows, the very *desire* for it are forbidden in Israel's *ḥerem* warfare. In other words, precisely because the scope of extermination is expanded beyond the usual class of male warriors to include goods and cattle, women and children, the motive of aggressive warfare as usual is undercut. In a principled way, moreover, this enlarged scope of *ḥerem* warfare turns against Israel when Israel violates the prohibition of coveting by taking booty, as the Achan story demonstrates.

All the same, contemporary readers may well feel relief at the consensus of critical scholarship that the historical representations of "genocide" (to speak anachronistically)[76] do not correspond to historical reality. Yet such relief would be false comfort insofar as the canonically authoritative text of Joshua in any case represents, and apparently commends, the utter extermination of foes in obedience to the will of God. Is that scriptural word a word of God spoken also to us?[77] If so, in what sense?

From Religious Ideology to Knowledge of God

We should not presume that any word of God recorded in scripture is a word of God spoken also to us. Scripture testifies to God's history with the particular people Israel, and it speaks also to us Gentiles (i.e., Canaanites) only under the conditions by which we, distant from this Israel of the scriptures by time and place and peoplehood, come also to belong to the eschatological Israel of God

---

75. Nelson, *Joshua*, 9.

76. For example, Pitkänen (*Joshua*, 75–76) offers a morally serious but anachronistic discussion of "genocide" based on the definition of the term by the United Nations in 2007.

77. For a discussion of the hermeneutical issues, see Paul R. Hinlicky, "Prima Scriptura: Saving Sola Scriptura from Itself," *Dialog* 55, no. 3 (Fall 2016): 223–30.

(Gal. 6:16). This transition or conversion is our Gentile crossing of the Jordan, the baptism into Christ crucified and risen. Consequently, any word from scripture that does speak to us also as word of God does so, not directly or immediately, but indirectly by the mediation of the scriptures and their ongoing theological interpretation in the ecclesia identified by Gal. 6:15. So Martin Luther taught in his commentary on Deut. 7, which is the canonical source of the Joshua narrative's *ḥerem* warfare. What is at stake in these qualifications regarding whether or how the command to *ḥerem* speaks also to us is a sharp and conscientious turn from religious ideology to the knowledge of God.

Deanna A. Thompson, to illustrate, has a helpful discussion of the issues involved in *ḥerem* warfare in her commentary on Deuteronomy but argues in conclusion that "the more prevalent images of Israel's God in Deuteronomy and in the Bible as a whole depict God as more compassionate and loving than violent. Still the tension persists without clear resolution."[78] Obviously, this is not a solution but only a restatement of the problem of deep and disturbing contradiction, not simplistically between Old and New Testaments, as Thompson rightly sees, but already within Deuteronomy (as well as within Joshua and within the New Testament) in regard to the knowledge of God. A theological resolution of conflict here moves beyond juxtaposing contrary presentations of God as "violent" and "loving" to one that yields knowledge of God in his own divine movement beyond the wrath of holy love to the mercy of it. But such a solution is, on the terms in which Thompson frames the question, not possible. She discusses the problem on the superficial plane of images or depictions of deity, asking which one predominates, as if it were a matter of quantification.

This common approach today reflects the conditions of modern theology since the time of Kant, who proscribed knowledge of God, leaving to the theologians only historical knowledge of various human constructions of deity in images or concepts. Modern theology accordingly discusses, not God, but ideas about God even though, if theologians are rigorously Kantian, they admittedly have no way of telling which of the competing ideas about God claiming revelation could be true. So they end up counting the votes or reducing theology to a campaign for votes. But knowledge of God is what is at stake in biblical revelation. The crucial point with respect to Deuteronomy and Joshua is not that they contain a putatively minority-report image of a violent God but that they knew God

---

78. Deanna A. Thompson, *Deuteronomy*, Belief: A Theological Commentary on the Bible (Louisville: Westminster John Knox, 2014), 85.

in the demand for *ḥerem* warfare and obeyed. A minority-report image we can readily discard according to our own majoritarian preferences, but what are we to do with Israel's knowledge of God in the holy and uncompromising demand for *ḥerem* warfare?

The crucial differentiation to be made here with Luther, as we shall shortly see, is that the various presentations of God in scripture are unique and unrepeatable events within God's history with Israel. The history of God with Israel becomes, through the mediation of scripture, the history of God with us today in the community of faith that receives these texts, including Joshua, as Holy Scripture by virtue of our baptismal inclusion in the eschatological Israel. But that mediation entails an act of hermeneutical violence in which in some way original meaning is transformed in specific acts of appropriation. Whether and how words of God once spoken to Israel are also spoken to us, then, is a question of how this new creation, the Israel of God, both cancels and fulfills the old and failed Israel of Joshua's prophecy at the end of the canonical book in order to speak also to us—that is, we who are ungodly Gentiles and Canaanites who would nevertheless cross the Jordan to enter the Israel of God.

On the other hand, it is perhaps our identification by the book of Joshua with the fortified cities of Canaan and their kings that explains why "our age cheers the liberation of Israel's exodus but abhors the destruction of its conquest . . . [even though] the eradication of Canaanite nations is continuing what the contest with Pharaoh started."[79] So writes Telford Work, who better grasps the sanctity of the command for *ḥerem* warfare in Deut. 7 when he locates the audience of the book of Deuteronomy (and Joshua) in the exilic situation of dispossessed Israel. Demoralized and dispossessed, readers looked back on what had gone wrong in the kingdoms of Israel and Judah and came to understand how the descendants of Joshua and his generation were "tempted as Pharaoh was to harness [political power] for their own purposes, eventually turning Israel into an empire, a client state, or pagan society. Ridiculous as it sounds, Israel is not dominating the nations it destroys [in *ḥerem* warfare]. Covenanting, showing mercy, and marrying from its position of temporary advantage would be futile efforts to master, manage, and exploit them."[80]

To be sure, it *does* sound "ridiculous" to *deny* that the extermination prescribed in Deut. 7 and executed in the book of Joshua is an act of domination, but we

---

79. Telford Work, *Deuteronomy*, Brazos Theological Commentary on the Bible (Grand Rapids: Brazos, 2009), 107.
80. Work, *Deuteronomy*, 104.

should linger on our nervous giggle in reaction to hearing this counterintuitive judgment because it reveals something more about ourselves than about the book of Joshua. Giggling aside, it is the painful work of understanding the holiness of *herem* that charts out the path forward, as Work argues, to the "relentless logic of Christ's victorious grace undo[ing] humanity's chronic calculus of temporal advantage and disadvantage, of sexual selection and political association, of pride and shame—and ultimately of hate—and creat[ing] a beloved and loving fellowship."[81] If that remarkable claim holds up in the interpretation of the book of Joshua made in the commentary to follow, we discover that "Moses's old instructions and Jesus's new instructions fundamentally cohere, even if the former involves systematic violence and the latter involves systematic nonviolence."[82] In either case, the spiritual sacrifice—that is, the personal renunciation of all objects of idolatrous desire—is demanded but also given by the victorious grace of Christ. "No one can serve two masters; for a slave will either hate the one and love the other, or be devoted to the one and despise the other. You cannot serve God and wealth" (Matt. 6:24).

Even as objects of idolatrous desire change with the times and conditions, clarity on the meaning of the spiritual sacrifice required by the obedience of faith comes with the second Joshua, the victorious Christ, who sacrificed himself for others once and for all. This is the critical insight that Luther brings to theological interpretation of *herem* warfare in Joshua and its basis in Deut. 7. God commanded this work of *herem*, Luther writes,

> not because he wanted this to be a permanent obligation of his people but because he had decreed to destroy those Gentiles completely on account of their sins, a work for which he had wanted to use his people. He who overthrew Sodom without using another nation is wont at times to punish one nation through another nation. Therefore one should not apply this literal and fleshly understanding of the first commandment to Christians, whose business it is to kill Gentiles and cast down images with the sword of the Spirit (Eph. 6:17). For this task was assigned specifically to this nation for a time, just like everything else that is commanded to this nation, for example, the rules concerning marriage, covenants, and all outward ceremonies.[83]

Luther not only confines the literal command for *herem* warfare to a unique historical episode bound to the law of Moses and the one-time dispossession of the

---

81. Work, *Deuteronomy*, 105.
82. Work, *Deuteronomy*, 108.
83. *Luther's Works* (hereafter LW), ed. Jaroslav Pelikan, Helmut T. Lehmann, and Christopher Boyd Brown, 75 vols. (Philadelphia: Muhlenberg and Fortress; St. Louis: Concordia, 1955–), 9:31.

Canaanites, but also teaches in principle that (apart from the first commandment, understood "spiritually") "Moses in nowise pertains to us in all his laws, but only to the Jews, except where he agrees with the natural law, which, as Paul teaches, is written in the hearts of Gentiles (Rom. 2:15)."[84] Thus, "it is now certain that among Christians the godless should not be killed with the physical sword."[85] A rueful reflection is mandatory here: if only Luther had minded his own counsel when he put to pen his late in life attack on the Jews. To teach the law rightly and to live it out truly, however, are not one and the same thing. Calvin too, in any case, held this position in parallel to Luther:

> It is now proper to consider how far this doctrine is applicable to us. It is true a special command was given to the ancient people to destroy the nations of Canaan, and keep aloof from all profane defilements. To us, in the present day, no certain region marks out our precise boundaries; nor are we armed with the sword to slay all the ungodly; we have only to beware of allowing ourselves to become involved in fellowship with wickedness, by not keeping at a sufficient distance from it. For it is almost impossible, if we mingle with it, spontaneously to avoid receiving some spot or blemish.[86]

So the spiritual renunciation of wicked objects of covetous desire remains in force—a policy of self-purification, not a politics of other-purgation.

With an eye to the contemporaneous teaching of erstwhile disciple but now iconoclast rabble-rouser Thomas Müntzer, Luther warns that Müntzer's hermeneutical assumption that all words of God recorded in Scripture also speak directly to us would force him and his followers

> to kill the whole world; for it has images even if it does not worship them. The command to kill the Gentiles is as explicit here as the command to destroy images;

---

84. LW 9:81. Luther thus refuted "untenable claims to institute Old Testament law in a theology that claimed to work by Scripture alone. For Luther, the civil, religious and ceremonial legislation of Moses for ancient Israel imposes, qua positive law, no abiding obligation on Gentile Christians. Not only is it outmoded, it was never addressed to them and so does not speak to them as law, although historically and theologically interpreted, it may as Scripture have heuristic value illuminating how contemporary formulations of positive law can be informed by the double love commandment. It is the law of love, as the law of creation itself, which abides for Luther as the rule of rules. In his writings against the antinomians, indeed, we find the statement, *Solus decalogus est aeternus*—a claim that is intelligible when we take the Decalogue, as Luther did with Augustine, as the *ordo caritatis.*" Paul R. Hinlicky, "Antinomianism—the 'Lutheran' Heresy," in *Lutheran Theology and Secular Law: The Work of the Modern State*, ed. Marie A. Failinger and Ronald W. Duty (New York: Routledge, 2018), 28–38.
85. LW 9:80.
86. John Calvin, *The Book of Joshua* (North Charleston, SC: CreateSpace, n.d.), 246.

if they affirm the one, they must necessarily concede the other. In fact here [in Deut. 7, God] commands the killing of the Gentiles first as an act more necessary than the destruction of the images. . . . Therefore no one who sees the iconoclasts raging thus against wood and stone should doubt that there is a spirit hidden in them which is death-dealing, not life-giving, and which at the first opportunity will also kill men, just as some of them have begun to teach.[87]

Given real-existing humanity, an insatiable politics of purity, drawing sanction from scripture as literally as indiscriminately, must descend into endless bloodbath.

But what does Luther's rejection of biblical literalism mean for Joshua's theology of the Divine Warrior? Does it mean for Luther that the scriptural command to *ḥerem* warfare in no way speaks as word of God to Christians? He affirms that it does speak spiritually, though not literally, as an instantiation of the first commandment. As he had commented on Deut. 10:18,

> See, this is what it means to interpret the First Commandment. This is the commentary of Moses himself. Thus he teaches the understanding of what it means that there is a God, what it means to have God, what it means to fulfill the First Commandment. Oh, what great fountains just these words have been for the prophets! From the source they have drawn whatever they shout forth about the concern of God for the infirm, the lowly, the poor, the sinners, the widows, the orphans, the judged, the condemned, the afflicted, and the wretched; also whatever they thunder against the wealthy, the tyrannical, the mighty, the critical, the violent, the hard, and the proud about the wrath and vengeance of God. For all these flow from the great ocean of the First Commandment and flow back into it, so that no richer consolation or voice is more plainly heard or ever will be heard, yet none harder or severer, than the voice of the First Commandment: "I am the Lord your God."[88]

What Luther means here by "spiritually" is actually derived from the same exegesis of the book of Deuteronomy, which itself had called for the circumcision of "the foreskin of your hearts" (10:16). The apostle Paul took up this summons to spiritual renunciation of idols, the correlate of Deuteronomy's summons to the wholehearted love of God, in Rom. 2:29, explicitly contrasting inward and spiritual circumcision to outward and literal circumcision. In Luther's words, pointing to a tension within the law, "Amazing indeed is the legislator who at

87. LW 9:80.
88. LW 9:112.

one and the same time commands works and yet condemns them when they are done! But He does this that they may know that the law is fulfilled not by works of the law, but from the circumcision of the heart, and that such works are good truly only when they proceed, not from the compulsion of the law but from the heart which was circumcised before."[89] Similarly, this "spiritual" move into the hidden region of the human heart and its loves was taken up by Jesus in his explicating and radicalizing the commandments in the Sermon on the Mount to expose the motives of action to the sight of the heavenly Father. In fact, this Deuteronomic command for wholehearted devotion to God, sacrificing all that gets in the way by clinging to God in the obedience of faith, teaches Christians to "know that before God there is no difference between you and the Gentiles, . . . that if you do not fulfill the word of God and do not slay these Gentiles but enter into pacts and marriages with them, the same wrath will wait you also. . . . The fact that the punishment is the same indicates that before God [you] will be guilty of the same godlessness, that [you] may know that [you] are better than those Gentiles only by virtue of the word of God."[90] So also Wyschogrod from the Jewish perspective: "In the context of the messianic future, the prophets speak of the circumcision of the heart that will complete the circumcision of the flesh, which seems to have left the heart insufficiently transformed. Israel has remained hardhearted; the word of God has not entered into [Israel's] spirit but only its flesh, and this does not please God."[91]

In this "spiritual" way, then, the command to *ḥerem* indeed speaks as word of God to believers today. Israel and Canaan from the book of Joshua accordingly become spiritual as tropes for the beloved community of God and the reprobate *civitas terrena*, respectively, such that if Christians do not spiritually fulfill the first commandment to love God above all and all things in and under God by true *fides ex corde*, they will fall victim spiritually to the same *anathema* (the Greek word that the LXX uses to translate *ḥerem*) that falls on the idolatries of the nations and the disobedience of unfaith—on reflection, with some further nuance, a fair summation of the message of the book of Joshua as a whole!

In fact, according to Luther the command to *ḥerem*, more carefully considered in the light of its actual execution in the book of Joshua, shows that "God does not decree that these nations be destroyed outright, but only if they continue to be obstinate. Otherwise peace was to be offered them, and they were to be

89. LW 9:110–11.
90. LW 9:84.
91. Wyschogrod, *Body of Faith*, 19.

endured if they were turned to Israel. So it happened to the Gibeonites and the harlot Rahab."[92] In the course of the book of Joshua the commentary will show this very movement away from a politics of purity and toward the politics of reconciliation.[93]

Even if Luther somewhat overstates the claim, he rightly grasps the neutralizing impetus vis-à-vis literal *ḥerem* warfare of the Rahab and Gibeonite stories in the book of Joshua and intimates therewith a politics of reconciliation fulfilling and canceling the politics of purity. Given real-existing humanity, a politics of reconciliation is urgently needed and it is this need that is exposed in the book of Joshua by the interplay of the divine demand to execute *ḥerem* and the human failure to accomplish it by virtue of obedience to other imperatives of Torah. The true tension is not between Christianity and Judaism, then, but a tension within the law itself.

Thus the acute theological problem presented by the book of Joshua of the wrath of YHWH, a "holy and jealous God," who fights for Israel according to his own sovereign purpose, remains as *crux intellectum* in moving from religious ideology to the knowledge of God. Strawn cites Jewish theologian Abraham Joshua Heschel aptly as to this decisive question: YHWH's "anger is aroused when the cry of the oppressed comes into his ears" (citing Exod. 22:21–24).[94] True, for also Gentiles, like the Egyptian slave masters, are responsible to the one true God, creator of all. But more precisely for Israel, Wyschogrod writes, "God's anger when Israel is disobedient is the anger of a rejected lover. It is above all jealousy, the jealousy of one deeply in love who is consumed with torment at the knowledge that his beloved seeks the affection of others. To much of philosophical theology, such talk has been an embarrassment in urgent need of demythologization. But theologians must not be more protective of God's dignity than he is of his own because God's true dignity is the sovereignty of his choice for genuine relation with man."[95]

---

92. LW 9:79. Was Luther here relying on a piece of rabbinic wisdom handed down to him through the scripture commentaries he studied? It is fascinating to point out with Weinfeld that "the rabbis indeed could not conceive the removal of the Canaanites in such a cruel, radical manner and circumvented plain Scripture by interpreting Joshua's conquest as follows: 'Joshua sent out three proclamations (*prostagma*) to the Canaanites: he who wishes to leave shall leave; he who wishes to make peace shall make peace; he who wishes to fight shall do so." *Deuteronomy 1–11*, 384.

93. For probing exploration of this movement, see Ted A. Smith, *Weird John Brown: Divine Violence and the Limits of Ethics* (Stanford, CA: Stanford University Press, 2015).

94. Abraham J. Heschel, *The Prophets* (1962; repr., New York: Perennial Classics, 2001), 365, cited by Strawn, *Old Testament Is Dying*, 116n57.

95. Wyschogrod, *Body of Faith*, 64, 95, 124.

Strawn accordingly warns against cutting the Gordian knot in the fashion of the second-century heretic Marcion, whose "better God . . . does not fully solve the problem of divine wrath" any more than a literalistic insistence on God's vengeance does. But God's justice and God's goodness "must *proceed together*. God's justice is fully compatible with God's goodness; indeed, the combination of God's goodness with God's justice *enhances* the perfection of God's character. This is part of what it means to speak of the oneness of God: God's goodness is God's justice is God's love. Marcion's notion of God's goodness is anything but divine, since it is devoid of God's justice. As a result, Marcion's god is simplistically and solipsistically 'good,' meaning 'nice' and 'without judgment.' That is why Marcion's god is a false god."[96] But this canonical framing of the question about the unity of God points interpreters forward to the cross of the second Joshua, where the God of love justly overcame the wrath of his love against sin to achieve the mercy of it once and for all.

Usurping the Usurpers of the Earth

We are still by way of introduction trying to frame the question about YHWH who fights for us that is to be answered in the commentary to follow. This entails now a new clarification: skepticism regarding historical *representations* in the book of Joshua is not tantamount to denial that the book of Joshua makes historical *reference*. It does indeed speak about a past epoch when Israel inherited the land of Canaan by dispossessing and/or assimilating its preexisting peoples. As mentioned, this historical reference is important because it weaves together what precedes and follows canonically—that is, between the promises made to Israel's nomadic ancestors and their fulfillment with the united kingdoms of David and Solomon. But Joshua also bridges between this fulfillment and the divided kingdoms' later collapse in the Assyrian and Babylonian conquests. Indeed, as also mentioned, it was from the perspective of the catastrophic loss of the land of promise that canonical Joshua received its final form, and it is from this perspective that we inherit and read the book as ingredient to the church's Bible. The perspective of perplexity and loss of the promised land raises, and indeed insists on, a probing question that will help frame our inquiry: In what sense does YHWH fight for Israel if the land can be lost? And this question generates the messianic intimations in the book of Joshua.

To be sure, just as the book of Joshua refers to a historical event, Israel's possession or, better, *inheritance* of the land of Canaan, it also makes a spatial or

96. Strawn, *Old Testament Is Dying*, 114.

geographical reference that can be neither overlooked nor underestimated in its theological significance. As Nelson observes, "For exilic and postexilic readers, the land represented both fulfilled promise and defaulted legacy."[97] But what exactly does the "land" refer to here? Here as elsewhere the danger of anachronistic presentism that retrojects fallaciously onto the text of Joshua current ideas of political sovereignty and land title to private property must be identified in order to hear precisely what it is that YHWH liberates and bequeaths to his people Israel.

In an important study, Ellen F. Davis sheds much light on the theology of the land in Old Testament scripture by interpreting its testimony through an "agrarian" lens.[98] While possession of the land is arguably the central gift YHWH gives to Israel in the book of Joshua, it is a mistake of anachronism to think that this possession of Canaan consists in *political sovereignty* over the land in the sense of the modern nation-state or, for that matter, the ancient city-states that YHWH usurped in his advent into Canaan. Possession of the land is rather what Joshua consistently describes as an "inheritance" (Hebrew *nakhalah*)—that is, a plot bequeathed to generation-spanning families of the twelve tribes, as one scholar cited by Davis summarizes, for the "preservation of multiple family holdings in relative equality and freedom."[99] Regarding the book of Joshua, the observation is manifestly true; there is as yet no such thing in Israel as political sovereignty (as the following book of Judges ruefully observes in conclusion, 21:25). Yet the absence of political sovereignty in Joshua is precisely to the book's point: here and now YHWH alone reigns by the ministry of his servant-in-training Joshua, dethroning the kings of the Canaanite city-states and demolishing their fortifications in order to liberate the land from their kind of possession.

Recalling the statement from the conclusion of the Song of the Sea in Exod. 15:17 (to which she could have added Josh. 5:13, 15), Davis argues that from the beginning of the exodus story

> Canaan as a whole is conceived of as a holy mountain and a sanctuary for Israel's God, long before the temple has been built. From this perspective, the land itself is the primary sanctuary, with the temple standing as a symbol or replica of it. . . .
>
> In turn, Canaan becomes Israel's covenantal allotment held on the condition of obedience from generation to generation. Conceived as *naḥălâ*, the land of

---

97. Nelson, *Joshua*, 16.

98. Ellen F. Davis, *Scripture, Culture, and Agriculture: An Agrarian Reading of the Bible* (New York: Cambridge University Press, 2014).

99. Davis, *Scripture, Culture, and Agriculture*, 102, citing Christopher J. H. Wright, *God's People in God's Land: Family, Land, and Property in the Old Testament* (Grand Rapids: Eerdmans, 1990), 63.

Canaan and any part of it is the possession of all Israel (Deut. 4:21; 15:4, etc.), of the tribe (Josh. 11:23; 17:6, etc.), or of an ancestral house within Israel (Josh. 24:28; Judg. 2:6, 1 Kings 21:3 etc.). It is . . . as the property of a family through the generations that *naḥălâ* is a genuinely agrarian concept, . . . "one that . . . honors healthy, enduring bonds between people and place, and that situates users within a social order that links past or future."[100]

This is a veritable "covenant of the generations" (Edmund Burke). As Wyschogrod develops the thought: "Abraham is not offered escape from death. Instead, what is offered to him as something good is not for him but for his descendants, and Abraham is more than satisfied because the welfare of his children means more to him than his welfare. This is the kind of fellowship of the generations that is made possible in Abraham. It is a love of children that far surpasses in importance the conquest of death."[101]

We have here, then, alternative conceptions of the possession of the land: between familial inheritance in perpetuity under covenant with YHWH on one side and political sovereignty according to which privatized property can be exchanged as a commodity on the other. Davis illuminates this contrast with the story of Naboth's vineyard in 1 Kings. When Naboth refuses King Ahab's financial offer for his vineyard, he says that it would be defilement/pollution for him before YHWH if he were to sell his ancestors' *nakhalah* to Ahab.[102] As YHWH's gift and the family's trust, the land is sacred and may not be subjected to the marketplace as backed by political sovereignty and thus turned into a commodity. The latter use is rather a usurpation of the royal claim of YHWH, who has come to destroy the usurpers of the earth by reclaiming the land as *nakhalah* bequeathed to the covenant people, Israel.

Two things of relevance for the interpretation of Joshua's theology of the land are to be noted from this brief sampling of Davis's rich study. First, Israel's possession of its inheritance in the land of Canaan—not referring then to a clearly bounded territory so much as to a system of political sovereignty—is conditional, not merely upon obedience to the letter of the law but, more profoundly, to the law's deeper requirement of the obedience of faith. For it is faith which ever remembers the land as a divine gift, thus understanding possession as a trust and task of stewardship for the

---

100. Davis, *Scripture, Culture, and Agriculture*, 106, quoting Eric Freyfogle, "Private Property Rights in Land: An Agrarian View," in *The Essential Agrarian Reader: The Future of Culture, Community, and the Land*, ed. Norman Wirzba (Lexington: University Press of Kentucky, 2003), 237.

101. Wyschogrod, *Body of Faith*, 123.

102. Davis, *Scripture, Culture, and Agriculture*, 111.

sake of coming generations. Second, recalling the perspective of readers of canonical Joshua following the loss of the land in the exile, Davis cites Ps. 37, telling how "the psalmist speaks to and for the 'vulnerable' (*'ănāwîm*), who, it seems, are currently landless"—that is, the dispossessed. Accordingly, she translates verses 9 and 11,

> For the evildoers will be cut off,
> but those who hope in YHWH, *they* will possess the land. . . .
> The vulnerable will possess the land,
> and they will take delight in an abundance of *šālôm*.[103]

So also the latter-day Joshua would speak shalom: "Blessed are the meek, for they will inherit the earth" (Matt. 5:5). The promise of the inheritance of God following the loss of the land of Canaan thus becomes messianic and eschatological, though not otherworldly, just as Israel, figured in the person of Joshua in anticipation of Spirit-anointed Jesus, becomes the representative of all the earth. And a third point here needs to be made for us today: just as the military policy of the book of Joshua is not literally any word of God for us today, so also the economic policy of land reform in the book of Joshua is not literally any word of God for us today.[104] Rather, the spirit of these words, expressing the mind of the Creator and Redeemer of the earth at war with the usurpers of the earth, would capture also the hearts and minds of contemporaries and empower in us more just and wholesome stewardship of the earth.

So what does the Spirit say? Against whom does YHWH fight, in Joshua prefiguring Jesus? He fights against the usurpers of the earth, those who possess the earth as a commodity and exchange it for profit extraction at the expense of future generations, backed by the powerful pretensions of political sovereignty. So Mary Theotokos sang, echoing Ps. 37,

> His mercy is for those who fear him
> from generation to generation.
> He has shown strength with his arm;
> he has scattered the proud in the thoughts of their hearts.
> He has brought down the powerful from their thrones,
> and lifted up the lowly;

103. Davis, *Scripture, Culture, and Agriculture*, 115.
104. For an education in the complexities of contemporary land reform, see Catherine Boone, *Property and Political Order in Africa: Land Rights and the Structure of Politics* (New York: Cambridge University Press, 2014). Thanks to a colleague Joshua Rubongoya for this reference.

> he has filled the hungry with good things,
> and sent the rich away empty. (Luke 1:50–53)

YHWH fights for the redemption of the common body, bound as it is organically to the good earth and through the good earth each body to the other. "For the creation waits with eager longing for the revealing of the children of God; for the creation was subjected to futility, not of its own will but by the will of the one who subjected it, in hope that the creation itself will be set free from its bondage to decay and will obtain the freedom of the glory of the children of God. We know that the whole creation has been groaning in labor pains until now; and not only the creation, but we ourselves, who have the first fruits of the Spirit, groan inwardly while we wait for our adoption, the redemption of our bodies" (Rom. 8:19–23). YHWH fights for the redemption of the body, formed from the earth and returning to the earth, against the usurpers of the earth. These usurpers, objectified in the Canaanite city-states and their kings, become in time the anti-divine figures of powerful sin and death, personified as the Evil One, the New Testament's devil.

If this is the one against whom YHWH fights, notwithstanding the book of Joshua's geographical reference to Israel's inheritance of the land of Canaan once upon a past time, the gospel of Joshua cannot be contained by this ancient reference to the land of Canaan whose time had passed away already for the first readers of canonical Joshua. The book's historical references to the fathers before and the failures and loss to come afterward, as also its geographical reference to the land of Canaan as Israel's inheritance, transcend fore and aft the course of Joshua's narrative. In this respect, the meaning of the book of Joshua remains open to both Jewish and Christian appropriation. Acknowledging this objective uncertainty, what specific theology, then, can a close literary reading of the book of Joshua provide, bounded as it is at the beginning by the commissioning of Joshua upon the death of the servant of YHWH, Moses, and the warning of Joshua to the covenanted people at the end when he too at last receives the same title, servant of YHWH?

This brings us to the messianic or christological sense of the book of Joshua, which may be Jewish as well as Christian. According to Wyschogrod, "authentic Judaism must be messianic Judaism," and indeed "messianic faith is very much alive among Jews. Jewish life could not have survived the Holocaust without it, nor could Israel have come into being."[105] Great as these events of survival and new

---

105. Wyschogrod, *Body of Faith*, 255–56.

birth are to the eyes of faith, they are but tokens of the future still outstanding and expected. "The apocalyptic dimension of messianism stresses the extraordinary magnitude of the coming transformation, which is seen as cataclysmic, since nothing ordinary can put an end to the tired and broken world of history as we have known it."[106] This is one way of making sense of the testimony of the book of Joshua—namely, as a transient episode of victory pregnant with the divinely promised future, a token of light illuminating a path through a very long trail of tears. With intellectual honesty and a definite moral courage, Wyschogrod's Jewish reading of Joshua leaves standing the grim contradiction between personal and public morality, insignia of the dark historical tragedy in which God's chosen people yet wander, waiting for the end of days. It is a contradiction that only the fabulous coming of the reign of God in power and glory overcomes.

Christian theological reading of Joshua in the spirit of Christian realism can certainly say no less than this, but in what follows we will attend to the Christian-messianic way of making sense of Joshua's inconclusive conclusion. It points forward to the best of news breaking into the human world still aching in sorrow and shrouded under the power of death. For the Christian theologian, the paradox of Christ crucified is not a senseless contradiction in terms as if to say, "Joshua put to the sword—end of story." Nor is it, for that matter, the end of the story, but rather a new beginning within it.

Joshua and the New Joshua

Optimally, as we have heard, close literary-spiritual reading is one in which the text gets not only to speak in its own voice but also to question the reader with its own claim to truth, which is Joshua's gospel that *YHWH fights for us.* Needless to say, an element of subjectivity is introduced here since the reader/commentator of Joshua varies, beginning with this reader/commentator who is your author and you who take this book up to read and respond to his reading of Joshua. This element of subjectivity is hardly to be ignored in theology but rather acknowledged and explicitly thematized in a subject-object-audience relationship.[107] More concretely, the production of theological knowledge by a theological subject through close reading of scripture is undertaken by and for members of the community of faith that holds to these particular writings as sacred—that is,

---

106. Wyschogrod, *Body of Faith*, 257.
107. Paul R. Hinlicky, *Beloved Community: Critical Dogmatics after Christendom* (Grand Rapids: Eerdmans), 82–84.

selected by the Holy Spirit from an infinity of texts and so set apart or sanctified for the community's encouragement and hope through the knowledge bestowed of the saving God. Having thus recalled the primary ecclesial location of theological subjectivity, it is, however, also true that any theological subject is also at the same time someone from the nations—that is, a member of some tribe, of some class, and of some gender and that these atheological factors, although passé in principle (Gal. 3:26–28), also influence, if not corrupt, the reading of scripture. The book of Joshua deals with this problem of the double nature of theological subjectivity in its poignant narratives of Rahab, the Gibeonites, and even the tribes that settle beyond the land of Canaan to the east of the Jordan.

As a consequence of this dual nature of theological subjectivity, the theological reading of scripture can never settle on a once-and-for-all fixed meaning but in an endless circulation of correction and reproof proceeds toward the better reading as bounded by the tradition's rule of faith and the scope of the ecclesial community—a process that is especially on display in Josh. 22, as we shall see. The reason this is so in Christianity is that scripture is *not* the foundation of faith but rather its authorized matrix.[108] The foundation of faith is the word from God spoken in the gospel promise that YHWH fights for us, a promise that finds its Yes and Amen, as we shall show in the commentary, in the resurrection of the crucified Jesus. Hence the lordship of Jesus Christ is what qualifies membership in race, class, or gender as passé, subjected now to baptismal union with Christ and through Christ with all who are so united to him.

In Christian perspective, what makes the book of Joshua cohere as knowledge of God who surpasses the wrath of his love to find the mercy of love is ultimately its paradoxical reference, seen in the retrospect of Easter morn, to the crucified Joshua. It is Jesus Christ who enacts the triumph of God by an act of solidarity with history's losers, thus forming a new creation out of one old and dying. Ultimately, as per Rom. 11, this triumph of God includes all Israel, including the particular people of God who lost the promised land but will never be lost to God's new and coming heaven and earth. In the apostle Paul's Christian perspective, this Israel of old will not be lost to God because in the fullness of time one of their own, a suffering son of Israel and servant of YHWH, took upon himself the fate, not only of lost and suffering Israel, but also of all the Canaanites slaughtered at the edge of Israel's sword, with their kings hung on trees to die in disgrace, in

---

108. Paul R. Hinlicky, "Scripture as Matrix, Christ as Content: A Response to Johannes Zachhuber and Anna Case-Winters," in *Luther Refracted: The Reformer's Ecumenical Legacy*, ed. Piotr J. Małysz and Derek R. Nelson (Minneapolis: Fortress, 2016), 299–317.

the place of curse, anathema. Appreciation and appropriation of these profound christological paradoxes, however, depends on a faith in their final coherence, formed in the matrix of the scriptures but generated by the singular word of God, the gospel of Easter morn, enacting and therefore clarifying precisely how it is that YHWH fights for us—namely, in the resurrection of the crucified Jesus as the new Joshua who triumphs on behalf of us all. "For God has imprisoned all in disobedience so that he may be merciful to all" (Rom. 11:32).

Thus what will chiefly interest us in the commentary is the christological cor-relation between the first Joshua, son of Nun, and the second Joshua, Jesus son of Mary and Son of God. This is a genuine task of discovery. This commentary will therefore not impose dogmatically from the rule of faith in such a way that obscures the primary literary sense of the text regarding Joshua the son of Nun. The task is rather to use the rule of faith (to wit, the previously referenced politics of reconciliation from Rom. 15:4 and Gal. 6:15–16) to discern the Holy Spirit's purpose in the literary sense and from there fittingly to develop further senses of the knowledge of God. The church father Origen was undoubtedly the first master in this regard, and with due caution to avoid supersessionism we shall make ample use of his *Homilies on Joshua* in what follows. Reading the Greek of the Septuagint, Origen realized that the Greek translation of the Hebrew name Joshua (meaning "YHWH is salvation") was the same word as the Greek trans-lation of the Aramaic name for Jesus. Joshua is really Jesus! It is not that Jesus supersedes Joshua but that Joshua servant of YHWH who saves really is Jesus in advance. Summarizing the account of Joshua in the Pentateuch in combination with the opening of the book of Joshua appointing him as successor to Moses, Origen asks, "To what then do all these things lead us?" And he answers, "Obvi-ously, that the book does not so much indicate to us the deeds of the son of Nun, as it represents for us the mysteries of Jesus my Lord."[109]

Making this connection, Origen saw in this christological typology a redemp-tive theology of *Christus victor*. The Joshua of ancient Israel cryptically refers to the Jesus of the new covenant, who conquers not with sword of bronze or chariot of iron but with the word of God, not then over Canaanite troops but over our sins, the Canaanite within. But how do we then account for the striking differences in the literary representations of the bloody conquest of Canaanites by Joshua and of Jesus the Christ victorious over sin and death by bloody self-sacrifice? The scheme of shadow to promise can be notoriously unprincipled

---

109. Origen, *Homilies on Joshua*, 29.

and thus turn the Old Testament text into clay in the New Testament potter's hand. Origen's default answer is that the dark and dangerous representations of literal Joshua literally slaying the literal Canaanites fall away like a snake's shed skin when the spiritually illuminated reader sees through the words of Joshua to our merciful Jesus hidden beneath, "who came not to be served [like an earthly king] but to serve [like an earthly slave] and lay down [like a priest] his life [like a sacrifice] a ransom for many" (Mark 10:45).

Without discounting the great value of this christological typology, which this commentary will also employ, Origen's account for his insight lent itself too easily to arbitrary appropriations from the book of Joshua that did not account for all the evidence in the text. As a result, the real and important difference or dissimilarity between Joshua and Jesus becomes obscured as does also the christological sense of the theologoumenon "YHWH fights for us," which in Origen virtually reduces to the ascetic Christian's internal battle against sinful impulses. While this is not wrong, it is but a microcosm of the cosmic-apocalyptic conflict between the *civitas Dei* and the *civitas terrena*.

What is interesting is that the resolute literalness of the Geneva reformer John Calvin's equally christological reading of Joshua—to which we shall also resort regularly in what follows—unravels in the same difficulty, notwithstanding the exegetical superiority of Calvin's treatment in comparison to Origen's. Hartmut N. Rösel helpfully elaborated on Calvin's strengths and weaknesses as a commentator on Joshua. The strength is that "Calvin is sensitive to inconsistencies and difficulties in the biblical tradition. If these difficulties are theological in nature, Calvin strives to reconcile them"—that is to say, *harmonizes*. One such difficulty in Joshua that troubles Calvin greatly is the contradictory accounts of complete and incomplete conquest. Calvin's solution to the contradiction is that "the Israelites acted faithlessly and cowardly and the outcome was that they did not conquer the entire Promised Land." The complete conquest promised by God, on the other hand, is "directed towards future realization in the kingdom of Christ, exemplified in David and his reign."[110] Thus Calvin's harmonizing issues in seeing Joshua as a royal figure, a position that Nelson in his commentary similarly adopts in seeing Joshua to prefigure the reforming king Josiah. Whether we read Joshua as prefiguring Israelite monarchy or rather as protesting it (as in 1 Sam. 8) is an interesting question that we will address throughout the commentary. In any case, there is much more to offer from Calvin's commentary (and also to

110. Rösel, *Joshua*, 11, citing Calvin.

criticize), especially regarding a key notion found in his repeated emphasis on the "obedience of faith." This is a significant concept, which opens and closes the apostle Paul's letter to the Romans (1:5; 16:26). But the notorious genitive construction is ambiguous: Does it mean that obedience that is faith itself, or does it mean an obedience that follows from faith and thus actually confirms (or disconfirms) faith by human works?

The modern historical-critical scholar, in any case, prefers source criticism to see conflicting antecedent traditions, if not ideologies, at work in the crude synthesis visible on the surface of canonical Joshua, the product of a sloppy editor. The historical-critical scholar prefers this reduction of the text to contending religious ideologies not least of all because, as Rösel points out, the perceived cost of Calvin's rigorously literal/typological theology of Joshua is too great. In his theological intention Calvin reconciles the difficulties, Rösel writes, by his "important principle" that "God is always right, but man (including the commentator) often is not in the position to understand and evaluate all the reasons for God's doing. . . . When no human explanation is possible . . . it remains only that we bow down and subjugate ourselves to God's ungraspable decisions."[111] It is certainly possible that in this obscurantist way muddle protects itself from criticism by cloaking its own confusions in a mantle of divine mystery. To the extent that Calvin in fact reads Joshua theologically according to his rule of faith regarding the unsearchable sovereignty of God, it not only offends the modern sensibility of the historical-critical commentator but also overrules a more discerning literary exposition of the dramatic coherence of the book of Joshua, in the light of its gospel that YHWH fights for us.

In any case, a Christian theology of liberation, *if* it is indeed *theology*, knowledge *of God*, turns on this good news of Joshua: "the book of Joshua is a theological confession, summarized in the creedal statement: 'YHWH fought for us' (10:14, 42; 23:3, 10)."[112] "Ultimately God himself is the reason for the continuity. He guarantees implementation of his program. Human generations change, leaders change, history changes, but God does not change"[113]—at least not in his militant resolve of grace to fulfill his purposes with humanity and establish his reign on the earth over his redeemed people, the Israel of God. In this way Joshua, son of Nun, prefigures the *Christus victor* who is Jesus, son of Mary and Son of God.

---

111. Rösel, *Joshua*, 12.
112. Nelson, *Joshua*, 17.
113. Rösel, *Joshua*, 26.

PART 1

YHWH USURPS THE USURPERS OF THE EARTH

(JOSHUA 1–12)

YHWH COMMISSIONS JOSHUA
TO SUCCEED MOSES

1:1–9

YHWH speaks, announcing the death of Moses and thus the termination of his service. "Now therefore"—the commissioning of Joshua arises as a consequence of the departure of Moses from the scene. The character for whom the book of Joshua is named is thus introduced to the reader by YHWH who calls him to follow Moses in his service. Readers of the canonical book of Joshua will already know about the death of Moses from the conclusion of the preceding book, Deuteronomy, as they will also know of Moses's service from Deuteronomy as well as from the books preceding it—namely, Exodus, Leviticus, and Numbers. They will also know from these sources something of Joshua the son of Nun, and relevant details from these sources will be called to mind throughout canonical Joshua.

We are to see in YHWH's words in what kind of relationship Joshua stands to Moses, as successor to predecessor, and hence what role Joshua can be expected to play in what follows. The Hebrew *'ebed yhwh* (slave/servant of YHWH) is a title at the outset reserved for Moses alone, while another word is used to characterize Joshua's previous ministering to Moses. The priority of Moses in the Moses-Joshua relationship is thus indicated. But what kind of priority is this? What Joshua goes on to do is in some sense derivative of the initiation accomplished by Moses in the exodus, the wilderness wanderings, the deliverance of Torah at Sinai and the covenant-making there, and even victory in battle as Israel approached the promised land. But equally Joshua will somehow complete what Moses has begun. Thus by the end of the book, Joshua too will be awarded the title of "servant of YHWH" (24:29). While some commentators see this Joshua-in-training to prefigure Josiah the king of Judah, associated with the discovery of the book of Deuteronomy and the reform of worship,[1] it is better, as our commentary will show, to see the ministry of Joshua in priestly terms.[2]

Origen reviews this background material extensively at the outset of his *Homilies* with a view to explaining how it is that Joshua succeeded Moses. He sees that it was not by continuing Moses's work as lawgiver since his instruction has become now a settled deposit of faith recorded in "the book of the law." Rather, Origen discovers in the background material of the Pentateuch the warrior whom Moses himself had already commissioned to accomplish the promises of YHWH on behalf of Israel. Moreover, for Origen, it is in this role as warrior that Joshua figures forward "Jesus, my Lord and Savior, [as it is he who now] assumed the leadership."[3] This is how Origen understands the priority of Moses and distinguishes the law from the gospel, the old covenant from the new, letter from spirit. The church fathers generally embraced this explanation of the typology. For example, Lactantius: "For that Jesus [Joshua] was a figure of Christ. Although he was first called Hoshea, Moses, foreseeing the future, ordered him to be called Joshua (or Jesus), so that, since he was selected leader of the soldiery against Amalek who was attacking the children of Israel, he might overcome the adversary through the figure of his name and lead the people into the land of promise. And for this reason also he succeeded Moses, to show that the new law given through Jesus Christ succeeded the old law which was given through Moses."[4] But both Origen and Lactantius overstate the difference between law and gospel by treating it as a supersession, when in fact, as we shall see, what is involved is a tension within the Torah between its indicatives and its imperatives.

---

1. Richard D. Nelson, *Joshua: A Commentary* (Louisville: Westminster John Knox, 1997), 29, who acknowledges that it is difficult to prove some sort of traditional installation genre behind the call of Joshua. But Dozeman notes to the contrary, "Joshua kills kings; he does not model them." Thomas B. Dozeman, *Joshua 1–12: A New Translation with Introduction and Commentary*, Anchor Yale Bible 6B (New Haven: Yale University Press, 2015), 212.

2. "P also lays the foundation for the leadership role of Joshua son of Nun who, in the JE tradition, is merely regarded as Moses's assistant or attendant. In P's historiography, Joshua emerges as a tribal chieftain and as the heir apparent, ultimately ordained by Moses to carry on after his death as leader of the Israelites. He will lead the Israelite conquest of Canaan. In presenting Joshua as a leader, the priestly writers may have taken their cue from the Deuteronomist (Deuteronomy 1:38, 3:21, 28)." Baruch A. Levine, *Numbers 1–20*, Anchor Bible 4A (New York: Doubleday, 1993), 71.

3. Origen, *Homilies on Joshua*, ed. Cynthia White, trans. Barbara J. Bruce, Fathers of the Church (Washington, DC: Catholic University of America Press, 2002), 30.

4. Lactantius, *The Epitome of the Divine Institutes* 4.17, in *Joshua, Judges, Ruth, 1–2 Samuel*, ed. John R. Franke, Ancient Christian Commentary on Scripture: Old Testament 4 (Downers Grove, IL: InterVarsity, 2005), 2 (hereafter cited as ACCS).

For the sixteenth-century reformer Calvin, by contrast, the human and historical figure of Joshua stands to Moses as obedience stands to faith or as imperative
stands to indicative. The career of Joshua is presented to illustrate

> the property of faith to animate us to strenuous exertion, in the same way as un-
> belief manifests itself by cowardice or cessation of effort . . . [so that] we may infer
> from this passage, that bare promises are not sufficiently energetic without the
> additional stimulus of exhortation. For if Joshua, who was always remarkable for
> alacrity, required to be incited to the performance of duty, how much more neces-
> sary must it be that we who labor under so much sluggishness should be spurred
> forward. . . . The only way in which we can become truly invincible is by striving
> to yield a faithful obedience to God.[5]

Here, by contrast to Origen and Lactantius, the difference between law and gospel is understated, and the directness of YHWH's speech to Joshua, as direct
as YHWH ever spoke to Moses, weighs in favor of Origen rather than Calvin:
"For if we do not understand how Moses dies, we shall not be able to understand
how Jesus reigns."[6] Thus from the outset we see that knowing the distinction
between the law and the gospel is no easy or self-evident matter. We shall see
that the priority of Moses to Joshua is not one of dignity but of mission, which
is why the warrior Joshua can figure the messianic Savior to come who resolves
the tension internal to the law between its indicative and its imperative by his
own performance of the obedience of faith on behalf of those who have failed
to keep the covenant.

The mission Joshua is to take up is consequential indeed: at YHWH's command Joshua is to lead this particular people, Israel, encamped at Shittim on
the eastern side of the Jordan River, across the Jordan into this particular land
of Canaan that YHWH is giving to them in fulfillment of the promise he made
to their ancient ancestors. Israel is a "people," a particular people whose name
contains the word "God" (*El*), a particular people chosen by God to strive with
God until blessing is won, if we hearken back to the episode in Gen. 32. There
the ancestor Jacob night-wrestled with God at the river Jabbok until blessing
was bestowed and so received this new name, Israel, meaning one who "strives
with God." The blessing in question is the grant of land now at last about to be
realized after many detours and long wanderings.

5. John Calvin, *Book of Joshua* (North Charleston, SC: CreateSpace, n.d.), 13–14.
6. Origen, *Homilies on Joshua*, 37.

Such word from YHWH thus initiates the action about to take place and indeed throughout the book. The pattern of divine word–faith–obedience repeats throughout the narrative; thus the imperative that directs the behavior of Joshua and Israel following is firmly, indeed exclusively and repeatedly, grounded in the indicative of YHWH's word telling what he is about to do on Israel's behalf.[7] Wyschogrod states emphatically, "Covenant, as moral demand, does not arise in a vacuum. It arises in the context of man's gratitude to God when God has mercifully saved him from some great danger. Receptivity to the command is therefore rooted in gratitude for salvation, for bringing into being (Adam), for saving from nonbeing (Noah) and bondage (children of Israel)."[8] Promise and faith are correlative just as faith that receives—passively and without merit—the divine promise becomes active as obedience. As YHWH is the one who brought Israel out of Egypt, the house of bondage, just so Israel is to have no other gods in place of YHWH, lest Israel, failing to hear YHWH and thus to follow YHWH, fall back into bondage. In YHWH's holy zeal to reign over liberated Israel on the soil of liberated Canaan, YHWH is a "jealous God" (Josh. 24:19) who will not overlook infidelities, for they are lethal. Divine and holy love is against what is against love. The love of YHWH is thus militant. By the same token, the sin of infidelity is the unforgivable sin. It is no venial sin within the covenanted relationship that may be repented, atoned, and thus forgiven. It is mortal sin that violates to the point of destruction the covenant relationship itself. Such sin is real and not fictitious destruction. Sin destroys. Infidelity is lethal.

The striking expression about gaining the land wherever Joshua's feet tread on the soil foreshadows the lightning campaign that Israel under Joshua will conduct, traversing the land north, south, east, and west. The meaning is not so much that Israel will actually take possession of the land to this extent in the lifetime of historical Joshua as that Israel will mark claim.[9] The boundaries actually specified in 1:4 in fact extravagantly surpass the territory on which Joshua and Israel will tread in the course of the narrative even as they equally surpass any political dominion actually achieved in the united kingdoms of David and Solomon, as the author's first readers will surely have known.[10] This vast territorial claim is thus first of many anomalies in canonical Joshua.

7. Nelson, *Joshua*, 32–33.

8. Michael Wyschogrod, *The Body of Faith: God in the People Israel* (Lanham, MD: Rowman & Littlefield, 1996), 29.

9. L. Daniel Hawk, *Joshua*, Berit Olam (Collegeville, MN: Liturgical Press, 2000), 8.

10. Hartmut N. Rösel, *Joshua*, Historical Commentary on the Old Testament (Leuven: Peeters, 2011), 32.

The hyperbole here at the beginning is thus an instruction about how to read Joshua. In literary reading, hyperbole is a figure of speech that exaggerates to make a point. "The verb *ntn* 'give' appears in this context eight times in chapter one with YHWH and Moses (once) as subject. . . . The special quality of life in the land given by YHWH is 'rest' (root *nwh*; 1:13, 15)"[11]—that is, not simply legal claim to possession but generation-spanning security on fruitful land. Ingeniously, Origen employs his christological typology here to render the striking expression about the footprints of Joshua as promising "to us" who are in Christ that we shall "crush Satan under [our] feet" (Rom. 16:20). Likewise, he redescribes the Canaanites of old as the "pride, jealousy, greed, and lust" within us today: "within us are the Canaanites; within us are the Perizzites; here are the Jebusites."[12] Thus in the gift of our own bodies and the gift again of their obedience in the Spirit, we are also given a little piece already of that promised land at rest from war.

The heir to Moses is assured of the same unfailing divine presence as had accompanied his predecessor. But the presence of the Divine Warrior with Joshua has the specific content that YHWH will be present to lead the armies of Israel to victory in battle as they enter Canaan; by the same token, however, a defeat in war, as will be found in the first skirmish outside of Ai in 7:4–5, will indicate that YHWH has forsaken Israel. This promise of presence in battle is the divine indicative. In the power of this promised presence, Joshua will not be fearing any man; rather others will fear him and shrink from his face. YHWH exhorts, "Be strong and act the man!" (1:6, 7, 9 AT). The promise of divine presence going into battle generates in Joshua the courage of faith, a new disposition that animates obedient action. What YHWH commands (imperative), as the true King of Israel, YHWH first gives (indicative) in a performative word, a word that does what it says and thus elicits trust. The divine imperative extends this grace to new behavior and thus enables Joshua's sacred agency, causing this people, Israel, to inherit the land that YHWH swore to give to their fathers. In faith Joshua becomes more than a mortal warrior. He becomes, step-by-step through the narrative, the man who commanded sun and moon to hold still at Gibeon—the man, unlike all other men, whom YHWH himself obeyed (10:12–15)!

As a sacred agent Joshua will thus cause things to take place. But this divinely willed and provided new agency of Joshua, who in the course of the narrative becomes "servant of YHWH," is correlative with the sovereign agency of YHWH

11. Nelson, *Joshua*, 31.
12. Origen, *Homilies on Joshua*, 34.

who elected the ancestors of Israel and swore to give them this land and is now fulfilling his word. Thus Joshua's holy agency remains subject to the sovereign purpose of YHWH as that is spelled out in the course of the narrative. He has the covenanted freedom of a servant to do the master's will—or not. The master's will in this case is to dispossess the Canaanites, liberate the land, and bequeath it to the tribes of Israel.

Joshua's agency as a courageous man of war is summoned a second time. This time, however, the summons accentuates the conditional status of Joshua's agency as subject to the sovereign purpose of YHWH. Therefore, quite surprisingly in a military context,[13] Joshua is now required carefully to guard himself from deviating in any direction from the path marked out by the commandments that YHWH gave to Moses. Success in YHWH's war depends on the obedience of Joshua's faith in his divine commissioning as heir to Moses—Moses who instructed Israel in the will of YHWH. Exactly what this Torah heritage means is made clear by reference to "the book" of the law, the Pentateuch, perhaps especially the book of Deuteronomy, preceding the canonical book of Joshua. Joshua is to win wars not by studying war but by studying and keeping the law, both its divine indicative of Israel's gracious election and its equally divine and gracious imperative for the obedience of such faith. For the apostle Paul this correlation is decisive: the saving righteousness of God is enacted and thus manifest in the obedience of Christ in the power of the Spirit. It is not the mere epiphany of a transcendent quality but the very deed and achievement of the saving God on the earth.

For Israel, consequently, all is *not* fair in love and war; loving YHWH above all means waging war, *not* by hook or by crook, but in strict conformity to the commandments of Moses, including *ḥerem*, as we shall see. The warrior agent Joshua is thus simultaneously embedded in a counterintuitive contemplative life of Torah study that is to issue in an active life of concrete obedience limiting his freedom of action, also in the life-and-death situation of combat. War is to be won not by casting off the yoke of the Torah but by wholeheartedly assuming it. Calvin is certainly right to comment here that "it is added as a true source of fortitude that Joshua shall make it his constant study to observe the law . . . because by following it as a guide he will be sufficiently fitted for all things. . . . By submitting entirely to the teaching of the law he is more surely animated to hope for divine assistance."[14] Hearing and meditating on law forms the dispositions

13. Hawk, *Joshua*, 34.
14. Calvin, *Book of Joshua*, 14.

of the heart to the fortitude that hopes defiantly against all odds in YHWH's fabled aid. Thus we might add to Calvin's thought that the conduct of war under these limiting conditions of Torah study and observance can only succeed with fabulous divine assistance!

Commentators notice the tension in this opening section between the unconditioned divine assurances of victory and the conditional stipulations regarding courage and obedience to the law.[15] Glancing back to the end of the book of Deuteronomy (31:1–29), moreover, Hawk even holds that "divine anger overshadows the entire episode of Joshua's investiture" because Israel proves incapable of covenant fidelity.[16] Perhaps better stated: Israel's incapacity *will become* clear gradually and thus only explicitly be pronounced in the conclusion of the book of Joshua. Calvin caught this ambivalence of countervailing trajectories within the law between indicative and imperative and made it a central feature of his commentary: "The people had it in their power to obtain possession of the prescribed boundaries in due time; they declined to do so. For this they deserve to have been expelled altogether."[17]

Nevertheless YHWH's opening address to Joshua concludes with a confident reiteration of divine promise, firmly anchoring the imperative to courageous obedience in the indicative of YHWH's militant presence accompanying Joshua wherever he treads. It is YHWH his God, the God of exodus and Sinai, who has so commanded Joshua to be strong and courageous, neither frightened nor dismayed before mortal opposition. The command to courage foreshadows, by contrast, the uncanny panic that the Divine Warrior will send on Joshua's enemies, causing them dismay in battle. YHWH's promise of presence, we should note, respects no boundaries; it transgresses territorial markers as the divine Presence will shortly cross the Jordan in victorious pomp as a liturgical procession headed by the ark of the covenant. Although Israel is YHWH's chosen people, YHWH is God over all nations—so YHWH crosses the Jordan at the head of the Israelite procession to take possession of what is already his own, to give it now to a people who were no people, but in covenant have become his people Israel.

15. Nelson, *Joshua*, 33–34.
16. Hawk, *Joshua*, 12.
17. Calvin, *Book of Joshua*, 12.

PREPARATIONS FOR THE BATTLE
OF THE KINGDOM OF YHWH

1:10–18

As YHWH commissioned Joshua, so Joshua now gives the officers of Israel specific instructions for the people in camp to prepare food for the passage over the Jordan to the land promised by God as their inheritance. We have here an echo of the hasty preparations for the exodus from Egypt. Yet the narrative next takes an odd detour from implementing the instructions as we have just been made to expect.[1] Joshua speaks instead to the tribes settling on the east bank of the Jordan River according to the arrangement Moses had made with them, recalling to them that it was YHWH through Moses who provided this eastern land to them as a place of rest (Num. 32:1–42; Deut. 3:12–22). "Rest" provides another significant qualification of YHWH's gift of land: land is not only an inheritance and thus a vocation of stewardship envisioning future generations of the covenant people but also a sanctuary from strife and struggle, conflict and war; the land is to be a place of shalom, not a peace of inner tranquility but the peace of finished victory— ultimately land cleansed and so prepared for the dwelling of YHWH with his people Israel. Although they are already settling down in land to the east of the Jordan, they are reminded that they have not yet arrived to this inheritance *as a place of rest*. The reason this is so is that the eastern tribes cannot have a separate peace in a separate land, belonging as they do to the *whole* people, Israel, which remains in trial and struggle to the west of the Jordan. Israel thus forms a body; it is a corporate reality. If one suffers, all suffer; if one has rest, all must enjoy rest.

1. Pekka M. A. Pitkänen, *Joshua*, Apollos Old Testament Commentary 6 (Nottingham, UK: Apollos; Downers Grove, IL: InterVarsity, 2010), 117; Hawk, *Joshua*, 15.

Israel is an organic solidarity—Wyschogrod's "body of faith"—that decomposes if torn apart into its constituents.

But why does this address to the eastern tribes interrupt the instructions for the crossing? Why is their participation with all Israel in the crossing into the land of Canaan significant at just this junction? "Their territory was not 'Canaan' in the traditional sense." The eastern tribes settling outside Canaan are highlighted here "in order to emphasize the 'all Israel' theological scheme of Joshua."[2] In other words, by the time canonical Joshua is written, a burning question has arisen concerning the solidarity of those descendants of the twelve tribes who yet remain in the land of Canaan with others dispersed and settled beyond the holy land. They are only together "all Israel." The issue of all-Israel solidarity introduced here returns near the end of the book in Josh. 23.

In the meantime, it appears that Joshua is commanding the eastern tribes to leave defenseless their women, children, and livestock when he orders their armed forces to join their tribal brothers in the impending campaign for the land west of the Jordan. Quickly, the clarification comes that the eastern tribes have already received "rest" in their own territory; their inheritance there is secure. Thus the departure of the warriors does not leave the women, children, and livestock in danger. Joshua's counsel to the eastern troops returning home in chapter 22 that they are to share their booty with their brothers, however, implies that a contingent remained there to safeguard the women, children, and livestock. Here it is rather the case that the men of war will not enjoy their inheritance in security until all Israel can enjoy together rest from war.

The eastern tribes answer Joshua, pledging their obedience to his instruction that they join their brothers-in-arms in the campaign for the west. They acknowledge that Joshua has inherited the leadership from Moses so that their obedience to him will be identical to the obedience they gave to Moses, the servant of the Lord, provided only that the Lord is with Joshua as he was with Moses. This proviso comes as an exhortation to Joshua: "*Only* YHWH be with you as with Moses. . . . *Only* be strong and courageous" (1:17–18 AT). Does this soft exhortation "hint that their assistance and loyalty, like YHWH's, will depend on [Joshua's] resolve . . . ?"[3] This conditionality suggests to Hawk that there is a reciprocity being promoted in the book of Joshua between divine choosing and human choosing, between being chosen by YHWH and choosing YHWH in

2. Pitkänen, *Joshua*, 33.
3. Hawk, *Joshua*, 17.

turn, between indicative and imperative. That impression of reciprocity is formally defensible, but one wonders about the tacit assumption that the command to choose YHWH presupposes Israel's ability so to choose. What if the narrative, taken as a whole up to the denouncement in Joshua's statement of 24:19, intends to expose a certain impotence in this regard? The difficulty attending Hawk's suggestion is that in this conclusive statement of his final speech, Joshua will deny that Israel can succeed in making the necessary reciprocating choice for YHWH. Something therefore does seem to be missing in the assumed reciprocal relation of divine indicative and divine imperative: the presupposed ability to obey that is generally taken as a condition of intelligibility for imperative statements. Against this presupposition and taken as a whole, the book of Joshua seems rather to reveal an impotence hindering the reciprocation by Israel of YHWH's gracious purpose for his people Israel.

Origen has a different solution, picking up on the easterners' assurance that they will obey Joshua just as they had obeyed Moses. This statement causes Origen to recall John 5:46, where Jesus says, "If you believed Moses, you would believe me." Moses pointed to Joshua who succeeded him as the warrior who would accomplish what YHWH promised. This pointing forward for Origen makes a veiled reference to the Johannine Jesus. The Christian reader may wonder, then, whether Origen's supposed insight that Joshua is really Jesus incognito is what Israel lacks and that this lack of Christian knowledge of who Joshua really is explains Israel's ultimate failure to choose YHWH. Surprisingly, however, Origen is not satisfied with such an easy answer: "I think that probably not even in the coming of Jesus or in his incarnation do we learn what is perfect and complete. . . . We still have need of another who uncovers and reveals everything to us." As Joshua signifies the Johannine Jesus for Origen, the allusion is now to the Johannine Paraclete: "None of these things will be considered perfect in anyone for whom is lacking the Holy Spirit, through whom the mystery of the Blessed Trinity is fulfilled."[4]

The critic of lazy Christian readings may all the same wonder if Origen's leap to the Holy Spirit is not all the more a wild and supersessionist one by the Christian interpreter criticizing the Jewish text for what is *not* there. Or may it be a keen observation about what is in fact not *there* in the text of Joshua? The book of Joshua is throughout devoid of any mention of the Spirit of YHWH. For the Christian reader this is the person of the Trinity who does the choosing in

4. Origen, *Homilies on Joshua*, 45.

believers of the God and Father who has chosen them in the person of the second Joshua, not the son of Nun but the Son of God come in the flesh, the son of Mary Theotokos, who sings with Israel a song of praise at the announcement of his coming. Does the absence of the Spirit in this book's concluding prophecy about Israel's inability to choose YHWH account for that failure? Origen suggests it does. But we will revisit this question time and again between now and the end of the book.

RAHAB, CONFESSING YHWH, TRICKS HER KING, SAVING JOSHUA'S SPIES AND HER OWN FAMILY

2:1–24

This "theologically constructed story"[1] of Rahab (together with its foil in the story of Achan in Josh. 7) takes prominent place at the outset of the book of Joshua, framing the crossing of the Jordan and the defeat of Jericho. It serves literarily to introduce a conflict "between the absolute demands of the ban in Deuteronomy and the rescue of the Canaanite Rahab,"[2] who, according to the rules of *ḥerem* warfare, should not have survived the divinely decreed slaughter of the people of Jericho. "Rahab, of course, embodies 'otherness' in the fullest sense (in ethnicity, gender, and social station). It is therefore significant that hers is the first story which treats the issue of Israel's social definition."[3]

The story goes like this. Joshua sends out two men secretly to scope out the land and Jericho. It is unclear precisely what "secretly" refers to; the ambiguity may be deliberate. Does Joshua keep a secret from YHWH—indicating some hesitations about YHWH's assurances and wanting instead a more rational assessment of Canaanite military power? Calvin asks, "Are we to approve of his prudence? Or are we to condemn him for excessive anxiety, especially as he seems to have trusted more than was right in his own prudence, when, without consulting God, he

1. Dozeman, *Joshua 1–12*, 236.
2. Dozeman, *Joshua 1–12*, 236.
3. Hawk, *Joshua*, 200n41.

was so careful in taking precautions against danger?"[4] Or is it that Joshua keeps a secret from the rest of Israel encamped in Shittim? Or does "secretly" simply mean that the two young men were sent incognito as spies (although later they are designated "messengers")? As also will happen in the story of the covenant with the Gibeonites in Josh. 9, Israelites in the course of the story make a forbidden covenant with a Canaanite without properly consulting YHWH. As in Josh. 9, here too faithless covenant-making is an exercise in prudential politics-as-usual that catches the Israelites in a bind: because of an oath made before YHWH with Canaanite Rahab, they are now bound to this degree to disobey YHWH's command to *ḥerem*.

In any case, the story hastens to show how the two young men failed to maintain secrecy. They went as Joshua commanded but straightaway entered the house of a prostitute and laid down there! It is important to notice the naming of Rahab in contrast to the anonymity of the two spies. Not only is she the protagonist of the story, as we have heard above, but as such she personifies the Canaanite outsider who, by her choice for YHWH, which is the Deuteronomic choice for life and not death,[5] will come to live inside Israel even as her survival from Jericho's destruction, strictly speaking, violates *ḥerem*. As mentioned, she thus stands literarily as a foil to Achan, a *ḥerem* violator but well-pedigreed Israelite whose story is told after the fall of Jericho. Achan is an insider of insiders, a son of the tribe of Judah who in the end is banished from Israel in literal lethality for violating *ḥerem*. Achan personifies disobedient Israel on whom the same judgment falls that obedient Israel executes on the Canaanite city-states and their kings in obedience to the command of their king, the invisible YHWH seated on the processional throne that is the ark of the covenant.

The business of the spies going into Rahab's house is left to the reader's imagination, but what they are scoping out seems to be neither land nor city and its defenses. There is thus perhaps a subtle allusion here to the story in Num. 25:1–5, when in Shittim (the place of the camp to the east of the Jordan River from which Joshua sends the spies) the Israelite men went after the Moabite women, who led them into the worship of other gods. Given the strict prohibition against sexual intercourse with the indigenous population expressed in the legislation of Moses in Deut. 7:2–4 (where the command and rationale for *ḥerem* is stipulated), Rahab may be seen at first glance to symbolize the Canaanite sexual temptation

4. Calvin, *Book of Joshua*, 27.
5. Hawk, *Joshua*, 32.

that threatens virile Israel's identity more profoundly than their vaunted military might. The narrative's hint of indiscretion on the part of the men of the covenant would thus threaten to bring down the divine retribution of abandonment in warfare, jeopardizing the intention of YHWH to give the land to Israel under the proviso of strict obedience (which had just been enjoined and confirmed by the officers of Israel and the eastern tribes in the previous chapter).

Only later in 2:8 does the narrator clarify that the two men had not yet laid down—that is, until they laid down under the flax with which Rahab hid them—perhaps a playful indication that the sin intended in the house of the prostitute was not the sin accomplished. The Hebrew name Rahab is a form of the Hebrew word for breadth; Rahab is, by a vulgar pun, a "broad." Origen recognizes this etymology and turns it to his theological advantage: "What is breadth, therefore, if not this church of Christ, which is gathered together from sinners as if from prostitution?"[6] The comment is not merely clever; it rightly captures the import of Rahab's story as the remarkable inclusion of those by divine right excluded. Without resort to the etymology of the name, Calvin comments to the same effect, "In the fact that a woman who has gained a shameful livelihood by prostitution was shortly after admitted into the body of the chosen people, and became a member of the Church, we are furnished with a striking display of divine grace which could thus penetrate into a place of shame, and draw forth from it not only Rahab, but her father and the other members of her family."[7] Calvin's commentary, too, is in keeping with the import of the text. The saints are not found saintly but become so in being found by grace. "Is it not wonderful, then, that when the Lord condescended to transfer a foreign female to his people, and to engraft her into the body of the Church, he separated her from the profane and accursed nation?"[8]

All the same, the two young spies evidently were not as secretive as Joshua's commission required, for report of their presence in Rahab's house of ill repute immediately comes to the king of Jericho. This is the first mention in canonical Joshua of a king of the Canaanite city-states who as a class will be, as we shall see, the special target of *herem* warfare. The report to the king presupposes a general knowledge among the Canaanites of the looming invasion of the people Israel from across the Jordan River and thus a well-founded suspicion that the discovery

6. Origen, *Homilies on Joshua*, ed. Cynthia White, trans. Barbara J. Bruce, Fathers of the Church (Washington, DC: Catholic University of America Press, 2002), 47.

7. Calvin, *Book of Joshua*, 28.

8. Calvin, *Book of Joshua*, 29.

of two of their men in the midst of their city indicates their purpose of military espionage. The king of Jericho accordingly sends a message to Rahab, telling her to expel from her house the men who have entered it, as the Canaanites of Jericho suspect, not in order to employ her as a prostitute but rather to spy out Jericho's defenses. But in the interim Rahab, who also shares the awareness that her visitors represent an impending invasion force, apprehends the danger the men are in and hides them so that "they are lurking in the house; their life hangs upon the tongue of the woman, just as if it were hanging by a thread."[9]

But Rahab dissembles before the king's messengers, saying first that it was true the two men came into her house—as might be expected—but that she did not know where these men were from. Plausible enough, Rahab's lie is further spun out, however, and succeeds in misleading the king's messengers. When the city gate was closing at dark, she tells them, the men from Israel went out, but *Quick! If the king's messengers hurry to pursue, they will overtake them.* As the reader perceives, Rahab has committed felony upon felony in acts of false testimony amounting to treason against Jericho and its king. According to Calvin, she has also violated the moral law in committing treason and by lying, and thus it is "by the kindness of God [that] the fault is suppressed and not taken into account.... The principal action was agreeable to God because the bad mixed up with the good was not imputed."[10] Perhaps, but what precisely is the "principal action" of Rahab that trumps legal imputation of Rahab's transgressions?

She has aided and abetted the enemy; she has lied elaborately to the king's officials and deliberately sent them on a wild-goose chase. Thus the folklore genre of the "trickster tale" suggests itself here. The protagonist of the trickster tale typically has a marginal social status but by self-reliant wit effects change and in the process entertains hearers/readers of her tale by ridiculing the pretensions of the powerful.[11] Appealing to us postmoderns as is this insouciance, for moderns Rahab violates the Kantian obligation to treat others as ends, never as means. Deception is unworthy of the moral agent whose dignity consists in being a bearer of reason and whose obligation as such is to treat others as bearers of reason like oneself. Moderns cannot universalize Rahab's action, while postmoderns would like to (think of the conflicting valuations of American whistleblower Edward Snowden). But manifestly, this entire discussion of Rahab as trickster proceeds as if YHWH were not God in heaven and on earth, and as if her concrete act of

9. Calvin, *Book of Joshua*, 29.
10. Calvin, *Book of Joshua*, 30.
11. Dozeman, *Joshua 1–12*, 238.

ḥesed were not his master rule governing all other rules. Because YHWH is the true and coming king, the king of Jericho is revealed in turn as a usurper who does not deserve the truth. Because *ḥesed* is Torah's rule of rules, Rahab is right to overrule the rules against false testimony for the sake of truthfulness and against treason for the sake of loyalty to a higher authority. So also Dietrich Bonhoeffer, who wrestled with his ethical obligations to Gestapo interrogators, argues.[12]

Only now do readers learn how Rahab hid the two men of Israel on her roof under the harvest of flax set out to dry in the sun. Deceived, the royal police take off on the way to the Jordan River. The text adds an interesting detail here that the pursuers went to a known passage through the river, to a ford, indicating that a perfectly natural passage through the river was available to friend and foe alike. Another interesting detail is that the city gates were shut after the pursuers went out. These details serve as negative foils foreshadowing the gratuitous nature of the miraculous passage of Israel over the Jordan River to come, as well as the collapse of the city's walled defenses after seven days of parading the ark of the covenant around it—anticipating war instructed by Torah and conducted by way of liturgy!

The narrative next gives us a flashback to the moment on the roof before the men laid down to be hidden under the flax by Rahab. The Gentile prostitute's speech articulates remarkable knowledge of God: she knows that YHWH has given the land to Israel. Accordingly, she reports, terror has fallen on the Canaanites, and their courage to resist the impending invasion is melting away. In 2:9 she virtually quotes verbatim from Exod. 15:15–16. The source of her knowledge of God is the gospel—that is, the word of YHWH's saving deeds in battle on behalf of Israel, specifically the rescue at the Red Sea from Pharaoh's chariots and the defeat of the Amorite kings Sihon and Og under the leadership of Moses when Joshua first became a warrior. Mention of these past events serves literarily to foreshadow the reiteration of YHWH's saving deeds of battle in the new history being made as Israel crosses the Jordan to take possession of the land promised to them from the Canaanites. The prostitute who receives the spies "becomes, instead of a prostitute, a prophet," Origen writes. "You see how that one who was once a prostitute and impious and unclean, is now filled with the Holy Spirit: she makes confession of past things, has faith in present things, prophesies and foretells future things."[13] But Origen here supplies the Holy Spirit, mention of whom is not found in the text.

---

12. Dietrich Bonhoeffer, *Ethics*, ed. Eberhard Bethge (New York: Macmillan 1978), 363–72.
13. Origen, *Homilies on Joshua*, 48.

We have here the first mention in the book of Joshua of the *crux intellectum*: the verb translated into English variously as "utterly destroy" or "devote to YHWH" is the Hebrew *ḥerem*. Rahab confesses that terror from God falls on the Canaanites through hearing the word of Israel's election. The "widespread rumor of miracles, hitherto without example, had impressed on the minds of all that God was warring for the Israelites."[14] It is then "because of you"—that is, because of Israel as God's chosen—that Canaanite courage melts away. In the polytheistic environment of the day, however, Israel's special relationship with its God could readily be taken as no more than a particular claim of one tribal deity over against particular claims of other nations each with their own warrior god. One would then brace for a battle of the gods in wars between the nations representing clashing civilizations. But Rahab's Gentile confession of YHWH, Israel's God, as "God in heaven above and on earth below" (2:11), reframes the usual military theologies of the times: YHWH is the *one true* God—that is, the *one who is truly* God *over all*, echoing Deut. 4:39. As Calvin rightly sees, "The faith of Rahab takes a higher flight, while to the God of Israel alone she ascribes supreme power and eternity. These are the true attributes of Jehovah. She does not dream, according to the vulgar notion, that someone, out of a crowd of deities, is giving his assistance to the Israelites, but she acknowledges that he whose favor they were known to possess is the true and only God."[15] Wyschogrod puts the same point this way: "The biblical narrative never totally integrates God into a framework wider than himself. God always remains the overwhelming and mighty Creator of heaven and earth and therefore the creator of all frameworks, to none of which he is subject."[16]

By the same token, however, this claim for the universality of YHWH's dominion does not represent a demythologizing turn toward abstract or philosophical monotheism positing an ineffable, generic deity behind and beyond the many gods of the nations. The claim is that the particular God of Israel, YHWH, is the one who is truly God over all; the claim embedded in Rahab's confession "probes the religious inclusivity of YHWH's universal rule within the literary setting of a book that is extreme in its exclusive ideology."[17] YHWH is sovereignly enacting his own purpose in Israel's election and the impending grant of Canaanite land to Israel as covenant inheritance. YHWH does not need to battle with the gods of

14. Calvin, *Book of Joshua*, 32.
15. Calvin, *Book of Joshua*, 32.
16. Wyschogrod, *Body of Faith*, 196.
17. Dozeman, *Joshua 1–12*, 244.

the Canaanites, for they are idols that have no true divine existence. The Divine Warrior's power over heaven and earth will be on display in the fabulous events to come.[18] Divine rage coming down from above targets the down-to-earth Canaanite kings as those who emblematize the usurpation of the good earth in regimes of malice structuring injustice; thus are they doomed to destruction, as they must be, when the reign of YHWH advances against them. Just so Rahab's confession, by predicating universal dominion to the particular, *herem*-commanding God of Israel, creates an antinomy within the law. By what right of hers may this one true God heed her challenge? And just what does it mean exactly that a particular deity should be God in heaven and on earth?

The narrative now brings us to an interesting development of Rahab's "character as . . . a trickster who lives on the margins of urban life in the city of Jericho."[19] The trickster now pleads for a covenant (though the word "oath" is used instead of the word "covenant") with the two spies, representatives of Israel, and indeed she invokes YHWH, Israel's God, as witness and guarantor. "Here's the trade: Rahab saves the messengers while the men of Jericho are in control, and the messengers are to save Rahab later once the Israelites are in control."[20] The plea for a new covenant is based on her own gracious act of *hesed*, showing lovingkindness to the endangered Israelites.

The theological question that arises here concerns the motivation of change, not only in Rahab or in the spies, but in YHWH who has been invoked as guarantor of the oath about to be made. "The central role of *hesed* in fashioning an exemption to the divine law of the ban is not surprising, since it is the one virtue that is able to change divine commands in the Pentateuch." Citing the story of Moses's intercession in Exod. 34 after the apostasy of the golden calf, Dozeman points to *hesed* as the basis in God for nullifying the previous death sentence. *Hesed* in this case "not only indicates a change in the Deity but also indicates the spontaneous nature of the virtue. . . . The same spontaneity characterizes Rahab's *hesed* toward the spies, who also had no legal basis for expecting her help."[21]

Elsewhere in the Hebrew scriptures what is hinted here in the figure of Rahab becomes explicit. Spontaneous divine *hesed* can overrule equally divine judgment, as in Hos. 11:8–9. This theological hint will not be made explicit in the book of Joshua, but the hint is there in the figure of Rahab. In Walter Brueggemann's

18. Nelson, *Joshua*, 52.
19. Dozeman, *Joshua 1–12*, 224.
20. Pitkänen, *Joshua*, 124.
21. Dozeman, *Joshua 1–12*, 247.

words, the triumph of *ḥesed* indicates that an "upheaval has occurred in Yahweh's life and character that impinges on Yahweh's sense of self-regard. We are not told whether this upheaval is irreversible nor how deep it is. What we are told is that . . . Yahweh had ample grounds on which to withdraw from the relationship with Israel in justified self-regard, yet Yahweh did not do so." In the figure of Rahab we are thus permitted "to watch while Yahweh re-decides, in the midst of a crisis, how to be Yahweh and who to be as Yahweh."[22] As a result of this novelty of *ḥesed*, through an oath "the mutual relations and obligations characterized by *ḥesed* become reaffirmed like a contract."[23] Rahab's plea for reciprocity in *ḥesed*, interestingly, extends not only to herself but also to her family—in manifest contradiction to Deut. 20:10–20.

What are we to make of such theologically significant contradictions? "How else can we explain [what is figured here in Rahab, YHWH's] constant swinging from anger to love that the Bible describes?"[24] In our culture of decadent Puritanism, we still sentimentally confuse the anger of love with malice and the force of love with violence, but the prophet Amos thunders, "hate evil and love good, and establish justice in the gate" (5:15); the apostle Paul confirms the prophetic teaching, saying, "Let love be genuine; hate what is evil, hold fast to what is good" (Rom. 12:9). The center around which the contradictory judgments pivot is YHWH's "infinite, eternal, and absolute love for Israel. This is the central theme of the Bible. Nothing else ultimately matters. Everything must be seen in its light. Only because it is true is everything else true. Only because of this love is there anger. [YHWH's] humiliation of being rejected by Israel presupposes this love and cannot be understood without it. It is, of course, easy to be free of jealousy if one does not love."[25]

This interesting fact reflects the low regard for the miserable of the earth within Canaan, not "loose" women but destitute ones, the refuse of the city-state structure of injustice animated by malice, driven to prostitution to support an equally destitute family. Rahab "bargains with so much presence of mind, and so calmly, for her own safety and that of her family. And in this composure and firmness her faith, which is elsewhere commended, appears conspicuous. For on human principle she never would have braved the fury of the king and people, and become a

22. Walter Brueggemann, *Theology of the Old Testament: Testimony, Dispute, Advocacy* (Minneapolis: Fortress, 1997), 302.
23. Rösel, *Joshua*, 50.
24. Wyschogrod, *Body of Faith*, 108.
25. Wyschogrod, *Body of Faith*, 118.

suppliant to guests half dead with terror. . . . She was endowed with a lively faith."[26] Covenant fidelity with this God who fights for Israel aims at and finds in Rahab the beginnings of new structures of *ḥesed* love at work in justice—even at the expense of God's own rules and strict justice. As Calvin rightly comments, Rahab has hit on the weightier matter of the law; "in Hebrew, to do mercy and truth, is equivalent to performing the office of humanity faithfully, sincerely and firmly."[27]

John H. Walton and J. Harvey Walton have argued an impressive case that *ḥerem* warfare is to be understood not as punishment (of Canaanites) but as purification (of Canaan). Their case is built on the fact that nowhere within the canonical book of Joshua are the Canaanites condemned to destruction because of moral wickedness. The immediate objection to the thesis is that canonical Joshua follows upon Deuteronomy and Leviticus just as Joshua the warrior follows upon Moses the legislator. The Waltons try to meet this objection by appealing to Deut. 7:25 and the Hebrew word there, *tôʿēbă*, designating "something outside the covenant order. . . . The Canaanite nations are *tôʿēbă* by default, since the covenant was not made with them, and everything in the land that is *tôʿēbă* is to be *ḥerem* ('removed from use')." Consequently, the Waltons argue that the merciless warfare commanded refers to

> destroying identities, not people, as is indicated by the destruction of identity markers (that is, cult objects) in Deuteronomy 7:5. The list of things Israelites are to do consists of breaking down their altars, smashing their sacred stones, cutting down their Asherah poles, and burning their idols in the fire; it does not include killing every last one of them. . . . The references to nations . . . all refer to community identities, not individuals. . . . This is especially the case with the kings (Deut 7:24), who are the embodiment of the identity of the community they lead (which is why they are specifically killed throughout Joshua's campaigns).[28]

Undoubtedly, the Waltons are right in challenging the anachronistic imposition of the contemporary notion of genocide on Joshua by pointing to the cultural-religious matrix of *ḥerem* rather than to the modern racial-biological-genetic matrix of genocide and lifting up in turn the culturally transformative thrust of YHWH's sovereign election of Israel in the covenant. But the case they

26. Calvin, *Book of Joshua*, 30–31.
27. Calvin, *Book of Joshua*, 34.
28. John H. Walton and J. Harvey Walton, *The Lost World of the Israelite Conquest: Covenant, Retribution and the Fate of the Canaanites* (Downers Grove, IL: IVP Academic, 2017), 193.

make overreaches in trying to eliminate the motif of retributive justice visited upon the Canaanite nations and, theologically, the identical divine wrath that threatens to fall on Israel when Israel defects from covenant identity to become again religiously Canaanite. The statement in Deut. 9:4–5 is presupposed by canonical Joshua: it is "because of the wickedness of these nations the LORD your God is dispossessing them before you, in order to fulfill the promise" to the ancestors. Likewise Lev. 18:27–28 employs the graphic image of vomiting to say the same: "(For the inhabitants of the land, who were before you, committed all of these abominations, and the land became defiled); otherwise the land will vomit you out for defiling it, as it vomited out the nation that was before you." Purification of the land and judgment on the human sinners who have polluted it are not alternatives in Joshua but proceed side-by-side.

In other words, read canonically the book of Joshua presupposes the moral as well as cultic indictments of Canaanite culture in Deuteronomy and again in Leviticus: "Do not defile yourselves in any of these ways, for by all these practices the nations I am casting out before you have defiled themselves. Thus the land became defiled; and I punished it for its iniquity and the land vomited out its inhabitants" (Lev. 18:24–25). Theologically, the difficulty raised by the Waltons' overreach in this connection is that it threatens to reduce YHWH to nothing more than Israel's covenant God battling the other gods of other nations outside the covenant, rather than claiming title as the living God in heaven and on earth to whom all nations belong and to whom they are thus in some way responsible, even if it is not the way of Israel's covenant. Returning to the present story: How else could Rahab, outside the covenant, have recognized any claim on her by the God of Israel or dare to lay claim to the God of Israel unless the God of Israel were somehow also her God to whom she could appeal in making an oath?

The endangered spies hastily exclaim their acceptance of the exchange of vows Rahab has proposed: if Rahab does not reveal the spies, thus saving their lives, then they will redeem her life from the *ḥerem* death sentence when it falls on Jericho.[29] When YHWH so acts to give them the land, they will treat her with lovingkindness in return as befits covenant fidelity. Covenant justice consists in this reciprocity of *ḥesed* even as it is instituted by an exchange of vows before YHWH, life for life. At this point, however, the narrative evidently forgets that this entire scene has been a flashback when it tells us that after the spies pledge

29. Perhaps—the LXX puts the statement in Rahab's mouth rather than the spies. The MT has Rahab imposing the oath on the spies; cf. Dozeman, *Joshua 1–12*, 232–33.

fidelity, Rahab leads them to escape down a rope from her window in the city wall, where her house is located. The detail is striking, of course, because it is precisely the city walls that will miraculously collapse when Israel cries victory in the name of YHWH on the seventh day. But it is even more striking when we realize how Rahab and her family will be saved from death in the very place where death befalls Jericho and its inhabitants.

Rahab compounds her disloyalty toward her city by instructing the fleeing spies to hide in the hills for three days—Israel's future home—while the pursuers seek them in the opposite direction, toward the river Jordan and the ford. Just as the spies are now bound by oath to violate the strict law of *herem*, her act of lovingkindness initiating a covenant relationship with Israel, as represented by the spies, entails a breach with her native loyalties and allegiances. Loyal to YHWH, God of Israel and in heaven and on earth, she is disloyal to the *civitas terrena*.

The men reply to Rahab on their way out, delaying their presumably urgent escape, to negotiate a few codicils to the oath. They will be free from the binding commitment of the oath they have sworn if the sign is not displayed by which Rahab and her family will be recognized and thus saved from death: a scarlet cord hanging from the window in the wall through which the spies escape. This required sign recalls the night of the Passover from the canonical book of Exodus: as the vengeance of God is visited on the hardened hearts of the slave master and his regime, taking their firstborn, only those within their domain will be spared from death whose lintels are marked out by the red blood of the Passover lamb (Exod. 12:1–32). So Rahab's crimson-marked house becomes a sanctuary within a wall otherwise fated to collapse on a city destined for destruction. Likewise the occupants of this sanctuary house become a symbol of the unlawful breach of an ostensible boundary between Israel and the Canaanites initiated by spontaneous *hesed*. Origen develops this lead ecclesiologically. "By that sign"—that is, the crimson cord suspended from Rahab's window signifying the blood of Christ the paschal lamb—"all persons attain salvation, all those who are found in the house of the one who was once a prostitute, all those cleansed in the water and by the Holy Spirit and in the blood of our Lord and Savior Jesus Christ, 'to whom is the glory and the dominion forever and ever. Amen!'"[30]

This final negotiation of the spies with Rahab represents a "legal discourse on the rights of non-Israelites who were allowed to live in the Promised Land despite

---

30. Origen, *Homilies on Joshua*, 50.

the absolute demands of the ban."[31] Bloodguilt will thus be distributed: anyone who leaves the sanctuary becomes responsible for their own death. But if anyone within the sanctuary is harmed, the guilt falls on the Israelites who have made this agreement with Rahab. The spies add a further condition to their keeping the oath—namely, that Rahab keep the matter secret. This addition is somewhat perplexing since it is Rahab who will now be in danger after the spies escape with her help, while the king and his people have become aware of their hostile purpose and are in hot pursuit, albeit misled by Rahab's treasonous activity. Keeping the secret is for Rahab a no-brainer. So Rahab quickly concurs with the conditions the spies have attached to the oath, and having sent the spies on their way, she complies immediately by displaying a scarlet cord from her window.

So Rahab's stratagem of deception unfolds as planned: the spies flee to the hill country to the north and west of Jericho, land destined to fall into Israel's hands, while the misled pursuers futilely seek them on the way east to the Jordan River. In due time, the spies return to Joshua and report what YHWH has done. It is true already now, they say, that the land is coming into Israel's possession, because its inhabitants are seized with panic. The dread that falls on them will fatally condition the actual combat about to occur in Israel's favor. Report of warrior YHWH's deeds together with Israel's massing in camp at Shittim deprives the Canaanites of courage for the battle.

But what have the spies actually learned from their scouting mission other than to repeat almost verbatim what they have learned from Rahab? And that suffices. Neither reckless nor timid, the courage that comes from faith rests in the knowledge that YHWH is a warrior who promises to fight for Israel. But the reader has learned that this faith includes the courage of a Canaanite prostitute who endangers herself by confessing YHWH within the walls of fortress Jericho, a new faith correlative with spontaneous action of *ḥesed* love for the endangered spies.

---

31. Dozeman, *Joshua 1–12*, 224.

ISRAEL PASSES OVER THE JORDAN AND MEMORIALIZES THE EVENT

3:1–4:24

The account of preparations for the crossing of the Jordan can bewilder the reader; it seems to try to accomplish too much: "simultaneously to enhance the standing of Joshua, to include various personnel, to define the processional order, to boost the wonder of the event, and to explore its theological meaning."[1] Perhaps nowhere else in the book of Joshua as here (actually from here on to 5:12) does the interpreter feel the countervailing tugs of a literary reading of the text in its final form issuing knowledge of God (4:24!) on the one side and on the other the tug of a compositional source analysis excavating latent but conflicting tendencies in the sources behind the final text.[2] Theological commentary can hardly deny this tension.[3] Decisive for the present approach, however, is the literary insight that the "crossing of the Jordan is a liturgical narrative that . . . emphasize[s] key events through repetition."[4]

Joshua's command at the beginning of the episode that the people sanctify themselves and assemble behind the priests bearing the ark forward indicates the liturgical nature of the narrative. The liturgical understanding of the episode is confirmed by the unexpected appearance of the ark. "It has not figured prominently in the larger narrative."[5] Indeed, here is the first mention of the ark

---

1. Nelson, *Joshua*, 55. For his account of the "complicated history of composition and redaction" here, see ibid.
2. Nelson, *Joshua*, 55, 65; Pitkänen, *Joshua*, 129–30.
3. Dozeman, *Joshua 1–12*, 277. But Pitkänen, *Joshua*, 131; Hawk, *Joshua*, 58–59.
4. Dozeman, *Joshua 1–12*, 281.
5. Hawk, *Joshua*, 63. Cf. Exod. 40:21; Num. 3:31; 4:5; 7:89; 10:33–36; 14:44.

in the book of Joshua. But the surprising appearance of the ark at this juncture is intentional when we realize the episode's liturgical character. Israel will initiate the paradigmatic act of *ḥerem* warfare not by building siege ramps and catapults but by following the lead of priests bearing the ark of the covenant in procession. "This reflects the ancient near Eastern custom of carrying God images or standards as symbols and vehicles of divine presence before the troops."[6] The question concerns precisely how this is to be understood, for symbols are ambiguous until they are interpreted. The ark may be taken as the repository of divine law and thus the sacred place of instruction,[7] or as the visible throne of the invisible YHWH leading Israel to war, or in some way as both.

"When we cross over the Jordan, we cross over to battles and wars," but not, Origen hastens to clarify for his Christian audience, the literal wars of old, but rather, citing Eph. 6:12, "that we may subdue the chief city of this world, malice, and destroy the proud walls of sin. . . . Within you is the battle you are about to wage; on the inside is that evil edifice that must be overthrown; your enemy proceeds from your heart."[8] When sinful malice allures or lust for the goods of Canaan arises, Origen counsels resistance by preaching to oneself the gospel: "I am not mine, for I have been purchased by the precious blood of Christ."[9] So, as Israel followed the ark to cross the Jordan and enter into battle, Origen's Christian rebukes the allures of Canaan and stills anxiety before the battle, saying, "I follow Jesus, the leader, in whose power are those things that are about to be. Why should I have knowledge of the future things since those future things are whatever Jesus wants?"[10] As Israel follows Joshua, so Origen's Christian follows Jesus in the conviction and courage of faith that in this leader the divinely intended future is already pressing into the present. In all this Origen tacitly takes the ark as icon of the throne of YHWH leading his people into battle.

If we follow Origen's lead, then, the ark of YHWH takes on a prominent role in this episode, but not so much as the shrine containing the law of Moses and the site of divine oracles; rather, here it plays a military role as the visibly empty throne of the living but invisible YHWH. The procession thus harkens back

---

6. Pitkänen, *Joshua*, 65.

7. Origen connects the Levites who bear the ark in the procession to their catechetical task: "It is the Priestly and Levitical order that stands by the ark of the covenant of the Lord in which the law of God is carried, doubtless, so that they may enlighten the people concerning the commandments of God." *Homilies on Joshua*, 55.

8. Origen, *Homilies on Joshua*, 61–62.

9. Origen, *Homilies on Joshua*, 65.

10. Origen, *Homilies on Joshua*, 66.

to a poem in Num. 10:35–36 ascribing such military significance to the ark, which Moses was said to recite whenever the ark began to move or came to rest.[11] David L. Stubbs, however, rightly qualifies that "the goal is not simply the defeat of other nations and their subservience to Israel, but that the kingdoms of earth worship God. . . . The ark is not seen as a kind of Greek palladium or magical device that assures the victory of Israel; instead it is a symbol of the presence of God. . . . [Indeed,] in [Num.] 14:44 the presumption and misplaced confidence of the Israelites to defeat their foes without the ark of God and Moses led to their downfall."[12]

What on the level of human history appears as an improbable invasion by nomads marching against walled cities behind an empty throne held high is in divine perspective birth pangs of new creation. This military significance of the ark comports nicely, moreover, with the occasion of river crossing. "The chaotic Sea/River may be an insurmountable barrier for humans, but the divine warrior cuts it and crosses through it in the form of the ark."[13] We do not have here the radical act of origin, *creatio ex nihilo*, but a continuing of creation by a new and redemptive act of *creatio ex vetere*. Such is the advent of the reign of YHWH coming into Canaan, dethroning the usurpers of the earth, to the end that the land will have rest from war. In this way, this new creative story of landed Israel's origin has enduring power to challenge "present social, political and religious order."[14]

In the same apocalyptic vein, we may appreciate Origen's appropriation of the text: "Lest you marvel when these deeds concerning the former people are applied to you, O Christian, the divine word promises much greater and loftier things for you who, through the sacrament of baptism, have parted the waters of the Jordan."[15] Origen's spiritual interpretation here takes "loftier" quite literally. Citing 1 Thess. 4:17, he applies the passage promised in Christian baptism not to river waters here below but through the air above, rising from the dead to meet the returning Lord. Just as the waters flowing downstream wall up and cease to flow when the ark at Joshua's command enters the water, "there is nothing at all that the just one should fear. All creation waits upon that person."[16]

11. Dozeman, *Joshua 1–12*, 284; Nelson, *Joshua*, 60.
12. David L. Stubbs, *Numbers*, Brazos Theological Commentary on the Bible (Grand Rapids: Brazos, 2009), 111.
13. Nelson, *Joshua*, 68.
14. Dozeman, *Joshua 1–12*, 251.
15. Origen, *Homilies on Joshua*, 51.
16. Origen, *Homilies on Joshua*, 52.

"[The] ark of the covenant is brought forward like a banner to guide the way."[17]
Literally within the narrative that begins here and continues to the eighth chapter, this episode marks the first step of several in travel to Shiloh, where the ark settles into its other function as shrine of divine instruction and oracle. But for the present, as the visibly empty throne comes to a standstill in the midst of the river Jordan, it signifies the manifestation of YHWH as the living God in the wonder of walling up the waters for Israel to cross on dry ground. In a series of panels or scenes, the transition of Israel from a band of wandering nomads to a landed nation is depicted, "both the inward transformation of Israel, symbolized externally by circumcision, and the potential of the Israelites to inaugurate a new social order that lacks kings and royal cities."[18]

Leaving behind Shittim both literally and symbolically (as the site of apostasy by the men with the women of Moab), Joshua and all Israel rose early, eager to get going,[19] and advanced to the bank of the Jordan River, there to camp for three days of final preparations. Calvin recalls here the mention of a ford in the vicinity for crossing the Jordan from the previous chapter and connects this with the mention of springtime floods making the ford impassable. Arriving at the flooded Jordan, Israel sees no way forward. Such for Calvin is the typical situation of faith already in possession of the divine promise but not yet of its fulfillment. "That, in such apparently desperate circumstances, they calmly wait the issue, though doubtful, and to them incomprehensible, is an example of faithful obedience. . . . Not produced without the special agency of the Holy Spirit."[20] Like Origen, Calvin too supplies what is lacking in the text: the Holy Spirit. Faith is indeed this kind of divine "patiency," waiting on the promise God provided by the ministry of the Spirit. Calvin thus rightly adds mention of the Holy Spirit as the author of patient faith, although nowhere in the text do we find this. If the Spirit is present in Israel's patient faith, he is present incognito.

The officers of Israel go through the camp commanding the people to follow when they see the ark of the covenant of YHWH their God being carried forward by the Levites. Moving in procession and borne aloft by the Levite priests, the ark thus symbolizes and indeed sacramentally eventuates YHWH's assertion of sovereignty on behalf of his people Israel over the land of Canaan. "[It] was no

17. Calvin, *Book of Joshua*, 41.
18. Dozeman, *Joshua 1–12*, 251; Hawk, *Joshua*, 59.
19. Rösel, *Joshua*, 61.
20. Calvin, *Book of Joshua*, 41.

empty symbol of his presence that God had deposited with them. For Jordan was compelled to yield obedience to God just as if it had beheld his majesty."[21]

There is a sacramental union in which the sign and the thing signified become one in the event. The people are to follow this lead because the land is new and unknown to them. But in following they are to keep considerable distance from the ark itself, respecting its holy otherness. "For although God invites us familiarly to himself, yet faithful trust so far from begetting security and boldness, is, on the contrary, always coupled with fear. In this way, the ark of the covenant was, indeed, a strong and pleasant pledge of the divine favor, but, at the same time, had an awful majesty, well fitted to subdue carnal pride."[22]

Perhaps recalling Lev. 10 (or citing the noncanonical Gospel of Thomas), Origen calls on his readers at this point to remember that "it is written, 'Those who draw near to me, draw near to fire.'"[23] In recognition of the uncanny holiness of YHWH numinously seated on the ark that they are to follow, the people are to use the three days of patient and fearful waiting to separate themselves from all profane things in order properly to follow the ark's holy lead (cf. Num. 11:18). Calvin notes that the Hebrew verb translated as "sanctify" can also mean "prepare" and "either meaning is not inappropriate. . . . For faith prepares us to perceive the operation of God."[24] Proper following in the procession knows and respects the leadership of YHWH as king, as that becomes manifest in the wonder that the people Israel will witness at the crossing. At Joshua's command the procession begins.

Now YHWH speaks to Joshua to tell him (and of course also us who read the narrative) the purpose of the approaching wonder, the crossing of the Jordan. The goal of the scene is a "theophany."[25] As Moses led the people Israel on dry ground through the Red Sea when YHWH was first manifested to the escaping Hebrew slaves as the Divine Warrior drowning Egyptian chariots hot in pursuit, so now on the way to the battle of Jericho Israel will cross the Jordan River also on dry ground.[26] The Divine Warrior has thus left behind the posture of defense of Israel at the Red Sea and now assumes the posture of offense in leading Israel across the Jordan. The parallelism between Moses and Joshua

---

21. Calvin, *Book of Joshua*, 44.
22. Calvin, *Book of Joshua*, 41.
23. Origen, *Homilies on Joshua*, 56.
24. Calvin, *Book of Joshua*, 42.
25. Dozeman, *Joshua 1–12*, 288.
26. Pitkänen, *Joshua*, 135.

serves to confirm that YHWH is with Joshua as he was with Moses, both being exalted to a unique place of leadership under the sovereignty of YHWH now asserting itself. But new assurance is needed corresponding to the newness of an offensive campaign. So "the manifestation of his power given in the passage of the Jordan would be a sure presage of the victory which would obtain over all the nations."[27]

So YHWH commands Joshua to command the priests bearing his throne at the head of his covenanted people to come to the edge of the waters of the river Jordan and there to stand still. The chain of command is executed as Joshua calls together the sons of Israel to come near to him to hear the words of the Lord. As in Egypt YHWH displayed his sovereignty in the wonders performed against Pharaoh, his court, and his military, and so made known his name to his people Israel, the Israel of this present generation, too, shall know by what is about to transpire that YHWH, 'el khay ("the living God," 3:10; also in 1 Sam. 17:26; Ps. 42:3, 9; 84:3; Hos. 2:1), is in their very midst. This epithet means that the one true God is not aloof but acts in history; YHWH is the subject of transitive verbs. Supremely, he fights for Israel. According to Dozeman, what now transpires as YHWH moves to the water's edge "calls forth a reaction from both nature and humans."[28] The event proclaims the vital deity of "Yahweh in association with the ark, as 'God Who Lives.'" This one, Israel's God—not only a tribal or territorial deity, but God in heaven and on earth—was with Israel "when they crossed the symbolic boundary of the Jordan into the land."[29]

Knowledge of the living God whose sovereignty is over all, even if only Israel is enlisted into a special service by the knowledge of this identity of the one true God as YHWH, is thus no idle insight into transcendent being, some vague awareness of a Beyond that Israel undoubtedly shares with the wicked nations about to be driven out of Canaan. That God exists somehow someway beyond the temporal and spatial existence of creatures is an analytic truth, if one merely conceives the existence of a Creator of all that is not God. This is what the traditional ecclesiastical phrase "one true God" actually means—namely, the one who is truly God. YHWH claims this title and acts to demonstrate his claim in his history with Israel. But natural knowledge of such vague transcendence by which all creatures are in reality related to their Creator is not to the point here. The crossing is the theophany of YHWH as claimant of this title, the true and

27. Calvin, *Book of Joshua*, 43.
28. Dozeman, *Joshua 1–12*, 285.
29. Nelson, *Joshua*, 59.

living God, Lord of nations, not only of Israel.[30] Such knowledge of the living God is exactly knowledge of YHWH the Divine Warrior who will unfailingly deliver the land to Israel, not because his transcendent nature is invulnerable and immutable, but because his historical resolve to redeem and fulfill the creation brings eternity into time. "Here the living God is the One who will be alive and active in the coming events of conquest."[31]

Look and see! The ark-throne of the covenant God of Israel precedes Israel into the Jordan, causing the waters to wall up. The living God is once again characterized, now as the "Lord of all the earth" (3:11)—not just the earth of Canaan that Israel will soon possess as its inheritance, but of all the earth. "The title of ruler of the whole earth here applied to God is not insignificant, but extols his power above all the elements of nature, in order that the Israelites, considering how seas and rivers are subject to his dominion, might have no doubts that the waters, though naturally liquid, would become stable in obedience to his word."[32] Therefore this God "has both the power and the right" to take the land from the Canaanites and to give it to Israel as he had promised.[33]

He is the Lord who disposes over all the nations on the earth and who accordingly has his own history with each and every nation, which rises and falls at his bidding. Out of all these, it is Israel, however, who comes to know this God by name, and by obedience of faith learns his ways, so that Israel's history with God becomes representative and thus indirect revelation of all human histories. Likewise YHWH's assertion of sovereignty over the piece of the earth named Canaan is representative of his sovereignty over all habitable land fit for human dwelling. In the theology of Joshua, one does not deduce particulars from some allegedly universal principles or axioms as is the procedure in classical metaphysics up to and through Spinoza; but in theology one proceeds from the particular scriptural narrative revealing YHWH, living God and Lord of the nations who fights for us, to discover his claim to truthful title as the one true God, whose sovereignty over time and space has universal scope and thus also relevance.

Now twelve men, one representing each of the twelve tribes of Israel, are called out. Disclosure of the meaning of this muster, however, is delayed while Joshua tells the specific wonder that is about to occur, how the waters of the Jordan

30. Dozeman, *Joshua 1–12*, 289.
31. Nelson, *Joshua*, 61.
32. Calvin, *Book of Joshua*, 44.
33. Nelson, *Joshua*, 61.

descending from upstream shall be stopped and stand up in a heap like a great watery wall when the Lord of all the earth, represented by his earthly throne in the ark, enters the waters to provide safe passage through it for all Israel. The walls of cities, just like this wall of water, exist at YHWH's command and so also collapse at YHWH's command. Just so it came to pass, as the narrator's voice resumes, noting that the harvesttime flood has caused the waters to overflow the banks, thus making for an easier, less steep access into the river. The priests bearing the ark merely dipped their toes into the edge of the water when a wall of water arose and backed up as far as the city Adam beside Zarethan—far out of sight upriver from the crossing Israelites. The flow of water south to the Dead Sea ceased altogether. And so the people Israel passed on dry land into the land of Canaan, arriving opposite Jericho. But the priests who carried the ark of the covenant stood in the dried-up riverbed until all Israel went across. "Thus the river, though dumb, was the best of heralds, proclaiming with a loud voice that heaven and earth are subject to the God of Israel."[34]

All Israel has now passed through the Jordan River on dry ground. The memory of what happened with the previous generation at the Red Sea imbues the present event, but what of the future, when these present events at the Jordan have passed from living memory? "While the account of the crossing [in chapter 3] stresses the wondrous character of the event, the following passage focuses on its significance for the present and future generations."[35]

In the Northeast of the United States, wanderers in the woods often discover stone walls or other unnatural formations of stone and wonder what pioneers centuries before had once cleared this now overgrown land and sought to domesticate it. Likewise, Israel here imagines a future in which new generations discover artificial rock formations that elicit their curiosity and provoke a catechetical child-and-elder dialogue about their meaning. "The retelling of the story, which the stones elicit, will itself constitute a unifying activity by reminding the tribes of their common history and calling."[36] Binding the twelve tribes together in memory of their common origin as a nation, the twelve stones drawn from the Jordan River become one in the monument. (For "sign" see Deut. 6:8; 11:18; 28:46, and for "memorial" see Exod. 13:8–9.) Israel is one under the one true God who is YHWH, the saving God who creates in order to save and who saves by creating anew. Indeed, this is the insignia of YHWH as the one

34. Calvin, *Book of Joshua*, 55.
35. Hawk, *Joshua*, 67.
36. Hawk, *Joshua*, 67–68.

true God: "For God is the God of the humble, the miserable, the afflicted, the oppressed, the desperate, and of those who have been brought down to nothing at all. And it is the nature of God to exalt the humble, to feed the hungry, to enlighten the blind, to comfort the miserable and afflicted, to justify sinners, to give life to the dead, and to save those who are desperate and damned. For he is the Almighty Creator, who makes everything out of nothing."[37] Above all, this identity of the one God as inseparably creator and redeemer must be remembered and made known to every new generation; it is the indicative in which the obedience of faith rests, even as faith is ever active in love and hope.

As chapter 4 begins, Israel is described in passing as a "nation."[38] But this change is fraught with ambiguity. We have already seen in Joshua an "all-Israel" focus. "People," 'am, not "nation," goy, is the preferred term in the book of Joshua for Israel, occurring over fifty times. For this particular nation is first of all a people covenanted to the saving God, chosen from out of all the multitude of peoples on the earth to know and serve YHWH, to the end that a system of blessing may finally defeat and surpass the system of curse that has befallen a creation gone astray (Brueggemann). In this dual characterization of Israel as nation and people here, an ambiguity is expressed. "Having crossed the Jordan, Israel has . . . become like the peoples of Canaan—a settled nation bound to the land. But, we may wonder, how much like them?"[39]

Does the acquisition of the land continue as inheritance to be passed on to future generations by stewards faithful to the reign of YHWH? Is the miraculous work of YHWH in war respected, or will it be retooled as an ideology of a national security state invoking divine sanction for its conscriptions, taxation, fortifications, and wars of aggression? Does Israel remain united by faith or become divided by tribal-partisan politics? "Israel" qua people can exist at peace on the land, in other words, without nation-state political sovereignty, and this special existence of "all Israel," unlike the nations, is precisely what identifies Israel as the covenanted people of YHWH. But at this moment of its history, the people Israel for the first time obtains in the very possession of land the possibility, if not yet the actuality, of becoming a nation-state, a political agent. Thus, when this entire nation has now passed through the walled-up waters of the river Jordan, YHWH singles out Joshua again and addresses him.

---

37. *Luther's Works*, ed. Jaroslav Pelikan, Helmut T. Lehmann, and Christopher Boyd Brown, 75 vols. (Philadelphia: Muhlenberg and Fortress; St. Louis: Concordia, 1955–), 26:314.
38. Nelson, *Joshua*, 62.
39. Hawk, *Joshua*, 67.

E pluribus unum, "out of many, one." Twelve representatives, one from each tribe, are summoned and told to draw twelve stones from the place in the riverbed where the priests stood bearing the ark of the covenant and to create from them a single monument. The symbolism of the construction underscores the message of unity[40] as grounded in shared faith in YHWH who breaches barriers as well as faith in their own election as his people. So Joshua commands the twelve men (representing all Israel) to go to where the ark of YHWH stood in the midst of the Jordan River bed and for each to take on his shoulder a stone to represent each of the tribes of Israel.

Travelers in Europe sometimes witness in isolated and unsettled places small chapels or shrines that are clearly not meant as houses of worship. They may discover, however, that these cultic buildings have been erected over unusual natural phenomena like mineral springs bubbling up gaseous waters. What has happened in these places is the erection of a memorial of Christian missionaries who long ago "baptized" the sacred places of pagan peoples. Something similar happens here: Joshua takes over the Canaanite custom of erecting "pillars for worship . . . , [which] originally represented the goddess or her presence"[41] but have now been retooled as memorials to YHWH's saving deeds. "Deuteronomy clearly seems to speak against such stones (Deut. 7:5; 12:3; 16:22). Here, however, the function of the stones is purely memorial"[42]—a desacralization accomplished by the retooling of idolatrous pillars of nature-fertility religion into Yahwistic memorials of saving deeds in history. This raises an important theological issue.

For surely these stone monuments, which play a role throughout Joshua, signify something of religious importance and thus may be called "iconic." They are stones erected as signs, for the purpose of testimony, not merely boundary markers indicating territorial possession. One must be wary here not to confuse idols—sharply proscribed by Deuteronomy, a proscription sharply reiterated in Joshua—with literal images. What is prohibited in Israel is "engraving," which impresses on the raw material a form or likeness of deity of the idol-maker's own inspiration. That construction of deity is the target of the prohibition against idolatry—a construction that may occur intellectually as well as graphically, invisibly as well as visibly. The prohibition does not represent some kind of antithesis between graphic depiction and conceptual-intellectual comprehension as in the Platonic tradition's denigration of aesthetic communication. Images speak and

40. Nelson, *Joshua*, 69.
41. Rösel, *Joshua*, 72.
42. Pitkänen, *Joshua*, 140.

speech forms images in the reciprocating process of communication. The twelve-stone memorial constructed of unhewn rock signifies precisely that it is YHWH who has made "all Israel" out of the rude, rough tribes by leading them together through the Jordan to the promised land. The monument is thus unmistakably an image of YHWH's design and command signifying his will and purpose to bequeath to Israel the land of Canaan. So John of Damascus writes,

> Images are of two kinds: either they are words written in a book . . . or else they are material images such as the twelve stones which he commanded to be taken from the Jordan for a second memorial (such a mystery, truly the greatest ever to befall the faithful people!) of the carrying of the ark and the parting of the waters. Therefore we now set up images and remembrances of valiant men that we may zealously desire to follow their example. Either remove these images altogether, and reject the authority of him who commanded them to be made, or else accept them in the manner and with the esteem which they deserved.[43]

The text explicitly tells us that the stones signify that "the waters of the Jordan were cut off in front of the ark of the covenant of the LORD" (4:7). "This language is unique to the book of Joshua."[44] "Cut off" is not found in the accounts of the miracle of the Red Sea, but it reappears in one of the concluding speeches of Joshua in 23:4, where it is used to describe the defeat of the Canaanites who were cut off. The use of this verb here "connects with the circumcision of Israel about to occur in 5:2–9 where the foreskins of the Israelite men were cut off."[45]

What follows may be characterized as catechesis. Catechesis is the method of instilling into heart and mind the divine indicative of electing grace and the equally divine imperative of the obedience of faith employed by the book of Deuteronomy, as Calvin insightfully notes: "Because the covenant by which God had adopted the race of Abraham was firm in an uninterrupted succession for one thousand generations, the benefit which God has bestowed on the deceased fathers is, on account of the unity of the body, transferred in common to their children who were born long after. . . . [Consequently,] when the sons hear that the waters of Jordan were dried up many ages before they were born, they acknowledge themselves to be the very people towards whom that wonderful

---

43. John of Damascus, *On Divine Images* 3.23 (ACCS 4:21).
44. Dozeman, *Joshua 1–12*, 291.
45. Dozeman, *Joshua 1–12*, 292.

act of divine favor had been manifested."[46] Catechesis is the way in which the gospel is inscribed on the new generation, bringing forth adults educated in their covenantal heritage.

Careful analysis reveals the presence of two catechetical accounts of the memorial stone monument(s). The first "instruction [in 4:3–5] is fashioned [as] a question-and-answer catechism between a child and adult,"[47] focusing on the wonder. A second catechesis occurs with the ark exiting the Jordan in 4:20–5:1, which turns attention to "entering the land and taking possession of it."[48] Here the stones from the riverbed are placed where Israel now encamps at Gilgal on the soil of the promised land to be a sign to future generations, provoking the new generation to ask for their meaning. For ages to come the twelve-stone monument will be a sign that will provoke testimony to the sovereign power invested in and displayed by the ark of the covenant of YHWH, the sovereign power that unifies the twelve tribes and grounds their new existence on the land of Canaan.

In 4:8–9 the successive verses contradict each other. Verse 8 reports the obedience of the sons of Israel in erecting the twelve-stone memorial in the midst of the camp at Gilgal, while verse 9 tells that Joshua had the memorial erected in the riverbed where the ark had stood, commenting that it remains there (presumably submerged in the flow of the river) to this day—that is, to the time of the text's composition. Calvin frankly admits perplexity at this: "I admit that a monument altogether buried in silence would have been useless."[49] As implausible as this seems—a redundant memorial lost to sight in a flowing river—it may serve an obscure literary purpose.[50]

Be that as it may, the erection of the memorial(s) is in partial fulfillment of Deut. 27:2–13 and points forward to Josh. 8:30–35. In contrast to 3:1–17, which tells how Israel came to the Jordan from Shittim, 4:10–19 "relates Israel's *coming out* of the Jordan to Gilgal."[51] The contradiction left standing between 4:8 and 4:9 is explained at last with the note that the priests bearing the ark stood on the dry riverbed until all the business commanded by YHWH had been accomplished and thus after the people passed over in haste. Only then did the priests bring the ark out of the riverbed and past the people.[52] The unity between the

---

46. Calvin, *Book of Joshua*, 56.
47. Dozeman, *Joshua 1–12*, 291.
48. Dozeman, *Joshua 1–12*, 293.
49. Calvin, *Book of Joshua*, 51.
50. Hawk, *Joshua*, 69.
51. Hawk, *Joshua*, 70.
52. On the repetition in 4:10–11, see Nelson, *Joshua*, 69.

Transjordan tribes and the rest entering the land of Canaan once again comes to expression as it is explicitly noted that the warriors of the two and one-half tribes of Reuben, Gad, and Manasseh also passed through the Jordan with the others as Moses had commanded.[53] Combining the forces of the twelve tribes, it is written that forty thousand warriors passed before YHWH—that is, before the ark of the covenant—to the Jericho plain. Implausible as this enumeration seems, "the inflated numbers were simply a part of the ancient Israelite way of telling things, naturally recognized as hyperbolic exaggeration by the first readers of the book."[54]

By the miraculous passage through the Jordan, now resulting in the muster of the army of Israel ready for battle, YHWH has magnified Joshua, the mediator who conveyed YHWH's instruction to Israel. So Israel fears Joshua just as it feared Moses. The fear of YHWH is thus transferred to his human mediators, Moses first, now Joshua. Fear is a rational and healthy emotion, if it is a realistic assessment of objective danger. Courage in any case is not recklessness that blindly ignores danger by denying its reality. Courage acknowledges danger and proceeds in spite of it to do what is required for the sake of obedience to what is written in the book of the law. For the book of Joshua, however, this courage that YHWH both commands and inspires is not in the first instance that of the soldier but that of a student of Torah both to learn and to do the will of YHWH. The location of the comment in 4:14 about Joshua's stature "deflects any sense that Joshua was exalted because of the miracle at the Jordan.... Joshua is exalted because he faithfully carries out the commands of YHWH and Moses"[55]—just as the new Joshua will become "obedient to death, even death upon the cross. Therefore God has highly exalted him" (Phil. 2:8–9 AT).

Once again in 4:15 the sequence of the events seems scrambled. Now YHWH instructs Joshua that the priests bearing the ark of the "testimony" (a new term, ha'edut) should now leave the Jordan. So Joshua commands and the priests obey. As soon as the feet of the priests reach dry ground, the wall of cut-off water collapses, the pent-up waters flow, and the harvesttime flood resumes, returning to the high water level when the crossing began. But, as we have heard, the Jordan is not just an item of geography but a symbol. As a rite of passage, the narrative of the Jordan crossing, told and retold through the generations, "would create self-understanding and identity ... as twelve tribes forged into a single nation."[56]

53. Rösel, *Joshua*, 74.
54. Pitkänen, *Joshua*, 139.
55. Hawk, *Joshua*, 71.
56. Nelson, *Joshua*, 68.

At the same time, however, the text points to the historical uniqueness of the event of origin in "the particular emphasis given to their feet, and particularly to the soles of the feet (3:13; 4:18)." Obedience manifests in the motion and placing of feet! "By treading . . . , Israel appropriates the divine promise and claims all the terrain as its own."[57]

In 4:19 the event is dated to the tenth day of the first month of the year—namely, Nisan (cf. 5:10 regarding the dating of the Passover)—and the place of encampment is named, Gilgal, to the east of Jericho, which "will continue to be the headquarters for Israel (9:6, 10:6–7, 14:6). Here the stone monument is associated with covenant making in Exod. 24:4 as in Josh. 24:26 (also Elijah in 1 Kgs. 18:31–32)," once again stressing the unity of all Israel. "As the first month was the start of the new year and was associated with Israel's liberation from Egypt (see Exod. 12:2), in the same way, the Israelites crossed the river Jordan to the promised land in the first month, and, in this case, just when the Passover season starts (cf. Exod. 12:3 . . .), the conquest starts only after the Passover has been celebrated."[58] The geographical site, Gilgal, is uncertain though Deut. 11:29–30 "*may* locate it close to Mount Ebal and Mount Gerizim. . . . Gilgal serves as an important reference point in both early and later Israelite history."[59] In 4:20 the previous story thread is picked up and confirmed: the twelve stones taken from the Jordan are set up as a memorial sign in the Gilgal camp. The explanation of the memorials here "broadens the literary horizon of the crossing of the Jordan . . . to an event within the larger story of salvation history."[60]

As this chapter on memorializing the theophany of YHWH when Israel crossed over the Jordan on dry ground draws to its close in 4:21–24, Joshua speaks catechetically as a father to the "sons of Israel" about the time when they shall be fathers to their own "sons" who will ask them what these stones are. Then it is to be made known to the children how Israel crossed the Jordan on dry land. So they are to know God, themselves as his chosen people, and the land as his gift. They are to know God as the God of the exodus from bondage and thus also, for the same reason, as the warrior-king leading them to freedom in the promised land. But not only Israel! Through Israel's experience of YHWH's word and its fulfillment, hence through Israel's testimony to YHWH, all the peoples of the

57. Hawk, *Joshua*, 72.
58. Pitkänen, *Joshua*, 139.
59. Pitkänen, *Joshua*, 137.
60. Dozeman, *Joshua 1–12*, 295.

earth[61] are to know the mighty hand of YHWH and learn to fear him and interpret their own histories truly as histories with this God. This final verse "sets Israel's continued fidelity into the context of the nations, who themselves may come to know YHWH's power as the one true God."[62] Already in postexilic Israel, YHWH's claim to sovereignty over the earth transcends the turf of Canaan, which in this perspective turns out to be only a token of a comprehensive claim for the redemption of the creation.

61. On the ambiguity of the term "earth," see Hawk, *Joshua*, 73.
62. Nelson, *Joshua*, 68.

JOSHUA PREPARES THE NEW GENERATION AND IS PREPARED BY THE PRINCE OF THE ARMY OF YHWH

5:1–15

Word of YHWH's deed for Israel at the Jordan River spreads beyond Israel's camp at Gilgal, and fear of YHWH spreads with it over the indigenous regimes.[1] It is notable that the story once again begins by singling out the "kings" of the Amorites and the Canaanites on whom dread from YHWH falls, melting their hearts. Just as the miraculous crossing has united "all Israel" in the liturgical display of unanimity, it also unites the kings of the Canaanites and Amorites—Israel being united, however, in the courage of faith but the indigenous royalty in desperate despondency. "We have already seen elsewhere," Calvin comments, "how unbelievers, when smitten with fear, cease not to wrestle with God, and even when they fall continue furiously to assail heaven. Hence the dread which ought to have urged them to caution had no other effect than to hurry them on headlong."[2]

Yet we may rather liken this dread of the kings of Canaan to the shrieking of the unclean spirit when another Joshua had penetrated into the strong man's house to bind him and plunder his goods, "What have you to do with us, Jesus of Nazareth? Have you come to destroy us? I know who you are, the Holy One of God!" (Mark 1:24). The evangelist Mark seems indeed to have used the Joshua narrative as a template for his pioneering construction of the gospel narrative

1. Rösel, *Joshua*, 81. Cf. Josh. 7:7, 9; Deut. 1:7.
2. Calvin, *Book of Joshua*, 60.

telling of the new Joshua.[3] The comparison is suggestive: the entry of the holy ones of God terrorizes the usurpers of the earth in the knowledge that they have come to destroy the destroyers in their regimes of malice and injustice.

Ignoring such intratextual clues of canon criticism, however, Pitkänen regards this report of the terror falling on the Canaanite royalty as "hyperbole in typical Ancient Near Eastern fashion, but, presumably, the idea is to emphasize that the crossing of the Jordan nevertheless is part of psychological warfare to terrorize the opposition."[4] Such explanation betrays egregious modernization and to boot produces a particularly clumsy reading of the text. Consider the narrative context literarily: "Now Israel engages in further 'rites of passage,' moving from the shame of uncircumcision to circumcision and from wilderness manna to a settled agricultural economy."[5] The report in this literary way intends rather to introduce the sanctification/preparation of the ancient holy ones, the twelve tribes united as the holy agent (= the twelve apostles of Mark 3:14–19), just as Joshua the leader will be prepared/sanctified in prostrating before the Prince of the Army of YHWH (= the "holy one" of Mark 1:23–24, according to Calvin and the consensus of the church fathers[6]). This report of the dread of the Canaanite royalty in which the narrator speaks, together with the concluding episode of the theophany of the prince of YHWH's hosts in 5:13–15, frames the sanctification/preparation of Israel for the impending campaign in the rites of (renewed) circumcision and Passover, so that it is "Israel transformed [who] is now prepared to wrest the land from its inhabitants."[7]

In reporting this, the narrator cites almost verbatim the words of Rahab in 2:11, which the spies, returning to Joshua, had also repeated almost verbatim. By this device of repetition the question is reiterated, "Whose side are you on?"[8] The report of YHWH's sovereign and gracious initiative for Israel, in other words, does not take sides; it *makes* sides. It thus also opens up, as we shall see, the question of whether there will be a place in holy Israel for those unholy enemies who will nevertheless take sides with YHWH—that is, theologically, the question of the election of the rejected, the justification of the ungodly.[9] If so, a disruptive

3. Joel Marcus, *Mark 1–8*, Anchor Bible 27 (New Haven: Yale University Press, 2000); and Marcus, *Mark 8–16*, Anchor Bible 27A (New Haven: Yale University Press, 2009), 406, 421, 499, 758, 763, 765.

4. Pitkänen, *Joshua*, 149.

5. Nelson, *Joshua*, 74.

6. Calvin, *Book of Joshua*, 68.

7. Hawk, *Joshua*, 75.

8. Hawk, *Joshua*, 76–77.

9. Hawk, *Joshua*, 78.

question arises: How will these Gentiles be circumcised—that is, sanctified? The book of Joshua raises this question in the figures of Rahab and the Gibeonites but does not answer it, even as the Achan story demonstrates that not all the circumcised are true Israel.

The sanctification of renewed Israel moves to the place, Gibeath-haaraloth, the "hill of foreskins." Joshua 5:2 tells that Joshua circumcised the Israelites "again"— thus, a second time. It is not immediately clear what this temporal reference means. Calvin thinks it would be strange and monstrous if Israel had for so many years of wilderness wandering neglected the rite by which they signified their adoption as the people of God. He concludes that "a new people were then created to supply the place of perverse rebels" of the wilderness generation.[10] In any case an astonishing turn of events is related: forty thousand armed warriors of YHWH, who has just demonstrated how YHWH commands also the forces of nature on behalf of Israel, have passed in review. They are ready and poised for battle, massed on the outskirts of Jericho, their threatening presence no secret inasmuch as the dread of the YHWH-Israel covenantal alliance has fallen on the royal warlords presiding over the Canaanite city-states. But YHWH tells Joshua to take up primitive knives made from stone[11] with which he is then in effect to immobilize the forty thousand troops by performing a mass rite of circumcision.[12]

Calvin captures the incongruity: "The Lord waits till they are shut up in the midst of enemies, and exposed to their lust and violence, as if he were purposely exposing them to death; since all weakened by their wound must have given way at once, and have been slaughtered almost without resistance."[13] In support of this reading, Calvin reminds his reader of the cunning ploy in Gen. 34. Here Judah and his brothers avenged the rape of their sister Dinah by requiring her rapist-suitor, Shechem, with all his menfolk, to be circumcised for the proposed wedding to proceed. As these Canaanites lay crippled in pain from the operation, the brothers took advantage of their incapacity to slaughter them. Is turnabout fair play? YHWH now requires that the same disadvantage—Calvin calls it a "harsh trial"—be imposed on Joshua's warriors so that they will lie stricken in camp, vulnerable to their foes in Jericho should the latter sally forth. Why does Joshua

---

10. Calvin, *Book of Joshua*, 62.

11. Dozeman, *Joshua 1–12*, 297; cf. Nelson, *Joshua*, 76. See Exod. 4:25; 20:25. Joshua 24:31 in the LXX preserves a tradition on the fate of these knives, Rösel, *Joshua*, 82, a reading that Origen depends on.

12. Boyd Seevers, *Warfare in the Old Testament: The Organization, Weapons, and Tactics of Ancient Near Eastern Armies* (Grand Rapids: Kregel Academic, 2013), 26.

13. Calvin, *Book of Joshua*, 62.

at this strategic juncture choose to perform a Torah-mandated rite that amounts to self-imposed military impotence? Why indeed does YHWH require this?

We recall that from the beginning of the book Joshua has been instructed to do battle, not by usual military tactics and strategies, but by obedience to the book of the law. Israel is to do battle by keeping the Torah. If we look back to the canonical "origin of the ritual, recorded in Genesis 17:1–27," we learn that circumcision is confirmation of one's election as member of Israel inscribed on the male body at the site from which procreation proceeds. Through circumcision one receives the new identity of Israel by affirmation in one's own flesh at the very place in the body from which every new generation proceeds in fulfillment of YHWH's promises.[14] The ritual has the newborn receive and undertake the yoke of the Torah. In the present case, however, it is not male infants volunteered by parents but adult male warriors who submit. The volunteering is not understood individualistically. These ritually wounded warriors in Gilgal will someday also volunteer their own offspring for circumcision that they may inherit the covenant even as this generation will first inherit the land. Thus this act—at this time and place, with its collateral damage of self-imposed military impotence—"marks the reciprocal choosing of God and people."[15] An entrance rite constituting the covenant community, according to Exod. 12:44, 48–49, circumcision is prerequisite to participation in the observance of Passover, which follows next in Josh. 5.

Why is circumcision prerequisite to Passover participation? There is now a further twist to the renewal of this archaic ritual, which Calvin grasped when he remarked that by this new circumcision the people "were again consecrated to God, in order that their uncircumcision might not pollute the holy land."[16] The blood of (adult) circumcision by knives of stone here (bearing in mind that this is not bloodless circumcision of infants with a scalpel) recalls the blood of the Passover lamb and its significance. The blood of circumcision painted on the very body of the Israelite warrior, like the blood of the Passover lamb painted on the house lintel in Egypt, which shielded the inhabitants from the angel of death, marks those out in Canaan who are to be preserved from the *herem* death sentence.[17] A separation-sanctification[18] comes into effect, protecting the circumcised from the

14. Hawk, *Joshua*, 78.
15. Hawk, *Joshua*, 79.
16. Calvin, *Book of Joshua*, 63.
17. Dozeman, *Joshua 1–12*, 298. Compare with the story of Zipporah in Exod. 4:24–26; cf. Dozeman, *Joshua 1–12*, 297.
18. Interestingly, the LXX translates the Hebrew for "circumcision" in 5:4 into Greek as "purification," perhaps reflecting the call of Moses for "circumcision of the heart" in Deut. 18:10.

ḥerem curse about to be unleashed on the uncircumcised following the celebration of the Passover in 5:10–12—thus in the same sequence as happened in Egypt. In parallel, baptism into the death and resurrection of Christ marks out those for whom the holy *koinōnia* in the body and blood of Christ is provided—the meal that turns poisonous for those, like Achan, who fail to discern and honor the holy solidarity into which they have entered by baptism (1 Cor. 11:18–22, 27–31).

Stricken by the very sign that will prove to protect them, the Israelite warriors thus are taught that it is YHWH who fights for them. The obedience of patient faith required of them in submitting to circumcision at just this juncture contravenes military wisdom with its usual stratagems. They are to make war in such a way that everything finally depends on YHWH and his fabulous acts on their behalf. The time of impotence effected by receiving circumcision as adult warriors is the sign of this patiency of faith. Faith in its patiency is prerequisite to sharing in the Passover meal so that, arising from their convalescence, Israel's powerful agency will be true to YHWH who fights for Israel.

Citing 1 Cor. 5:7–8, Origen insists that "no one unclean celebrates the Passover, no one uncircumcised."[19] Thus what today is promoted as "radical Eucharistic hospitality" is no true hospitality at all but the marketing of a grace so cheap one can hardly give it away. Baptism is admission to the supper of the Lord when the baptized "gather together as church" (1 Cor. 11:18 AT), because it is baptism into Christ that makes Canaanites into Israelites by joining them to the death and resurrection of Christ; therefore it is the baptized who keep the feast of Christ our Passover as those who are in principle and in power freed from the thrall of malice working injustice that reigns over Canaan. Thinking of Rahab, Origen introduces here 1 Cor. 6:11, telling about prostitutes who are no longer prostitutes: "And this surely you have been; but you have been washed, you have been sanctified in the name of our Lord Jesus Christ, and in the Spirit of our God." Baptism into the death and resurrection of Christ marks one with the prostitute Rahab's scarlet cord and works the true and spiritual circumcision of both circumcised and uncircumcised.[20]

To be certain, then, Christian baptism should not be understood as a mere rite of passage welcoming all infants into the world and as such superseding parochial and patriarchal Jewish circumcision limited to males. Christian baptism must rather be understood and received as the Spirit's intention of true and lifelong

19. Origen, *Homilies on Joshua*, 68.
20. Origen, *Homilies on Joshua*, 75.

"circumcision of the heart" for both Jew and Gentile. "But because God loves every soul, he did not utterly abandon either the circumcised or the uncircumcised. For he sent Jesus, who circumcised both the worthy and the unworthy at the same time, not Jesus the son of Nun—for that one did not circumcise the people with the true and perfect circumcision—but Jesus our Lord and Savior. For he is the one who truly cut off the pollution of the flesh from us and purged the filth of our sins from our heart and soul."[21] This Pauline true circumcision of the true Israelite—the very circumcision of the heart that the book of Deuteronomy *demands*—is what, according to Origen, Jesus our Lord and Savior *gives*.

We now receive an explanation of this "second" circumcision: all the men of war in Israel who had come out of Egypt had died on the way in the wilderness. During the time of the wilderness wanderings, moreover, there had been no circumcision. The renewal of the covenant ceremony at this juncture signals a fresh start for Israel, contrasting with the disobedience of the wilderness generation that perished en route. Receiving circumcision here and now signifies the obedience of the new generation that will inherit the land. The disobedience of the wilderness generation is characterized as an unwillingness to listen and believe the voice of YHWH. On account of this unbelief and its practical implications in disobedience to YHWH's commands, that wilderness generation would not live to see the land "flowing with milk and honey" promised to their fathers (Exod. 33:3; Num. 14:8; 16:13–14; Deut. 6:3; 11:9). This passage, then, points back to Num. 14 and its account of rebellions in the wilderness.[22]

So it is the children of the disobedient who are now circumcised, completing the replacement of that faithless generation, which, in addition to all other disobedience of unfaith, had not circumcised their sons on the way.[23] This narrative placement reinforces the significance of circumcision as a gracious crossing from the time of covenant disobedience to the new time of obedience. Joshua 5:6, which continues in the voice of the narrator, quite unconsciously uses the pronoun "us" in reference to the recipients of YHWH's renewed promise; it thus makes contemporary readers/auditors also members of the new generation of covenant obedience that YHWH raises up in place of the old one by crossing the Jordan. Just so, the entire armed force in the camp in Gilgal lay prostrate in pain and vulnerable to surrounding enemies—and we readers with them in the patient solidarity of faith—until they/we heal.

21. Origen, *Homilies on Joshua*, 67.
22. Stubbs, *Numbers*, 198.
23. Hawk, *Joshua*, 79.

The camp is in Gilgal, and we are now provided an etymology of the name. The Lord speaks to Joshua upon the completion of the circumcision, declaring that on this day he has "rolled away" (Hebrew *galal*) the reproach/shame/disgrace of Egypt that lay upon the Israelites. The meaning of the metaphor is obscure. With stunning imperception, the usually perceptive Calvin mistakenly argues that the reproach was the stigma attaching to the escaped Hebrew slaves as "rebels against legitimate authority."[24] Was the disgrace a lack of circumcision already in Egypt or rather the humiliation of slavery there?[25] Or both? The text does not tell us, but what is clear is that "Egypt and everything associated with it have been exorcised from Israel."[26] Egypt lived on in the rebellious wilderness generation, which hankered after the fleshpots of Egypt. Now Egypt has died within Israel and Israel emerges a new creation, truly born anew.

Having healed, the newly circumcised generation of covenantal obedience keeps the Passover on the evening of the fourteenth day "like the one envisioned in Deuteronomy 16 and carried out by Josiah (2 Kings 23:21–23)."[27] Having celebrated the Passover, on the next day the people for the first time eat the food of the promised land. The manna from heaven that YHWH had given Israel to eat during the wilderness wanderings ceases when they begin to eat the grain, the milk, and the honey of the promised land (cf. Exod. 16:35). Despite the disobedience of the wilderness generation—Joshua and Caleb are notable exceptions—the new generation inherits through them the annual memorial of the people's liberation from bondage in Egypt. In this legacy there is continuity between generations discontinuous in their covenant obedience.

But this very continuity raises a question concerning admission to the Passover meal that troubles Calvin: If there was no circumcision during the years of the wilderness, how could Passover have been observed? The sanctification of circumcision was prerequisite to eating the Passover meal "lest it should be profaned." Yet somehow Passover was preserved through the wilderness generation. "Should anyone object that it was absurd to celebrate the Passover in uncircumcision, I admit that it was so according to the usual order. For none were admitted to the Passover or the sacrifices save those who were initiated into the worship of God; just as in the present day the ordinance of the Supper is common only to

24. Calvin, *Book of Joshua*, 63.
25. Rösel, *Joshua*, 84; Dozeman, *Joshua 1–12*, 298.
26. Hawk, *Joshua*, 80–81.
27. Nelson, *Joshua*, 79. The MT and LXX diverge; see Pitkänen, *Joshua*, 148.

those who had been admitted into the church by baptism."[28] But regular order can bend under exceptional circumstances for the sake of mercy. Calvin reckons with a special dispensation by which the Lord "might choose for a time to alter the ordinary rule."[29] Indeed, Calvin's YHWH can and does for reasons of *ḥesed* mitigate or even suspend his own regulations. Pastoral supervision of the holy meal may accommodate justice to mercy and in this way also discern and honor the holy solidarity into which one enters by baptism. As we shall see by the end of the book of Joshua, *ḥesed*, as leaven that leavens the whole lump, desires that aliens and sojourners in Israel also participate in its holy life.

Chapter 5 concludes with a theophany that displays "the central role of the Deity as the divine warrior."[30] The theophany is uncanny and enigmatic. As Nelson observes, "This stunted, cryptic narrative seems to break off before any real plot has a chance to develop and twists into a jarring ending that connects only ambiguously with the following story." Admittedly, that is one way the episode can be characterized, representative of the historical-critical perspective in being informed more by ancient Near Eastern parallels than by the narrative course of the book of Joshua. From the cultural sources of the ancient Near East now available to scholars, Nelson tells, one would expect that "such [appearances of divine] figures occur in the context of confidence-building oracles as pledges of victory and signs of military power. . . . But such words fail to materialize" in Joshua's uncanny encounter.[31] One wonders, however, if *absence* of the usual religious war *ideology* is not precisely the literary *point* of the story! A literary explanation of the strangeness of the theophany is possible along these lines and as such provides a *crux intellectuum* for the theological reading of Joshua.

To begin with, Joshua is strangely and suddenly "in Jericho"[32]—not in the camp in Gilgal where the reader might expect him to be found from the preceding. It is here in Jericho that he is told to remove his sandals, for the ground is holy. Questions multiply. Does the location mean that Joshua is in Jericho city or in the vicinity of Jericho, its wider territory? Moreover, is the holiness attributed to the place at which a divine theophany occurs, or is it meant to designate Jericho as *ḥerem*—that is, devoted to, made holy to God?[33] Origen recognizes the strange

28. Calvin, *Book of Joshua*, 62.
29. Calvin, *Book of Joshua*, 62.
30. Dozeman, *Joshua 1–12*, 328.
31. Nelson, *Joshua*, 81.
32. This location "is original and must be explained." Rösel, *Joshua*, 87.
33. Hawk, *Joshua*, 83.

fact that Joshua is in Jericho while "the enemies occupy the city and have not yet been conquered," coupled with the even stranger fact that the ground on which he stands is said to be holy. For Origen this means that "the chief of the Army of the power of the Lord sanctifies every place in which he comes, for Jericho itself is not a holy place. . . . The presence of the Lord has sanctified the place."[34] But it is doubtful that Origen has captured here the double-sided aspect of YHWH's holiness, which destroys even as it creates.

In any case Joshua has a vision, as the dramatic language in 5:13 (*Behold!*) indicates. As mentioned, the war literature of the ancient Near East often contains apparitions of the nation's deity assuring its presence together with the heavenly armies in support of the earthly combatants. We see something similar in Israel (cf. 1 Kgs. 22:19; Ps. 103:21; Judg. 5:2; 2 Sam. 5:24). The phrasing about a man standing "opposite" Joshua, however, is unusual and is meant to give the impression of threat. Joshua sees a warrior with drawn sword—certainly a threatening posture.[35] Thus Joshua approaches, asking the ominous figure's intentions:[36] Will this man of war fight for us, for Israel, or against us, for Jericho? But the mysterious warrior "rebuffs the question"[37] and replies, "No! I have come as prince of the army of YHWH" (5:14 AT). This "terse and noncommittal response is particularly strange,"[38] although saying he has "arrived" reinforces the impression that "the stranger belongs to the heavenly sphere and that this is where he has come from."[39] Thus we gather that "he represents a third force in the conflict, the Army of YHWH."[40]

If we take these odd features of the episode as clues to the meaning of the story at this juncture in the Joshua narrative, we begin to see with Dozeman that "the designation of Jericho [as] holy is the rationale for the execution of the ban against cities in the book of Joshua; it makes their extermination a sacrifice to YHWH and the ban against booty absolute." Yet a historicizing objection to this interpretation of the clues is that the sudden, indeed fabulous, relocation of Joshua into the unconquered city of Jericho, let alone its designation as "holy," is implausible. Nor does it fit the ancient Near Eastern genre. But the story as told may well intend to *subvert* the genre. Defending his thesis against the objection

34. Origen, *Homilies on Joshua*, 71.
35. Hawk, *Joshua*, 83.
36. Rösel, *Joshua*, 88.
37. Rösel, *Joshua*, 89.
38. Hawk, *Joshua*, 84.
39. Rösel, *Joshua*, 89.
40. Nelson, *Joshua*, 73–74.

regarding plausibility, Dozeman replies that the objection "ignores the fantastic nature of the book of Joshua in general and of this episode in particular. . . . The theophany to Joshua has a prophetic function in the book of Joshua, since it anticipates the destruction of Jericho as a divine act of holy war."[41] The objection also misses the double-sided nature of holiness as blessing to the holy but curse on the unholy.

Thus the retort "No" to Joshua's question of whether the divine warrior is for him or against him is best understood as "neither." The figure in the vision defies the framework presupposed in Joshua's question with his answer, in effect saying, "I am neither on your side nor on the side of your enemies." YHWH has his own agenda; YHWH has his own reign to inaugurate with his own battles to fight. For YHWH is a warrior and his invisible forces manifest momentarily in Joshua's vision of their commanding officer *already* at work, even holding sway *within* Jericho.

But what, then, is the benefit of the vision if it is not an unconditional assurance that YHWH sides with Israel? Calvin's answer captures the intention of the text: "For although [Israelites] boasted in lofty terms of having been planted by the hand of God in a holy land, they were scarcely induced by all the miracles to acknowledge in good earnest that they were placed there as God's vassals. This vision, therefore, must have been beneficial to all ages, by leaving no doubt as to the divine kindness bestowed"[42]—the "severe mercy"[43] of being made *vassal* of YHWH!

As Joshua recognizes the divinity of this figure and the figure's terse reply to mean in effect "I am not on your side but you are to be on mine," thus a reinforcement of Joshua's vassalage as servant of YHWH in training, he prostrates himself. He puts his face to the earth before the prince of the army of YHWH and addresses him as lord—therewith identifying himself as vassal.[44] He surrenders his own agenda, asking what his lord would have to say to his servant. The response to Joshua's question here too is at first cryptic. The prince of the army of YHWH declares the holiness of the land on which Joshua lies prostrate with the command that he remove his sandals so that the bare soles of his feet tread on the ground.

41. Dozeman, *Joshua 1–12*, 306, 322–23.
42. Calvin, *Book of Joshua*, 67.
43. Augustine, *Confessions*, trans. Henry Chadwick (Oxford: Oxford University Press, 1991), 150–51.
44. Calvin, *Book of Joshua*, 67. Calvin, however, also interprets the prince's "no" to Joshua's question as a denial of his being a mortal man and thus an intimation of his divinity.

What kind of message is given by this cryptic conclusion of the episode? First, we may recognize how Joshua is made parallel to Moses, who had his own theophany at the burning bush involving a similar ritual of removal of sandals on holy ground. In addition, the land of Canaan that is about to be conquered beginning "in Jericho" is designated as holy land, provided we bear in mind the double-sided meaning of holiness as blessing to the holy but curse on the unholy. Finally, the reader is made to understand that the heavenly army will fight the imminent wars.[45] In light of the promise of 1:3, "wherever *the soles* of your feet touch" (AT), then, "what was once alien land has now become YHWH's land, holy land (compare 22:19; 1 Sam. 26:19–20; 2 Kings 5:15–19)."[46] But fortified Jericho has become holy in the negative sense of *herem*.

45. Rösel, *Joshua*, 90.
46. Nelson, *Joshua*, 82.

THE WAR PROCESSION
OF THE THRONE OF YHWH

6:1–27

Levitical theology is of first importance for understanding this famous story of the miraculous fall of Jericho's walls. Israel's holy agency in this event consists in a liturgical enactment of the revealed word of God. Here again Israel "participates in YHWH's mighty work through the performance of a specific ritual act."[1] Not only do the priests in liturgical procession bearing the ark-throne of YHWH signal the impending conquest of Jericho by YHWH's royal power and the consequent nature of Israel's land possession as inheritance, but the fabulous nature of the victory has ethical consequences for the future. The importance of the Jericho story in the book of Joshua therefore "is above all literary,"[2] providing the paradigm for Israel's warfare to follow. This fabulous story (cf. 2 Chr. 20:1–34), as we shall see, warrants the equally fabulous economics of the Year of Jubilee. Literarily, the inescapably *supernatural* event prefigures a promised future that has yet to be accomplished in the earth, on the earth, for the earth. Like all biblical miracles, this signal miracle works less as an explanation of the present order than as an inauguration and revelation of the future that YHWH wills and undertakes for the sake of Israel.

Origen grasps the thrust of the Jericho narrative with its fabulous depiction of the fall of its humanly impregnable walls: "The sword is not drawn against it; the battering ram is not arranged, nor is the spear hurled. The priests and the

1. Hawk, *Joshua*, 93.
2. Pitkänen, *Joshua*, 156–57.

trumpets alone are employed, and by these the walls of Jericho are overthrown."[3] The trumpets of the priests, leading Israel in procession, are indicative of liturgy as "a certain disposition of concordance and unanimity, . . . the whole people . . . united and of one mind."[4] The story consequently includes for Origen an instruction to liturgical leaders, warning those "who do not consider that all of us who believe are one body, having one God who draws us into one and holds us together—Christ. You who preside over the church are the eye of Christ's body, so that you may especially keep an eye on everything, and examine everything, and even foresee things about to come. You are a pastor; you see the lambs of the Lord unaware of danger. . . . Do you not run [to them]? Do you not call them back?"[5]

The calling of the pastor who presides over the flock of Christ by ministering his word and sacraments is not for show, though show can display and enact this holy calling. Rather, the narrative suggests that the pastor leads the people liturgically into the battle of the kingdom of God. While Origen thinks of the pastor as a defender of the vulnerable flock against the predations of false teachers—hirelings, not true shepherds—the Joshua narrative portrays the priests leading the people by the obedience of faith in YHWH's offensive against the mighty fortresses of the dark Egypt of this world.

Paul Tillich once wrote that "the battle for the kingdom of God is fought first of all in the lives of its representatives, the churches."[6] This militant language, a genuine echo of the book of Joshua, was welcomed in the Western world after the horrific conflict defeating the Nazi menace, when hymns like "Onward Christian Soldiers" were sung with gusto—already in the North Atlantic when Roosevelt and Churchill rendezvoused on naval ships! It is part and parcel of the contemporary sentimentalization of Christian love[7] in the liturgical life of the churches to have become allergic to the eminently biblical militancy of divine grace, which cannot elect the forsaken and rejected apart from dethroning the powers that oppress them. Within the life of the churches, supposed "grace," undisciplined by the obedience of faith that entails the struggle of lifelong repentance for self-giving service, has cheapened beyond recognition into an easy salve for consciences that

---

3. Origen, *Homilies on Joshua*, 72. Origen speaks here of a consensus of the church fathers; cf. ACCS 4:32–34.

4. Origen, *Homilies on Joshua*, 76.

5. Origen, *Homilies on Joshua*, 81.

6. Paul Tillich, *Systematic Theology*, 3 vols. (Chicago: University of Chicago Press, 1967), 3:381.

7. Ann Douglas, *The Feminization of American Culture* (New York: Doubleday, 1977).

do not know their own deep complicity in structures of malice working injustice. But the God of the prophets searches and judges the heart!

The gates of Jericho were shut and locked so that none could enter and none could leave—such was its supposedly impenetrable defense against attack. Yet YHWH speaks to Joshua to tell him that *already* he has given the king of Jericho, smug behind mighty walls,[8] into his hand. "The perfect tense of the verb . . . makes the divine pronouncement about the future a completed event."[9] The completed event alludes, in the first place, to that otherwise hidden work, but now to Joshua revealed, of the prince of the army of YHWH, who has also already been operative in creating the dread of the enemy at the report of YHWH's deeds on behalf of Israel. Being in dread does not contradict the Canaanite sense of security behind their fortifications but corroborates it; the fortifications, shut tight and sealed, are the product of dread. In the second place, the "already" refers to the faith of Joshua impressed anew on him when he laid prostate as vassal before his lord, the prince of the army of YHWH: in this fresh impression on him of the patiency of faith, Joshua is given what is to him still future in the very act of surrendering his own agenda and taking sides with YHWH. The obedience of faith in turn activates in Joshua, rising up to embrace the promised future as something already given and present.

The indicative of YHWH's "already" word and promise grounds the imperative to faith in the face of the "not yet" of human experience. So Origen exhorts his Christian auditors to make for themselves trumpets to call down the defenses of this world: "You have in you, through faith, Jesus the leader. If you are a priest make for yourself trumpets . . . ; no, rather, *because* you are a priest. For you have indeed been made 'a kingly race,' and it has been said of you that you are 'a holy priesthood.' Make for yourself trumpets . . . from the Holy Scriptures[!]"[10] The defenses of this present Jericho against which Christians are to sound their trumpets of scripture, according to Origen, are "all the devices of idolatry and dogmas of philosophers, all the way to the foundation."[11] The dark Egypt of this world otherwise penetrates the mind with the dogmas of the philosophers even as it captures the desire of the heart with its glittering idols. But knowledge of scripture drowns out this chatter and dispels the glitter. Knowledge has causative power: as Israel in faith knows YHWH, it becomes YHWH's faithful Israel. In light of

8. Dozeman, *Joshua 1–12*, 335–36. Cf. Deut. 28:52.
9. Dozeman, *Joshua 1–12*, 308.
10. Origen, *Homilies on Joshua*, 76.
11. Origen, *Homilies on Joshua*, 75.

this knowledge of God, what is thus discerned as *ḥerem*—that is, as anathema—is therewith prohibited from being brought into the church, the people of God. These are, says Origen, "the solemnities of the nations"—that is, civic rites and sacrifices, horoscopes and augury[12]—the same civic liturgies that enthrall Joshua's Canaanite city-states.

What is the difference? Canaanite liturgies bargain with the gods for human advantage, but the liturgy of the reign of YHWH who fights for Israel, on display in the parade around Jericho, gives Israel no choice but the true choice to side with YHWH's sovereign purpose of a true Israel at rest on holy land where YHWH dwells with his people. In the same sense, the second Joshua gives no choice but the true choice to the people of God with the summons, "Strive first for the kingdom of God and his righteousness, and all these things will be given to you as well" (Matt. 6:33). In this light, Origen's Christian appropriation of the Joshua text is not incongruous with the literary sense of its narrative. Indeed, Origen grasps that liturgy with pastoral custodianship, learned in scripture and thus knowledgeable of YHWH's candidacy as the one true God, contends for the hearts and minds of the people; consequently, the alluring pagan religiosity of Canaan is being deprived of its attractions. In its place, the human desire of the people of God is being reformed and fortified in battle bonds as all Israel rises up in unity to follow Joshua/Jesus in the offense of the reign of God.

YHWH has given Jericho—the city-state, its king, and army—into the hand of Joshua. How then is Joshua to receive this gift? How is his faith obedient? Should he build a siege ramp,[13] erect catapults, or try to scale the walls by a frontal assault? YHWH instructs otherwise. The strategy provided is entirely counterintuitive militarily, inasmuch as the promised future of victory is no more presently visible to the eyes of believing Israel than to the eyes of Jericho, secure in its unbelief (excepting Rahab). Believing Israel, however, is obediently to circle the city in a procession featuring the ark of YHWH, borne aloft by priests, one circuit on each of six successive days. A parade?[14] Or a joke—"child's play, . . . sport with mere trifles"?[15] An intimidating show of force? Or a reckless revelation to the enemy of the strength of the prospective invader?

12. Origen, *Homilies on Joshua*, 79.

13. Rösel, *Joshua*, 98; Hawk, *Joshua*, 93.

14. Nelson, *Joshua*, 86. On the discrepancies and tensions in the chapter's revision of an earlier narrative, see Nelson, *Joshua*, 88–89; also Rösel, *Joshua*, 94. It is clear in any case that the story of Rahab's survival in spite of the absolute requirement of *ḥerem* warfare is integral. The battle of Jericho is a paradigm (Nelson, *Joshua*, 91) for all that follows.

15. Calvin, *Book of Joshua*, 74.

Deception, it is said, is the first art of war. That banal observation is already an indication of the radical sinfulness of war, canonically represented by the paradigmatic fratricide of Cain against his brother Abel. Inflamed with frustrated desire, Cain deceived his brother and then fell on him in a paroxysm of the rage that is fueled by envy. War is such coercion, destruction to the point of death, forcing the unwilling to do one's will to the point of destroying the enemy's will to resist once and for all, the final solution of utterly eliminating the perceived enemy. Anyone who plays this game of war falls short of the glory of God, even if within the dark Egypt of this world it remains an urgent and necessary task to discern the relative distinction between perpetrators and victims and so to defend victims by stopping perpetrators (as the Cain story in Genesis itself acknowledges, Gen. 4:13–15; 9:6). If, within the sinful world of violence and counterviolence, it is a strange divine work to defend victims by stopping perpetrators with counterviolence, then those divine hands, not only or chiefly those of its human servants, also become stained with blood in war.

So the God of Israel is responsible—guilty, if you prefer—for the warfare of Israel in Canaan. Having bound himself to Israel, God falls with Israel short of his own glory in this strange work of destructive love. One must apprehend without flinching this divine kenosis into the work of rough justice in an unjust world. One cannot protect God from his own choice in the sovereign election of Israel with all that that entails, as Michael Wyschogrod rightly insists.[16] Nor can Christians have an "incarnational" theology without bringing God all the way down, even into human warfare, thus thickly concealed within the moral ambiguity of violence and counterviolence. If, however, lacking this theological courage to see clearly, we historically relativize the case by assimilating Israel's warfare into the customary practices of the ancient Near East, excusing the savage excesses of the people of God as an accommodation to those primitive times, we miss the little bit of leaven that leavens the whole lump. For the advent of the reign of YHWH into Canaan begins a long slow work in human history, far from finished, of discrediting war and its immoral arts.

YHWH, at the outset of this paradigmatic battle, instructs Israel to show its hand, disguising nothing—not once but repeatedly. As Calvin sees, "should the inhabitants of the city suddenly sally forth, the army would, without difficulty, be put to the rout." Calvin confirms the war stratagem of divine masquerade in the Jericho procession in Pauline fashion: "With the same intention, the Lord often,

16. Wyschogrod, *Body of Faith*, 62, 95, 124.

for a time, conceals his own might under weakness . . . that his weakness may at length appear stronger than all might, and his folly superior to all wisdom"[17]— and, we may add, divine sinfulness more righteous than human righteousness. For behind the mask of liturgical parade, it is YHWH who is deceiving Jericho while simultaneously exercising Israel's faith in a fashion that has now become a pattern of boundary-breaking.[18] The theme of faith's patiency in performing this liturgical parade thus sounds again through Calvin's pen: "There is nothing better than to leave the decisive moments and opportunities of acting at [the Lord's] disposal, and not, by our haste, anticipate his providence, in which, if we acquiesce not, we obstruct the course of his agency."[19] This militarily reckless limitation of proactive, offensive warfare by the patiency of faith, on display in a liturgical parade around the fortifications and trusting in incalculable divine agency, simultaneously mitigates the human impulse to arms and alarms. It forbids zealotry. It denies that anyone captures the kingdom of God by human force. The odd liturgical parade around Jericho forces on Israel this lesson in the patiency of obedient faith.

The reason for the details of the spectacle is now given, seven being the number of perfection or completion. Preceding the ark, itself preceding the column of Israel's warriors, the priests shall carry seven ram's horns, and on the seventh day, after circling the city seven times to the point of human exhaustion, the trumpet shall sound. At the trumpet signal the warriors will cry out with a great shout of the victory YHWH has already given, and the walls defending the city of Jericho will collapse before them. YHWH's mighty command to the walls that they fall before him, just as the river waters of the Jordan walled up and then collapsed at his word, will coincide with Israel's faithful shout of victory. So the promised future becomes present for all, both those of faith and those of unfaith, to see. Only then may the warriors of Israel rush in to finish the work as holy agents of the holy destruction of unholy Jericho by the holy YHWH.

The text equivocates on the role of the priests blowing the horns, using two terms for the horn, one of which is associated with the announcement of the Year of Jubilee according to the book of Leviticus. What is of chief literary concern here is not the details but the invocation of Levitical theology. Certainly in our text it is not clear whether the priests blow the horns repeatedly on the six days or only on the seventh day at the decisive moment. In any case, "the blowing alone

17. Calvin, *Book of Joshua*, 74.
18. Hawk, *Joshua*, 88.
19. Calvin, *Book of Joshua*, 74.

was not the reason, but the shouting of the people was necessary to cause the miracle: this motif constitutes the main difference between the final circuit and the previous ones."[20] Why then the trumpets? Broadly speaking, "trumpets have a role in some of the festivals and holy days described in Leviticus (Lev. 23:23–24, 25–29)."[21] More specifically, the priestly trumpeting of the ram's horn, the shofar, calls to mind the Levitical Year of Jubilee as if a similar reassignment of land to rightful heirs were now being heralded.

The law of Jubilee underscores the holiness of the land coming into Israel's possession as inheritance. Inheritance is the axle on which the law of Jubilee turns—namely, "the permanent tie that exists between a family and its land. The land may be sold but may remain in the possession of the new owner only until the [fifty-year] Jubilee releases it [so that it reverts as inheritance to the original family]. However, the practice also denies any essential connection between the people and their land, for YHWH declares that 'the land is mine; with me you are but aliens and tenants' (Lev. 25:23). By evoking the Jubilee, the narrator [in describing the paradigmatic fall of Canaanite Jericho by the sounding of the shofar] also deflects any notion that Israel's coming possession constitutes ownership," as in a legal land title that could count for the right of possession in a pagan court. "The land is YHWH's to give, and Israel will possess the land only because YHWH has promised that it will be so."[22] By the same token, Levitical YHWH warns Israel against accommodating itself to the religious culture of the ancient Near East: "Do not defile yourselves in any of these ways, for by all these practices the nations I am casting out before you have defiled themselves. Thus the land became defiled; and I punished it for its iniquity, and the land vomited out its inhabitants. . . . Otherwise the land will vomit you out for defiling it, as it vomited out the nation that was before you" (Lev. 18:24–25, 28). Just as Israel's war policy is not a word of God directed to us today, however, neither is Levitical land-reform policy something spoken directly to us today. Rather, these policies have heuristic value for us today, encouraging hope for the earth on which the cross of Jesus stood, and firing the imaginative reason of those seeking greater justice and peace on the earth—and also with the earth.

The liturgical enactment of an otherworldly possibility for this-worldly living is not some linguistic magic, say, a performative utterance that effects what it says. On the contrary, Israel acts in the power of sacramental real presence:

20. Rösel, *Joshua*, 99; Pitkänen, *Joshua*, 157.
21. Pitkänen, *Joshua*, 158.
22. Hawk, *Joshua*, 95.

the utterance of the divine promise performs, giving what it says. "YHWH is flatly identified with the ark,"[23] the ark being the movable throne of the invisible but "living" God advancing to reclaim the land of Canaan for his reign of *ḥesed*, which in turn consists in his covenant with Israel (cf. Num. 14:44; 1 Sam. 4). The organization of the procession accordingly has the human soldiers "frame" the "main forces," represented by the shofar priests and the ark. This arrangement of the parade "means that not human force but YHWH brings about the conquest of the city."[24] So organized, the whole company of Israel is instructed to move forward around the city while the armed men are to go on before the ark of YHWH. "What is happening here is that YHWH himself is circling the town."[25] These verses give the impression that the priests bearing the shofars are blowing them vigorously during their daily procession before the ark of YHWH with the armed forces following around the city. Thus in 6:10 Joshua instructs the company not to raise their human voices until the seventh day when Joshua will give the command, "Shout!" This instruction would indicate that it is not the trumpet blast but the voice of Joshua summoning the war cry of Israel that will trigger YHWH's deed, collapsing Jericho's defenses. All this proceeds in the dark, as it were, although the parade takes place in full daylight. The text tells us that neither Joshua nor the people Israel were informed in advance that YHWH would collapse the walls before them at this juncture. They would be as surprised by this turn of events as the defenders of Jericho.

When Joshua has had the ark of YHWH circle the city just once on this first day, the whole company returns to camp for the night. Dozeman sees here a "polarity of camp and city [that] accentuates a central theme in the book of Joshua between rural and urban that is manifested in a religious conflict between aniconic worship, on the one hand, and the manufactured images and metal objects that are associated with kings and city states, on the other." We have previously noted that Dozeman's contrast here is overdrawn in that Israel's worship is not in any case correctly categorized as aniconic—for what else is the liturgical procession featuring the ark but a dramatic icon in motion, a visible word, displaying faith in sacramental real presence? Perhaps the iconic ark, as the visibly empty throne of the invisible YHWH, is an anti-idol in the sense Dozeman intends, but all the same it is a paradoxical "aniconic icon." In truth, most all riches of urban Jericho

23. Nelson, *Joshua*, 93–94.
24. Rösel, *Joshua*, 100.
25. Pitkänen, *Joshua*, 158.

will be treated as "unclean and infectious,"[26] and its mighty walls of defense are never to be rebuilt, as indicated in Joshua's curse pronounced over the ruins at the end of the chapter. But these ruins are made into a memorial—another form of iconography. The memorialized ruin of Jericho is the negative reflection of the icon-in-motion that is the circumambulating ark of the covenant, visibly empty throne of the invisibly present but active YHWH.

On the second day Joshua rises, eager to get going, and has the procession repeated again; the priests are said to blow their shofars continually but then return to camp. So it happens for the next four days. Rising at the break of dawn on the seventh day, once again eager to get going, Joshua and the company of Israel repeat the procession as in the preceding days, but this time they make six additional circuits of the city: seven circuits on the seventh day—perfect, albeit to the point of human exhaustion! "Israel will mark a full seven-day cycle. . . . The seventh day, with its echoes of Sabbath and Jubilee, marks a conclusion."[27] At the completion of the seventh circuit as the priests blow the trumpets, Joshua at last commands the people to raise their battle cry of victorious faith in YHWH, who has already given them the city. From this point on, its work having been accomplished, the ark of YHWH fades from the narrative screen, while the somewhat confused account of the blowing of the shofar momentarily takes center stage.

But the confusion in the account is immaterial. "For the ancient reader, the story was perhaps less extraordinary: he knew that God participates in war; he also knew that miracles happen; and he knew that walls collapse precisely after a seven-day war (1 Kings 20:28–30). . . . So for that reader the cultic character of the story was possibly more important than the exact details of the miracle. Decisive for him was that in the final analysis God, not trumpets, caused the miracle. The story, about the first conquest in the land of Canaan, highlights that the whole conquest is a miracle performed by God."[28] Although these observations of Rösel are correct, one should not minimize the fabulous nature of the event by relativizing it as a superstition from a bygone era held in common by ancient Israel and its foes, which moderns may conveniently disregard as readily as Rösel (and many other commentators) also disregards Israel's warfare of extermination as an accommodation to ancient Near Eastern culture.

Resort to cultural accommodation does not come close to accounting for this narrative's integral reliance on the fabulous. Not even in that superstitious

26. Dozeman, *Joshua 1–12*, 334.
27. Hawk, *Joshua*, 98.
28. Rösel, *Joshua*, 93.

epoch would any king go out to war calculating on the miraculous collapse of the enemy's fortifications, ignorant of this divinely provided outcome as Israel has apparently been in its vulnerable display of its forces throughout this militarily bizarre liturgical procession. But neither is the point of the paradigmatic Jericho miracle in the Joshua narrative historical representation, as if archaeological excavation might validate or invalidate its claim to truth. As iconic paradigm, the Jericho narrative represents the already of the not yet, picturing by a narrative icon-in-motion the coming of the victory of God over the usurpers of the earth. The miracle at Jericho, as represented in the narrative, simply and solely refers to YHWH who fights thusly for Israel. To be sure, only theology sees this, insists on this, and accordingly knows this in advancing the best reading of the text, telling what the letters actually say in their causal sequence.

Or at least it is apocalyptic theology that knows God in the uncanny collapse of Jericho's fortifications.[29] The resort to "accommodation" to explain away the violence or implausibility of biblical narrative has always been a favored tactic of the interpretation of the canonical biblical narrative as "history of salvation," despite the fact that the history narrated in the sweep from Genesis to Revelation is hardly an unambiguous tale of salvation. Of course this term, "salvation history" (German *Heilsgeschichte*), which came into provenance in the nineteenth and twentieth centuries, can mean many different things, much of them innocuous. But strictly taken as a neologism of modern theology, salvation history reflects the idealistic and supersessionist-teleological scheme of "progressive revelation," in which human ideas of God advance in tandem with the evolution of human culture until they reach their summit in our present. This presentist conceit allows theologians, and also critical biblical scholars otherwise quite concerned not to be theologians, to discount the scriptural text's knowledge of God. In the treatment of theology as a culturally relative accommodation to a bygone stage, an apologetic and self-serving exoneration of Bible and interpreter by contextualization transpires in place of an intellectually honest exercise in what Bultmann called *Sachkritik*. But the book of Joshua knows YHWH in his fabulous act of tearing down the walls of Jericho no less than in YHWH's ensuing destruction of its survivors, who may also be us. As scripture, the canonical book of Joshua wants to impress on its reader this disruptive knowledge of God. The interpreter dare not evade this knowledge of

---

29. On apocalyptic theology, see Paul R. Hinlicky, "Käsemann's Critique of Salvation History," in *Luther and the Beloved Community: A Path for Christian Theology after Christendom* (Grand Rapids: Eerdmans, 2010), 236–42.

God, which tears down the scheme of "salvation history" not otherwise than YHWH once tore down the walls of Jericho. "Indeed, this is the most radically theocentric of Joshua's conquest stories."[30]

The root of *ḥerem* (to YHWH) occurs six times in 6:17, 18, and 21. As Calvin rightly put it, *ḥerem* is "that which had been set apart for God alone" and thus has "perished, in so far as men were concerned."[31] Calvin acknowledges that the ensuing enactment of "indiscriminate and promiscuous slaughter, making no distinction of age or sex, but including alike women and children, the aged and decrepit, might seem an inhuman massacre, had it not been executed by the command of God. But as he, in whose hands are life and death, had justly doomed those nations to destruction, this puts an end to all discussion."[32] Well, perhaps not. We have already indicated our judgment that Calvin's resort to mystery at this decisive point of theology in the interpretation of the book of Joshua is an evasion that goes against even his own better judgment. The extension in scope of *ḥerem* to noncombatants appears inhumane in Calvin's eyes, as he expressly confesses, yet his justification of the divinely commanded atrocity appeals at the same time to the just punishment of the wicked by the Almighty. But what are we to say theologically about divine and retributive justice when its execution of punishment leaves no survivors, no creation to vindicate, redeem, and fulfill? Can we take reprobation that seriously?

As discussed in the chapter on preliminary considerations, the modern reader will quickly and rightly object to Calvin's attempt to silence ethical protest against the book of Joshua's divinely commanded slaughter and his further attempt to muffle theological inquiry against the textually manifest inhumanity of God's just but terrible judgment, even though Calvin is correct at least in describing what the text actually says in 6:17–21. What difference can it make to insist against Calvin but also against our own humane instincts that we not evade knowledge of the divine horror presented by the story? Perhaps we are to learn from it *theological* revulsion, "recoil" in the "heart" of God (Hos. 11:8) at the horror of God descending into battle in order to cleanse the land—as in Noah's flood. So Calvin understands this campaign: "to purge the land of Canaan of the foul and loathsome defilements by which it had long been polluted."[33] Revulsion may at length teach us that *ḥerem* warfare is mutually assured destruction, a politics of

30. Nelson, *Joshua*, 92–93.
31. Calvin, *Book of Joshua*, 76.
32. Calvin, *Book of Joshua*, 77.
33. Calvin, *Book of Joshua*, 78.

purity in which no one survives in the end—*not even God* in his creative purpose, however just the punishment of the usurpers of the earth! Revulsion may thus train us to entertain the dilemma of the God of love who must be against what is against love. Revulsion may lead us to ask with the church father Athanasius, "What was God in his goodness to do?"[34]

But to return to the Jericho story: with respect to the nations of Canaan, *herem* serves to radically separate Israel from the inhabitants of the land. *Ḥerem* establishes "a boundary that must not be transgressed if Israel is to retain its unique status as the treasured possession of YHWH."[35] But how odd is this introduction of the relentless politics of purity here! "The paradoxical pattern of using the principle of annihilating foreigners as an opportunity to address the topic of their survival [is] a pattern that will occur in chapter 9 [regarding the Gibeonites]."[36] Odd indeed but dramatic; for it is only now that Joshua explicates the *herem* mandate to the troops poised for action: all the city is to be sacrificed to YHWH, removing from any human utility everything in it. Yet, at the same time, because of Rahab and the oath made to her before YHWH, the story raises a dilemma. "Will Joshua disavow covenant and oath made in the name of YHWH in order to keep the command of Moses? Or will Joshua honor the oath made to Rahab and therefore violate the command of Moses?"[37] Joshua's instruction is dramatic at this juncture because of the impending rescue of Rahab. So it turns out: as she saved Israel's "messengers," now she and her family are to be saved by them. In obeying YHWH's command for *herem*, Joshua at the same time disobeys it.

One might attempt to lessen the paradox here by rightly pointing out misleading translations of *herem* that conceive of the verb's root meaning as "utterly destroy." Destruction is but a means to an end, and the end in view is rather, as the Waltons point out, to remove something from human usage. In the context of warfare in the ancient Near East, the command to put all Canaanites to the sword "is an alternative to their normal expected fate, which was slavery. They were killed not for the purpose of making them dead but to remove them from use as slaves."[38] There is a difficulty, however, with this *historical-critical* reconstruction

---

34. Athanasius, *On the Incarnation of the Word* §6, in *A Select Library of Nicene and Post-Nicene Fathers of the Christian Church*, 2nd series, ed. Philip Schaff and Henry Wace, 14 vols. (Peabody, MA: Hendrickson, 1994), 4:39.

35. Hawk, *Joshua*, 101.

36. Nelson, *Joshua*, 94. The narrative motif of *herem* as a test that was failed may also be found in 1 Sam. 15 and 1 Kgs. 20:42.

37. Hawk, *Joshua*, 90.

38. Walton and Walton, *Lost World of Israelite Conquest*, 173.

insofar as it would mitigate the *literary* force of the conundrum that the Rahab exception to *ḥerem* imposes on the reader of Joshua's speech. It cannot make sense of the later fate of the Gibeonites who were enslaved, nor for that matter of the capital punishment of Achan and his family as Israelite victims of the law of *ḥerem*. Achan is destroyed precisely for the purpose of making him dead, in retribution for his crime of violating the law of *ḥerem*. It is more likely the case that, already by the time of the composition of the book of Joshua, the denotation "remove from human use" and the connotation "utterly destroy" had become inextricably intertwined. Only so can the Rahab story "work" literarily to call the relentless *politics of ḥerem purity* into question by the invocation of *ḥesed*, pointing to a surpassing *politics of reconciliation*, as we have previously indicated.

The narrator is quick, in any case, to explain that the awkward exemption from the demand to devote Jericho and all its inhabitants as a sacrifice to YHWH does not extend past Rahab and her family. Joshua sternly warns against any such presumption rationalizing greed for the booty of war. Anyone who wants to possess something designated as *ḥerem* comes instead to possess only the holy curse that lies on the booty—not only for himself but for the whole camp of Israel into which the forbidden booty may be brought. Like a contagion, the forbidden booty radiates the poison of what lies under divine curse to all around, portending disaster. The use here in 6:18 of the verb *'akar*, "to entangle, put into disorder, bring disaster," sounding similar to Achan's name, hints forward to his story.[39]

Beginning with Rahab, the application of *ḥerem* in the book of Joshua is oddly variable. "It seems that the extent of *ḥerem* was not constant, but could vary depending on the occasion. In some cases not everything falls under *ḥerem* (e.g. in Josh. 8:1–2 the people may take the booty and animals from Ai; cf. Josh. 11:12–14; Num. 31); however, in the case of Jericho *ḥerem* is to be total, except for Rahab and whatever is inside her house,"[40] although the exception of Rahab is also a variable! Even so, yet one more quasi-exception is now articulated: precious metals are declared holy—that is, sanctified to YHWH. And accordingly they shall be removed from ordinary human utility by placing them in the cult treasury for liturgical use. "The phrase 'treasury of the house of YHWH' is surprising since YHWH has no house or temple in the narrative world of the book of Joshua . . . although the Tent of Meeting appears one time at Shiloh (18:1), and a sanctuary of YHWH is also noted at the conclusion of the book (24:26)."

---

39. Rösel, *Joshua*, 102.
40. Pitkänen, *Joshua*, 162.

The point may be simply to create a contrast with the treasuries of the Canaanite kings.[41] It thus seems difficult to discover a constant rule for the scope of *ḥerem* with all these exceptions and exemptions. Things can be devoted to YHWH by way of destruction, as in the whole burnt offering sacrifice, removing the victim from any human usage. Or things can be sanctified to YHWH by placing them into service of the cult. Or persons can be devoted to YHWH by making them into slaves of the cult, as will be the fate of the Gibeonites. Or persons converted to YHWH like Rahab may escape destruction and live in the midst of Israel. One may observe that a law arbitrarily applied, flagrantly disregarded, and haphazardly enforced is in function no law at all in any realistic political sense.

The gruesome report matter-of-factly tells the utter destruction of all life in the city, from men to women, from young to old, the livestock too, all devoured by "the mouth" of Israel's sword as the Hebrew idiom has it—the sword devouring the enemy like shark's teeth. But seemingly Joshua interrupts the bloody mayhem underway to instruct the two spies who had sworn fealty to Rahab to find her and her people and bring them out to safety from the chaos of destruction. In striking contrast to the episode in Rahab's home, here Rahab is passive and the spies are active.[42] At the same time, the deliverance of Rahab turns out to be expansive, more than readers are prepared to expect. The young men find her and bring out not only her immediate kin but her entire clan (*kol-mishpekhoteha*). Delivered from the violence engulfing Jericho, Rahab and her people are given a place of "rest"—that is, security—to dwell outside the camp of Israel at Gilgal. Thus already this paradigmatic battle "shatters any idea that the land will be populated only by 'Israelites.'"[43]

Except for the precious metals sanctified for use in the "house of YHWH," all that remained of Jericho after the slaughter is consigned to fire, as if a whole burnt offering, reducing the once mighty fortress to a heap of ash and rubble. All the same, Joshua kept Rahab and her people alive, the narrator tells us, so that they have dwelt "in the midst of" (not, as above, "outside the camp of") Israel to this day. The spies are once again, after 6:9, called "messengers" in 6:17, which "puts the focus on what was really important about their mission, the message gleaned from Rahab and given to Joshua."[44] In this subtle way, the narrator tells

41. Dozeman, *Joshua 1–12*, 337.

42. Rösel, *Joshua*, 103. There are differences between the MT and the LXX versions of the story of Rahab (Dozeman, *Joshua 1–12*, 314–15).

43. Hawk, *Joshua*, 104.

44. Nelson, *Joshua*, 95.

us, the presence of the Canaanite Rahab with her clan in the midst of Israel to the present day has come about on account of the "message" she bore by her confession of faith in YHWH who fights for Israel, along with her corresponding act of *ḥesed*—the true obedience of faith in hiding the spies from the suspicious minions of the king of Jericho and deceiving them with false testimony. So Rahab, like Bonhoeffer when he decided to join the military conspiracy to assassinate Hitler, "sinned boldly but all the more boldly believed" (as Luther famously advised his scrupulous and wobbling partner, Melanchthon). Luther's teaching of this disruptive paradox is exegetically well-grounded here. This first story of the execution of *ḥerem* ends paradoxically with literally emphatic exceptions to its otherwise strict rules of engagement. "Competing obligations to sworn oath and Deuteronomic law collide."[45] The case of Rahab in Jericho exposes an antinomy between *ḥerem* and *ḥesed* within the law of Moses itself, an antinomy that arises from within the telling, hearing, and obeying of the Torah of YHWH.

Thus we have a case here of what Luther called "the law battling the law in order to become liberty" for all.[46] Similarly, in his essay seeking to restore Paul's letter to the Romans as the chief messianic text of Western civilization, contemporary philosopher Giorgio Agamben develops what I have elsewhere called a "positive dialectic" in Paul arising from the crucified Joshua's final exposure and resolution of this antinomy within the law by his own life of obedience even to death on a cross. This clarification advances theology beyond the clichéd "law-gospel" theology of historical Lutheranism precisely because it does not feed on a sterile and injurious confrontation between Christianity and Judaism, or a Marcionite opposition of New Testament to Old Testament, but discovers the problematic antinomy of *ḥerem* and *ḥesed* within the Torah, just as close reading of Joshua already finds us wrestling with. In Agamben's words, "Paul is able to set the *nomos pisteos*, the law of faith, against the *nomos ton ergon*, the law of works. Rather than being an antinomy that involves two unrelated and completely heterogeneous principles, here the opposition lies within the *nomos* itself, between its normative and promissive elements. There is something in the law that constitutively exceeds the norm and is irreducible to it, and it is this excess and inner dialectic that Paul refers to by means of the binomial *epaggelia / nomos*."[47]

45. Nelson, *Joshua*, 93.
46. Hinlicky, *Luther and the Beloved Community*, 242–53.
47. Giorgio Agamben, *The Time That Remains: A Commentary on the Letter to the Romans*, trans. P. Dailey (Stanford, CA: Stanford University Press, 2005), 95; see also 114, 118. This is, as Agamben points out, by no means a dialectic imposed on the Jewish law from the outside. The Kabbalists also

This commentary has introduced this tension within the law along the way as the one between the indicative of grace and the imperative of faith's obedience. When we recall that the Decalogue is founded on a promise of the liberating YHWH's faithfulness to rescued Israel, its claims and prohibitions are therewith relativized and ordered to the sustenance of the community of liberated Israel on the land YHWH is giving. When the commandments are detached from this gracious indicative, however, they inevitably become universalized as abstract principles (say, as "natural law" or "categorical imperative") and in this way become sheer imperatives, the "moral ought," removed from their covenantal context in the gracious, unilateral, and unconditional divine promise "I am the LORD your God." Thus they become *nomos ton ergon* and no longer *nomos pisteos*. But this detachment of imperative from indicative happens also when infidelity mortally violates Israel's covenantal identity, committing the unforgivable sin of disowning one's election by grace. Then the imperatives become law that only accuses, revealing the incapacity of lost and wayward Israel to live and work as freed people on the land—just as Joshua concludes, as we shall see at the end of the commentary. This conclusion, unsettling as it is, leaves us yearning for that excess of the element of promise and its christological/messianic accomplishment.

For the present, the curse that Joshua now pronounces in the presence of YHWH over the ruins of Jericho has less to do with historicizing etiology than with theology: YHWH has torn down the mighty defenses of the fortified city. Ruins remain, however, as an icon memorializing the living God who here fought for Israel, a "trophy," as Calvin puts it, "to prevent [Israelites] from burying the divine favors in oblivion; hence the spectacle, wherein the divine agency was made conspicuous to the people, was [to be] a kind of indirect censure of their ingratitude."[48] The question for the book of Joshua, as we have noted, is not whether there will be icons but of what the icons will be and to what end they will serve. Anyone who would rebuild these walls of Jericho as if to erect and defend some future fiefdom on the Canaanite model defies this definitive judgment of YHWH: no one is to build up again what YHWH has torn down. The ruins portray and memorialize this judgment.

Therefore Israel by YHWH's victory is not displacing the city-state with a royalty of its own in order to establish a well-fortified Israelite imperialism.

---

distinguish between the law of creation and the law of the unredeemed world (49). See further Brent Adkins and Paul. R Hinlicky, *Rethinking Philosophy and Theology with Deleuze: A New Cartography* (New York: Bloomsbury, 2013), 200–206.

48. Calvin, *Book of Joshua*, 79.

Rather, Israel will attain rest on the land in order to serve YHWH without fear, as Zechariah, "filled with the Holy Spirit," would one day sing, heralding the birth of John the Baptist:

> Thus he has shown the mercy promised to our ancestors,
>   and has remembered his holy covenant,
> the oath that he swore to our ancestor Abraham,
>   to grant us that we, being rescued from the hands of our enemies,
> might serve him without fear, in holiness and righteousness
>   before him all our days. (Luke 1:72–75)

To be sure, the foundation for a rebuilt Jericho may someday be laid (1 Kgs. 16:34), but the cost will be dear; fallen from grace, false Israel arises, building up again what YHWH has torn down. This false Israel becomes the very thing from which Israel had once been liberated by YHWH: a usurper of the good earth, an ethnic nation-state under its own self-proclaimed political sovereignty in defiance of the liberator God YHWH's purpose of life on the land—also with the Rahabs of the land.

The chapter concludes by attributing the defeat of Jericho to YHWH's presence with Joshua as also to Joshua's obedience of faith in YHWH.[49] The obedience of faith, which as *nomos pisteos* is the twofold trust in YHWH's election and one's inclusion in it, is a peculiarly theological kind of compatibilism, not like that of the philosophers who debate about the relation between fatal necessity in the nature of things and human freedom as a causal power to initiate new and naturally unmotivated sequences within the causal chain, conceived as spontaneous contingency. But as theology understands, Joshua presents a compatibilism of divine sovereignty and human freedom in the dialectic of election and its elicited obedience of faith: as Hawk puts it, "choosing one's chosenness," accepting one's acceptance, justifying one's justifier, freely surrendering one's will to the good and gracious will of God for oneself as also for all. This compatibilism always works as a "Gethsemane of the soul," which proves paradoxically more powerful than walled fortifications. As Martin Luther King Jr. once preached,

> One must learn to make the transition from "let this cup pass from me" to "nevertheless, not my will, but thy will be done." And God grant that as you face life with all of its decisions—as you face the bitter cup which you will inevitably face

49. Nelson, *Joshua*, 93.

from day to day—God grant that you will learn this one thing and that is to make the transition from "this cup" to "nevertheless." . . . This, you see, is the thing that determines whether you go through life devoted to an eternal cause or whether you go through life depending on your own finite answers, which really turn out to be no answers. This is the thing that determines whether you can rise out of your egocentric predicament to devotion to a higher cause. This is what Jesus was able to do and this is the lesson that he presents to us today.[50]

So the first Joshua did, and just so his notoriety spread across the land of Canaan. "YHWH is indeed with Joshua. The question of whether YHWH is with Israel, however, remains open (cf. 5:13–14)."[51] Hawk's literary analysis argues that as a whole the book of Joshua is exploring the question "Who really is the Israel for whom YHWH fights?" Even so, this focus begs a further question that cannot be settled on the plane of ecclesiology but requires theology, strictly speaking—that is, the doctrine of God: What is the difference between YHWH's assured accompaniment of Joshua for the sake of the Israel of God and Hawk's open question regarding Israel and its presumed capacity to choose its chosenness?

50. Martin Luther King Jr., "Garden of Gethsemane," sermon, Dexter Avenue Baptist Church, Montgomery, AL, April 14, 1957, https://kinginstitute.stanford.edu/king-papers/documents/garden
-gethsemane-sermon-delivered-dexter-avenue-baptist-church.
51. Hawk, *Joshua*, 105.

ACHAN COVETS

7:1–26

Rahab and her people were saved from Jericho's destruction. Why? Was it on account of the cunning of the oppressed, tricking the king's men into a wild-goose chase and the spies into a life-saving pledge of their lives in exchange for hers? Is this an ancient Hebrew dramatization of Hegel's dialectic of the master and the slave, in which the bitter experience of the slave at length equips the slave to master the master? Answers to the question of Rahab's salvation along these lines bear some interest and would be worth exploring so far as there is little concern for learning from the literary integrity of the canonical book its theological message. But according to the narrative that is given to us, it was Rahab's faith in YHWH's election of Israel, along with its dark side, the reprobation of Jericho by the warrior God, which led her to side against Jericho and hide the spies, enacting and then eliciting a reciprocating *ḥesed*. By the grace of Rahab's faith in grace, she was subsequently exempted from the exceptionless rule of *ḥerem* warfare that otherwise should have destroyed her for being on the wrong side, as it is said, of history.

"Rahab, in short, acts like an Israelite should and receives life in the land. Achan, on the other hand, suffers the fate of the inhabitants of the land."[1] By stark contrast to outsider Rahab, Achan is an insider, a family man and son of the notable tribe of Judah; he is "a true Israelite insider, one whose ethnic purity is established by patrilineal descent."[2] But he will be destroyed publicly, in the midst

---

1. Hawk, *Joshua*, 107.
2. Hawk, *Joshua*, 111. On the other hand, "the negative context betrays an anti-Judahite tendency here." Rösel, *Joshua*, 110. Dozeman (*Joshua 1–12*, 353) agrees.

of the people of Israel, because of his secretive breach of the covenant in the disobedience of unfaith when he coveted, stole, and then concealed booty snatched from the ruins of Jericho. "The ritually unclean Rahab is prudently kept outside the war camp (6:23), but it is Achan the pedigreed Judahite who contaminates the camp with *ḥerem*."[3] By means of this vivid juxtaposition of Rahab and Achan, "Joshua's narrator transforms the campaign at Ai into a program for identifying and resolving the problem of Canaanite difference *within*."[4] For, to paraphrase Paul the apostle, not all Israelites are true Israelites just as not all Canaanites are true Canaanites. Israel has just learned how to recognize false Canaan in Rahab, an Israelite "outside." How then is true Israel to recognize false Israel, the true Canaanite "within"?

Dozeman calls attention to an interesting shift to the noun form from the verb form of *ḥerem* that appears in the story of Achan. The verbal form, "to do *ḥerem*," predominates elsewhere in Joshua where the focus is external to Israel—that is, the act of removing the Canaanite nations from any human use by total extermination. But in the Achan story, the noun form predominates: "the ban is no longer about the Israelite participation in holy war, but about the restriction from sacred booty ... lest the objects contaminate the Israelites, making them like the indigenous nations."[5] Achan's act of taking booty, as designated by the noun form of *ḥerem*, therefore, was a "sacrilege." This is another Hebrew verb employed in 7:1, which is common in the Priestly literature of the Pentateuch; it means "to use something holy for a wrong purpose" and thus to profane it. This story of such sacrilegious misuse functions in the book of Joshua "in a similar way to the story of the golden calf in the Pentateuch."[6] For all the external focus in the book of Joshua on what threatens Israel from the outside, here the spotlight shifts to expose the "central" threat to Israel from within Israel. "Achan's appropriation of *ḥerem* was a most dangerous act because it transformed Israel and its camp into a state of *ḥerem*, subject to destruction."[7] It did so because in coveting the goods of Canaan, the object of Achan's desire, *pars pro toto* for Israel's desire, became idolatrous.

The first verse puts readers in the know.[8] What is presupposed in this literary revelation, however, is an assumption of the collectivity of guilt; this troubles

3. Nelson, *Joshua*, 103.
4. Hawk, *Joshua*, 110.
5. Dozeman, *Joshua 1–12*, 352.
6. Dozeman, *Joshua 1–12*, 340.
7. Nelson, *Joshua*, 101.
8. Nelson, *Joshua*, 100.

the modern reader immediately and elicits an individualist protest of injustice, but "Israel is a collective entity and must be pure as such."[9] More precisely put: Israel as covenanted to YHWH exists as an "all-Israel" solidarity whose health is jeopardized as such by mortal sin; mortal sin is sin that violates the covenant that is the sole basis of Israel's peoplehood, rendering it null and void. And thus sacrilege pollutes the whole of the sacred people like a rotting corpse unburied would spread corruption to all the living around. Achan has shattered Israel's "homogeneity by introducing what belongs outside,"[10] just as an infection comes from the penetration of an organism by a foreign body. The whole body becomes sick when one cell turns cancerous, traitor to its host's organic integrity. "It was a deed of an Israelite, hence of Israel. This has less to do with 'guilt' or similar categories and much more with 'contamination.'"[11]

True enough, but don't even we modern individualists recognize how the individual polluter, whether personally intending harm or not, is "guilty" of endangering others with whom we must share the earth? What else has coronavirus social distancing and sheltering in place enabled than a moral judgment on those who recklessly disregard the command to separate and thus infect others? Theologically, a progressivist scheme in which Old Testament collectivism is superseded by New Testament individualism helps little here. Calvin reminds those so inclined that the apostle Paul in 1 Cor. 5:4–6 "upbraids all the Corinthians with the private enormity of one individual, and inveighs against their pride in presuming to glory while such a stigma attached to them."[12] Modern individualism with its individualistic understanding of sin and guilt finds an ally against Joshua's teaching of Israel's collective guilt for Achan's sin neither in Paul nor in Calvin. But the cost of the true perception of social solidarity in sin seems to lead relentlessly to the ruthless politics of purity.

Of course also in Israel of old there was knowledge of personal liability and fault. While Achan is the individual agent guilty of the act of covenant infidelity, the harm of his deed as well as the contagion of his hidden booty extends to the sons of Israel, the "all Israel," the body of the people of God. YHWH's wrath against this lethal betrayal of his new creation from within is said to be kindled into a raging fire to consume one and all, such as the divine force that had just reduced Jericho to a heap of ashes: an indiscriminate cautery or chemotherapy, as

9. Pitkänen, *Joshua*, 176.
10. Hawk, *Joshua*, 111.
11. Rösel, *Joshua*, 111.
12. Calvin, *Book of Joshua*, 84.

it were, that kills healthy cells along with diseased ones. Jealous, zealous YHWH does not tolerate infidelity and holds all Israel responsible for the betrayal of one. Moreover, YHWH is not automatically on Israel's side but has his own holy agenda to which Israel has been enlisted—certainly, for Israel's ultimate good. But that is the good that comes after judgment on the betrayal: "His winnowing fork is in his hand, to clear his threshing floor and to gather the wheat into his granary; but the chaff he will burn with unquenchable fire" (Luke 3:17). Penultimately, this ultimate good consists in Israel's solidarity, whether in evil or in good, in sickness as in health, in death as in life.[13] That solidarity of all Israel is integral to the covenanted people's existence through time because the good YHWH intends is the inauguration of his sovereignty on earth made holy by his coming to reign—not merely, then, over the territory of Canaan but much more in the peoplehood, Israel. Stunningly, this good has included the otherwise excluded Rahab, as we have seen. We now see how it can also exclude the otherwise included Achan, just as happens to the traitor Judas, that one of the twelve chosen who betrays the second Joshua.

There is much food for thought here in connection with the profoundly polluting and too often concealed sin of the sexual abuse of minors by Christian clergy in recent times. The pious temptation to cover up these crimes as a merely private indiscretion for the sake of saving the public reputation of the church succeeds only in concealing, as Achan concealed, what is hateful with the further sin of hypocrisy. Exposure, when it does *not* come as the fruit of the new Israel's self-discipline, is deeply and rightly discrediting of the church's calling to be a place of holy truth-telling. For modern churches feeding on the thin gruel of cheap grace, more spiritual courage to face these difficult betrayals is needed than seems available. Because the victim's call for justice in exposing the crime is inevitably also a call for punishment, indeed for retribution, the church should receive exposure as a "severe mercy."[14] Premature calls that the "healing begin" before the wound is exposed to antiseptic sunlight do not restore the missing equilibrium to the solidarity of the church disrupted by vicious crime hypocritically concealed. The fate of Achan should cause us to ponder Calvin's comment in this connection, how "severe punishment" wipes away "the scandal which might otherwise have existed; hence we gather that when occasion has been given to the wicked to blaspheme, the church has no fitter means of removing the opprobrium than

13. Wyschogrod, *Body of Faith*, 242.
14. Augustine, *Confessions*, trans. Henry Chadwick (Oxford: Oxford University Press, 1991), 150–51.

that of visiting offenses with exemplary punishment."[15] As with Achan, there is no putting a pretty face on this abomination of sexual exploitation until the crime is faced, the perpetrator is identified, and reparation to the victim provided.

The narrative next turns to the military advance following after Jericho, the nearby city of Ai. A temptation to pride among the victorious tribes after the stunning defeat of Jericho is evident in the description of the action. Without further inquiry to YHWH and word from him, Joshua again sends spies, thinking either that his spying would be effective preparation for battle or that a rote repetition of the previous stratagem against Jericho would guarantee a similar result. Seeing a temptation to pride in these preparations for the assault on Ai is reinforced by the evident presumption of the returning spies. They counsel Joshua to keep the main body behind and only send a smaller detachment to take care of Ai. Joshua assents, but the ensuing division of forces breaks the covenantal all-Israel solidarity/integrity necessary for success. Keeping solidarity keeps Israel covenanted to YHWH, the Divine Warrior. It is as "all Israel" that battles are won against the fragmented Canaanite peoples.[16] But "the Israelites are overconfident and . . . they trust in their own abilities rather than relying on YHWH's favor,"[17] and so they presumptuously divide their forces.

The book of Joshua rarely gives detailed battle accounts, so the level of detail now given is "exceptional."[18] True, but the "exceptional" level of detail that is reported about the engagement focuses narrowly on the disgraceful flight of Israel's warriors with the hot pursuit of the soldiers of Ai on their heels. We are told that thirty-six warriors of Israel were killed in action in a flight that began at the gates of Ai and continued on for miles through the valley. The hearts of valiant warriors are often likened to steely frozen blocks of ice, unwavering before danger. But the unexpected defeat reduces the ice-hard fighting mettle of Israel to a quivering puddle of melted water—an image previously used to describe the Canaanites in 2:25 and 5:1. The text thus tacitly turns attention to the human self, what a human creature is before YHWH (the *coram Deo* relation in distinction from the *coram mundo/hominibus* relation). Corresponding to the imminent exposure of Achan's hidden sin of coveting, here "the heart appears as the seat of the will";[19] to see past superficial appearances based on outward behavior is

15. Calvin, *Book of Joshua*, 85.
16. Hawk, *Joshua*, 112.
17. Pitkänen, *Joshua*, 177.
18. Rösel, *Joshua*, 112.
19. Rösel, *Joshua*, 114.

the prerogative of YHWH, who searches and judges the heart. Unlike human judges YHWH is not deceived by outward behavior. The text invites readers to share in this divine perspective, seeing into the cowardly hearts of the Israelites in flight from the enemy. Thus the reader is led by this divine inspection of the soul to the provocative realization that "Israel bears an uncanny resemblance to the peoples of the land."[20]

In a fashion reminiscent of Num. 14:44–45, Joshua now realizes that he has acted presumptuously by not taking counsel with YHWH. "Divine initiative" has played no role. Israel has mimicked "the peoples of the land, relying on its own might and ingenuity."[21] Such methodological reliance on the flesh, which is unreliance on the Spirit, is precisely what *herem* warfare prohibits. Panicked, knowing that something has gone wrong, fleshly Joshua has difficulty therefore recognizing "the Canaanite within"—not in the first instance the covetousness hidden in Achan's heart that shamefully concealed the booty hidden in his tent, but in Joshua's own self-reliance as a military leader. In desperation, Joshua along with the elders humbles himself before the ark-throne of YHWH, seeking relief from the punishment that is falling on Israel, if not yet from the sin that elicited punishment.

What follows is another intriguing portrait of the human self—this time of Joshua's desperation *coram Deo*, the narrative painting the inverse image of his pride and presumption that has led to the defeat in battle. Calvin is inclined to defend the piety of Joshua, who felt the deepest sorrow bordering on despair, he says, fearing for the disgrace brought on his holy calling. But Calvin adds the sharp observation that it is not a new thing "for pious minds, when they aspire to seek God with holy zeal, to obscure the light of faith by the vehemence and impetuosity of their affections."[22] In the confusion of grief at the setback, Joshua casts about looking for relief. Superficially, he imitates Moses's celebrated prayers of intercession for sinful Israel by appealing to YHWH's reputation, but, as Hawk points out, his prayer in fact does not seek to inquire for the cause of wrath but on the contrary gives precise echo to the complaining of rebellious Israelites in Num. 14:2b–3![23]

Thus Joshua misdiagnoses the failure at Ai, speculating that it was sinful greed to acquire more land than the Transjordan held that had motivated Israel to

20. Hawk, *Joshua*, 114.
21. Hawk, *Joshua*, 113.
22. Calvin, *Book of Joshua*, 87.
23. Hawk, *Joshua*, 114–15.

cross the Jordan for conquest, so that YHWH is now punishing greedy Israel, delivering them to the Amorites, by whom they are now surrounded. "Better to have remained in the Transjordan"[24] echoes the complaints of the wilderness generation when they hankered after the fleshpots of Egypt in preference to the rigor of responsible freedom. The desperate soul thus comes to doubt YHWH's deeds for Israel in the crossing of the Jordan and at Jericho—a doubt-induced wish, tantamount, Calvin comments, "to abrogat[ing] the covenant altogether." In this way and that, Joshua searches for understanding, baffled that the victorious warriors of Israel, fresh from the spectacular triumph over Jericho, have played the coward and shamefully turned their backs to the enemy, fleeing in terror, publicly disgraced! As previously the hearts of the Canaanites were said to have melted at the news of YHWH's deeds on behalf of Israel, now word of YHWH's abandonment of Israel, Joshua fears, will reverberate through the land; emboldened, the Canaanites will unite and surround Israel, erasing their name from human memory. The narrator's characterization of Joshua's prayer "indicates that the reason for the defeat was unknown to Joshua. He must have assumed that it was divine arbitrariness, or God's ungraspable will."[25] Most darkly, he imagines that a sinister YHWH has double-crossed Israel.

So a desperate Joshua has diagnosed the situation and makes his final plea: What happens to YHWH's great name when YHWH's people are thus destroyed? But this very prayer of Joshua betrays his own contamination by the as yet undetected pollution hidden within Israel. His appeal is "patently manipulative"[26] and shows no evidence of contrition for sin or need of divine mercy.[27] By the same token there is no genuine inquiry into and hence confession of sin in it, let alone contrition. He wants relief from punishment, not deliverance from sin. An intervention—an apocalypse—is needed to unveil what really is going on beneath the visible surface of Israel's history as history with the God who searches and judges the heart.

The portrait of Joshua at prayer raises the question, equally terrible and radical, of whether the believer loves God for God's sake or for the sake of the benefits of God. To love God for the sake of presumed benefits is not merely "patently manipulative," but it enthrones the believer as if king in place of the saving kingship that YHWH asserts. Thus Joshua would do a cost-benefit analysis, assuming the

24. Rösel, *Joshua*, 114.
25. Calvin, *Book of Joshua*, 87.
26. Hawk, *Joshua*, 116.
27. Dozeman, *Joshua 1–12*, 358.

position of a religious consumer with her own self-diagnosed perceived needs, determining what benefits are worth the cost of loving God for his sake and to his glory. But to love God for God's sake is to renounce religious consumerism along with the devil and all his pomp and circumstance. It is to regard God as the true and living God in heaven and on earth, the creature's supreme and only true good—a wholehearted and whole-minded love from the seat of desire that relativizes all other goods in and under God's dominion.

Origen entertains a version of this penetrating question, though its force is somewhat muted. God alone knows, he writes, who "is kindled by the desire of the good itself to do what is good, and who of us, out of fear of Gehenna and the terror of eternal fire, strives toward the good and is diligent and hastens to fulfill the things that have been written. It is certain that the nobler ones are those who do what is good by the desire of the good itself and by the love of blessing, rather than those who run after the good through the fear of evil."[28] It is true enough that one who loves God out of fear of punishment loves in servile, not filial, fashion. But the book of Joshua, taken as a whole, presses a more radical question than assumed in the moral truism that all by nature seek the good, asking sharply in the end, "Who can love God for God's sake truly and purely?" It pushes, in other words, the politics of purity to its ultimate self-cancellation, recognizing how even a sublime calculation of reward and blessedness can corrupt love. But the purity of the heart is to will one thing: *soli Deo gloria*.

In reply, YHWH sovereignly overrules confused and desperate Joshua. The command to stand up like a man is also a rebuke for having fallen on his face in the first place in sinful doubt of what YHWH already has done for Israel in the crossing and at Jericho. The guilty self wants only to evade the consequences of guilt rather than to discover and eliminate the cause of guilt and ensuing punishment: "He sees and thinks and knows crookedly even in relation to his crookedness."[29] So YHWH commands Joshua to stand up straight in order that he see straight the cause of the defeat at Ai. The people have fled like cowards in battle because the people have *sinned*. We are not to think here of trivial, readily visible transgressions but, as the narrative shows, of something sinister and hidden from view. How are we to understand "sin"?

The book of Joshua uses this weighty Hebrew word *khata'* meaning "to miss the mark" ("to fall short of the glory of God" in Pauline paraphrase), translated

---

28. Origen, *Homilies on Joshua*, 102.

29. Karl Barth, *Church Dogmatics*, vol. IV/1, *The Doctrine of Reconciliation*, ed. G. W. Bromiley and T. F. Torrance (Edinburgh: T&T Clark, 1956), 360.

into English as "sin," only here in YHWH's diagnostic (7:11) and again later when Achan publicly confesses, "I have sinned" (7:20 AT). The grievous term, accentuated by this rare usage, seems to be reserved, not for venial transgressions that can be repented by means of restitution and atonement from within the covenant relationship, but for lethal sin, sin that destroys the covenant relationship itself, specifically here for violation of the exacting stipulations regarding *ḥerem* warfare.[30] Israel has sinned—broken the covenant that binds the people to YHWH—and thus as a consequence YHWH as warrior is no longer bound to them in battle, but the opposite. The frightful consequence of divine abandonment is the exposure of hapless little Israel in the midst of the powerful Canaanite city-states and their alarmed warlord-kings. That is not all. It is the warrior YHWH who has actively turned against Israel for their violation of the covenant.

How have they violated it? They have stolen, they have lied, they have concealed devoted things among their possessions in the camp, a deed that veritably transforms Israel into not-Israel. The violator is said to have committed an "outrage in Israel," an expression in the Hebrew Bible "used mostly for grave crimes in the sexual sphere that endanger the basis of the community. . . . Here too the issue is the breach of a taboo, which endangers the existence of the community."[31] The transference of a term used commonly in the sexual sphere, however, is not inappropriate for the lethal sin of Achan, which violates the covenant relationship in an act inspired by wayward desire. This "outrage" is likened elsewhere in the Hebrew Bible, notably in the prophet Hosea, to infidelity. Deuteronomy 7:25b–26 states the statute forbidding desire of Canaan's ensnaring goods. The other Hebrew verb used in these verses for "sin" (*maʾal* in 7:1) has the priestly connotation of pollution, as if to say, "I have polluted myself before YHWH." While the metaphor of pollution is more medical than juridical, one should not thereby divest it from the connotation of sin and guilt, as the narrative goes on to show us.

Exposing, disowning, and executing punishment on the sin of Achan is thus made the collective responsibility of all Israel by YHWH's apocalypse of the corruption to Joshua. Until it is purged by treating what is *ḥerem* as the rule of *ḥerem* warfare requires, all Israel is under the kindled wrath of the Divine Warrior about to erupt into a devouring inferno. The cowardly flight of the warriors of Israel from Ai is exposed: they have become themselves the thing accursed by

30. Dozeman, *Joshua 1–12*, 359.
31. Rösel, *Joshua*, 115; cf. Nelson, *Joshua*, 101.

YHWH. The thirty-six dead were thus removed from any human purpose by way of destruction at the hands of the enemy, who has now acted as the instrument of YHWH who fights against Israel. The strict justice that was applied against Jericho is now turned against Israel—even against Joshua, at the head of this people.

What is to be done? The danger is real and impending. The polluted people are commanded to sanctify themselves. Sanctification, in the liturgical sense here required, begins to remedy pollution by a ritual act of separation; separation will make the source of the people's pollution stand out by contrast for discovery. So YHWH commands Joshua to have the people separate themselves from the source of the pollution by separating themselves anew to YHWH, the God of the covenant. The prophetic formula "Thus says the LORD . . ." prefaces Joshua's new, divinely given diagnosis of the defeat at Ai: until Israel exterminates the stolen booty along with the thief who stole it and his family who enabled the crime, Israel will be exterminated by its enemies, who become the instrument of YHWH who now fights against Israel. The fate that belongs to devoted things must single out the guilty one who personally crossed the strict line drawn by the covenant and then brought back into the camp of Israel forbidden gain, in so doing bringing down curse in place of blessing on Israel. The punishment is "death by fire" as in Jericho (6:24), Ai (8:8, 19), elsewhere (11:6, 9, 11).[32] Fire vividly figures of the wrath of YHWH.

Tribe by tribe, family by family, household by household, man by man, the people of Israel will pass before YHWH in the morning; so the sanctification of Israel is renewed as those innocent of violating the ban are separated from the guilty one, who will be discovered in the process. We are not told how the selections were determined,[33] but "with surgical precision, the nation separates itself from those within who are 'not one of them,'" from the "Canaanized insider (a subject) who has infected the nation, rather than Canaanite outsiders (an object)."[34] It is only important for the narrative that the process of discovery is under the direction of YHWH, who himself identifies the guilty son of the tribe of Judah, Achan. The name Achan, incidentally, is curious; it has no decipherable Hebrew etymology but is similar to the Hebrew word for Canaan, suggesting that Achan represents the "hidden presence of Canaan within Israel"[35] just as

---

32. Dozeman, *Joshua 1–12*, 360.
33. On casting lots, see Pitkänen, *Joshua*, 178.
34. Hawk, *Joshua*, 119.
35. Hawk, *Joshua*, 120.

the persistently reviving "old Adam" in the sanctified Christian life needs daily to be exposed and drowned by the remembrance of baptism.

Achan has been publicly exposed by the God of Israel and for this reason Joshua implores him, as a father to a son, to glorify God and give thanks, since the true source of Israel's pollution is now known and can be purged. By confessing his sin, the one who has fallen short of the glory of God restores in principle the glory to God, from whom he robbed it by his faithless deed. Thus Achan's confession of sin is at the same time a confession of praise in that the direct object of his sin is YHWH, the God of Israel, and just so indirectly Israel as the covenanted people of God. But employment of the first-person singular pronoun, "I," singles out the offender and separates him from all others. "With the self-accusation formula 'I have sinned' (v. 20; 1 Sam. 15:23–24; 2 Sam. 12:13; 19:21 [19:20 ET]; 24:17), Achan acknowledges his own responsibility," thus concurring in the separation/sanctification of the people as a whole from him in his personal culpability.[36] So Calvin: "Nor does he only acknowledge the deed, but by renouncing all defense, and throwing aside all pretext, he condemns himself in regard to its atrocity. I have sinned, he says; this he would not have said had he not been conscious of sacrilege, and hence it appears that he did not pretend mistake or want of thought."[37]

His pollution exposed, Achan does not deny or protest but gives God glory in that he may now come clean and so overcome the pollution by which he has brought harm upon his people. He takes the harm he has done to others upon himself in the process, implicitly as just retribution. In an agency like that of the one thief on the cross in Luke's passion account, Achan confesses emphatically: "I have sinned against YHWH." This is indeed occasion for doxology, because "the most perilous difference is the one that is not apparent, that lies hidden within the midst of the community." Yet the account raises an acute question even in the process of resolving the crisis: "How can Israel recognize the presence of Canaan within itself if what is Canaanite is not always open to view?"[38] Is true insight into sin itself only a divine possibility and thus a gift? In the event, YHWH has now acted to open Achan's hidden heart to the view of all Israel and, being exposed, Achan assumes the responsibility of a true agent, owning the deed and acknowledging it as his own: "I have sinned."

How remarkable is the statement! There is no easy distinction to be made between the sin of the soul and the crime of the body, and overly easy discourse

36. Nelson, *Joshua*, 106.
37. Calvin, *Book of Joshua*, 93.
38. Hawk, *Joshua*, 120.

about loving the sinner but hating the sin will not spare Achan any more than it saved the penitent thief on the cross from paying for his crime. Criminal justice questions aside, the spiritual reality is that, for all eternity, the one and only body-and-soul who is Achan remains the one who betrayed the covenant and brought the disaster of defeat on Israel at Ai at the cost of thirty-six lives. In this "hell of the irrevocable"[39] now found out and made public, Achan's only remaining agency consists in the choice to give glory to God by confessing the sin as his own deed and taking the harm of it from others back upon himself. His reward is an excruciatingly, excessively just—indeed ruthless, relentless—retribution: his life and his family's for the thirty-six fallen Israelite warriors.

Observing the spectacle, we readers are left to ponder what sin of Achan's heart was at the root of the crime. *Khamad*, the Hebrew verb used here, means "to delight in, to desire greatly" especially that which is not one's own. It is the "coveting"[40] forbidden by the final commandments of the Decalogue. The church father Prudentius waxed poetic in describing this:

> And Jericho had seen in her own ruin
> Our hands control, when conquering Achan fell.
> Renowned for bloodshed, proud of leveling walls,
> He fell a victim to the enemy's gold
> When from the dust he gleaned the stuff accursed
> And snatched the mournful plunder from the ruins.[41]

The forbidden objects of Achan's delight were not his to enjoy, and he knew it. Deception and self-deception are the bribes that a shamed conscience pays to knowledge of the commandment of God. Covetous Achan had to bury the booty within his tent to keep others from knowing what he had acquired, lest they see the disobedience. The location within the tent, moreover, implicates his immediate family as enablers in the deception. The irony is that in his shame he is not able to enjoy the objects of his desire but has ever to live with the torturous fear of being exposed.

As previously discussed, the ordinary motive for wars of aggression in Israel's time was precisely to acquire such desirable property of others, a crime motivated

---

39. Josiah Royce, *The Problem of Christianity* (Washington, DC: Catholic University of America Press, 2001), 162–63, 169, 175.

40. Dozeman, *Joshua 1–12*, 347.

41. Prudentius, *The Spiritual Combat* 536–46 (ACCS 4:42).

by the sin of coveting. Shameless as it was, there was never anything hidden about this motive in warfare as usual in the ancient Near East. Destruction of the enemy's war-fighting capability—hence the slaughter of enemy combatants, namely the males of fighting age—for the sake of acquisition of the women and children, livestock, and other goods was the very point of going to war. As we have seen, just this motive is disallowed by the covenant rule of *ḥerem* warfare. The war is YHWH's, and it is Israel's only so far as Israel is and remains covenanted to YHWH in his sovereign purpose of forming a new humanity at rest from war on the good earth. When Israel succumbs to the avarice motivating the warring nations, the curse on Canaan falls equally on Israel, concretely now in the person of Achan, who has acknowledged his hitherto deeply concealed sin of covetousness with its collateral crimes of theft and deception. The sin of coveting is magnified in the eyes of readers by the mention of the particular booty that Achan took. The "robe of Shinar" is likely a cryptic reference to Babylon, which, for the dispossessed Israelites of postexilic times reading the story in the book of Joshua, would allude to their own temptation to covet the goods of Babylon in preference to the ruins of Jerusalem.

Achan's confession is verified when messengers sent by Joshua discover the loot hidden in the tent and bring it to Joshua and all the sons of Israel, displaying it before YHWH. The sin against YHWH and the crime against Israel thus publicly verified, the terrible retributive justice of *ḥerem* now expunges the source of their pollution: with his sons and daughters, livestock, and all he owned, Achan is brought to the Valley of Achor, where Joshua pronounces the lex talionis sentence of "trouble for trouble."[42] The reason why that is so is that the wage of covenant apostasy is death. The brutal execution by stoning enacts what is prescribed in Deut. 13:17.[43] The burning anger of YHWH deflects from all Israel to focus narrowly on the ones who endangered all Israel by coveting the things belonging to God rather than willing to will and to do the will of God. All Israel in turn ritually participates in the return of trouble on Achan and his family by the stoning and then having the remains consumed with fire—the burnt offering of *ḥerem*.

Calvin acknowledges the "harsh, nay, barbarous and inhuman" punishment; "it seems a cruel vengeance to stone and burn children for the crime of their father; and here God publicly inflicts punishment on children for the sake of their parents, contrary to what he declares by Ezekiel." He laconically reflects

42. Dozeman, *Joshua 1–12*, 353.
43. Hawk, *Joshua*, 108–9.

that it may be that "death proved to them a medicine; but if they were reprobate, then condemnation could not be premature." Calvin is not unaware of the horror contained in his reflection up to and including the dark thought of eternal reprobation. "What remains for us, but to acknowledge our weakness and submit to his incomprehensible counsel?"[44] But it is too easy a solution to mask subtheological ignorance of God by the assertion of a putative knowledge of the mystery of God's incomprehensibility and in the process to let stand without question a sinister portrait of God as harsh, barbarous, inhuman, and cruel. That is arguably not the intention of the text, which wants the event to be remembered as a warning of the ruthless, relentless politics of purity. Just as the righteousness of God in the second Joshua will surpass the civil understanding of justice among philosophers and jurists and Moses too, so also does the justice of God executed by the first Joshua surpass the self-serving justice of walled cities under political sovereignty when it turns inward to judge unfaithful Israel. But to know God one must know these differences and say how they are so. The Achan story forces this theological task upon us.

To this day, the narrator tells us, a great heap of stones marks the place of this execution, where YHWH executed his burning anger on the Canaanite within through the hands of Israel and so turned it away from all Israel. The valley takes its name from the Hebrew word for "trouble, disturbance."

44. Calvin, *Book of Joshua*, 95.

ḤEREM CONSUMES AI AND ITS KING

8:1–29

The source of Israel's pollution now having been eliminated with Achan's execution, YHWH again takes the helm in Israel. With each passing episode, the narrative turns to clarifying further what is at stake in *ḥerem* warfare as the inauguration of the reign of YHWH advancing into Canaan. To begin with, it is made clear that "the destruction of the king of Ai is as important as that of the city. . . . The themes of the introduction (king, city, booty) return at the finale (booty, city, king) to produce a satisfying feeling of completion."[1] Permission is granted for the taking of lesser booty like cattle in the same breath as the royalty of the Canaanite city-states are identified as the special target of *ḥerem* warfare. The new tactic of ambush announced by YHWH further illuminates theological compatibilism: "From YHWH's perspective success may be guaranteed; from the human standpoint it requires tactics and subterfuge. These two perspectives are brought together by the sword brandished by Joshua [as the battle unfolds], as both human signal and medium of divinely assisted victory (cf. Exod. 17:11)."[2]

A new literary technique in the account of the battle of Ai provides alternating vignettes displaying the perspective of the king of Ai (which serve to underscore the king's arrogance) and YHWH's cunning (as executed by Joshua). The story here invites comparison with the story of the Benjaminite conquest of Gibeah in Judg. 20,[3] but within the framework of canonical Joshua, this chapter's account of *ḥerem* war not only balances and thus further clarifies the sense of the foregoing

1. Nelson, *Joshua*, 112–13.
2. Nelson, *Joshua*, 113–14.
3. For details, see Rösel, *Joshua*, 122–23. Pitkänen (*Joshua*, 175) mentions also 1 Sam. 14–15 and Num. 14.

battle of Jericho and the sin of Achan, but also prepares for "the final stage in the northward journey of the ark . . . [to] Ebal and Gerizim."[4]

In sharp contrast to the cowardly flight of the detachment in the first skirmish with Ai, and indeed in continuing reprimand of Joshua's own display of misery at news of the defeat, YHWH now forbids fear and dismay. This renewed imperative is grounded in the indicative: YHWH has *already* given the king of Ai with his people, the city, and the land into Joshua's hand. The obedience of faith at this good news this time has Joshua deploy *all* the fighting men of Israel to go up to the place of the earlier debacle. It is certainly true to observe here that "whether the military success is achieved by divine miracle or by human activity does not matter; God is always involved."[5] But such banal commentary misses too much and misstates the real contrast in the narrative between two equally *human* forms of Israel's cooperation with the Divine Warrior in *ḥerem* warfare: victory by public parade in Jericho and victory by the stealth of ambush in Ai.[6]

As mentioned, it is once again the king of the city-state who is specified as YHWH's target and assigned to the same fate as occurred to Jericho and its king: destruction (though previously we had not learned of the particular fate of Jericho's king). Origen takes occasion here to elaborate a redemptive theology of Christ the victor based on a twofold literary interpretation of the story. He claims that the city name, Ai, means "chaos" and is to be understood as "the place or habitation of opposing powers, of which the Devil is the king and chief."[7] And he interprets Josh. 8:29 to mean "hanged on twofold wood." Combining these two, he writes, "For the Son of God was indeed visibly crucified in the flesh," but invisibly the devil too "with his principalities and authorities was affixed to the cross"—an allusion to Col. 2:14–15.[8] Seeing the human Christ being crucified, the voracious predator-devil pounced to devour but in the process was himself impaled on the hidden divinity that, like a fishing hook, bore the bait of the dying humanity. Nonetheless, Origen's paradoxical victory of Christ as crucified over the devil by the trick of bait and switch (surely Athanasius's previously mentioned "divine dilemma" is an advance over this scheme) shares with the book of Joshua the "already/not yet" schema: "Truly, one coming of Christ in lowliness has been accomplished, but another is expected in glory." Thus Origen's Christians are not

---

4. Dozeman, *Joshua 1–12*, 362. The MT and LXX versions diverge considerably; see ibid., 366–69.
5. Rösel, *Joshua*, 108.
6. Dozeman, *Joshua 1–12*, 384.
7. Origen, *Homilies on Joshua*, 86.
8. Origen, *Homilies on Joshua*, 87.

yet secure but steel themselves for battles against "those demons deeply within, whose dwelling place is chaos and who rule in the abyss." These Christians are to destroy. How? "If we sin, they have life; but if we do not sin, they are destroyed."[9] Conquest of sin *is* liberation from the devil's tyranny.

The strength of this kind of Christian appropriation of Joshua is that it delivers readers from "disgust or distaste [at] those things that are read because of the narration of them seems to be less pleasant"—as Origen gingerly references the graphic accounts of *ḥerem* warfare.[10] Battles of extermination against Canaanites are reconfigured as battles against the devil and the sin that he locates within the saints-in-struggle, their battle already begun but not yet completed. The weakness of this kind of appropriation, however, is that the transindividual configuration of the forces of evil represented in the regimes of the Canaanite cities and their kings is reduced to the pious Christian's internal struggle with wayward passions.

Wyschogrod, on the other hand, denies that Judaism's tension between the already and the not yet is shared with Christianity. He is certainly correct about triumphalist and supersessionist Christianity, which imagines that it has already arrived in the kingdom of glory and consequently lords it over others remaining in the darkness. This posture represents what scholars call "realized eschatology," and this is precisely what Wyschogrod accuses Christianity of: "Unlike Christianity, Judaism does not believe that the central event of its history or of human history has taken place. The central event, the advent of the Messiah and the redemption of Israel and the world, has not yet taken place; it is still being awaited, and it is this waiting that characterizes the condition of humanity."[11] But what else can justification by faith—"the just will live by their faith" (Rom. 1:17 AT), citing the prophet Habakkuk—mean but such waiting on a salvation assured but not yet realized?

"Now, by divine fiat, what was declared *ḥerem* at Jericho is rendered into something that may safely be incorporated into the nation, again demonstrating that Israel's boundaries are defined by YHWH."[12] True enough, the observation here regarding the difference between the Jericho and the Ai directives is correct, but it is questionable whether it is best to call this change a "fiat" in the sense of an arbitrary decree warranted by nothing other than the sheer superior power and

9. Origen, *Homilies on Joshua*, 92.
10. Origen, *Homilies on Joshua*, 85.
11. Wyschogrod, *Body of Faith*, 225.
12. Hawk, *Joshua*, 124–25.

arbitrary whim of YHWH the Divine Warrior who dictates rules as he pleases. In respecting the freedom of God in theology, one must be careful not to divinize caprice. Does a more careful reading of the narrative provide theological reason for this relaxation of the rules of *ḥerem* warfare?

A relaxation of the absolute rule of *ḥerem* is certainly now provided by the narrative: the spoils of war, especially the livestock, are allowed to the victors. "The topic of acceptable booty for profane possession is often tied to the theme of intermarriage in the Hebrew Bible," as in Deut. 20:10–15. "In the book of Joshua the only acceptable booty for profane possession is the general spoil and the animals."[13] This restriction of permissible booty to livestock seems to be based on the rationale provided for *ḥerem* warfare in Deut. 20:18, "so that they may not teach you to do all the abhorrent things that they do for their gods, and you thus sin against the LORD your God." Cattle, presumably, are not capable of issuing such deviant religious instruction. In other words, "for the author, all humans are excluded from becoming war booty; only animals and more general spoil of war are allowed to become possessions of the Israelites."[14] Rösel suggests that the unrealistically strict rule in Jericho was the result of a literary need to make the Achan story work: "The difference must be explained in that the episode of Achan demands the harsher sanctions."[15] But Dozeman is closer to the truth in suggesting that what the Jericho and Ai *ḥerem* directives have in common is a concern to prevent intermarriage with Canaanites. The sin of the men of Israel at Shittim with the women of Moab is in the background here. Until the consequences of violation of *ḥerem* have been made utterly plain in the story of Achan by strict prohibition of all booty and strict enforcement against violators, the narrative dare not lower the bar. Having accomplished this literarily, lesser booty is permitted in the narrative course of the book of Joshua without relaxation of the ban on human life on account of the continuing danger of syncretism through intermarriage with the Canaanites. Of course, one still wonders about little ones.

The change in tactics is announced: not parade this time, but ambush. Deception is the first rule in the art of war. Recall, however, that just this was the rule that was deliberately jettisoned by the seven-day parade around Jericho. But in this new case a tactic of deception is commanded by YHWH the Divine Warrior, and his battle plan will succeed by means of Israel's obedience to it, just as before at Jericho. In contrast to the counterintuitive display of Israel's military

13. Dozeman, *Joshua 1–12*, 385–86.
14. Dozeman, *Joshua 1–12*, 385.
15. Rösel, *Joshua*, 123.

capability in the processions around Jericho, now Israel's military prowess will lie in wait out of sight while a detachment similar to the first engagement at Ai will act as bait, luring the enemy out of the safety of its city fortifications. The contrast in tactics is important and inescapable: public procession as opposed to covert ambush. But the objective is the same: showing the impotence of walled fortifications against YHWH the Divine Warrior.

So the tactic of deception begins to unfold. Joshua handpicks a contingent of thirty thousand mighty men of valor and sends them off under the cover of darkness. He tells them how they are to lie in wait and then ambush the city from the rear; he instructs them to stay close and be ready for battle on his signal. In the morning Joshua with the rest of Israel's warriors will approach the city so that when the defenders of Ai see them, they will come out to battle as before, thinking easily to repeat their previous victory—an equivalent act of arrogance as in Israel's first foray against Ai. Just so, Joshua and his troops will feign flight, giving the warriors of Ai the opportunity to repeat their previous rout. As Israel had failed on account of the sin of pride in the first engagement, so now the same sin of pride will overtake the pursuing warriors and deceive the remaining defenders of the city. They too will bargain on mere repetition of the past, ignoring the intervening will of YHWH in his providential purpose and corresponding ordering of events. Thus the enemy forces will twice be drawn out from the safety of the city walls in pursuit of the feigned flight of Israel, as Pharaoh and his chariots had once foolishly pursued Israel to the cusp of and then through the midst of the Red Sea. Sin in this way becomes its own punishment as YHWH, the God of Israel, hands the king of Ai over to his pride and its consequences; and likewise the remaining defenders of the city came out to complete the slaughter of Israel, but in the process let the unguarded city fall into the hands of Israel's mighty men of valor waiting to spring the trap. Those lying in ambush will then arise and capture the city after its defenders have left it wide open, defenseless, in their rush to judgment. According to the word of YHWH, the captured city is then to be set ablaze as Jericho had been.

Joshua mediates this command of YHWH. At the heart of the new strategy is reversal in roles between the tempter and the tempted. As Hawk sees, "Conquering the people of the land through beguilement promises mastery over Canaanite seductiveness. By successfully tempting the tempters (and destroying them), Israel frees itself from their [seductive] power"[16] (cf. Deut. 7:1–5; 12:29–32; 29:17–

16. Hawk, *Joshua*, 126.

29). Thus the instruction is clear. Faith has heard afresh the word of YHWH and, trusting in it, obeys. "The aspects of human and of divine acting merge: everything must take place at God's direction, as stated in verses 1–2, to which Joshua's instructions correspond."[17] Represented is *theological* compatibilism as YHWH's assertion of rule commands and enables Israel's obedience of faith. "The plans also affirmed Joshua's position as a victorious conqueror, reestablishing the unity of God, leader, and people."[18]

The party sent by night to lie in ambush takes a position on the west side of Ai while Joshua spends the night in the camp at Gilgal in the midst of the people. In the morning Joshua musters his forces and leads them along with the elders of Israel to the vicinity of Ai.[19] When Joshua and company draw near, they encamp on the north side with a ravine between them—and now, it is written, he sends five thousand troops to lie in ambush on the west side of the city.[20] If the reader is confused here by the shifting perspectives and accounts of the ambush, "the confusion has the odd effect of placing the reader alongside the king of Ai. Both know that something is up, but neither can see with clarity."[21] That interpretation may make a virtue of necessity. In any case, Joshua's new encampment in the north on a ridge top was visible to Ai, while the others waiting in ambush lay hidden to the west. Joshua spends the night in the valley (or on the ridge top?) at the main encampment visible to Ai.

"The reader notices that the decision to erect the camp near Ai is an important difference from the first, abortive, attempt of chapter 7 to conquer the city."[22] Just as planned, when the king sees Israel's position, he musters his forces quickly and, exiting the city, descends into the valley for battle, not suspecting the ambush waiting in the west. "Israel's visibility on the opposite ridge triggers the king's reaction. There is emphasis on how completely the enemy is fooled: 'did not know,' 'no one was left,' 'left the city open.'"[23] Likewise as planned, Joshua and his forces fake defeat by flight to the wilderness. Seeing the unfolding rout, all the king's forces remaining in Ai rush from the city to join in pursuit. In foolish pride,[24]

---

17. Rösel, *Joshua*, 125.

18. Hawk, *Joshua*, 125.

19. Mention of the elders here is unusual. Only in Joshua are the elders also portrayed as leaders in war. Dozeman, *Joshua 1–12*, 389.

20. The numerous discrepancies in the account are explained in a number of ways by scholars; cf. Nelson, *Joshua*, 109–10.

21. Hawk, *Joshua*, 127.

22. Rösel, *Joshua*, 127.

23. Nelson, *Joshua*, 114.

24. Rösel, *Joshua*, 128.

they leave the city unguarded. This is dramatized by display of the alternating perspectives between Joshua and the Israelites on the one side and the king of Ai and his forces on the other. Similar to the portrait made of Pharaoh in Exod. 14–15, where the "arrogance of Pharaoh was underscored through point of view," the narrative's provision of the king of Ai's perspective allows the reader to see that the "king of Ai is arrogant and ignorant in his quest for power, which forces him to run headlong into a doomed battle."[25]

In a scene reminiscent of Moses's leadership in battle, YHWH at this moment commands Joshua to hold up his spear toward the unguarded city. Commentators are divided on whether Joshua's raised weapon is meant as a signal to spring the trap or as a talisman, as it were, a lightning rod channeling divine power to the troops of Israel, but most probably it is meant as both. "Its meaning is less strategic and much more theological in nature. That the weapon was extended towards Ai, not the ambush, is significant. . . . This accords with verse 26, according to which Joshua held his weapon extended until the ban was completely executed."[26] Yet further complicating the picture (or reflecting the fog and friction of battle), we are told that at that Moses-like signal the ambush party rose up to take the city and set it on fire. In either case, "it is the divine power channeled through the sword."[27] At the site of the smoke rising from the city, Joshua's party turned back from their feigned flight to face their pursuers while the warriors of Ai now realize that they had been flanked front and back and entrapped.

The Hebrew uses an idiom in 8:20 to portray the despair that now overcomes the surrounded men of Ai: they "no longer had hands [= power] among them to flee anywhere" (AT). In other words, "the men of Ai, who have been delivered 'into the hands' of the Israelites, no longer have 'hands,' while Joshua's hand is extended against them [holding up the spear]."[28] And so Joshua with the main party smites the demoralized enemy as those who captured the city now join the battle from the rear: none could escape the closing jaws of Israel's swords devouring like shark's teeth.

Instantiating a consistent pattern, focus now shifts to the king of the city-state, captured alive and brought to Joshua. But this focus is interrupted no sooner than it is introduced. We are told first about the devastation of the warriors of Ai, trapped and surrounded on the way to the wilderness. When the utter

---

25. Dozeman, *Joshua 1–12*, 389–90.
26. Rösel, *Joshua*, 129.
27. Dozeman, *Joshua 1–12*, 390.
28. Hawk, *Joshua*, 129.

extermination is complete, the forces of Israel then return to the burning city to kill any survivors: twelve thousand killed, both male and female. All human life remains under the rule of *herem*, although, as mentioned, cattle and spoil are permitted to the conquerors by the word of YHWH that Joshua relayed. The divine destruction complete, focus now returns to the captured king. At the end of the devastation, Joshua hangs him on a tree and then, at the close of day, buries the corpse at the gate of the city under a heap of stones. To display the enemy leader's body was a public humiliation[29]—hanged on a tree, a form of execution that marks him as accursed (8:29; cf. Deut. 21:22–23; Gal. 3:13).

Calvin's commentary on this is particularly obtuse as it is colored by his concern to defend in principle the divine legitimacy of established political sovereignty: Joshua, he apologizes, "seems to have treated the king with great severity in order to satisfy the hatred of the people"[30]—although there is no hint of this motive in the text. Just as Joshua pronounced a curse over the defeated ruin of Jericho, so also here Joshua curses to the effect that both these ruined royal cities are, and are to remain in perpetuity, under divine curse because the point is "to eliminate both [kings and their cities] from the promised land."[31] So the city of Ai was reduced to a heap of ashes, a "mound of devastation" ever since (the city name, Ai, is similar to the Hebrew word for "ruin").[32] To this day at the gate of the destroyed city lies a great heap of stones covering the body of the defeated king, signifying the demise of the Canaanite city-state political regime. In executing this curse, "the nation, Joshua, and YHWH act as one."[33]

"One God, one leader, one people"—this was a slogan of the now notorious German Christian party of those Protestants in the 1920s and '30s who sacralized the National Socialist movement of Adolf Hitler and encouraged the "coordination" of church and theology to its worldview. The resemblance of the slogan to the book of Joshua's presentation of "YHWH, Joshua, and all Israel" in union raises the volatile and painful question mentioned in passing in the chapter on preliminary considerations: the cruelly ironic possibility that the theology of Joshua is a source in Western civilization of what, unwittingly, has come to be named the Holocaust (the "whole burnt offering"), the *herem* executed on Europe's Jews. This possibility of interpretation is a brutal instance of the objective

---

29. Nelson, *Joshua*, 115.
30. Calvin, *Book of Joshua*, 106.
31. Dozeman, *Joshua 1–12*, 391.
32. Pitkänen, *Joshua*, 182–84.
33. Hawk, *Joshua*, 130.

danger involved in any reading of Joshua. But the vulnerability to such appropriation comes not from theological-literary reading, such as undertaken here, but from naïve literalism and its supposedly "plain sense" reading. What it means for Israel to be elected or chosen is not at all obvious on the surface of things, nor can it be understood apart from theology—that is, knowledge of the electing God and his purposes. And what we are seeing is that the aim of the book of Joshua is to eliminate both kings and their cities from land redeemed for the dwelling of the beloved community.

No contemporary interpreter has so forcefully argued for the reality of this misappropriating possibility of interpreting Joshua and its supposed holy-war ideology as a source of Nazism as has Richard Steigmann-Gall in his study *The Holy Reich*[34]—even if in his painfully obvious ignorance of theology he attributes the danger to the "interventionist God of history" in Christian fundamentalism rather than to its source in the Hebrew Bible, and in particular this book of Joshua. As we have seen, the gospel of Joshua is its knowledge of God, YHWH who fights for Israel, and this in human time and space. It is to be emphatically conceded that there is no foolproof defense against reckless reading and violent misappropriation of Joshua's knowledge of God as religious ideology that can be defeated only by careful theological reading of Joshua as scripture, as this commentary has proposed, according to the rule of faith articulated in Gal. 6:15. As Origen puts it, "For we who are of the Catholic Church do not reject the law of Moses, but we accept it if Jesus reads it to us. For thus we shall be able to understand the law correctly."[35] That defense of correct reading—a defense not of faith but against the abuse of faith by the willfully ignorant, be they foe or supposed friend—has been the strategy of this commentary.

In that light any equation of the pro-Nazi religious motto, "One God, one leader, one people," with the book of Joshua's theology of all Israel as covenanted to YHWH who fights for us by the ministry of Joshua, the servant of YHWH, can be exploded with the stroke of a pen, as the Barmen Declaration did in its first thesis: the new Joshua is not Adolf Hitler but Jesus Christ, whose kingdom is not of this world and who just so teaches us to read the law correctly as instruction in "militant grace."[36] But theology must continually be at work to make this

34. Richard Steigmann-Gall, *The Holy Reich: Nazi Conceptions of Christianity, 1919–1945* (Cambridge: Cambridge University Press, 2003).
35. Origen, *Homilies on Joshua*, 104.
36. Philip G. Ziegler, *Militant Grace: The Apocalyptic Turn and the Future of Christian Theology* (Grand Rapids: Baker Academic, 2018).

identification of YHWH who fights for us against the idols of Canaan concealing the demons that bewitch with their kings and fortifications (of which Hitler was a reprisal), when these allure the people of God to coveting their goods, captivating desire to their unholy service. To believe YHWH who fights for us is to disbelieve the idols and to exorcise the demons.[37]

Like Menno Simons, Origen appropriates the theology of Joshua's YHWH who fights for us from the canonical perspective of the dispossessed and persecuted, by which it becomes a lens interpreting his own experience: "For the kings of the earth have assembled together, the Senate and the people and the leaders of Rome, to blot out the name of Jesus and Israel at the same time. For they have decreed it in their laws that there be no Christians. Every city, every class, attacks the name of Christians. But just as at that time all those kings assembling against Jesus were able to do nothing, so even now, whether princes or opposing authorities, they have been able to do nothing to prevent the race of Christians from being propagated more widely and profusely. For it is written, 'the more greatly they abased them, the more they multiplied and they increased mightily'"[38]—an allusion to Exod. 1:12.

---

37. Christopher Morse, *Not Every Spirit: A Dogmatics of Christian Disbelief* (Harrisburg, PA: Trinity Press International, 1994).

38. Origen, *Homilies on Joshua*, 107.

COVENANT RENEWAL
IN THE PROMISED LAND

8:30–35

The account of the victory over Ai culminates with an impressive ceremony pronouncing unconditional blessing on all Israel at a place a little to the north: here the ark of the covenant of YHWH has come to rest within the narrative of the book of Joshua. Certainly this ceremony reasserts the covenant identity of Israel,[1] although the narrator makes a point of noting the presence of sojourners/aliens as well as the women and children in the midst of an all-Israel ceremony (8:33, 35)—yet another anomaly if *herem* warfare succeeds in executing a radical politics of purity. All the same, the episode here "appears like a foreign body."[2] The location at the mountains of Ebal and Gerizim near Shechem is problematic, since in the next episode Israel encamps at Gilgal (9:6). Is this episode an interpolation? Is it a deliberate interruption in the narrative? If so, what kind of interruption is it?

If we read the account in 8:30–35 as a reiteration of what was already pronounced in the first chapter of Joshua, the ceremony presently at the mounts of Ebal and Gerizim is only a repetition of the theme of Torah-keeping.[3] Is the episode, then, a deliberate redundancy, made for the sake of emphasis? So that "chastened by experience" after the initial debacle at Ai, Israel now "stands united in complete obedience to the Mosaic commandments"?[4] It can seem so. The concluding verse tells us emphatically that "not a word of Moses" (AT) was

1. Hawk, *Joshua*, 131.
2. Nelson, *Joshua*, 116.
3. Rösel, *Joshua*, 132.
4. Hawk, *Joshua*, 131.

omitted from Joshua's public reading of the Torah at the ceremony. Thus one can read the episode as a thoroughly Deuteronomic interpolation portraying Joshua as prefiguring Josiah, a "royal figure . . . taking what would be the king's role in the time of the monarchy." So Nelson argues, even while conceding some "idiosyncratic twists" in contrast to the ceremony instructions stipulated in Deut. 27: "Blessing dominates here (v. 35b) rather than cursing."[5] In that case Joshua's idiosyncratic twist is meant to project "a powerful and effective act of blessing, [which] completes Israel's return from the deviation of the Achan episode . . . and prepares the reader for the legal dilemmas to be presented by the upcoming Gibeonites episode."[6] An interpreter can for these reasons join Nelson in reading the story in this way. But it is unsatisfying literarily. Why?

If the victories over the kings of Jericho and Ai signify the inauguration struggle of the reign of YHWH, who has led Israel in the paradoxical "aniconic icon" of the ark, visible throne of the invisible God in heaven and on earth, the covenant ceremony comes about instead as the very goal and fulfillment of these paradigmatic opening battles. "The altar on Mt. Ebal therefore symbolically underscores the end of the old, nomadic social order" by establishing a permanent sanctuary.[7] To be sure, the ceremony at the mounts of Ebal and Gerizim takes place for the most part as Moses had instructed in the "book of the law"—that is, Deut. 27.[8] The altar is made of stones uncut by human hands, as required by Deuteronomy, and Joshua is said to have copied onto them the words of the law of Moses. But, in clear deviation from what is plainly required in Deut. 11 and 27, the reader should be struck by the remarkable fact that only blessing is spoken from the two mounts (8:33, even though the curses are later added in 8:34, perhaps to correct this omission of the curses as too obvious a deviation from what the law expressly requires—namely, that *both* blessing *and* curse are to be read out on the solemn occasion). We are thus confronted here with a seemingly small but highly significant deviation from the passage's overall comportment with Deuteronomy.

The deviations, however, number several more and they are significant; all seem to depict complete fulfillment of the unconditional promises of YHWH, whose ark has now come to rest on holy land with an altar erected and the law publicly displayed in the vicinity of Shechem. Significant as well, the other theme from Deuteronomy in Joshua about the condition of obedience for the fulfillment of

---

5. Nelson, *Joshua*, 119.
6. Nelson, *Joshua*, 119.
7. Hawk, *Joshua*, 134.
8. Rösel, *Joshua*, 135.

the promises (1:7–8; 8:34–35; 22:5; 23:6) seems absent in the present episode of pure blessing. What are we to make of this triumph of the indicative of blessing over the conditional imperative with its threat of curse?

Indeed, a concluding ceremony in the book of Joshua will also take place in Shechem (24:26), but with rather different implications for the future. Perplexities abound. We find in this Shechem location for altar, ark, and covenant-reading ceremony another, more notable deviation from Deuteronomy. "Jerusalem is identified as a Jebusite city. . . . [And] the author states that the Jebusite population of Jerusalem was never eliminated and that the city remained a source of pollution, which continues to plague the Jews who lived there 'to this day' (15:8, 63)."[9] There is manifest tension, then, not only between Deuteronomy and Joshua regarding the one sanctuary for all Israel destined for Jerusalem, but also within the book of Joshua between unconditional promises of YHWH and the condition for their fulfillment in Israel's obedience, corresponding to total and partial accounts of the conquest of Canaan. In the present passage we have a reiteration of unconditional election in fulfillment of divine promise with unqualified blessing on Israel now established on holy land: a triumph of the indicative over the failure of the imperative, hence not dependent on the conquest of Jerusalem.

Any hermeneutical act of retrieval entails a certain violence against the original since its own horizon of meaning cannot be taken over wholesale but only converted into the interpreter's horizon of meaning. Acknowledging that is a matter of intellectual honesty; with honesty the viability of a retrieval of meaning from the past for the present is in fact enhanced. Despite dissonances, the present episode in the book of Joshua on the whole retrieves the theology of Deuteronomy but for its own purposes. Moses had forbidden use of iron tools in the construction of the altar (Deut. 27:5–6). "The stones must be in their natural form, unworked: human processing would profane them."[10] Joshua, in counterpoint to the heap of rubble over the defeated city of Ai and the memorial mound of stones at its gate covering the body of its executed king, built a *mizbeakh*, an "altar" to YHWH, the God of Israel, on Mount Ebal. In this matter the book of Joshua is following for the most part what is stipulated in the book of the law of Moses concerning an altar to be built of uncut stones, untouched by iron tools, for cultic sacrifice:[11] the whole burnt offerings completely consumed by fire; the offerings of well-being, of which only a part was consumed on the altar; and the

9. Dozeman, *Joshua 1–12*, 392; cf. 394–96.
10. Rösel, *Joshua*, 137.
11. Nelson, *Joshua*, 120.

rest "consumed by the participants in the ceremony for a holy meal."[12] Moreover, Joshua does not allow this altar to be subject to varying interpretations. Rather, on this altar Joshua inscribes a copy of the law of Moses[13] in the presence of the sons of Israel—the elders, judges, and officials being singled out.[14]

So here within the episode "again the continuity from Moses to Joshua stands out."[15] What is forbidden is not the icon but the ambiguity of symbols that are accordingly to be explicitly interpreted by the words of God. The purpose of stone monuments, in general, was "lasting effect," memorialization of the founding of an institution that is to exist in perpetuity.[16] So all Israel, both *kagger* and *ka'ezrakh*, sojourner and native, assemble on opposite sides of the ark of the covenant of YHWH, half before Mount Gerizim and the other half before Mount Ebal, for the blessing that Moses commanded. And when this blessing has been pronounced, Joshua reads all the words of the law, both the blessing and the curse, as it is found written in the book of the law. So all of Moses's words are read to all the congregation of Israel, as the text now explicitly notes, including the women, the children, and the sojourners/aliens that walked among them. "The reader now knows who some of these aliens are and how [Israel] encompasses men, women, children, and even Canaanites, indeed all who express obedient devotion to YHWH."[17] These unlikely groups singled out for emphasis are, moreover, "relatively powerless"; thus their deliberate inclusion "stresses the importance of making fair provision for everyone within Israelite society," just as also the "keeping of the law is everyone's responsibility."[18]

In this way the theology of Deuteronomy is both retrieved and modified for the book of Joshua's narrative purpose of exploring the conundrums resulting from execution of *ḥerem* warfare. Wyschogrod calls this the "paradox of Jewish existence . . . : the applications of the apocalyptic demands for justice to the infinite ambiguities of concrete situations that remain after the prophets have delivered

12. Rösel, *Joshua*, 137.

13. Rösel, *Joshua*, 137; cf. Hawk, *Joshua*, 132.

14. Origen is curious about how such a large book could be written on an altar of uncut stones, and takes the curiosity to indicate a new and different kind of writing of the law by the Spirit of the Lord Jesus on the hearts of his believers: "But even now, through these things that we are speaking, Jesus is writing Deuteronomy in the hearts of those who receive these things that are set with the sound faith and with all their mind; who listen with their whole hearing and whole heart, not with the corrupt and false mind concerning the faith, and to retain what is set." Origen, *Homilies on Joshua*, 101. This is Origen's doctrine of the priesthood of all believers.

15. Rösel, *Joshua*, 138.

16. Pitkänen, *Joshua*, 190.

17. Hawk, *Joshua*, 134.

18. Pitkänen, *Joshua*, 191. Cf. his lengthy excursus on the archaeology of Mount Ebal (192–204).

themselves of their fiery orations. Here the concrete instances of clashing rights demanding qualification, discussion, and patience will not go away. And in this darker realm the full light of justice is rarely seen."[19] Concluding this way, the episode stands as a corrective theological interpretation of the "conquest," not as the interpolation of a foreign body interrupting an unambiguous narrative of conquest, and as such it points forward to the next episode.

19. Wyschogrod, *Body of Faith*, 23.

THE PARADOX OF THE GIBEONITES

9:1–27

"According to the Torah the story [about to unfold] should not have happened; the Torah rules that a covenant between Israelites and the people of Canaan is not possible."[1] By "the Torah" here, Rösel is referring to "the book of the law" just mentioned in the preceding chapter (8:34)—that is, to Deuteronomy. Thus this story, which weaves its way to the punishment of the Gibeonites as slaves in the service of Israel's sanctuary, "cannot be of Deuteronomistic origin." He finds further support for this conclusion about yet another anomaly in the execution of the law of *ḥerem* in the ambiguous reference to an odd figure, the "man of Israel" (grammatically singular but interpreted collectively as the fighting men of Israel) introduced in 9:6–7, as distinguished from Joshua, and also, from outside the book of Joshua, the mention of the covenant with the Gibeonites in 2 Sam. 21:2.[2] When we combine all of this evidence with the narrator's note that the Israelites did not consult YHWH before concluding the pact with the Gibeonites, however, we can be led to the surprising conclusion that "these verses introduce the major military campaigns of chapters 10–12."[3]

Surely, it could seem so from the opening in 9:1–2, which tells of remaining Canaanite nations uniting "to fight Joshua and Israel." Calvin likewise thinks so. He sees an implicit contrast between the motivation of the Gibeonites suing for peace with Israel and the motivation of the alliance of the Canaanite kings. These latter display the insane defiance of hardened hearts: "instead of being

---

1. Rösel, *Joshua*, 142.
2. See further Nelson, *Joshua*, 127–28.
3. Rösel, *Joshua*, 145.

overcome by manifest miracle, they continue to rage like wild beasts against the unassailable power of God . . . tak[ing] up arms against heaven."[4] Behind this "insane" behavior is divine operation, that "their hearts should be hardened, and that they should perish."[5] But should we not by the same token then probe the divine intention in the Gibeonites' cunning pursuit of peace with Israel? What goes unnoticed with such explanation is that precisely this motive for the Canaanite alarm is *not* provided in the present text, as it had been earlier, while the target of the Canaanite alliance here is *not* YHWH who fights for Israel, but rather "Joshua and Israel."

If the point of the story in chapter 9 is to introduce the blitzkrieg[6] that follows in chapter 10, the introductory purpose of the story of the Gibeonites should be to illustrate how the campaign of *ḥerem* warfare will be accomplished. But what a strange introduction this story makes! How could a story of the Gibeonites successfully and by trickery escaping the death sentence of *ḥerem* ever do that? In the preceding accounts, moreover, the Canaanites are depicted as being paralyzed with terror, "resulting in passivity," but in the present chapter the Canaanites are portrayed as "active, preparing for war."[7] Such active preparation, however, can also take the unexpected form of the preemptive deception-cum-negotiation of the Gibeonites with Israel as well, not only the more usual military alliance-making of the Canaanite kings. Certainly the story of the Gibeonites bridges from the initial and paradigmatic victories over Jericho and Ai to the sweeping campaigns to the south and west and then to the north in chapters 10–12. But to draw the conclusion that the *purpose* of the story of the Gibeonites here is to introduce the ensuing military campaigns of *ḥerem* warfare is to miss the literary point. Rather, the literary point is to continue the cascade of conundrums befalling the execution of *ḥerem* warfare that began with Rahab in Jericho. As a result, "the shadow of possible disobedience to the law and the problematic presence of conquered peoples left in the land (15:63; 16:10; 17:12–13; 23:4, 7, 12–13) has started to loom over the book of Joshua."[8]

There appears to be a difference, however, between the MT and the LXX versions of the story that here as elsewhere indicates genuine early perplexity about

4. Calvin, *Book of Joshua*, 114.
5. Calvin, *Book of Joshua*, 115.
6. I cautiously employ here the Nazi military term to indicate a superficial resemblance that I will in due time demolish.
7. Rösel, *Joshua*, 145.
8. Nelson, *Joshua*, 132.

what kind of story the book of Joshua is trying to tell, especially as we come to this crucial juncture in chapter 9. One might argue that in the MT version, the cunning Gibeonites appear as "tricksters, who are seeking their survival. . . . The fear of YHWH plays no role in the MT version of the story." Their seemingly pious professions of YHWH's power in 9:9 and 9:24–25 are to be dismissed, in other words, as also "part of the trick." By contrast, the LXX version seems to change "the character of the Gibeonites, since they are now motivated by theological reasons, rather than political survival."[9] But this tendentious differentiation is, in literary perspective, exaggerated; not only does it disregard the virtual repetition of Rahab's confession of faith by the Gibeonites, which cannot be a literary accident, but the thesis about the difference between the MT and LXX in this episode emerges as part and parcel of some intricate reasoning in a tenuous historical-critical reconstruction of the composition of the text according to which Josh. 9, as a unified narrative, turns out to be a polemic against the postexilic "leaders of the congregation" for permitting "the cultic service of the Gibeonites" in Jerusalem.[10]

The final forms of the canonical text in both MT and LXX, however, tell a rather different story. The story has a very "Priestly" tone, to be sure, both in vocabulary and in concern for service to the cult, in spite of the obviously Deuteronomic cast of the narrative.[11] The survival of the Canaanite Gibeonites is not "outside the camp," nor merely "in the midst" of Israel, but at the *center* of Israel's life: in service to the cult. In literary appraisal, consequently, the story continues to expand on and explore the accumulating paradoxes that emerge in implementing *ḥerem* warfare.

The new episode, as mentioned, begins once again with sharp focus on "all the kings" of Canaan remaining on the west side of the Jordan. Now, despite varied ethnicities and discrete sovereignties, they come together against Israel's threatened subversion of their dominions. The place names and nationalities given to these kings in the text are vague and stereotypical; the list provided is "precisely and distinctively that of Deuteronomy 20:17."[12] As such, the list serves simply "to define all Palestine, not Judah alone."[13] A pluralistic Canaanite alliance is thus juxtaposed to all Israel under the one God led by the singular figure of Joshua on

9. Dozeman, *Joshua 1–12*, 401.
10. Dozeman, *Joshua 1–12*, 413, 423.
11. Pitkänen, *Joshua*, 207–8; cf. Nelson, *Joshua*, 124.
12. Nelson, *Joshua*, 124.
13. Rösel, *Joshua*, 146.

his way to acquiring the title "servant of YHWH."[14] The many Canaanites unite against the one Israel—with one glaring exception, as is now explored in the story of the deception of Israel by the Gibeonites, who turn out to be natives of Canaan.

When these dwellers of Gibeon hear of what Joshua had done to Jericho and Ai—the reference is undoubtedly to the utter destruction of life—they too resort to the first rule of the art of war: deception. As Joshua has just employed deception to defeat the city of Ai, now the Gibeonites, presumably having heard of this, employ deception to avoid their own destruction at Joshua's hand. Calvin chastises equally the Gibeonites' "recourse to fraud" and the "foolish credulity of Joshua and the rulers,"[15] but the Gibeonites acted prudently from their own perspective—cunningly, to be sure, from Israel's perspective.[16] They put on a front with a scarcely plausible masquerade of worn-out clothing, and dried-up bread as fake travel provisions to boot, all this to represent themselves as foreigners sojourning in the land of Canaan. "They" put on the act—it is notable that no king of the Gibeonites is mentioned inasmuch as "the Gibeonites are governed by elders."[17] "They" send these messengers disguised as foreign travelers to Israel, still encamped at Gilgal. There they perform before "the man of Israel" the elaborate but scarcely plausible lie that they are travelers from a far country who have a right qua foreigners—a right based on Deuteronomic law (e.g., Deut. 20:10–18)—to ask for a covenant with Israel (cf. Deut. 29:10–12, 15).

There will be two rounds of negotiations. In the first round, only the "man of Israel" asks questions. Who is this? "The collective 'man of Israel' was the body consisting of every adult male citizen of Israel. In other stories the core of warriors is meant, namely the Israelite army."[18] The "man of Israel" whom the Gibeonites first address initially objects, suspicious that these sojourners are native Canaanites. Literarily, this figure of the man of Israel "provides an ironic twist by raising the essential objection and then heedlessly falling for the trick anyway."[19] We should notice, however, that "the Gibeonites, from the beginning of the episode, bear an essential resemblance to Israel"—that is, without king, wanderers from afar, and displaying a sophisticated knowledge of the Torah![20] Are they not also, then, a part of Israel?[21]

14. Hawk, *Joshua*, 138.
15. Calvin, *Book of Joshua*, 114.
16. Rösel, *Joshua*, 147.
17. Nelson, *Joshua*, 133.
18. Rösel, *Joshua*, 148; so also Dozeman, *Joshua 1–12*, 43.
19. Nelson, *Joshua*, 125.
20. Hawk, *Joshua*, 139.
21. Nelson, *Joshua*, 126.

Appealing over the head of the suspicious "man of Israel," the Gibeonites turn to Joshua, announcing themselves "in a markedly obsequious gesture"[22] as his "servants" (the same word used as a title for Moses and later for Joshua, "servant" of YHWH). The gesture has a double meaning in that the Gibeonites in this way "anticipated their own punishment at the start of the story,"[23] when they will survive the death sentence of *herem* warfare by instead doing service as cutters of wood and haulers of water for the house of YHWH. Joshua too, however, wants to know whether his new, would-be "servants" are native dwellers of Canaan or sojourners from afar. Similar to Rahab in Jericho, the Gibeonites tell a truth within the context of their larger deception of being from a far country. The truth they tell is that they know the reputation of YHWH, Israel's God, on the basis of what he did for Israel in Egypt and in the Transjordan. So these new outsiders putatively visiting Israel from afar make a Rahab-like confession of faith in Israel's election by the God claiming therewith to be the living God in heaven and on earth and thus rightfully asserting kingship over the land of Canaan by usurping the usurpers of the earth. Their deception of Joshua is thus based on a truth, no matter whether the Gibeonite profession of faith is sincere or the false front of trickery.

The commentary of Origen here on the faith of the Gibeonites will resonate with any reader who has enjoyed the burden of pastoral responsibility for the *corpus permixtum* that is the real existing church:

> There are in the church certain ones who believe in God, have faith in God, and acquiesce in all the divine precepts. Furthermore, they are conscientious toward the servants of God and desire to serve them, for they also are fully ready and prepared for the furnishing of the church or the ministry. But, in fact, they are completely disgusting in their actions and particular habit of life, wrapped up with vices and not wholly "putting away the old self with all its actions." Indeed they are enveloped in ancient vices and offensive faults just as those [Gibeonites] were covered over with old garments and shoes.[24]

Let these new Gibeonites, Origen continues, who "exhibit no inclination to also improve their habits, correct impulses, lay aside faults, cultivate purity, soften the violence of wrath, restrain avarice, curb greed"—"let them know that they

---

22. Hawk, *Joshua*, 142.
23. Rösel, *Joshua*, 149.
24. Origen, *Homilies on Joshua*, 110.

will be assigned a part and lot with the Gibeonites by the Lord Jesus."[25] Rant of pastoral exasperation notwithstanding, Origen reiterates his characteristic theological compatibilism when he finally counsels his new-day Gibeonites "to hasten back to your liberty, . . . demand your liberty"[26]—the Johannine insight that sin is slavery to what is not God and therefore vicious, but true freedom serves righteousness.

The disguised Gibeonites continue their appeal to Joshua, explaining that their elders, on behalf of the people, delegated them for this mission—namely, to come and submit to Israel as covenanted servants, or *vassals*, as such covenant relationships were generally understood in the ancient Near East. To make the ruse more plausible, they present Joshua with dry and moldy bread, which, they claim, had been taken hot from the oven on the day of their departure from that faraway place. Likewise, they show Joshua wine skins that have burst and clothing that has worn out during the long journey they have supposedly made. This charade too reflects Gibeonite knowledge of Torah (Deut. 29:4–6).

And so "they" (Joshua is not specified) eat from the unappealing provisions offered by the Gibeonites without inquiring of YHWH[27]—another parallel to Rahab and the Israelite spies. "The point is made that the Israelites believe the story without consulting YHWH for guidance."[28] Meager fare as the moldy bread is, the Israelites partake of it and so seal the proffered covenant by shared meal. Curiously, then, "the Gibeonites have acknowledged YHWH and claim that YHWH's deeds have drawn them to Israel. But the Israelites seem, for the moment, to have forgotten YHWH. Is this just an oversight?" Or is something darker intimated? "Did the temptation of subjecting another people prove too powerful for Joshua and the Israelite leaders?"[29] The story thus hints that the Israelites did not want to know the truth about the Gibeonites because they envied Canaan and wanted slaves of their own. At this juncture Joshua emerges again from the storytelling mists: it is he who makes peace (*shalom*) with the Gibeonites by agreeing to let them live—and more, as we shall see shortly. He has the leaders of Israel swear to it before YHWH, and an oath in "the sacred name of God is more precious than the wealth of the whole world,"[30] the sacred

25. Origen, *Homilies on Joshua*, 112.
26. Origen, *Homilies on Joshua*, 113.
27. Rösel, *Joshua*, 150.
28. Pitkänen, *Joshua*, 212.
29. Hawk, *Joshua*, 143.
30. Calvin, *Book of Joshua*, 119.

oath constituting another parallel with the Rahab story. In the success of this
negotiation "the Canaanite actors are distinguished by their cunning and their
prudence, as well as by their fear of God. As a result their lives were saved and
their existence in Israel secured."[31]

In three short days, however, Israel learns that the Gibeonites were in fact
near neighbors, dwelling in the midst of the land promised to Israel. So Israel
marches on their cities, reaching them on the third day to make war. But the text
continues by announcing immediately what will be the conclusion of an "intra-
Israel debate"[32] yet to unfold—namely, whether the Israelites should refrain from
destroying the Gibeonites because their leaders invoked YHWH, the God of
Israel, as witness and seal of the treaty of peace. Just this debatable deviation from
the strict rule of *ḥerem* warfare provokes "murmuring" in all the congregation
against the Israelite leaders—a phrasing reminiscent of the rebelliousness of the
people during the wilderness wanderings. The leaders suppress the murmuring by
explaining to the congregation that they were bound not to destroy the Gibeonites on account of the invocation of the name of YHWH over the treaty of peace
made with them. So they will have to let them live, for violating a covenant made
before YHWH would bring wrath (*qetseph*) on them.

Of course, the murmuring people might well be imagined to have continued the protest inwardly: "Violating *ḥerem* also provokes YHWH's wrath!"
For postexilic readers of this intra-Israel debate about the forbidden presence
of foreigners in their midst in conflict with the obligation to keep the vows
made before YHWH, the later fate of the family of Saul for breaking a solemn
oath as recorded in 2 Sam. 21 will come to mind. It is a genuine dilemma. "Do
the Israelites carry out YHWH's commands against the Canaanites and thus
profane the oath they have sworn? Or do they honor the oath and thus break
YHWH's commands?"[33] The dilemma polarizes the murmuring community. In a
fresh attempt to respond to the dilemma, the leaders offer an explanation: Since
the Gibeonites offered themselves to us as servants, we deigned to let them be
cutters of wood and drawers of water for us all. That's a win-win, isn't it? Slavery
in exchange for life!

Once again, Joshua emerges from the shadows to take center stage in this intra-
Israel debate by confronting the Gibeonites with their deception. The Gibeonites,
exposed with the truth about their deception, once again reveal an uncanny

31. Rösel, *Joshua*, 150.
32. Nelson, *Joshua*, 130.
33. Hawk, *Joshua*, 145.

knowledge of what YHWH, Israel's God, commanded through his servant Moses—namely, that in giving Israel all the land, they were to exterminate all its native inhabitants. So we did what we did, the Gibeonites explain in justification for their cunning act, because we feared for our lives. But now the truth is out and we are in your hands. So do to us what seems right and good. Because of the fraud, Joshua pronounces them indeed cursed to servitude as cutters of wood and drawers of water. In Calvin's view this curse is fitting retribution because "nothing would be more unbecoming than to allow tricks and wiles to be profitable to those who employ them. . . . [Joshua] puts the blame of their servitude upon themselves, because they bear nothing worse than they have deserved by their guile or perfidy."[34] Perhaps, although deception is the first rule in the art of war. But in distinction to what the elders have just said, Joshua goes on to specify that their service will be "to the house of my God" (9:23)—that is, to the tabernacle/temple. So Joshua thus keeps the elders from indulging in retrograde greed-as-usual for the acquisition of slaves that *herem* forbids; he does so by putting the Gibeonites to work as slaves to the cult, an exception that *herem* can be stretched to accommodate. In the process, however, Joshua creates yet another dilemma as previously noted: what is accursed is now located at the center of Israel's life.

What seemed right and good to Joshua, the narrator tells us, was to deliver these Gibeonites from the ready-to-hand sword of angry, murmuring Israel. "Joshua in his wisdom found a way between Scylla and Charybdis: on the one hand he had to save their lives so as not to violate the oath. On the other hand he invoked a dreadful curse on them, far harsher than an ordinary punishment, to serve as a fairly appropriate substitute for the ban."[35] The Hebrew idiom for making a covenant is "cutting a covenant," but here another form of the verb "to cut" is used. Joshua says literally, "Slavery will not be cut away from you"[36]—in this way punning on the kind of cut-rate "covenant" that has been cut with the Gibeonites. Even so, "in a final irony, Joshua therefore assumes the role of Gibeonite savior."[37]

The episode ends establishing a supreme paradox in regard to what proves to be the actual impossibility of executing the strict demands of *herem* warfare: the accursed Gibeonites "are also privileged people, set apart for service to the altar."[38] This is all the more true if the formulaic phrase about the place that YHWH will

34. Calvin, *Book of Joshua*, 120.
35. Rösel, *Joshua*, 155.
36. Dozeman, *Joshua 1–12*, 407.
37. Hawk, *Joshua*, 148.
38. Hawk, *Joshua*, 148.

choose for his name to dwell is an anachronistic reference to the (future) temple in Jerusalem.[39] The temporal reality but also the final impossibility of divine wrath is thereby indicated, recalling the question of Athanasius, "What was God in his goodness to do?" The question intimates the inclusion of the ungodly by the mediation of Joshua, who finds a way to graft the deceiving Gibeonites—through no merit of their own, indeed in spite of their demerit—into Israel, the beloved community of God. The paradoxes that have been building through the Joshua narrative to this point bring us to the book's messianism, its inchoate Christology.

39. Rösel, *Joshua*, 156.

THE MESSIANIC PARADOX

10:1–15

Chapter 10 is composed of several interacting themes: "battle success, elimination of survivors, defeated kings, and YHWH's combat for Israel."[1] It betrays some kind of relationship with the report in Judg. 1 regarding the war against a king, Adonizedek (compare Josh. 15:63 to Judg. 1:21). It contains the fabulous account of sun and moon standing still at Joshua's command, giving time for YHWH the warrior to rain destruction on the foe. Above all, however, from this point forward in the book of Joshua, the nature of the narrative changes dramatically. We leave behind the interlocking, carefully developed, and indeed sophisticated stories of Rahab in Jericho, the sin of Achan, and the conquest of Ai, with the contrasting tactics of parade and ambush, concluding in the Gibeonite conundrum where paradoxically Joshua emerges as savior of Gentiles. Henceforth we will read a monotonous chronicling of battles, regularly punctuated by ice-cold reports of the execution of *herem* destruction on the Canaanites, interspersed with interpretive remarks by the narrator. But that is not the only midcourse change in the narrative, as we shall see.

"The ban is executed on a much larger scale than before [in Joshua]. The modern reader recoils from this account; his only consolation is that the stereotypic description does not reflect historical reality."[2] "Modern" this historical skepticism may be, but regarding *herem* warfare as fiction is false consolation theologically, even if it is the typically "modern" theological consolation, as H. Richard Niebuhr once captured its idea, "of the God without wrath who brought men

1. Nelson, *Joshua*, 139.
2. Rösel, *Joshua*, 161.

without sin into a kingdom without judgment through the ministrations of a Christ without a cross."[3] Fundamentally it misses, if not evades, the literary point. In this connection John H. Walton rightly chastises, "Sensitivity to the poetics of ancient historiography complicates both critical scholars' dismissal of the validity of biblical historiography and confessional scholars' apologetic approaches and doctrinal convictions. Critical scholarship needs to rethink its imperialistic and anachronistic imposition of modern standards and values on ancient texts. Confessional scholars need to rethink precisely what constitutes the truth of the text that they seek to defend in light of the text's own poetics and perspectives."[4]

To be sure, the employment of terse battle reports as sources, beginning in Josh. 10, invites "the comparison of Joshua to Ancient Near Eastern conquest accounts [which] show that the juxtaposition of heroic actions and divine intervention in the same story of war is commonplace."[5] Thus there are many parallels between Joshua's "accounts of battle and the ancient Near Eastern campaign reports," but comparison unveils a crucial difference: Israel's faith in YHWH the warrior was not harnessed to "the power of the king as in the texts from Assyria or Egypt, but their own national identity as the people of a powerful God and as the legitimate masters of Canaan."[6] This historical-contextual insight, however, must be carefully handled if it is not to transpose theology into religious ideology.

Nelson concludes from such comparison and contrast that "title to the land is the ideological issue at the core of all three of these conquest narratives" in chapter 10. It is strange, however, for a scholar of such precision to employ here the concept of land title—the kind of anachronism against which Walton warns. With greater literary sensitivity to ancient poetics, one might rather see in the change of narrative style commencing in chapter 10 a merging or fusion of the identities of YHWH who fights for Israel with Joshua who commands sun and moon. Certainly the God rendered by the narrative is YHWH in his "decisive participation as divine warrior."[7] But just as certainly Joshua is increasingly rendered messianically as a singular servant of YHWH—a mediator between the holy God reclaiming his creation and the unholy world resisting his reign. What accounts for the narrative change commencing in chapter 10 is not title

3. H. Richard Niebuhr, *The Kingdom of God in America* (New York: Harper & Row, 1959), 193.

4. John H. Walton, *Ancient Near Eastern Thought and the Old Testament: Introducing the Conceptual World of the Hebrew Bible*, 2nd ed. (Grand Rapids: Baker Academic, 2018), 209.

5. Dozeman, *Joshua 1–12*, 440.

6. Nelson, *Joshua*, 139.

7. Nelson, *Joshua*, 139.

to the land, for Canaan already belongs to the living God as God in heaven and on earth, nor title for Joshua's postexilic readers to land that has been in any case lost, but hope for a new Joshua bringing a new heaven and earth.

An initiative to form a military alliance to punish Gibeon for its separate peace with Israel is announced and attributed to the Jerusalem king, whose name is Adonizedek. "This is the first appearance of the name Jerusalem in the Bible."[8] Adonizedek is motivated by fear. He has heard how Joshua, having captured Ai, executed *ḥerem* warfare on it and its king, just as he had previously done to Jericho and its king. Adding to the terror is news of how the residents of Gibeon have made a separate peace to dwell in Israel's midst, in spite of the fact that Gibeon was a greater city than Ai and defended by mighty warriors. Why, wonders Adonizedek, should they have feared Israel, betrayed us, and sued for peace with them? It is interesting to observe here that Adonizedek betrays no knowledge of YHWH, as had the Gibeonites and Rahab. Corresponding to this ignorance of YHWH in Adonizedek, "the narrator renders the impending conflict as a contest between the kings and Joshua (rather than YHWH or Israel)."[9] This narrative elevation of Joshua's status, however, should not be seen at the expense of the status of YHWH, the God of Israel, who is its sole king; rather, YHWH fights for Israel in the person of Joshua, who at length is to be awarded the messianic title "servant of YHWH."

Adonizedek rallies the neighboring kings of the Canaanite city-states to join him in punishing turncoat Gibeon. Consequently, five kings of the Amorite city-states marshaled forces and joined together to lay siege to Gibeon. The Gibeonites now claim their new "friendship with Joshua" and send word to him at Gilgal that he, whose name means "YHWH saves," come quickly now to save his "servants," lest he abandon them on whom Joshua's own enemies have turned with a vengeance. "The premise is that the covenant between these partners provides for military assistance."[10] Joshua responds by mustering his mighty men of valor and marching to Gibeon. YHWH speaks, saying to Joshua that he is not to fear because not a single warrior of the Canaanite alliance will stand before him. Joshua moves quickly by night, advancing on the enemy already surrounding Gibeon. "Joshua and his army come upon the Canaanite enemies suddenly—he surprises them. . . . This implies the notion of double causality, which is not restricted to the Old Testament. Success is the result of prudent human action jointly with

8. Rösel, *Joshua*, 164–65.
9. Hawk, *Joshua*, 149–50.
10. Rösel, *Joshua*, 167.

God's help."[11] True, but once again the theological profile of this compatibilism is clumsily expressed, as if to say, "God helps those who help themselves," a sentiment that eclipses the sovereignty of YHWH's gracious election and initiative that transpires on the earth in the new agency apparent in Joshua's servant leadership. The purpose of God is Israel redeemed and at home and at rest on the good earth, inclusive of alien and sojourner.

The theological compatibilism gives a choice that is, as it were, the no-choice between life and death; the only freedom in it is the freedom of obedience by faith that trusts in YHWH's election of Israel, for disobedience is slavery to the lethal structures of malice and injustice whose wage is death. Perhaps better: YHWH's word-in-action elicits and sustains proper human action. Increasingly the narrative displays this theological compatibilism by displaying Joshua's obedience of faith by virtue of which YHWH fights for Israel, constituting a saving synergy. Origen explains this synergy, which is really the Pauline exchange of lordships from the dominion of sin to the dominion of the Spirit, with his characteristic focus on the individual believer's battle with sinful impulses: when the five senses of the human organism, he writes, "are subdued through Jesus so that infidelity and disbelief are expelled from them and when their sins die so they desist from the service of sin, then the soul uses these very servants to work the righteousness of God."[12] Consequently, in an exchange of predicates, Joshua's human action becomes the action of YHWH and vice versa, as the narrative continues.

YHWH acts, throwing the enemy surrounding Gibeon into a great confusion (cf. Exod. 14:24; 23:27; Deut. 7:23; Judg. 4:15; 1 Sam. 7:10; 2 Sam. 22:15), so that Israel falls on the enemy with a great slaughter and pursues them. But YHWH is not yet finished; "God is fighting from heaven."[13] As the enemy flees, "YHWH himself"[14] showers large hailstones from the sky so that more die from that heavenly barrage than are put to the edge of Israel's sword. In coordination with YHWH's acts of casting panic on the minds and then hailstones on the bodies of the enemy, Joshua acts. In the hearing of Israel, Joshua, believing the promise that not a single enemy will remain standing, commands the sun to be still and also the moon. And the heavenly bodies obey. If the reader is not bedazzled by this spectacle of the fabulous, she may comprehend what has actually

11. Rösel, *Joshua*, 167.
12. Origen, *Homilies on Joshua*, 118.
13. Calvin, *Book of Joshua*, 127.
14. Rösel, *Joshua*, 168.

transpired here. "YHWH and Joshua virtually reverse roles. YHWH fights and pursues the enemies, while Joshua stops the sun and moon."[15]

An exchange of attributes or communication of idioms transpires: this man commands sun and moon; this God fights on the earth. The narrator concludes by noting how the sun remained still in the sky for an elongated day that the battle might conclude as YHWH promised. The Divine Warrior "does battle using heavenly auxiliaries,"[16] and yet the text tells us that it was the human Joshua who took the initiative and spoke daringly and authoritatively[17] to YHWH in the presence of Israel, commanding prolongation of the day of battle to accommodate its promised conclusion. Calvin attributes the divine work of Joshua to the "power and privilege of the faith which Christ inspires (Matt. 17:20; Luke 17:6) that mountains and seas are removed at its command. The more the godly feel their own emptiness, more liberally does God transfer his power to them, and when faith is annexed to the word, he in it demonstrates his own power. In short faith borrows the confidence of command from the word on which it is founded."[18] Such Christ-inspired faith is not human opinion, the lowest form of knowledge according to Plato. It is divine faith, a theosis of Joshua by which God will "transfer his power" to him, prefiguring the humanity of God in the person of the second Joshua. For in Jesus Christ, the eternal Son humbles himself to take on the form of a servant; and the human servant by his obedience, even to death on a cross, is exalted to reign over the redeemed creation. This once-and-for-all event of Jesus Christ is communicated by the Spirit in the proclamation of joyful exchange—precisely not the usual calculation of a quid pro quo in which at best anyone gets what they deserve. But it is a joyful exchange because in it faith in the faith/faithfulness/obedience of Christ out of divine love for the undeserving receives precisely what is not deserved: righteousness, life, and peace.

The book of Joshua is quoting here from an ancient poem, as the narrator himself notes, making a rare reference to a source, the Book of Jashar, which is generally regarded as "an old collection of poetic pieces."[19] In that case, the question arises whether the speaker who addresses sun and moon in the poem is YHWH, in which case "cosmic power is personified but is under the control of YHWH." If the speaker is human, however, the implication is that "the sun is part

15. Hawk, *Joshua*, 152.
16. Nelson, *Joshua*, 144.
17. Hawk, *Joshua*, 153.
18. Calvin, *Book of Joshua*, 128.
19. Martin Noth, quoted in Rösel, *Joshua*, 169.

of the divine entourage, the object of an incantation, . . . [a] form of solar worship," which Dozeman regards as an idolatrous "feature of royal religion associated with the king"[20]—a plausible hypothesis if the Canaanite city-states and their royalties are extensions of Egyptian imperial power and its famous sun worship. In fact in the quotation cited from the Book of Jashar, sun and moon are addressed as if "the references are to local thinking of the sun and the moon as deities, which should be seen to be under YHWH's control during the battle."[21] Whatever the source may have intended, Joshua in our canonical narrative is clearly the speaker of this statement addressed to sun and moon; consequently, "the voice of Joshua is more authoritative than royal solar cults, since his command to YHWH can control the sun to defeat kings."[22] And so "the sun remains at its zenith. The day is prolonged thereby, and the victory can be fully exploited."[23] More precisely stated (lest we be dazzled by the fabulous but miss its literary point), "the miracle . . . allows for the hanging of the kings during the day (v. 26) and their burials in the cave at sunset (v. 27)."[24]

The event, to be sure, was singular; nothing like it, we are told, occurred before or ever since. An exchange of idioms or attributes, indeed of subjectivities, occurred in this singularity: as YHWH fought for Israel, YHWH became the servant, listening to and obeying the human voice of Joshua, who acted as Lord in commanding heavenly powers.[25] The intended sense of the story is thus plain if acutely paradoxical: "It glorifies Joshua as the leader whose extraordinary request for extended daylight was uniquely heeded by YHWH."[26] So the reader is made to wonder, Who, then, is this whom even sun and moon obey (cf. Mark 4:41)? It is undoubtedly true that the text "points decisively away from astral powers and directly to Israel's God, who listened to Joshua's request." Yet one might ask if it is any less a "mythopoetic notion" than found in the primitive poem's belief in astral powers that it was YHWH, God in heaven and on the earth, who "obey[ed] the human voice" to suspend the course of sun and moon.[27]

We have occasion here, therefore, to comment on the element of the fabulous that saturates the Joshua narrative. Ever since the rise and success of the natural

---

20. Dozeman, *Joshua 1–12*, 442–43.
21. Pitkänen, *Joshua*, 224.
22. Dozeman, *Joshua 1–12*, 444–45.
23. Rösel, *Joshua*, 170.
24. Dozeman, *Joshua 1–12*, 453.
25. Hawk, *Joshua*, 154.
26. Nelson, *Joshua*, 141.
27. Nelson, *Joshua*, 145.

sciences, and the prestige rightly accorded to them, theology in the modern world finds itself at a loss in dealing with the biblical resort to the fabulous. Many have tried to diminish the role played by biblical miracle, but any and every attempt to explain away our modern embarrassment destroys the narrative and forces it into saying something other than what it wants to say. Here the insight of New Testament theologian Gerd Theissen in his study of New Testament miracles, however, is as penetrating as it is pertinent: miracles have no other function than to indicate the one true God to whom all things are possible and to reveal his creative and redemptive purposes.[28] Consequently, any attempt to explain *how* miraculous events happened is a categorical mistake that misses the literary point. The literary point is that the one who is truly God, as creator of everything that is not God, has possibilities beyond human comprehension and imagination. This one true God may freely exercise such possibilities, not to replace nature, but wisely and therefore parsimoniously to reveal his power and goodwill in it for the sake of eliciting and empowering the messianic theological compatibilism—which we have observed throughout the book of Joshua—anticipating the miraculous person of the second Joshua.

Faith in YHWH as the living God in heaven and on earth—that is, in the God of Israel as the one who will prove at last to be the one true creator of all that is not God—brings about a metaphysical revolution over against the deification of apathy worked by the ancient philosophers who were embarrassed at the tales of the gods in their own cultures, as the church fathers grasped. Nemesius of Emesa, commenting on the miracle at Gibeon, writes,

> What we say is that God not only stands outside the power of all necessity; he is its Lord and maker. For in that he is authority and the very source whence authority flows, he himself does nothing through any necessity of nature or at the bidding of any inviolable law. On the contrary, all things are possible to him, including those we call impossible. To prove this, he established once and for all the courses of the sun and the moon, which are borne on their way by inevitable laws, and forever and ever will thus be borne, and at the same time to prove that nothing is to him inevitable but that all things are possible that he may choose, just once he made a special "day" that Scripture sets forth as a "sign," solely that he might the more proclaim, and in no way invalidate, that divine ordinance with which, from the beginning, he fixed the undeviating orbits of the stars.[29]

28. Gerd Theissen, *The Miracle Stories of the Early Christian Tradition*, trans. Francis McDonough (Philadelphia: Fortress, 1983), 291, 232. See Paul R. Hinlicky, *Beloved Community: Critical Dogmatics after Christendom* (Grand Rapids: Eerdmans), 407–8.
29. Nemesius of Emesa, *On the Nature of Man* 38.55 (ACCS 4:59).

"YHWH fights for Israel"—how is this most fundamental good news of the book of Joshua to be understood? "The statement is much more important than the details of YHWH hurling hailstones at the enemy and influencing the behavior of sun and moon. Understandably, however, it was these motifs of mythological flavor that left their imprint on human imagination for all future generations. The motif of sun and moon obeying YHWH can be connected to later conceptions of the entire universe being God's creation and under his rule."[30] True, but be it noted that such lame commentary misses utterly the messianic point, which is "the strange reversal of roles: YHWH has been the fighter, Joshua commands."[31] The literarily inextricable miracle anticipates the person whom Joshua foreshadows.

---

30. Rösel, *Joshua*, 160.
31. Hawk, *Joshua*, 154.

THE CAMPAIGN AGAINST
THE SOUTHERN KINGS

10:16–43

After the battle at Gibeon, Joshua with all Israel returns to the camp at Gilgal. Having announced that, the narrator's focus returns forthwith to the five Canaanite kings who have allied against Gibeon, the new and strangely covenanted Canaanite servant of Israel. The kings escape from battle and hide themselves in a cave. When they are discovered and word is sent to Joshua, Joshua orders the mouth of the cave be blocked and establishes a guard to keep them trapped inside (cf. Matt. 27:65–66). Leaving the guards behind, the rest of Israel is ordered to pursue the enemy and keep them from refortifying in their cities. "YHWH fights for you! He has given them into your hand!" So the slaughter ensues until the remnant of the enemy enters the fortified cities. Then all the people return to Joshua in the camp at Makkedah, and no one wags their tongue any longer at the sons of Israel.

Joshua next orders that the kings captured in the cave be brought to him. After they are brought, Joshua summons the troops of Israel to watch as he orders the captains of the Israelite warriors to come near and put their feet on the necks of the captured royalty. This public humiliation is a "ritual act of subjugation" of the hostile powers.[1] Calvin is duly offended and resorts, as he too frequently does, to the incomprehensibility of God's commands along with the duty to unquestionably obey. He writes, "It would argue boundless arrogance and barbarous atrocity to trample on the necks of kings, and hang up their dead bodies on gibbets. It is

1. Dozeman, *Joshua 1–12*, 454. Cf. Ps. 110:1; 1 Cor. 15.

certain that they had lately been raised by divine agency to a sacred dignity, and placed on a royal throne. It would therefore have been contrary to the feelings of humanity to exult in their ignominy, had not God so ordered it. But as such was his pleasure, it moves us to acquiesce in his decision, without presuming to inquire why he was so severe." In fact, however, Calvin goes on not only to inquire into but also to explain the severity of Joshua's, and presumably God's, judgment as the necessary outcome of the politics of purity: it was necessary that thus "the land be purged of all pollution."[2] Such unprincipled commentary, oscillating arbitrarily between comprehension and incomprehension of God, yields the worst of both possible interpretations: it interprets the dramatization in the Joshua narrative of *herem* warfare according to an unchastened, indeed fanatical, politics of purity, and at the same time misses *herem*'s special target in the political regimes of Canaanite royalty. In the process, unsurprisingly, it misses the christological reference to the second Joshua, who, having suffered ignominy in death and in burial like these five Canaanite kings, will rise from a guarded tomb (Matt. 27:65–66) to wage war until he hands the kingdom over to God the Father, "after he has destroyed every ruler and every authority and power. For he must reign until he has put all his enemies under his feet" (1 Cor. 15:24–25).

Joshua, unlike his commentator Calvin, does explain the meaning of the humiliating display: Israel is never to fear nor to panic like these kings with their armies did when YHWH fought for Israel against them. They are to fear only YHWH and therefore nothing else in heaven and on earth. In the fear of YHWH, Israel is to be strong and courageous, counting on YHWH to do the same to all their enemies in battle. When he finishes speaking, Joshua executes the kings and hangs their corpses, one each on five trees, until evening. As commanded in the book of the law of Moses, Joshua has the corpses removed from the trees at dusk and cast into the very cave where they had hidden. "The hiding place becomes a grave, with the entrance covered by stones,"[3] which remain as a memorial to the narrator's very day.

What does the grave memorial intend? Nelson argues that "these stones [are] visible signs of Israel's territorial claims . . . marking the graves of the land's previous claimants"[4]—thus marking land title in perpetuity. But this interpretation mistakes regime change for land title. And theologically it can lead to the disastrous interpretation of the reign of YHWH as consisting in the turf claimed by

2. Calvin, *Book of Joshua*, 132.
3. Pitkänen, *Joshua*, 225.
4. Nelson, *Joshua*, 146.

the religions of Judaism or Christianity. But YHWH's regime-change battles are not intended to replace one form of political-sovereignty-cum-land-title with another one backed by yet another religious ideology, with the result that the more things change, the more they remain the same. A revolutionary *new* beginning is intended, a *fabulous* revolution, to be sure, that comes *from above* but appears *below* in the messianic figure of Joshua, whose special target on the earth is the Canaanite royalty and whose special outcome is the new humanity, the Israel of God, in which the will of God is done on earth as in heaven. In turn, the book of Joshua, in which Priestly themes are evident throughout and increase as we near the midpoint of the narrative on to the end, fairly exudes the Levitical statement of YHWH *against* so-called land title: "The land shall not be sold in perpetuity, for the land is mine; with me you are but aliens and tenants" (Lev. 25:23).

The grave-memorial of the Canaanite royalty is rather intended to balance the stories of Rahab and the Gibeonites, which have made room in Israel for Canaanites who join themselves to the cause of YHWH, participating in YHWH's purpose for a new humanity in Israel. The inclusion of these Canaanites does not by any means, however, include the old regime of political sovereignty that cannot analogize the reign of YHWH. "You know that among the Gentiles those whom they recognize as their rulers lord it over them, and their great ones are tyrants over them. But it is not so among you; but whoever wishes to become great among you must be your servant, and whoever wishes to be first among you must be slave of all" (Mark 10:42–44). These are the words of the second Joshua, indicating how he too would be "servant of YHWH": "For the Son of Man came not to be served but to serve, and to give his life a ransom for many" (Mark 10:45).

The balancing of inclusion by the exclusion marked by the grave-memorial of the Canaanite royalty "illustrate[s] the elasticity of Israel's national boundaries."[5] Pope Francis re-presented the message here when he said in 2016, "A person who only thinks about building walls, wherever they may be, and not building bridges, is not Christian."[6] Borders without bridges are mighty walls with gates shut up tight so that no one can come in or go out—the only security that the political sovereignty of Canaan imagines. Such are the walls of those who think that they

---

5. Hawk, *Joshua*, 156.
6. Christina Wilkie, "Pope Francis on Donald Trump: 'This Man Is Not Christian,'" *Huffpost*, February 18, 2016, https://www.huffpost.com/entry/pope-francis-donald-trump-christian_n_56c5f9c8e4b0c3c5505402d1.

are above others, finding shelter within them from the nomad, the wanderer, the refugee, and resident alien below—shelter that YHWH's revolution from above brings crashing down here below through the messianic labors of Joshua. In fact, the proud kingdoms of the dark Canaan of this world become prisoners within their own imagined fortresses. Borders, certainly, are necessary all the way down to cellular biology, for they constitute the individuation that separates a life form from its environment and thus protects the integrity of its metabolic order, on which any individual life depends. But no such living individual, bounded and therefore finite, is an island. Without portals permitting life-giving exchange with the external environment, an organism quickly dies in the would-be security of pure isolation. Borders with bridges are the great necessity—all the way up from cellular life to the social life of human communities. Borders with bridges in social life preserve the coherence of a community from the disintegrating effects within of alien allegiances, but only if they are sufficiently "elastic" to integrate aliens and sojourners who would join in YHWH's cause for the wholeness of Israel on good land at rest from war. Neither individualism nor collectivism but beloved community constitutes the Israel of God.

Although we have been told earlier that Joshua returned to Gilgal, we now see that Joshua continues the battle on that very day after the rout at Gibeon, capturing the fortified city of Makkedah according to the rule of *herem* warfare. With the "mouth of the sword," *herem* is executed, devouring everyone in the city; not a soul remained. And Joshua does to the king of Makkedah as he did to the king of Jericho—a theme that is repeated with matter-of-fact monotony in all the battle reports that follow. But we grasp by now the genre of this literature as eschatological and ecclesiological rather than historical and political. Origen responds bluntly to the offense that gnostics take at Joshua's bloody wars, predicated on their hermeneutical literalism, thus lacking the Spirit to read the narrative rightly as foreshadowing messianic redemption: "The kingdoms of earth are not promised to you by the Gospels, but the kingdoms of heaven." Citing the Christian interpreter's linchpin text from Eph. 6:12, "Your fight will not be against flesh and blood," Origen belabors what is "spiritually" obvious: "We shall not fight in the same manner as the ancients fought."[7] Instead, under the lordship of Jesus the servant-Son of God, Origen's properly instructed Christian prays to "crush the spirit of fornication with my feet and trample upon the necks of the spirit of wrath and rage, to trample on the demon of avarice, to trample down

7. Origen, *Homilies on Joshua*, 121.

boasting, just crush the spirit of arrogance with my feet, and when I have done all these things, not to hang the most exalted of these exploits upon myself but upon his cross."[8] The lever on which this battle turns is the "spiritual" re-formation of human desire by the Holy Spirit, "so that no disposition of desire for any evil may be preserved in me . . . [and that I may be] purged from all former evils and under the leadership of Jesus."[9] Indeed, such Pauline "crucifixion" of the former self is the "unavoidable and chief" work of "the word of God: to pluck up by the roots the sprouts of sin, and to tear out and consume by fire every plant that the heavenly Father did not plant."[10] Spiritually, the politics of purity here become a policy of lifelong repentance.

Returning to the text of Josh. 10, the following "battle reports in Joshua are modeled after the Deuteronomic account of the Transjordanian conquests (Deut. 2:24–3:11),"[11] in this way forging a strong connection between east and west of the Jordan. The narrative continuity pulls the data together from the battle reports "to create for its readers the sense of an impressive blitzkrieg campaign in the southern part of the country."[12] From Makkedah Joshua is said to turn against Libnah, which YHWH gave into the hands of Israel for *ḥerem* along with its king who received the same treatment as the king of Jericho. From Libnah Joshua encamps against Lachish, which falls on the second day and receives the same treatment that Libnah had. When the king of Gezer comes to the defense of Lachish, Joshua exterminates him and his people. From there Joshua goes on to besiege Eglon, which falls on the very same day and receives the same treatment as Lachish. From there Joshua at the head of Israel goes against Hebron, taking it and its king and all its towns, destroying all the life therein. From Hebron, the lightning warfare turns against Debir; as Joshua has done before, so he does now to Debir and its king. Joshua's campaign even reaches Gaza, the territory of Goshen as far as Gibeon. In sum, Joshua, in a quick-as-lightning campaign, smites the entire land in the south of Canaan with all their kings. In obedience to the command of YHWH, the God of Israel, he leaves none alive but utterly destroys all that has breath. Then Joshua with the army of Israel returns to the camp at Gilgal. "The ideological goal of the entire chapter is reached in v. 42,"

8. Origen, *Homilies on Joshua*, 123.

9. Origen, *Homilies on Joshua*, 127.

10. Origen, *Homilies on Joshua*, 128.

11. Hawk, *Joshua*, 159. See Hawk's illuminating side-by-side charts displaying this relationship (161–67).

12. Pitkänen, *Joshua*, 226.

when YHWH, fighting for Israel, conquers "in one swift stroke."[13] So argues Nelson. But—to the cognitive disappointment of secularizing scholarship, which in fact displaces knowledge of God with discovery of some religious "ideology" in "real" history—Joshua will *not* make himself king over Israel in place of the Canaanite royalty (cf. John 6:15).

13. Nelson, *Joshua*, 148.

THE ALLIANCE OF THE
NORTHERN KINGS AGAINST
ISRAEL AND THEIR DEFEAT

11:1–15

Israel led by Joshua, and Joshua led by YHWH, now advance to the north in a campaign that reproduces the sweeping victory just recorded in the south. Chapter 11 mirrors chapter 10.[1] The royalty in their fortified cities are yet again the special target of the offensive. This antimonarchical thrust, as we have had repeated occasion to observe, is crucially important for understanding the messianism of the book of Joshua, which, once again, is not so much about "title" to the land or an insurrectionary ideology of "holy war," not to say "genocide" and "ethnic cleansing," as it is about the advance of YHWH, the living God in heaven and on earth, to establish his reign in Canaan for the sake of his new humanity, the Israel of God, to the ultimate end that the earth have rest from war. This new creation out of the ruins of the old entails the destruction of the structures of malice and injustice that are figured in the Canaanite city-states and personified in their kings, just as the righteousness of the reign of YHWH is figured in the anti-king servant-of-YHWH-in-training, Joshua. This knowledge of God is the harvest of our literary-spiritual reading thus far. But this reading, as we have noted in passing, is in tension already from the origin of the book with any otherwise plausible literalism that would read the book as representational history. The book belongs in the genre of the fabulous; it is inchoate apocalyptic disclosing to

---

1. Nelson, *Joshua*, 151–52.

suffering faithful, postexilic losers themselves dispossessed, the hidden meaning of contested history.

In this light it is not incongruous with the message of the book of Joshua when Origen affirms that "doubtless the wars that are waged through Jesus, and the slaughter of kings and enemies must also be said to be 'a shadow and type of heavenly things,' namely, those wars that our Lord Jesus with his army and officers—that is the throngs of believers and their leaders—fights against the devil and his angels." Origen takes the king of Hazor to be a figure of the devil, and his court to be the dominion of "the prince of this world." Origen would thus have us consider "how the new things harmonize fully with the old."[2] This spiritual congruity with the literal sense of the Old Testament speaks against Origen's contemporaneous opponents, the gnostics who reject the book of Joshua and its God, YHWH who fights for us, on the basis of their literalistic but hostile hermeneutic. By the same token, it also speaks against "that Israel that is accord-ing to the flesh"—his trope for literalists (n.b., not only "the Jews" but also fellow Christians) who "understood nothing in [Joshua], except wars and shedding of blood, from which their spirits, too, were incited to excessive savageries and were always fed by wars and strife." Just as Luther criticized Müntzer, as noted in the chapter on preliminary considerations, Origen too criticizes literalists: "If we understand this according to the letter, it will be necessary for us to shed blood incessantly."[3] The root of the problem is that in fact both parties, literal-ist gnostic opponent and would-be literalist apologist, share a representational epistemology unlettered in the rhetoric and poetics of proper reading; they di-vide consequently only in repudiating or affirming what they take to be Joshua's bloody representation of reality.

Neither party reads Jabin, king of Hazor, as a figure of the "prince of this world" holding sway over a captive world, a usurped earth, until a new and "stronger" Joshua breaks in, one who "may both 'bind' him and 'carry away what he pos-sesses'" (cf. Mark 3:27).[4] But a child should be able to ask the obvious literary question at this midpoint of the book of Joshua about how rest from war on the good earth could truthfully be predicated of Joshua the son of Nun "when the earth never entirely rested from wars in his time." The manifest contradiction borne by literal reading cries out for recognition in a literary reading that the text does not point behind itself to a historical reality in the past as the thing signified

2. Origen, *Homilies on Joshua*, 120.
3. Origen, *Homilies on Joshua*, 149.
4. Origen, *Homilies on Joshua*, 133.

by the sign—no matter whether one affirms this naïvely and dogmatically with the apologist or skeptically and critically debunks it with gnostics old and new. Instead the sign points forward messianically, as Origen sees: rest from war "is fulfilled in my Lord Jesus Christ alone. . . . Your land has ceased from wars if you still 'carry around the death of Jesus Christ in your body' so that, after all the battles have ceased in you, you may be made 'peaceable' and you may be called a 'child of God.' . . . Then rest will be given to you."[5]

So in parallel to Israel on the way to rest from war in the book of Joshua, in Origen's Christian the battle is already inaugurated but not yet complete in victory. "I observe that today we are not able to overwhelm all those powers [of sin and devil], nor to destroy them all, but they will be entirely taken away tomorrow, that is, after the consummation of this age."[6] The consummation of this age is the end of all things figured by the conclusion of *herem* warfare in Joshua, when at last the land will have rest from war so that the meek inherit the earth. But the war of extermination against the usurpers of the earth has been the necessary prerequisite once and for all to end the demonic rebellion and restore the reign to God; it figures horribly the final judgment as Origen cites Matt. 25:41: "Go into the eternal fire that God has prepared for the devil and his angels." He comments, "Then, if following Jesus the leader, we have conquered and have been able to take possession, even we shall occupy the kingdom that the Father has prepared for his saints."[7]

This Christian appropriation of the already/not yet dialectic in Joshua is apropos. "Joshua 11 . . . serves as a broad conclusion to the wars of extermination."[8] Yet "v. 18 indicates that Joshua fought against the Canaanites for a long time."[9] As Wyschogrod puts it theologically, "Judaism thinks of man as the inhabitant of an unredeemed world in which Israel clings to the promise that it has received, but is also aware that there is something that remains outstanding that has not yet occurred but has been promised and will therefore occur. . . . It believes the promise, but it can also accept failure."[10]

It is worth noting here that the LXX and the MT diverge throughout Josh. 11, seemingly on account of divergent theologies of "holy war"; for example, "the statement in the MT of verse 19 that no nation made peace with Israel is absent

5. Origen, *Homilies on Joshua*, 150.
6. Origen, *Homilies on Joshua*, 136.
7. Origen, *Homilies on Joshua*, 137.
8. Dozeman, *Joshua 1–12*, 459.
9. Pitkänen, *Joshua*, 231.
10. Wyschogrod, *Body of Faith*, 14.

in the LXX."[11] As the LXX translation of the Hebrew was written for Jews in the postexilic Greek-speaking diaspora, there appears to be a tendency in it to downplay apparently subversive implications in MT Joshua as these might appear to host cultures in the Greek-speaking world. Despite the divergence, the theology remains fabulous: victory comes from above without reliance on the apparatus of statesmanship or of military prowess. Joshua's good news must remain fabulous in our literary reading if Joshua is not, with disastrous consequences in human-all-too-human zealotry, to be taken literally and ideologically so that we put God's putative works into our own bloody hands. From its origin, the book accomplishes this necessary resort to the fabulous, disrupting any immediate reduction of the indicative to the imperative, through the snowballing aporias in its telling of *herem* warfare, crying out for figural-messianic reading to know the God rendered in its story as the one who

> has shown strength with his arm;
>> he has scattered the proud in the thoughts of their hearts.
> He has brought down the powerful from their thrones,
>> and lifted up the lowly;
> he has filled the hungry with good things,
>> and sent the rich away empty.
> He has helped his servant Israel,
>> in remembrance of his mercy,
> according to the promise he made to our ancestors,
>> to Abraham and to his descendants forever. (Luke 1:51–55)

The report of YHWH's deeds personified in his servant Joshua has now catalyzed reaction by the Canaanite kings, this time in the north, for the final time in the book of Joshua.[12] The report—that is, the gospel that YHWH fights for Israel in the figure of Joshua at the head of all Israel—evokes resistance by the Canaanite powers that be. Thus, when the king of the northern city-state Hazor, Jabin, hears of Israel's success in the south, he sends word to the kings of the other northern city-states, both Canaanite and Amorite. In a great alliance—armed to boot with horse and chariot and a multitude of warriors vast "like the sand on the seashore" (11:4)—they come out against Israel, pitching their camp at the waters of Merom, poised for battle against Israel. Hyperbole "presents the coming conflict

11. Dozeman, *Joshua 1–12*, 461.
12. Hawk, *Joshua*, 169.

in climactic terms, as though all of the kings and peoples of the land are gathering for a final attack against Israel"[13]—a proleptic Armageddon. The stage is thus set for what will appear as a massive battle ranging beyond the north to all of Canaan.

In the narrative of the military campaigns in the canonical book of Joshua, the possession by the enemy of advanced weaponry like chariots heightens the tension: here is a qualitatively greater danger than hitherto faced by Israel. Just so, however, YHWH speaks a fresh word of assurance to Joshua that by this time on the next day the vast army assembled against him will be slain. Calvin comments on how often the promises are reiterated throughout the book of Joshua, fresh in every new situation and countering the forgetfulness, sloth, and fickleness of believers: "For unless new nourishment is every now and then given to faith, they forthwith faint and fall away." The repetitiveness readers endure in reading Joshua (and which this commentary's paraphrase has tried to imitate) draws Calvin's further remark, "And yet such is our perverse fastidiousness, that to hear the same thing twice is usually felt to be irksome."[14] The repetitiveness is not idle, however, for the gospel must be proclaimed again and again in order to be claimed again and again in the obedience of faith. In other words, it is to be heard ever fresh as the word of the living God; it is not an ordinary datum that can be registered and mastered in a moment and then filed away in the memory banks to be recollected as desired or needed. In the pitch of the eschatological battle that rages on the earth against the usurpers of the earth, the promise of God must be newly enunciated at every twist and turn in the fog and friction of eschatological war. This enunciation of divine promise is the perpetual liturgy of covenant renewal, so long as the struggle will last.

Joshua, when victorious over the vast horde of the Canaanite alliance, shall, according to the instruction of YHWH, cut the hamstrings of their horses and burn their chariots with fire; the instruction calls to mind Ps. 20:7: "Some take pride in chariots, and some in horses, but our pride is in the name of the LORD our God." The directive is not gratuitous animal cruelty, let alone guidance on battle tactics, but rather "a way of making the warhorses useless for future battles. . . . [It is] a sort of *ḥerem* by making the devoted animals and military equipment" unserviceable.[15] Calvin sees in this a further and deeper motive, reminiscent of the military vulnerability displayed in the act of mass circumcision and then the liturgical parade circling Jericho at the beginning of the invasion. The instruction

13. Hawk, *Joshua*, 169.
14. Calvin, *Book of Joshua*, 144.
15. Nelson, *Joshua*, 153.

was meant to keep Israel from assimilating to the tactics and technology of the ancient Near East and instead to rely only on YHWH and his fabulous interventions on Israel's behalf.[16]

Fortified by this divine assurance and therewith reminded to trust in YHWH alone, Joshua and his army make a surprise attack on the encampment of the enemy at the waters of Merom. No details of the battle are provided, however, other than YHWH's deliverance of the enemy into the hand of Israel, who slays them and pursues them far and wide until none remain alive. Terse historical narration betrays the fundamental literary-theological intention of the text to underscore YHWH's promised victory realized through obedience to YHWH's commands.[17] Accordingly, Joshua does precisely as YHWH commanded, disabling the warhorses and burning the chariots[18]—as if also in the process to preserve Israel from the temptation, as Calvin sees, to rely on the captured technology of organized warfare rather than on the fabulous power of YHWH that descends from above to give the victory (cf. Deut. 20:1).

Calvin accordingly notices the messianic aura in a "distinct statement of what had not yet been expressed . . . namely, that Joshua faithfully performed his part, by fulfilling everything which the Lord had enjoined by Moses. It is just as if he had placed his hands at the disposal of God."[19] Thus Calvin recognizes the literary shift from chapter 10 onward in which Joshua virtually becomes the figure of YHWH in action on the earth. This new humanity, Israel personified in Joshua, servant in the making, does not desire what the Canaanite city-state system regards as desirable; its goods are evil for Israel. If the reader wonders literalistically what earthly king, counting the cost, would chance initiating war without the best available weaponry—that is precisely the point being made in the Joshua narrative, reflecting on the failure of kingship in Israel and Judah. Reliance on the fabulous power of YHWH is integral to Israel's war against any system of political sovereignty that relies ultimately on its own brainpower or muscle power or both—that is to say, relies on the flesh rather than the Spirit (to put the matter in Pauline terms).

Turning from the scene of battle at the waters of Merom, Joshua takes the northernmost city Hazor, which has been at the head of the alliance. The narrative spotlight once again shines on Hazor's king, whom Joshua slays with the sword. Likewise, *ḥerem* warfare requires the utter extermination of the living until none

---

16. Calvin, *Book of Joshua*, 144.
17. Hawk, *Joshua*, 170–71.
18. On the chiastic structure of 11:6–9, see Hawk, *Joshua*, 170.
19. Calvin, *Book of Joshua*, 145.

are left to breathe; then the city is consumed with fire. "The special attention given to Hazor contrasts with the indeterminate nature of the rest of the summary," a "contrast which will arise during the description of tribal territories."[20] Why this southern bias in historical-geographical and battle report is so will concern us later when we come to the distribution of the land.

Despite this difference between Josh. 10 and 11, "the destruction of Hazor represents the ideal of the author of Joshua; it mirrors the fate of Jericho and Ai."[21] In portraying this, the narrator announces that Joshua did just as Moses the servant of YHWH had commanded. Yet in the same pen stroke, it seems, the *ḥerem* conundrum makes a new appearance. The narrator simultaneously notes that, of the cities built on tells, only Hazor was burned. Simultaneously, while all the Canaanites were slain, the sons of Israel kept the booty and the cattle for themselves. In other words, "Joshua did not burn the towns in the north, save for Hazor. Only people are killed, and the possessions of the victims plundered."[22] The discrepancies attending the execution of *ḥerem* warfare thus continue to appear.

There are several possibilities for explaining this new contradiction. First, the narrative in this way gives tacit recognition to a historical fact: Joshua's campaign did not succeed in defeating most of the cities in the north, and that is why he did not succeed in razing them and burning them to ruins. Military weakness then required exploitation of Canaanite booty when it became available. Another possibility of historical explanation is that Joshua did succeed but kept the cities for Israel to occupy as the later text in 24:13 seems to indicate. Another historical answer, then, to the apparent contradiction would be that there were various sorts of *ḥerem* warfare; presently, this "sort of *ḥerem* . . . did not destroy captured towns, but appropriated them, thus realizing the principle of Deuteronomy 6:10–11 and Joshua 24:13."[23] In this case, Hazor got the same exceptional treatment as Jericho because it was the head of the northern alliance, and its treatment is to be taken as paradigmatic. The reporting is contradictory, then, because the history was contradictory, and to boot, the law divides against itself—a messy analysis with a messy conclusion! Historically, *ḥerem* is in application apparently not the rule but the exception to the rule! But this historical-critical speculation makes a literary hash of the book of Joshua, which now cashes in on its accumulating account of the conundrums of *ḥerem* warfare.

20. Hawk, *Joshua*, 171–72.
21. Dozeman, *Joshua 1–12*, 475.
22. Pitkänen, *Joshua*, 234.
23. Nelson, *Joshua*, 154.

THE HARDENING OF THE HEARTS
OF THE CANAANITE KINGS

11:16–20

So Joshua captured all the land from north to south, everywhere taking and slaying their kings. Despite the representation of a lightning campaign, as we have already seen, it is also acknowledged that the warfare against these kings that Joshua waged took a long time. For there was no other city that made peace with the sons of Israel except the Gibeonites. Therefore all the others had to be taken in battle. One cannot but wonder at reading this: Why did the Canaanites continue their futile resistance? Why did the war take so long? And why was it ever and always incomplete, since "at the heart of each [report], the narrator points to exceptions which revealed the incompleteness of the conquests"?[1] Thus Pitkänen claims that "it would seem better to make sense of the narratives on the basis of glowing hyperbolic statements to which there is added some small print about the actual state of affairs."[2] But such commentary is stunningly shallow on a literary level and no explanation at all. It only restates the difficulty. Attending to the difficulties, however, is the first order of business in literary interpretation and the launching pad for theological exegesis.

What is the reason for the failure of historicizing interpretation? Like all modern theology in its anthropological reductionism, it takes the thing signified in the text to be a wholly secular human history really existing behind the narrative. In this, however, it is no different in principle from its traditional opponent of medieval allegorical reading and its invention of hidden senses behind the

1. Hawk, *Joshua*, 173.
2. Pitkänen, *Joshua*, 235.

literary text waiting to be revealed by clever eisegesis. Historicizing interpretation is another turn on the very same wheel. But read as scripture, biblical narrative here in Joshua as elsewhere refers theologically to YHWH who fights for Israel. The real explanation of the narrative paradoxes is accordingly theological. Just as of old when Moses commanded Pharaoh in the name of YHWH to let his people go but YHWH hardened Pharaoh's heart to resist his own command (Exod. 7–14), the same YHWH now hardens the hearts of the kings of the Canaanites and the Amorites so that they gather together against Israel; as a result of their willful and thus sinful but now divinely fixed resistance, they are utterly and mercilessly destroyed, if not at first, then at length. To be sure, then, the increasingly clarified agenda of *herem* warfare is the destruction of political sovereignty, not of Canaanite peoples per se; it is the sanctification of the earth for the indwelling of YHWH who reigns, not the acquisition of land title for an Israelite political sovereignty. This literarily clarified warfare of YHWH on behalf of Israel, to be sure, has its dark side—all the more dark for being clarified: the reprobation of the wicked.

Calvin articulates the horrible thought with steely determination: "It was wonderfully arranged by the secret providence of God, that, being doomed to destruction, [the Canaanites] should voluntarily offer themselves to it."[3] The kings and their royal cities represent the "antithesis of the author's religious worldview. ... [This worldview] is an extreme form of iconoclastic religion that leaves no room for compromise."[4] True enough, if iconoclasm is taken ideologically as a (very odd for being imageless) world*view*; what goes unnoticed by this scholar is Joshua's increasing stature as that servant of YHWH in the making, constituting a messianic-apocalyptic antithesis to the Canaanite political sovereignty. The deeper point remains, even if Calvin has expressed it with clumsy brutality: between God and the Canaanite kings, as between rival sovereignties, there can be neither reconciliation nor compromise, as if they were rightful equals.[5] Like the Canaanite kings, the devil of Christian imagination is the usurper of the earth. As the living God in heaven and on earth, YHWH compels such who resist his reign to resist utterly until resistance culminates in their utter destruction as a consequence of being handed over to the consequences of their own sin. There is no liberation apart from usurping the usurpers of the earth, who must be destroyed *willingly*, preserved in their own *chosen* defiance and handed over

3. Calvin, *Book of Joshua*, 148.
4. Dozeman, *Joshua 1–12*, 479.
5. Calvin, *Book of Joshua*, 148–49.

to its consequences temporally and eternally. The narrative theology of Joshua exaggerates brutal extermination to make this theological point; the hyperbole of *ḥerem* has this literary purpose.

This narrative theology once again ties Joshua to the exodus tradition and reinforces his growing stature as successor of Moses who realizes what had been promised through Moses, by way of the true obedience of faith to all that Moses had commanded in the name of YHWH. It is YHWH in battle for his own cause of new creation, the Israel of God at peace on the earth, who magnifies the malice of the Canaanite kings, hardening it into their fortified walls and chariots of iron in order to bring the whole machinery of sovereignty and war as usual tumbling down on itself at the right time of YHWH's own choosing. Origen timidly observes, "God is said in like manner to permit, even to excite, opposing powers to go out into battle against us so that we may see the victory and they may pursue destruction."[6] Calvin is notoriously less reserved, criticizing those (like Origen?) who "only allow God a permissive power, and in this way make his counsel dependent on the pleasure of men." On whose side is the text in this darkest question of the knowledge of God? Calvin is undaunted; he affirms that the Spirit speaking through the text says that "the hardening is from God, who thus precipitates those whom he means to destroy."[7] One *must* think this thought, but *not* remain with it.

6. Origen, *Homilies on Joshua*, 146.
7. Calvin, *Book of Joshua*, 149.

DEFEAT OF THE ANAKIM
AND THE END OF BATTLE

11:21–23

Joshua then wages *ḥerem* war against the Anakim (cf. Num. 13:22, 28, 32–33; Deut. 1:28; 2:10–11, 21; 9:2). The Anakim were a putative race of giants residing in Canaan.[1] Joshua utterly destroys these remaining monstrosities with their cities so that none remain in the land of the hill country inherited by the children of Israel, but only in Gaza, Gath, and Ashdod, cities on the coastal plain that later are occupied by the Philistines. A brief notice rounds out the book of Joshua's account of the wars. "So Joshua," it is said, "took all the land according to all the words that YHWH had spoken to Moses. And he distributed the land as an inheritance to the tribes of Israel. And so the earth became quiet after the din of battle" (11:22 AT). Really? "Why does the land have rest from war when Canaanites still occupy much of the territory promised to Israel?"[2] Is *ḥerem* completed or not? Or, can the best of news be proclaimed in a world that still remains in sorrow and struggle?[3]

---

1. Dozeman, *Joshua 1–12*, 469.
2. Hawk, *Joshua*, 175.
3. J. Louis Martyn, "Epistemology at the Turn of the Ages: 2 Corinthians 5:16," in *Christian History and Interpretation: Studies Presented to John Knox*, ed. W. R. Farmer et al. (Cambridge: Cambridge University Press, 1967), 269–87.

THE END OF CANAANITE SOVEREIGNTY

12:1–24

"Between chapters 1–11 and 13–21 the book's strategy for bolstering national identity and land ownership changes, and the attention shifts from capture in war to land distribution."[1] So it may seem. Chapter 12 breaks down into three distinct sections that recapitulate Israel's advance from the wilderness into Canaan: first Moses's victories over Sihon and Og in the Transjordan; then, second, a brief account of the territory gained, indicating that as Moses distributed portions in the Transjordan, so also Joshua would grant inheritances in the land of Canaan to the other nine and a half tribes; and finally, third, the impressive list of the dethroned kings/destroyed kingdoms. This list has resemblances to Deut. 2:26–3:22 and Num. 21:21–35; it dominates chapter 12 and is important for understanding the nature of the grants of land about to be distributed in chapter 13 and following.

The tone is set early on in 12:2–5: the death of Og as the last of the Rephaim, reported in verses 4–5, "ends the mythical institution of the royal ancestors, who provide cosmological support for political kingship. . . . In this way, the war of Moses in the Transjordan provides the paradigm for Joshua."[2] The ubiquitous cosmic mythology of the ancient Near East grounded political sovereignty in the eternal nature of things, forming a "great symbiosis" between the gods and political sovereignty;[3] but dynasty so rooted ideologically in the nature of things is dethroned in the new worldview, or, better, "Godview," of the narrator

1. Nelson, *Joshua*, 159.
2. Dozeman, *Joshua 1–12*, 498–99.
3. Walton, *Ancient Near Eastern Thought*, 99.

of Joshua—that is, as described above, by the good news of exclusive monotheism, in which YHWH who fights for Israel claims title as creator of all that is not God. This YHWH who fights for Israel consequently claims exclusive right to give and to take away as living God in heaven and on earth. Here a corresponding new sovereignty is instituted on the earth on the basis of YHWH's free decision and gracious election of the people Israel. Accordingly, what we have actually seen transpire to this point in Joshua's ministry to YHWH for Israel is how "the previous political organization of petty kingships was decisively shattered, king by king. . . . All Israel together, south, north, and east of the Jordan, properly organized into its foundational tribes, enjoyed possession of the land under the unified leadership of Moses, the servant of YHWH, and Joshua his successor."[4]

There is an odd addition of the numeral "one" in the MT after each king's name, as if counting on one's fingers; this "suggests that the list may have been refashioned to focus on a single king for each city, rather than the city itself,"[5] since at the end of the impressive list a count of all these "ones" is totaled to "thirty-one kings in all." Thus the focus we have noticed on the kings as the special target of *herem* warfare in the book of Joshua up until this point now comes to its culmination, making the negative point that the land grants to follow are *not* to be more of the same under a new name. A radical alternative to political sovereignty is being presented in the land grants. "The repetitive listing. . . [of the] kings of the land, here revealed in all their multiple majesty ('thirty-one kings in all') have been overcome by unified Israel under the command of Joshua."[6] This distribution will thus be the work of the anti-king, the man Joshua, whose name denotes his person: "YHWH saves," a salvation incarnate in his life's work as servant of YHWH in the making.

So what kind of "occupation" of the land is to come? The term "possession" (*yerusha*) is introduced in 12:7 in reference to Moses's grant to the Transjordanian tribes. The verb form, *yarash*, in the Hebrew Qal means "to possess" but in the Hiphil means "to drive out" or "to dispossess." Both Qal and Hiphil forms "take a more prominent role in the second half of the book of Joshua, indicating that the motif in Joshua 12:1 has a transitional function in the book."[7] Dispossessing political sovereignty of its tyrannical grip on the earth, which it pretends to possess as a commodity, portends a future of "having, as having not": a "possession"

4. Nelson, *Joshua*, 159.
5. Dozeman, *Joshua 1–12*, 495.
6. Hawk, *Joshua*, 176.
7. Dozeman, *Joshua 1–12*, 496–97.

that is and essentially remains a trust from YHWH for future generations, never a disposable commodity to be bought and sold for profit based on extraction rather than conservation of the land for the well-being of future generations. Israel, as Wendell Berry understands, is meant to *settle* on the land for good, at home on the good earth now liberated under the gracious reign of YHWH from the usurpers of the earth.[8]

There are other features of note in chapter 12. The kings and cities in verses 16b–18 have no precedent in Joshua.[9] Along the same lines, another scholar lists a series of historical incongruities here; it is very possible that verses 7–24 in particular telescope things that happened somewhat later, seeing Joshua and the Israelites of the initial conquest and settlement as their ultimate cause. In fact, the additional mention of "the Israelites" in verse 7 in particular seems to allow for conquest after the time of Joshua. Also, the fact that "the kings are described as defeated does not necessarily mean that their land was taken, or held conclusively by the Israelites; the list may also reflect hyperbolic features and the [mere] claims of Israel to the land."[10]

As opposed to such historicizing apologetics, however, the incongruities in chapter 12 may rather mean that defeat of the kings, not possession of their land, is the narrative point: the land is *already* the possession of YHWH, God in heaven and on earth, which he will distribute as a stewardship conditional on the covenant; but the regime of the usurpers of the earth is *not yet* finished off. Like the boundary descriptions to follow in chapter 13 onward, the book thus provides vague markers indicating that reference, not representation, is the point of the text's report of the land distribution to the tribes. The historical truth to which the theology of the book of Joshua points is that, *yes*, Israel came to inherit the land of Canaan *but* in the peculiar way described above: as a trust from YHWH for the sake of future generations to the end that the meek inherit the earth, upon which peace will prevail. The varied representations of this historical truth serve only to point away from the fragmentary and preliminary inauguration of the reign of YHWH to its still future realization.

It is a fundamental misreading of the canonical book of Joshua, therefore, to take it as a literal report about a fanatical military power armed with a ferocious religious ideology invading an alien nation of peaceful natives and subjecting them to colonization, let alone ethnic cleansing or mass extermination. This

---

8. Wendell Berry, *The Unsettling of America: Culture and Agriculture* (Berkeley: Counterpoint, 2015).
9. Nelson, *Joshua*, 160.
10. Pitkänen, *Joshua*, 238–39.

dire construction tells us more about us contemporaries—still reeling from the twentieth-century catastrophes of Hitler, Hiroshima, and Stalin—and how some contemporaries have used the book of Joshua than it does about the canonical book. This is so for multiple reasons. In the first place, the children of Israel have entered Canaan as wandering nomads, refugees escaped from slavery in Egypt who, as they found similarly situated Canaanites on the margins as figured in Rahab and the Gibeonites, incorporate those who are willing to betray existing political sovereignties in Canaan to align themselves with the cause of YHWH by confession of his name and deeds. In the second place, the royal cities in the land of Canaan are understood as extensions of Egyptian colonial-imperial power; thus by way of numerous literary parallels with the book of Exodus, the exodus from Egypt is understood to continue in the re-creation of Canaan as a land of promise by the overthrow of its political sovereignty, including the despoiling of the usurpers of the land in appropriating their cattle, goods, and even cities. In the third place, the ideal of *herem* warfare brutally-all-too-brutally, but just so forcefully, forbids colonialist instrumentalization of alien peoples for imperial purposes; more profoundly, precisely as it is spiritualized, it roots out of the human heart the very coveting of Canaanite luxuries, even as its demand for the literal extermination of Canaanites simultaneously proves impossible of consistent execution and thus fails.

Herem warfare thus becomes in Christian literary-theological interpretation and appropriation a figure of the wrath of God to come from which the crucified, risen, and ascended Jesus delivers those who await him, those who have thus turned from idols to serve the living and true God (1 Thess. 1:9–10). *Herem* warfare, taken spiritually, concludes and so ends with the eternal defeat of the evil one and his minions (Rev. 20). Devoting such Canaanites to YHWH places them, along with their vicious goods, beyond any possibility of human desire, bringing about the eschatological state *non posse peccare*! In the same way as the Levitical whole burnt offering gives the life of the sacrificial victim back to YHWH, God in heaven and on earth, the Christian believer devotes the usurpers of the earth to spiritual destruction by sacrificing her allegiance to them. This spiritual sacrifice is, on the one hand, the renunciation of their seductive and addictive claim on the desires of the human heart; on the other hand, it is daily practice of the patiency of faith, by those beloved in the Beloved who never avenge themselves, leaving room for the wrath of God (Rom. 12:19). It is to this true and living God that persistent and impenitent Canaanites of hardened hearts must render eschatological account—these would-be kings who preside over the ruin of the earth by building human structures of malice as if injustice were scripted into the nature of things. Literal extermination by Joshua and spiritual threat of eternal loss by Jesus differ significantly in the way that a politics of purity differs from a politics of reconciliation with its policies of repentance and renunciation, with the result that the beloved are not to be "overcome by evil, but [to] overcome evil with good" (Rom. 12:21). Nonetheless, the theological problem of the wrath of God that they both represent is one and the same. *Herem* warfare is the figure of the eternal wrath of the God of love against all that is against love.

It is necessary to add emphatically that even if we who read the book of Joshua spiritually as Christians succeed in hearing its message that YHWH fights for us on its own terms as a figure for the eternal defeat of the devil and his minions, that implies no consent to *herem* warfare taken literally as extermination of ethnic others as any kind of word of God spoken to us today. For the Christian reader, that emphatic *No* to literal Joshua requires taking the anti-king Joshua and his battles spiritually as a type of Christ. Why is it that chapter 12 at the literary center of the canonical book lists in seemingly endless repetition the kings defeated first by Moses in the Transjordan and then by Joshua in the Cisjordan? It is not the case that YHWH gives this land to Israel simply as an unconditional gift in fulfillment of the promise he made to their nomad fathers and mothers. So far as YHWH has piecemeal done this, he nevertheless is executing his own agenda in this gift, which is the inauguration of his reign on the land that he makes holy by his very coming to reign over it—which, coming in fullness, is its final rest from war. As the kingship of YHWH advances, then, the kings of the Canaanite city-states need fall away into oblivion along with their malicious structures of injustice posing as eternally grounded political sovereignty. This struggle of the kingdom of God remains, a perpetual task, suspended in the tension between the already of the inaugural victories of YHWH who fights for us on land not yet at rest from war.[11]

Such spiritual reading of Joshua is not a foreign imposition on the text but can in fact claim to be a true reading of the literal sense that takes its anomalies and dissonances as literarily purposeful. If we have read closely and carefully, we begin to see that Joshua's literary "emphasis on the ban clarifies that . . . it is a story of identity formation, which is articulated through the imagery of extermination as an act of sacrifice to the Deity."[12] In other words, by literarily pushing the literal

11. Nelson, *Joshua*, 156.
12. Dozeman, *Joshua 1–12*, 456.

mandate to *ḥerem* warfare to logical extremity, literal *ḥerem* in Joshua is reduced step-by-step to political absurdity through a crescendo of self-contradictions and thus literally self-destructs as a politics. It survives metaphorically as an ecclesiology of hope predicated on the practice of repentance, just as the distinction between political sovereignty and ecclesiology that emerges from this is an inchoate form of the doctrine of the two humanities of Adam and Christ (Paul), the two cities, heavenly and earthly (Augustine), or the two kingdoms of God and the devil (Menno *and* Luther).

PART 2

TO INHERIT
THE EARTH

(JOSHUA 13–21)

UNCONQUERED CANAAN

13:1–7

The chronology of the book of Joshua, as we have seen, oscillates in and out of focus. One has the impression from the first twelve chapters that lightning warfare thundered through Jericho and Ai and then immediately swept over the south and thereafter the north until coming to a halt in apparent finality with the narrator's announcement that the land had rest from war. And yet, as we have noted, there are interspersed comments throughout this account of *herem* warfare indicating that it took a long time and was never completely successful. Here, past the midway point of the book and at the beginning of the distribution of inheritances to the tribes of Israel, the contradiction is openly acknowledged: Joshua has grown old and warfare has not succeeded in gaining all the land promised to Israel. Thus "the long passage of time between the story's beginning and the present narrative moment,"[1] which would be that of the book's first readers, is indicated. That was the time after exiles returned to the ruins of Jerusalem, as recounted in the books Ezra-Nehemiah. Certainly we have insisted from the outset of this commentary that in any case the book of Joshua must be read from the ironic perspective of those dispossessed of the very land that YHWH once gave their ancestors to possess as an inheritance. Can the geography of Joshua provide further clues?

Geographically, the description provided of the "land that remains" reflects a "tradition of expansive borders over much of Syria-Palestine also found in Numbers 34:1–12 and Judges 3:3." This "land that remains" is essentially "Canaan," as this name designates an area of former Egyptian control, a "territorial sweep

---

1. L. Daniel Hawk, *Joshua*, Berit Olam (Collegeville, MN: Liturgical Press, 2000), 182.

represent[ing] almost pure promise, never matched by reality"[2]—as the postexilic first readers of canonical Joshua surely realized. Given this expansive description of the land that remains, one must say consequently that the reign of YHWH reasserting over all the usurped earth was inaugurated with Joshua's foray into Canaan hitherto described, but that its coming in fullness has not yet taken place either temporally or geographically.[3] Indeed, the narrative has its coming continually resisted, both, as we have seen and will further make note in what follows, from within Israel and from the outside. Thus the reign of YHWH in fullness over the redeemed earth is delayed even as the postexilic generation sees little political or military hope for restoration of what little had been gained in the united kingdoms of David and Solomon. Politically desperate, it is reduced to faith in the fabulous—that is to say, to faith alone in the promise of God alone.

Origen sees that a similarly defiant "hope against hope" attends the Christian company that remains in affliction and struggle: in the "first coming of our Lord and Savior . . . , he took possession of all the earth by casting of seed alone. . . . He sowed the word and propagated the churches. This is the first possession of all the earth." Much earth still "remains" unworked and has not yet been "placed beneath the feet of Jesus," who is "certainly to possess all. . . . In the second coming Jesus will obtain this extensive land that still remains."[4] Centuries after Origen's death, the ecumenical church condemned the doctrine of the reconciliation of all things attributed to him for implying universal salvation, even of the devil. But here, in congruity with the literary sense of Joshua read theologically in Christian perspective, Origen retains the figure of *ḥerem* warfare for the eternal wrath of God: at the parousia of Christ, he maintains, if "anyone has become subject out of compulsion, then, when even 'the last enemy, death, must be destroyed,' there will no longer be grace."[5]

It is just as difficult to regain this needed perspective of the dispossessed for reading Joshua rightly. "In the modern world, the land of Israel/Palestine is again being contested, by the Israelis and the Palestinians. The radical Jewish settlers still refer to Israel's ancient occupation of the land as justification of their acts of appropriating territory to themselves. Also, indigenous people all around the

2. Richard D. Nelson, *Joshua: A Commentary* (Louisville: Westminster John Knox, 1997), 167.

3. Nelson, *Joshua*, 165; Pekka M. A. Pitkänen, *Joshua*, Apollos Old Testament Commentary 6 (Nottingham, UK: Apollos; Downers Grove, IL: InterVarsity, 2010), 267.

4. Origen, *Homilies on Joshua*, ed. Cynthia White, trans. Barbara J. Bruce, Fathers of the Church (Washington, DC: Catholic University of America Press, 2002), 153–54.

5. Origen, *Homilies on Joshua*, 154.

world have suffered and are still suffering conquests, dispossession and other forced measures by people groups stronger than they are. Whether in ancient or in modern settings, theology and ideology are important driving factors for the actions of people."[6] Bad theology that reads Joshua literally and therefore wrongly as providing a religious worldview or ideology, however, is countered only by good theology that reads Joshua literarily and therefore spiritually to harvest its knowledge of God in repentance and a new policy of reconciliation. The modern conceit that historical reconstruction can settle interminable and nonjudicable theological disputes has succeeded more or less in discrediting theological literalism, but it has not succeeded in settling disputes about the meaning of the book of Joshua and its import for us today. Indeed, as a discipline, historical criticism in principle evades such theological questions or in undisciplined fashion merely opinionates on the basis of presumed historical-critical expertise with no attention to the hermeneutical problems.

Postliberal[7] or postcritical theology, such as employed in this commentary, is precisely not a return to the literalism of precritical dogmatism, which under modern conditions issues in reactionary fundamentalism: "God said it. I believe it. That settles it. End of discussion." Much is at stake, then, in a properly critical and precisely so a genuinely theological reading of Joshua for today. Having similarly rejected fundamentalism with the historical critics, Karl Barth continued with the penetrating judgment that the problem with the historical critics is that they are not radical enough. What is radical is *theology*—that is, *knowledge of God* as it is freshly gained by close reading of the biblical text itself as placed into the hands of the Holy Spirit to speak the word of God for us today. The historical critics in any case gain no traction with fundamentalists because in principle these critics will not read the texts as Spirit-selected sources of the knowledge of God. To this extent, literalists rightly pay them no mind when the point is to read the biblical book as scripture written from faith for faith, having been preserved as scripture and passed on as scripture to be the book of the church. Consequently, it is postliberal literary-theological reading that emerges as the one effective tool for the disarmament of the willful ignorance of fundamentalist appropriations of Joshua by hoisting "Bible believers" on their own petards. The reason is that theology reclaims Joshua's gospel of YHWH who fights for us—the ungodly, even we who have lost Eden, the land of promise, and are found like Rahab and

6. Pitkänen, *Joshua*, 275.
7. Peter Ochs, *Another Reformation: Postliberal Christianity and the Jews* (Grand Rapids: Baker Academic, 2011).

the Gibeonites (and Caleb the Kenite as we shall shortly see) on the margins of the apparently triumphant earthly city. Properly understood, Joshua does not tell a story of *our* victory, least of all of our victory *on behalf of God*, but the very reverse: of God's triumph for enemies, *all* of us, then, and in spite of all—the eternal victory of the heavenly city, the eschatological Israel, the beloved community of God.

The correlation between the destruction of the Canaanite city-states with their monarchs and the distribution of the inheritance of the land to the tribes of Israel that now commences is thus also highly significant. No monarchy akin to the political sovereignty of these preexisting city-states is instituted by Israel in its new beginnings on the land. Joshua is, to be sure, a divinely appointed and divinely attended leader, YHWH's servant in the making, but he has neither claim nor aspiration to a throne for himself; he has come not to be served but to serve, and when his mission is accomplished, he will lay down his sword for a small inheritance of family land in trust for the future. Thus the land is distributed socially to the twelve tribes, their clans and families, for a land stewardship in perpetuity that is to be passed on from generation to generation. We should be cautious, moreover, about projecting back the modern connotation in the word "inheritance" as transference of property title. We moderns no sooner "inherit" something than we put it on the auction block to extract value and be freed from the burden of its care. But this is not the meaning of inheritance in Joshua. Paired with the noun form "portion" and the verb for dividing, inheritance in Joshua "serves the purpose of ordering the community, establishing the place of social units within it, and permanently fixing the resultant configuration." So the new creation of Israel on the promised land orders chaos into cosmos by the distribution of land; the priority of theology over geography and land title in this is emphasized "by intermittent reminders that the tribe of Levi receives no land as their inheritance (13:14, 33; 14:3–4; 18:7) and by the institution of Levitical cities within the territories (21:1–40)."[8]

The diffuse presence of the priestly Levites throughout the territories of the twelve tribes (and throughout the book of Joshua!) indicates that the divinely gifted land is not "private property" in any modern sense; if we describe it as "property" at all, we would have to call it a kind of "public property," though quite decentralized in comparison to modern ideas of the public as the domain of nation-state political sovereignty, with its corporate oligarchies, military-industrial

8. Hawk, *Joshua*, 180.

complex, and regulatory bureaucracy, all of which indeed more resemble the Canaanite city-states and their royalty than Israel's projected new life on the land. Rather, "the statements that all these allocations were 'for their clans' is more than just rote formula. . . . It was the clan's duty to redeem and restore land for its constituent families."[9] Israel's possession of the land by inheritance given to the clans and families of the twelve tribes, with the priestly Levites dispersed among them, is not and is not to be a mere exchange in political sovereignties, another earthly city this time but all the worse for being decked out in the veneer of a heavenly city. Israel's inheritance is rather, and fundamentally, an alternative to the earthly city as an expression on the earth of the sovereignty of YHWH.

Fundamentally, then, Israel's task of taking "possession" of the land is bound up integrally with the radical breach that has been made with political sovereignty in favor of the reign of YHWH. The book of Joshua thus presents today as an "Anti-Leviathan," if we may pose it over against Hobbes's decisive political tract of the modern age. Joshua read theologically intrudes the specter of the city of God with its ever incalculable disruption of the earthly city—the Augustinian specter of two cities, not one, which Hobbes sought to exorcise from the very foundations of modernity when he subordinated religious authority to the absolute political sovereignty of the national security state. Reality disrupted in this fashion is hence in a volatile state of contestation. The territories not yet possessed, therefore, are frankly acknowledged at the beginning of chapter 13 and listed along with the nations inhabiting them. YHWH tells Joshua that he will drive these peoples out for the sons of Israel to enter in. But already now Joshua is to make the distribution, even though possession of the land is not yet accomplished. In other words, the distribution of inheritances that follows is an act of faith in a promised future only partially present, or rather present only to the eyes of faith in YHWH's promise. But first a retrospect intervenes on the distribution that Moses had already made before Israel crossed the Jordan into the promised land.

9. Nelson, *Joshua*, 173.

THE TRANSJORDAN

13:8–33

By the time the final form of canonical Joshua was completed, the territory in the Transjordan had been "lost for generations."[1] Yet for these readers, Joshua was long ago commanded to complete the distribution to the nine and one-half remaining tribes to the west of the Jordan. Previously the half-tribe of Manasseh with the Reubenites and the Gadites had received their inheritance from Moses, the servant of YHWH, who gave them the land east of the Jordan River—the land of Sihon, king of the Amorites, and all the kingdom of Og, who alone was left of the remnant of the Rephaim, whom Moses had defeated and driven out. Surprisingly again, since at the beginning of the book of Joshua we were assured that the Transjordan settlement was secure, there is here frank acknowledgment of failure: the foreign peoples Geshur and Maacath have lived among Israel there until this day. This acknowledgment of foreign presence in the Transjordan raises critical questions about the description of this land that go unanswered in the text. Consequently, the careful reader asks, "How can geographical (and ethnic) boundaries be fixed when they cannot be clearly determined?"[2] Such questions arise from the very beginning of the distribution and continue to its end.

The special status of the tribe of Levi is now mentioned in anticipation of Josh. 21: Moses gave no inheritance of land to Levites, but rather their inheritance was to be the priestly duty of offering to YHWH on behalf of Israel; sacrifice by fire to YHWH, the God of Israel, is to be the Levite inheritance. Is this special mention a signal of Israel's postexilic fate? In any case, if the cult is the soul of culture where

---

1. Nelson, *Joshua*, 170.
2. Hawk, *Joshua*, 188.

the desires of the community's heart are articulated and formed, negotiated and transacted, so also Levitical sacrifice is the thing signified by the sign of *ḥerem* warfare. In the act of worship one returns to the Source a token of what has been given so that the gifts are not severed from the Giver but acknowledged as the gifts that really they are, received in trust and held as stewardship. In 13:33 the notice that the tribe of Levi did not receive an inheritance of land is repeated in a new formulation: YHWH, the God of Israel, becomes their inheritance—an even more pregnant signal, perhaps, of Israel's postexilic fate when all (that remains of) Israel has become Levite, a priestly people. If sacrifice is the form of worship articulating desire, inheritance of the God of Israel is its substance, satisfying desire, the promised land of rest from war. "Behold, the tabernacle of God is among the people, and He will dwell among them, and they shall be His people, and God Himself will be among them, and He will wipe away every tear from their eyes; and there will no longer be any death; there will no longer be any mourning, or crying, or pain; the first things have passed away" (Rev. 21:3–4 NASB). The sacrificial cult of Israel by its very nature points beyond itself to the reign of God as sign to thing signified. While Levitical ministry is distributed throughout the inheritances of the tribes in the ancient land of Canaan, these inheritances are themselves rich signs of an inheritance that is in heaven and yet to come on the earth, when the will of God is done in principle, in power, and in fullness.

In this interim between the already and the not yet, the Levitical ministry signifies for Origen the theological vocation of those special priests among the priestly people of God who are ordained to minister to the word and sacraments by which the cult forms and continually reforms the culture of the people of God in the world as yet unredeemed: "Few persons, exceedingly rare, who give attention to wisdom and to knowledge, keep their minds clean and pure, and cultivate normal virtues for their souls. Through the influence of teaching, they can illumine the way for the other more simple ones to walk and arrive at salvation. These persons are probably designated here under the name of Levites and priests, whose heritage is said to be the Lord himself, with his wisdom, which they dearly loved above all other things."[3] Origen knows that "divine discourse"— that is, scripture—"and the reading may become tedious to hearers if it does not receive an explanation."[4] But even for theologians who pastor by teaching, whose calling it is to explain the difficult and dark passages of the scriptures so that they

---

3. Origen, *Homilies on Joshua*, 159–60.
4. Origen, *Homilies on Joshua*, 174.

lead to salvation, this is a taxing discipline. Even those who are theologians by vocation "may not reject [dark passages], even if we do not understand them."[5] *Lectio divina*, Origen says, reveals "a certain strength in Holy Scripture that may avail the reader, even without explanation."[6] In any case, also for the theologian, "the aid of God is truly necessary in order to be able to explain these things, and it is utterly impossible for any humans to discourse about these things unless enlightened by the grace of God."[7] The illumination worked by the Holy Spirit in "all the individual teachers of the churches" turns "the letter of the law into gospel speech and discussion."[8] In the Spirit they understand the words of the Spirit, kindling light in the darkness. To be sure, this is an ongoing task on the gospel's way through the world.

Specific distributions to the half-tribe of Manasseh, Reuben, and Gad are now recounted. In 13:21–22 the narrator mentions Israel's slaying of the "dukes" of Sihon as well as Balaam, the soothsayer (cf. Num. 22–24, 31). Joshua 13:32 summarizes the Transjordan territory as the plains of Moab on the other side of the Jordan, east of Jericho.

5. Origen, *Homilies on Joshua*, 177.
6. Origen, *Homilies on Joshua*, 178.
7. Origen, *Homilies on Joshua*, 179–80.
8. Origen, *Homilies on Joshua*, 181.

THE CISJORDAN

14:1–5

In 14:1 the Hebrew verb for "to possess" and "to inherit" (*nakhal*) is the same, and so the translation here is a matter of interpretation. Obviously, not all possessions are inherited and inheritances can be alienated or otherwise lost from possession. Nelson leans toward the sense of possession; he gives these passages the genre-title "land grant narrative," and he tends therefore to assimilate the sense of "inheritance" to possession in that the distributions here recounted are intended, in his historical-critical reconstruction, to justify contested land tenure in the postexilic situation by pointing back to an endowment by an authorized figure (such as Joshua or Caleb) or to another ancestor. Accordingly, these passages in the book of Joshua set forth a legal case that legitimates the claim to ownership. In the postexilic situation, Nelson envisions the remnant of Israel thereby laying claim to disputed territory. One way to test this hypothesis, at least on a literary level, is simply to ask how solid a case for land tenure is actually accomplished in what follows.

Mentioned for the first time in the canonical book of Joshua is Eleazar the priest, who partners with Joshua along with the heads of the tribal households for the distribution of the "land of Canaan," the Cisjordan in distinction from the Transjordan previously discussed; it is, indeed, the land west of the Jordan that denotes the promised land, properly speaking. Eleazar "is undoubtedly, among other things, the representative of priests and Levites." His appearance here "reinforces the importance of priests and Levites in the book of Joshua,"[1] going back to the procession of the ark of the covenant across the Jordan, the

---

1. Pitkänen, *Joshua*, 277.

parade around Jericho, and thence the progress to Shechem for the covenant ceremony and, as most recently mentioned, the dispersal of the tribe of Levi throughout the tribes that they may sustain the cult of YHWH, cultivating thereby the soul of the new culture. The implicit distinction here between Israel settling to the west of the Jordan and the two and a half tribes that settle to its east will fester into the potentially volatile dispute considered at the end of the book of Joshua in chapter 22. The distinction already here figures the relation of Jews living in the territory of ancient Canaan to the Jews in diaspora living beyond the geographical boundaries of the promised land in the postexilic situation.

The distribution will take place by lot, as YHWH commanded Moses. Ostensibly, the boundaries are "the result of YHWH's gracious guidance."[2] We are reminded again by the mention of Moses how he had given the two and a half tribes their inheritance on the eastern side of the Jordan while he had given no inheritance of land to the Levites. Two of these tribes, Manasseh and Ephraim, descended from the sons of Joseph. Levites, however, were not given land of their own but rather cities to live in throughout Israel, yet with access to common pastures for their livestock. Despite assurance of divine guidance, in fact "tribes may occupy lands that they do not have claim to, and conversely tribes may claim lands that they do not occupy"[3]—an ambiguity accompanying all the coming accounts of land distribution.

As mentioned, the distribution proceeds in the acknowledgment that possession of the land has not yet been achieved. "All that Israel needs to do is trust in YHWH's promises. And Israel is to allot the land based upon this trust."[4] All this was commanded by YHWH through Moses, and all this the sons of Israel did when they apportioned the land. Calvin perceives the many anomalies within what follows and accordingly grasps the literary point figured in Caleb, whose inheritance is about to be described, that "he was contented with the mere promise of God, the true exercise of faith, consisting in a willingness to remain without the fruition of things which have been promised until they actually arrive."[5] Speaking of Calvin, I may note here that as commentator I too with him will "not be very exact in delineating the site of places, and in discussing names, partly because I admit that I am not well acquainted with topographical

2. Nelson, *Joshua*, 177.
3. Hawk, *Joshua*, 194–95.
4. Pitkänen, *Joshua*, 270.
5. John Calvin, *Book of Joshua* (North Charleston, SC: CreateSpace, n.d.), 179.

or chorographical science, and partly because great labor would produce little fruit to the reader; nay, perhaps the greater part of readers would toil and perplex themselves without receiving any benefit."[6] Yet one may wonder if this threat of perplexity in what follows were not already the case for the first readers of canonical Joshua!

6. Calvin, *Book of Joshua*, 177–78.

THE KENITE'S INHERITANCE

14:6–15

Joshua and Caleb were the two faithful spies according to the book of Numbers. Perhaps for that reason, "the Cisjordanian allotments are framed by the narrative about Caleb and Joshua's inheritances (14:6–15 and 19:49–50)."[1] Beginning with the story of Caleb, the Kenite's inheritance also serves to remind the reader of Rahab and the Gibeonites, for he too is of foreign origin. "The two parts of the story enclose the description of Judah's allotment, by far the most complete and detailed description of all the tribal territories."[2]

The descendants of Judah, now including adopted Caleb, a descendent of the foreigner Kenaz, approach Joshua. Caleb reminds Joshua of what YHWH said to Moses, the man of God, concerning the two of them in the wilderness at Kadesh-barnea. Caleb was forty years old when God's servant Moses sent him to spy out the land of Canaan, and when he returned, he reported to Moses with sincerity of heart. He spoke from his heart—but alas, his fellow spies on that mission terrorized the people of Israel when they reported on the fearsome inhabitants of Canaan, filled with the giant Anakim! In contrast to these doubting cowards, Caleb recounts, he fully followed YHWH his God. "Caleb's argumentation centers on the story of his loyalty."[3] Yet what is remarkable here is that zealous Caleb is another (semi-)foreigner, thus similar to Rahab, who has become integrated into the tribe of Judah by profession of faith. Caleb indeed follows YHWH with greater devotion than the native-born children of Israel.[4]

1. Pitkänen, *Joshua*, 279.
2. Hawk, *Joshua*, 195.
3. Nelson, *Joshua*, 178.
4. Hawk, *Joshua*, 198.

Moses swore on that day, Caleb continues, that the land Caleb had spied out, on which the soles of his feet had trod, would be an inheritance for him and his descendants forever. Forty-five years have passed. Caleb is now eighty-five years old. YHWH has kept him alive through all the wanderings and all the battles. Indeed, Caleb avows that he is as strong today as then and still ready for war—a wish shortly to be granted. Therefore Caleb concludes his appeal to Joshua to grant to him the hill country where the Anakim reside in great and inaccessible cities—"the very places that had intimidated his companions 40 years earlier!"[5] This precisely is the land on which the soles of his feet had then fallen. It may be, Caleb concludes, that YHWH is with him so that he will drive them out according to YHWH's word spoken to Moses concerning him. Upon hearing this, Joshua grants Hebron to him as an inheritance and pronounces a blessing. "Here Joshua's power-laden blessing provides a positive answer to Caleb's modest but hopeful 'perhaps' of the previous verse."[6]

And so Hebron became the inheritance of Caleb and his descendants to the present day, the narrator tells us; the reason is that he fully followed after YHWH, the God of Israel. Previously the name of Hebron was taken from the name of the greatest of the Anakim, but it became the inheritance of Caleb. And so the land grew silent from the din of battle—words spoken in anticipation of Caleb's yet to be accomplished defeat of the remaining Anakim in Hebron. Origen thinks that the name Hebron means "union" or "marriage" and deploys the etymology to express the "double becoming" of God as Israel's God and of Israel as God's beloved, akin to a marital union and frequent metaphor for the covenant. This "double becoming" he transfers also to his Gentile Christian: "Would that the share of Abraham and of Isaac and Jacob might also be given to me, and that my God might become mine, just as he became 'the God of Abraham and the God of Isaac and the God of Jacob,' in Christ Jesus our Lord, 'to whom is the glory and the dominion forever and ever. Amen!'"[7]

5. Hawk, *Joshua*, 197.
6. Nelson, *Joshua*, 179.
7. Origen, *Homilies on Joshua*, 167.

THE TERRITORY OF JUDAH
AND ITS SATELLITES

15:1–17:18

The imperative of reading the book of Joshua from the ironic perspective of the postexilic faithful—those who had been dispossessed from the land which they once possessed by dispossessing the Canaanites—is reinforced by the arrangement as well as content given to the distribution of the inheritances of the remaining tribes that occupies chapters 13–19. This becomes abundantly clear in the very ordering of the material. Hitherto, the progress of the ark of the covenant had been to the north, and its ultimate residence was taken at Shiloh/Shechem, likewise in the north; these are the territories that would become at length the northern kingdom of Israel in distinction from the southern kingdom of Judah. But here in Josh. 15 at the beginning of the allocation of territory to the remaining tribes by Joshua and Eleazar the priest along with the elders of Israel in premonarchic times, it is the tribe of Judah that predominates in sequence, in description, and in detail.[1] "Judah is preferred to all others."[2] This too constitutes evidence for the postexilic *Sitz im Leben* of canonical Joshua.

This literary predominance of Judah is more than, perhaps other than, a historical remembrance of Joshua's time. To be sure, "Judah's prominence here also reflects his prominence in a number of places in Genesis (including Gen. 49:8–12)."[3] But here, as the commentary will show, preeminence appears as Judah seems to be the chief survivor from among the twelve tribes after the devastations

1. Pitkänen, *Joshua*, 286.
2. Calvin, *Book of Joshua*, 178.
3. Pitkänen, *Joshua*, 297.

of the Assyrian and Babylonian conquests centuries later than the ostensible time of Joshua. Judah's inheritance is elaborated not only first in order but also more richly in detailed description and in geographical extent. Its territory, with its virtual absorption of the surrounding territories of Simeon, Manasseh, and Benjamin, takes pride of place in the presentation of the book of Joshua.

Narratively, this differentiation is marked by a shift in location back to the north, after the distribution to Judah, for the allocations to the remaining tribes in an assembly of all Israel at Shiloh in 18:1. It is also evident in the contrasting vagueness and lack of detail in the boundary descriptions of the northern tribes in comparison to the abundance of detail for the southern tribes, even though in the south too there is plenty of difficulty in making sense of the boundary descriptions. With Calvin,[4] as mentioned above, this commentator also leaves these historical perplexities and geographical difficulties to the detective work of the biblical scholars. For our theological purposes, it suffices to survey these chapters sufficiently to lift up their ironic function proclaiming YHWH who fights for the remnant of Israel as for those who have lost the land on account of covenant infidelity and who now struggle to rebuild on a fragment of it in hope against hope of future fulfillment.

The "lot" (cf. 16:1; 17:1; 18:11; 19:1, 10, 17, 24, 32, 40) for Judah was *not* determined, as it were, by Lady Luck in a throw of the dice. The lot was a method for taking the decision out of human hands and putting it into the hands of God. Such "casting of lots" is explicitly noted for the distribution to the northern tribes (18:10). But apparently Judah and the Josephites receive their inheritances by the decree of Moses (14:2) or the commandment of YHWH to Joshua (15:13; 17:4). Judah not only comes first but also receives by explicit divine decree the largest allotment of land, reaching south to the wilderness, east to the boundary with Edom, and west as far as the Wadi of Egypt to end at the Mediterranean Sea, drawing a line forming the southern border. The eastern border runs along the Mediterranean, and the northern border runs from there to the bay of the Dead Sea at the mouth of the Jordan. The detailed descriptions of the boundary lines, however, are beyond geographical reconstruction as almost all the place names provided are unknown to us today.[5] Manifestly, such boundary descriptions are incapable of serving as a word of God spoken also to us today, as Calvin acknowledges: "The object of defining the countries by their boundaries was to

4. Calvin, *Book of Joshua*, 164.
5. Pitkänen, *Joshua*, 290–97.

give a better display of the divine power by setting forth their extent; but this of course was only for those to whom their site was known. Hence, for anyone not acquainted with the geography to dwell upon the names, would be vain and foolish curiosity."[6]

Scholars distinguish between this boundary description in 15:1–12 and the list of towns given in 15:20–62, which "represents a reality somewhat different,"[7] to which we will return. For the present consideration of Judah's boundary description, Nelson lifts up a postexilic concern evident in this material. He observes that the narratives betray how "land grants often resulted from attempts to solve problems and disputes (v. 19; 17:3, 14–18). This indicates that even in the foundational period, YHWH's gift of the land was to some degree provisional and required a continuing struggle on the part of the people to realize it completely (v. 16; 17:18)."[8] If that provision had been true "already" at the beginning, how much more true was it now after the end of political sovereignty and the accompanying loss of land title—painful reiteration of the "not yet"! The progress of the reign of God is not a linear advance as Christians sang in a hymn that became popular in America after World War II: "From victory unto victory his armies he shall lead, till every foe is vanquished and Christ is Lord indeed!" Faith ever formed in the crucibles of the exile and placed there under a heavy cross remains faith in the triumph of God for all of us who have lost our way; it is never faith in our own victories, over which we plaster blasphemously the sacred name of God by means of religious ideology.

Intervening in the descriptions now is one such "problem-solving, dispute-resolving" story regarding Caleb's inheritance, which is paralleled in Judg. 1:10–15. The reader is reminded that he was given the city of Hebron according to the commandment of YHWH to Joshua (not to Moses as previously). And so Caleb, the narrative tells, takes possession there from the three sons of Anak. From there Caleb goes against the inhabitants of Debir, previously named Kiriath-sepher. Caleb vows to give his daughter Achsah in marriage to whomever takes Kiriath-sepher. Othniel, brother to Caleb and uncle of Achsah, captures the place and is given Achsah in marriage. Calvin, incidentally, anticipating the moral of the charming twentieth-century musical *Fiddler on the Roof*, takes occasion here to inveigh against arranged and involuntary marriage: parents "are not permitted to exercise tyrannical power and to assign [daughters] to whatever husbands

6. Calvin, *Book of Joshua*, 155.
7. Nelson, *Joshua*, 185.
8. Nelson, *Joshua*, 189.

they think fit without consulting them. For while all contracts ought to be voluntary, freedom ought to prevail especially in marriage that no one may pledge faith against his will."[9] Well said, but in this case it appears that Achsah is not in any need of defense, either from a tyrannical father or a tyrannical husband. After they are married, Achsah asks Othniel to request better land from her father, Caleb. Such deference might pass unnoticed as patriarchal business as usual. Nonetheless, in the event it is she who, upon dismounting her donkey, straightway approaches her father, who asks her what she wants. Achsah says to him, "Give me a blessing, for the land you have given me is in the desert; give me also springs of water" (15:19 AT).

Terse as the narrative is, it is perplexing in that Achsah herself makes the very request she induced her husband to make.[10] But the literary point of this peculiarity is that her husband, Othniel, who won his bride as a warrior, now "remains little more than a bit player in the drama" while Achsah communicates "her force of character through action and speech."[11] In reaction to her initiative, Caleb, who gave stingily, now gives generously land with not one spring but two. The little episode connects back to the beginning of the book of Joshua. While the stories of Rahab and the Gibeonites in effect "seriously damage the ethic of ethnic separation . . . , the stories [of] Achsah and Zelophehad's daughters [see below] challenge Israel's social configuration in a different way. . . . If women possess land, women are also Israelites in the most fundamental sense."[12]

An extensive list of towns, sometimes with their place locations and sometimes including surrounding hamlets, is provided in 15:20–62, followed by a note in 15:63 that the children of Judah were not able to dispossess the Jebusites occupying Jerusalem. The narrator concludes this second account of the allotment of Judah, declaring that the Jebusites coexist with the children of Judah and Jerusalem "to this day," because at the time of Joshua Judah was not able to dispossess them. The text seems to be indicating that ethnic coexistence prevails in the city of peace and persists indefinitely—perhaps long after the city was seized by David centuries later and made his capital for the united kingdom.

With this explicit announcement of anomaly, Calvin begins to develop a theme he carries through to the end of his commentary, explaining the failure of the complete conquest. Failure occurs on account of the sloth of the children of

---

9. Calvin, *Book of Joshua*, 183.
10. Nelson, *Joshua*, 187–88.
11. Hawk, *Joshua*, 201.
12. Hawk, *Joshua*, 199.

Israel: "It was owing entirely to their own sluggishness that they did not make themselves masters of the city of Jerusalem. This they were not able to do; but their own torpor, their neglect of the divine command from the love of ease, were the real obstacles."[13] The opposite of desperate and frenetic activism, sloth has at root the sin of unfaith whose fruit is hopeless apathy: "Because they were not fully persuaded in their minds that God is true, [they] stifled his agency by their own sluggishness. . . . Induced by filthy lucre, they preserved those alive [for slaves] whom God doomed to destruction."[14] Calvin passes over here the brutality of the requisite slaughter that in the context of *ḥerem* warfare serves as the alternative to the lazy business of enslaving others. This is a potential blind spot in all theologies that stress that believers be not hearers of the word only, but doers also (Jas. 1:22)—that is, that take the obedience of faith not as the peculiar obedience that faith in divine promise is, but as a requisite human work, predicated on faith to be sure, subsequent to faith. Activism not deeply formed by patient contemplation readily mistakes its own fervor for the will of God, its own hands for God's work, and consequently becomes imperceptive of the hidden unfaith at work in attempting to bring in the kingdom by force—to make, as it were, faith come true. Theology slides into ideology.

David L. Stubbs helpfully comments in this connection that Israel, in preferring idols, is "willing to settle for less. For this reason, Israel's sin is best named sloth or even despair."[15] "Despair" is precisely right, as this concept detects the loss of faith hidden behind a busy activism that superficially attacks the sloth of others when it should instead kindle and nurture faith in those who despair with the indicative of God. Reasserting the imperative, however, to those in despair amounts to beating a dead horse. The present point is that one can also make an idol of one's election, which remains from beginning to end the fabulous work of the God of Israel and thus works upon humans as a profound "suffering of divine things"[16] in all who believe the gospel of YHWH who fights for us. Whether by the apathy of despair or by the pseudo-activism that in truth is slothful reliance on others to do one's own work (as in slavery), the loss of faith in God's indicative conduces to such self-aggrandizing and other-abusing misuse of God's imperative.

13. Calvin, *Book of Joshua*, 185.
14. Calvin, *Book of Joshua*, 195.
15. David L. Stubbs, *Numbers*, Brazos Theological Commentary on the Bible (Grand Rapids: Brazos, 2009), 130.
16. Reinhard Hütter, *Suffering Divine Things: Theology as Church Practice* (Grand Rapids: Eerdmans, 1999).

The persistence of the Jebusites in Jerusalem also gives Origen occasion to discourse about the persistence of sin in the ecclesial life of the redeemed, although from a different angle than Calvin: "Even here in Jerusalem—that is, in the Church—there are certain Jebusites who lead an ignoble and degenerate life.... For while the Church is on earth, it is not possible to cleanse it to such purity that neither an ungodly person nor any sinner seems to reside in it, where everyone is holy and blessed and no blot of sin is found in them."[17] Origen clarifies that he is speaking of "doubtful or secret sins." He maintains that "those who are clearly and plainly sinful" should be banned because they scandalize the community causing the little ones to stumble. Such backsliders "by their contradictions shatter our hearts." But in reality "even the one who bears fruit and grows in the faith is not able to exterminate the Canaanite, the very wicked seed, that accursed seed, that ever inconstant seed, always unsettled.... It is certain that a Canaanite always dwells within the one who bears fruit and grows; for the tumult of temptation never ceases from him."[18] Thus Origen resources his Pauline battle of the Spirit and the flesh in the life of the redeemed with its prototype in the thorny persistence of Canaanites within Israel, careful to explain that "we are not enjoined to demolish and to destroy the natural impulses of the soul but to purge, that is to purify," the soul by the Spirit's penetrating analysis of the wayward desires of the human heart.[19] The good earth of God's creation and the good body-and-soul upon it have been usurped by, and now groan under, the tyrannies of sin and death, sighing for their new creation even as they simultaneously sigh against the captivation of desire by these unclean forces. The earth and the bodies on it are the objects of divine and redeeming love and as such the field of battle between the Holy Spirit and the unclean spirits.

There is a revealing discrepancy from the parallel account in Judges of the failure to dislodge the Jebusites from Jerusalem. "It may be significant that Judah is blamed for the inability to conquer Jerusalem here, whereas Benjamin is blamed for it in Judges 1:21.... The book of Judges was written from a strong Judahite perspective. However..., the book of Joshua was in contrast written from an all-Israelite perspective."[20] Such a tension may also be detected within Joshua reflecting a differentiation between the "all-Israelite" sources the narrator employs

17. Origen, *Homilies on Joshua*, 185.
18. Origen, *Homilies on Joshua*, 186.
19. Origen, *Homilies on Joshua*, 192.
20. Pitkänen, *Joshua*, 297.

and his own perspective as a postexilic Judahite, supporting "the central role of the tribe's heirs in YHWH's plan."[21]

We have here, if that is right, the biblical origins, but also limits, of Zionism as a theology. For Jewish theology, the geographical promise of the land centered on Mount Zion does not expire after the land of Canaan once given to the twelve tribes has been lost, nor also after the loss of Jerusalem and the destruction of the temple there in the first century—though of course that is beyond the historical horizon of canonical Joshua. The diaspora of Israel's remnant cannot in any case be permanent. Someday the scattered children of Israel must be returned to Zion as the place in which YHWH has caused his name to dwell. As Wyschogrod explains, YHWH "chose to elect a biological people that remains elected even when it sins. . . . If secular Zionism was sin because it rejected God as the source of Jewish redemption, it was the sin of the elect because, however secular its rationale, it was the longing for the holy soil of Israel. Even in sin, Israel remains in the divine service because the spiritual circumcision that has been carried out on this people 'is indelible.'"[22] So also another "Israelite, a descendent of Abraham, a member of the tribe of Benjamin," affirmed, "God has not rejected his people whom he foreknew" (Rom. 11:1–2), so that eschatologically "all Israel will be saved; as it is written, 'Out of Zion will come the Deliverer'" (11:26). A modest Christian Zionism may be articulated theologically on this basis.

The inheritance of Ephraim is described in 16:1–10, though the description of the territory is particularly hard to understand, difficult even to translate, and many of the site identifications are uncertain.[23] This chaos is striking; in "contrast to the coherence and completeness of Judah's section, . . . that concerning the tribes of Joseph is incomplete, confused, and fragmented."[24] This literary mishmash, however, mirrors "the fragmented makeup of Joseph itself"[25] as the two tribes of the sons of Joseph, Ephraim and Manasseh (with half of Manasseh, to boot, having settled on the far side of the Jordan), contend for full and equal allotments with the other tribes, although ostensibly these tribes are stemmed from nephews, not equals to the other brothers/uncles constituting the twelve tribes.[26]

21. Nelson, *Joshua*, 193.

22. Michael Wyschogrod, *The Body of Faith: God in the People Israel* (Lanham, MD: Rowman & Littlefield, 1996), 184.

23. Nelson, *Joshua*, 195.

24. Hawk, *Joshua*, 203.

25. Hawk, *Joshua*, 204.

26. Nelson, *Joshua*, 201.

The allotment for the sons of Joseph begins at the juncture of Jericho and the Jordan River, and from there goes on into the eastern desert through the hill country to Bethel and then downhill through the territory of the Archites and then the Japhletites and beyond, ending at the sea. Mention of the anomalous Archites and Japhletites draws attention "to the presence of peoples of indigenous or uncertain origin."[27] So Manasseh and Ephraim receive their inheritance. The border of Ephraim according to clans follows, including some towns with their satellite villages within the territory of Manasseh that are set apart for the Ephraimites. Here we may note a common phenomenon in what follows: "urban islands belonging to one tribe within the general territory of another."[28]

As mentioned at the end of the account of Judah's inheritance, candid acknowledgment is made here too concerning the failure of the Ephraimites to disinherit the Canaanites dwelling in Gezer, where instead, so it is claimed, these Canaanites have been made slaves to do forced labor. But this terse notice is embarrassing; it "only begs the question. Why didn't they exterminate them as Moses commanded?"[29] How can they have made slaves of alien peoples when precisely such human use of them as slaves is what is forbidden by herem warfare? Calvin captures this anomaly perfectly: "But their disgraceful sloth is more clearly expressed and their culpability greatly heightened by the fact that they made tributaries of those with whom it was not lawful to enter into any kind of arrangement. . . . The Ephraimites sin much more grievously by exacting tribute than if they had tolerated them without paction."[30]

More broadly, the confusion in representation, which is in fact evident here by literary analysis alone, should cause us to recognize how the tribal system was "an idealized simplification which was ideologically superimposed over a much more complex reality of kinship structures and political arrangements."[31] But if that is the case, the book of Joshua's accounts of the land distribution have little to do with an attempt to reestablish land title where none had ever existed in reality. What then? "Readers of the book of Joshua in its final form . . . would have found the theme of Israel's incomplete conquest significant. . . .

27. Hawk, *Joshua*, 205.
28. Nelson, *Joshua*, 197.
29. Hawk, *Joshua*, 207.
30. Calvin, *Book of Joshua*, 189–90. Interestingly, the LXX substitutes the statement about the failure of the Ephraimites with a totally different data point: "until Pharaoh the king of Egypt came up and took it and burned it in fire and massacred those Canaanites and Philistines who lived in Gaza, and gave it as a dowry for his daughter." This alternative rendering may be derived from 1 Kgs. 9:15–16.
31. Nelson, *Joshua*, 197.

Even Joshua had to concede some political realities. . . . Imposed forced labor ([16:]10), Israel's increasing strength (17:13), and the forecast that Israel would eventually dispossess the Canaanites (17:18) point readers beyond their present ambiguous situation to faith in the ultimate success of YHWH's people."[32] As with Hawk, so also with Nelson we find a tendency to supplant here knowledge of God with religious ideology; ecclesiology swallows up the messianism/inchoate Christology of the book of Joshua. Against this one has to press the question, What counts as "success" with respect to the earth usurped by anti-divine powers? Ecclesiastical turf? Land title?

With this question we arrive at a juncture at which Jewish and Christian readings of the text diverge. Christian theology has not traditionally endorsed the chiliastic hope to "restore the kingdom to Israel" (Acts 1:6), and the reappearance of chiliasm in the nineteenth- and twentieth-century dispensational theologies of American evangelicalism is fraught, in all the more acute form, with the problems previously discussed regarding "salvation history." Nothing prevents, however, post-Holocaust Christian theology from seeing the modern establishment of a homeland for the Jewish people in the state of Israel as a token of the restoration of all the suffering creation to the reign of YHWH who fights for that eschatological Israel of God in which there is no longer circumcision nor uncircumcision. As Origen bluntly puts it for the Christian reading, "Earthly inheritance ceases now that the inheritance of the kingdom of heaven was revealed."[33] Like the Jewish messianic hope, however, the Christian eschatological hope is for the coming of the heavenly kingdom to this earth on which the cross of Jesus stood. In either case, such faith disinflates enthusiastic religious ideologies accompanying modern Zionism.

The western inheritance of the half tribe of Manasseh is described in 17:1–13. "The main point to bear in mind regarding this chapter is that the amount of information is clearly less than for Judah in Chapter 15."[34] True so far as it goes, but the anecdote it contains about the daughters of Zelophehad merits theological attention. Manasseh was the firstborn son of Joseph who begat Machir, the father of Gilead, the man of war, to whom fittingly are allotted Gilead and Bashan. The rest of the male descendants of Manasseh receive allotments for their families. The sex of the descendants is mentioned here because inheritance was customarily passed through the male line. But a descendent by the name of

32. Nelson, *Joshua*, 197–98.
33. Origen, *Homilies on Joshua*, 158.
34. Pitkänen, *Joshua*, 304, 306.

Zelophehad had no sons but only daughters, by name Mahlah, Noah, Hoglah, Milcah, and Tirzah. These women approach Eleazar and Joshua and the other leaders, invoking YHWH's commandment to Moses in Num. 27:1–11 that they be given an inheritance in the midst of their brothers.[35] Indeed, the text of Num. 27:8 generalizes a rule from the incident: "If a man dies, and has no son, then you shall pass his inheritance on to his daughter."

Nelson's commentary here exaggerates what according to Numbers was standard operating procedure into a remarkable departure from the patriarchy: "It is remarkable that in making this land claim Israel's patriarchal culture . . . here preserves a 'memory' of mothers and daughters."[36] A deeper departure from "the patriarchy" might be sought and found, however, in questioning the very notion of title to land. In any case, in this passage of the book of Joshua as it is written, inheritance in the midst of the brothers of their father was given to the daughters of Zelophehad without much fuss and according to the word of YHWH. We should see that this ruling and its fulfillment in practice, like much else in Joshua, is not a patriarchal "memory" but an exilic aspiration. "The daughters thus personify what Achsah anticipates, that 'Israel' cannot be identified fundamentally in male terms only."[37] That is, the understanding of Israel in turn is clarified as naming not an ethnicity, let alone a land, but the beloved *community of God*.

Gilead and Bashan bequeathed to Manasseh, we are now told, are on the other side of the Jordan, so now ten portions of land fall to Manasseh, since the daughters have received an inheritance among the sons of Manasseh. The rest of Manasseh's sons are allotted the land of Gilead. It is impossible to sort out these places. Border description of the western territory now follows, which is said to intersect or even overlap with territory allotted to Ephraim, Asher, and Issachar. Once again the narrator concludes this description of Manasseh's territory declaring that the sons of Manasseh could not dispossess the Canaanite inhabitants of cities assigned to Manasseh even though they were on the territory of Issachar. Rather, when the sons of Israel gained strength, they enslaved these Canaanites rather than taking possession of their land, emulating the sinful violation of *ḥerem* by the Ephraimites in a practice that seems to be becoming habitual.

A protest of the tribe of Joseph is recorded in 17:14–18. The narrative suddenly reverts from discussion of the two tribes of Ephraim and Manasseh to the (one) tribe of Joseph—that is, their father and the brother of the other eleven

35. Nelson, *Joshua*, 202.
36. Nelson, *Joshua*, 202.
37. Hawk, *Joshua*, 209n61.

fathers of the twelve tribes of Israel, all the sons of Jacob. Here we are told that "Joseph started out with but one lot ... [but] in the end Joseph ended up with more than a single lot by wresting territory from the forests and the Canaanites."[38] What accounts for this odd divergence from the predominant schematization? Envy among the brothers of Joseph long before had incited them to sell their brother, favored son of Jacob, into slavery. Now Joseph's descendants are gripped with envy as they watch the apportionment proceed with such generosity toward Judah and the others, even though it came by the decree of YHWH as mediated by Moses and Joshua. They now object, appealing to experience over against the word of God: "Has not YHWH richly blessed this tribe and made it a great people—too great for just one lot for one of the smaller portions of the land of Canaan?" (17:14 paraphrased). In reply to the protest, Joshua hoists the Josephite protesters by their own petards.

Let us grant the premise of your complaint, Joshua replies, that you are a great people because YHWH has blessed you. If so great and blessed, Joshua continues, go beyond the territory allotted in the hill country to where the Perizzites and the giants dwell and clear the wooded land there for you to farm and to graze. The disappointed Josephites dispute with Joshua, saying that the forest hill country is in any case not big enough, while the valley lands below are occupied by Canaanites who have iron chariots at their disposal. We are outgunned! Yet Joshua "turns their own words against them."[39] Joshua concludes the dispute by pronouncing his judgment on the basis of the premise of the Josephites: "You are indeed a great and powerful people, so you will not receive only one lot. Therefore the wooded hill country to the farthest borders will also be yours—to clear the land and dispossess the Canaanites, notwithstanding their superior military power in the chariots of iron" (17:17–18 paraphrased).

In sum, thus far "the heritage of each tribe has been presented as incomplete, marred by foreign holdouts. ... [However,] Joshua leaves the impression that progress was being made."[40] Already/not yet!

---

38. Nelson, *Joshua*, 204.
39. Nelson, *Joshua*, 204.
40. Nelson, *Joshua*, 205.

CASTING LOTS AT SHILOH FOR THE SEVEN REMAINING TRIBES

18:1–19:51

Movement of the tribes from Gilgal to Shiloh initiates the action. Now all Israel gathers north to Shiloh to finish the apportionment. As Calvin detects, "these words intimate that up to that time the ark was pilgrimating . . . [until at length] Mount Zion was set apart for the temple." Pointing to Jer. 7:12, Calvin confirms that the initial placement of the cult of YHWH was in Shiloh.[1] Themes accordingly associated with the Priestly tradition, harkening back to the Levitical procession bearing the ark of the covenant from the beginning of the book of Joshua, now reappear in fullness. The text reflects "a compositional perspective similar to that of the priestly writing," beginning with the assembly of the community at the tent of meeting.[2] "The Tent of Meeting was the 'house' of YHWH, where he dwelt in the midst of the people of Israel (Exod. 29:43–45)."[3] Thus "chapters 18–19 form a unit held together by the brackets of 18:1 and 19:51 (Shiloh, tent of meeting) and by the general topic of the seven remaining tribes."[4]

Shiloh will henceforth be the place of assembly of all Israel where the tent of meeting is erected on land that has been "subdued" (*nikhbesha*). This is the same verb that is employed in the mandate to the human couple created in the image of God for likeness to God according to Gen. 1:28 (also a text associated with the Priestly tradition). There the "subduing" of the earth refers to the dominion

---

1. Calvin, *Book of Joshua*, 201.
2. Nelson, *Joshua*, 209.
3. Pitkänen, *Joshua*, 312.
4. Nelson, *Joshua*, 206.

over it that the human couple exercise in partnership under God in accord with the revealed blessing on humanity and the divine mandate of the living God in heaven and on earth; as we have seen, however, this subduing has become in the book of Joshua not only a "settling" of the land in perpetual stewardship—that is, domesticating the wilderness by clearing the land for human cultivation as Joshua just exhorted the Josephites. Now truly human dominion has also become rescue and redemption of the good earth from usurpers who would exploit it. Human subduing of the earth is a subset of YHWH's dominion. YHWH, overthrowing the usurpers, is now settling into the land of Canaan to bring about the new creation that is Israel settled on the land in a state of shalom.[5] This settlement is a messianic sign of YHWH's intended destiny for the whole earth.

Looking ahead, "Joshua 22 implies that the writer of Joshua thought that Shiloh was an exclusive place of worship at that time. Deuteronomy, chapter 12 in particular, speaks about an exclusive place for sacrifices"[6]—a concern for the cultic unity of the tribes by way of a single central place for sacrifice. This concern for true unity at the heart of culture, where desires are formed socially, will return with near vengeance in blood in Josh. 22, when the troops of the eastern tribes, returning across the Jordan to their allotments, pause to build what is to all appearances a rival altar. Certainly from a postexilic Judahite perspective, Shiloh could be viewed as the legitimate antecedent of the temple in Jerusalem. As the place of the tent of meeting where the ark was normally housed (Exod. 26:34), Shiloh at that time long ago represented an exclusive all-Israel worship (cf. Josh. 22:9–34). Looking down the narrative pathway, moreover, "the loss of the ark at the battle of Aphek (1 Sam. 4) was interpreted as YHWH's rejection of Shiloh. Conversely, the entry of the ark into Jerusalem [by the hand of David] signaled the election of the town by YHWH."[7] So these chapters, which detail the once-upon-a-time allotments to the northern tribes, are framed by concerns for the exclusive location of all-Israel worship, even though they center on Shiloh to the north rather than on the as yet unconquered Jerusalem to the south.

The purpose of the assembly at Shiloh is to finish the allotment of land to the "less important" seven remaining tribes in the north. The allotments here "are all smaller than those of the principal three tribes," the two Josephites, Manasseh and Ephraim, and Judah, and are "all approximately the same size."[8] But the assembly

---

5. Wendell Berry, *The Unsettling of America: Culture and Agriculture* (Berkeley: Counterpoint, 2015).
6. Pitkänen, *Joshua*, 312.
7. Pitkänen, *Joshua*, 56.
8. Nelson, *Joshua*, 207.

of Israel at Shiloh begins with a rebuke by Joshua, who asks the assembly what they are waiting for before going out to take possession of the land that YHWH, God of their fathers, has given to them. For the first time, a reason is provided for the failure of Israel already under Joshua fully to inherit the earth, which theologically is already theirs by the assured and continually reassured promise God gave to their fathers, vouchsafed by all that Israel has witnessed hitherto in the narrative course of the book of Joshua. The sons of Israel are *lazy*—and without excuse! Here Calvin's diagnosis of sloth finds a textual warrant. The tribes must be prodded into action by Joshua's exhortation that they become what already they are, with the imperative of the indicative. As we shall see, however, Joshua prods to no avail. Something deeper than sloth hinders them.

Calvin sees this role of the imperative grounded in the indicative as a stick to awaken the slothful from slumber. Throughout his commentary he has anticipated Joshua's diagnosis of sloth here, and now he accentuates it: "It is easy to infer from [Joshua's] speech that they had shown great alacrity at the outset, but that there had been no perseverance. . . . [But] by their delays [they] retard and suspend the effect of the divine goodness."[9] Generally Calvin holds that the will of the Lord is irresistible, yet he is quick, by a felicitous inconsistency, to acknowledge that the unfaith operative in slothful disobedience is somehow humanly able to resist the divinely irresistible. In that case, however, one wonders whether the stick of the indicative can resupply a motivating faith that is lacking. Origen has a rather different explanation of sloth even in the new generation of liberated Israel, taking sloth as a figure of "the horrible power of a demon": "Many prayers are employed, many fasts, and many invocations of exorcists. Yet deaf to all these things, the demon remains and persists in the possessed body and prefers to endure the punishments of the exorcists and the torments applied to it when the name of God is invoked, rather than to depart from the person whom it shamelessly and miserably besets."[10] By this figure, Origen hints at a deeper well of resistance at work in human sloth than the stick of the imperative can fathom or prod.

Joshua in any case takes the initiative to organize the irresolute tribes and prod them back into motion for the fulfillment of their mission in advancing the reign of YHWH over the land. Addressing the failure, Joshua conscripts three men from each tribe to be sent out to survey the land that remains and to write a

9. Calvin, *Book of Joshua*, 200–201.
10. Origen, *Homilies on Joshua*, 205.

description of it with a view to its allotment for the remaining tribal inheritances. And then they are to report back to Joshua.

With Judah and the descendants of Joseph already apportioned on the west of the Jordan, the remaining land is to be subdivided into seven lots for the remaining seven tribes. With descriptions of the territory in hand from the return of the scouting mission, Joshua will then cast lots in the presence of YHWH their God (usually a task of the priests, thus the addition of Eleazar at the conclusion of the allocations in 19:51) to distribute the seven lots to the seven tribes. Joshua reminds the assembly that the Levites have no allotment since the priesthood is their inheritance. Moreover, Gad, Reuben, and the half tribe of Manasseh also have already received their inheritance from Moses, the servant of YHWH, to the east of the Jordan. The distribution to Judah and its satellites is presupposed. So informed, the surveying team sets out under Joshua's charge that they describe the land and return for the casting of lots before YHWH in Shiloh.[11]

Origen devotes an entire homily to the matter of the lottery, perturbed by the apparently crude identification of fate or Lady Luck, seemingly represented by the lottery, with revelation of the will of God. After a wide-ranging survey of the lottery in the scriptures, he comes to the conclusion that "when prayer preceded, it was no longer by chance but by Providence that the lot announced divine judgment."[12] Citing the prophecy in Deut. 32 about the destinies of the twelve tribes, Origen holds forth on the predestination of God manifested in the lottery results: "Not even for a single one of us does anything come to pass except by a lot of this kind that is dispensed by the judgment of God. For example, each of us, immediately from birth, draws by lot this or that kind of life . . . that has been directed by a certain mystic dispensation of Christ."[13] This crucial reference to Christ indicates that divine governance of the world from macro level to micro level is less a foreordained prescription necessitating events than a foreordained intention to sum up all things in Christ, including even, according to Origen, the names given for places and persons in scripture—rich fodder in these chapters as elsewhere for those willing to work at unraveling the mysteries of Christ they contain.

Dietrich Bonhoeffer makes a similar point in his posthumous *Ethics* when he argues that (1) the so-called orders of creation are not to be taken as fixed institutions serving as bulwarks against historical change but rather as dynamic

11. Nelson, *Joshua*, 209.
12. Origen, *Homilies on Joshua*, 197.
13. Origen, *Homilies on Joshua*, 199.

and enduring creative mandates for humanity to fill the earth, subdue it, and have dominion over it, but (2) in a fallen world these orders of creation become orders of preservation resisting the avarice of the usurpers of the earth.[14] They have no autonomous authority, as the German Christians imagine in regarding an innovative "racial order" as revelation of God. Rather, the biblical mandates of sexual union in procreation, labor and economy, and government are issued for humanity to serve God's purpose insofar as they are subordinated to the reign of the risen Christ in the ongoing work, as we may say in the idiom of the book of Joshua, of usurping the usurpers of the earth. This more dynamic and Christocentric understanding of divine providence provides an alternative to Calvin's rather rigid insistence on fixed institutional authorities, as we have seen, especially in government. So Bonhoeffer reasoned his participation in the Rahab-like conspiracy to betray the tyrant.

For postexilic readers of Joshua, however, the account of the allotment by lottery to the northern tribes, which have since virtually disappeared from history, would bear witness that "national identity somehow still encompasses the 'all Israel' of past tradition."[15] The scouts accomplish their mission, describing the seven sections by the cities in it. And so it happens that Joshua begins to cast lots for the seven tribes in Shiloh and divides the land for them. "Benjamin comes first as centrally located and closest to Judah; then Simeon again because of its significance for Judah. The four Galilee tribes follow as more distant in space and Dan as more distant in time."[16] Even in the northern allotment Judah remains tacitly the hub of the wheel; we now follow the final distributions of territory, like spokes radiating outward from the hub.

The inheritance of Benjamin is told in 18:11–28 in significant detail.[17] Its territory lies between the allotments to Judah and Ephraim, forming a kind of no man's land between what would later become the northern kingdom of Israel and the southern kingdom of Judah. The level of detail in the boundary description correlates with Benjamin's nearness to these preeminent tribes. Next are listed the cities of Benjamin. The archaic name Jebus is included and then explained to be the previous name of Jerusalem. The overlapping or fluctuating state of the boundaries, detailed as they are in the case of Benjamin, is evident in 18:21–24, which lists "Benjaminite towns which were once part of the kingdom of Israel

14. Dietrich Bonhoeffer, *Ethics*, ed. Eberhard Bethge (New York: Macmillan 1978), 286–91.
15. Nelson, *Joshua*, 209.
16. Nelson, *Joshua*, 207.
17. Pitkänen, *Joshua*, 311.

and then of the Assyrian province of Samaria, but eventually were included into an expanded Judah presumably at the time of Josiah."[18] So Benjamin is described by its relevance for Judah. "As with Judah, the allotment of Benjamin communicates fullness, order, and coherence. The reader is therefore not prepared for the disordered and fragmented presentation of the last six allotments."[19] As Calvin acutely notes, "All we have here is a compendious description of the division as it was taken from the general and confused notes of the surveyors."[20]

The inheritance of Simeon is sketched in 19:1–9. Continuing the radiation outward from the tacit center in the preeminent tribe of Judah, the allotment to Simeon comes next after Benjamin: an odd territory in the midst of Judah, lacking a boundary description, which is finally explained on the grounds that the portion allotted to Judah is too great for the tribe to occupy. The desert lands bordering the wilderness to the south are given to Simeon. The inheritances of Zebulun, Issachar, Asher, Naphtali, and Dan are sketched in 19:10–48. Now the allotment turns far to the north, first to Zebulun, which will in a later century provide the setting in Galilee for the ministry of Jesus. Its eastern border was the Sea of Galilee. Next, Issachar is sandwiched between Zebulun to the north and Manasseh to the south. The descriptions of the tribal territories are becoming progressively thinner. The allotment to Asher extends far north to the border with the great cities of Tyre and Sidon in Lebanon. Naphtali receives the land with Zebulun to the south and Asher to the west and the Jordan to the east. Fortified cities are mentioned here, including Hazor—which a reader of the book of Joshua might have thought had been accursed and left to ruin after being devoured by the flames of ḥerem. In 19:47 we are told that Dan abandoned its allotted borders in the south and migrated to the north to attack Leshem, which they then dispossessed of its inhabitants by the sword and settled, renaming the territory after their ancestor. This terse report leaves many questions, perhaps provoking the Septuagint to provide an alternative account;[21] apparently this same migration north by the Danites is more fully described in Judg. 17–18. But remarkably, here in Joshua, this "campaign of possession, the only one yet recorded in its entirety, occurs apart from any divine initiative or authorization. The land that Dan settles is not the

18. Nelson, *Joshua*, 214.
19. Hawk, *Joshua*, 217.
20. Calvin, *Book of Joshua*, 212.
21. The LXX has a lengthy passage not found in the MT that seems to say that while the Danites were oppressed in the south by the Amorites, it was the sons of Judah who waged war against Leshem and conquered it, while Ephraim suppressed the Amorites and extracted tribute from them. Cf. Nelson, *Joshua*, 225–26.

land allotted to it. . . . Dan succeeds in securing a tribal possession but does so apart from the system that legitimates its claim to the land. What then defines Israel and the land, occupation or claim?"[22] Or neither? In any case, the many incongruities attending the accounts of the final six allotments to the northern tribes imply theologically that "the tribes either do not carry the program to its completion or modify it to suit their own ends. . . . Inheritances, which define and organize Israel's life in the land, fail to do either completely."[23]

The inheritance of Joshua in 19:49–51 brings this section to a conclusion. The chapter concludes describing Joshua's inheritance, forming a parallel to his colleague in spying from the old days, Caleb the Kenite. When the allotment to the tribes is finished, the sons of Israel give to Joshua an inheritance in their midst. Upon hearing the voice of YHWH, they give to him the city he requested, Timnath-serah in the hill country of Ephraim. Joshua settles there and rebuilds the city after he and Eleazar the priest with the tribal heads have finished the division by lot of the tribal inheritances before YHWH at Shiloh—a process that began in 14:1.[24]

Origen notices that Joshua "did not presume for himself a portion of the inheritance, but he received it from the people." To the end, Joshua was among the people as one who served.[25] Calvin devotes an extended meditation here to Joshua, servant of YHWH in the making: he is the anti-Achan who did not covet for himself, and the anti-king who humbled himself to obedience and was thus exalted.

> He does not give any heed to his own interest till the commonweal has been secured. . . . [He] thinks not of himself till the land has been divided. . . . Joshua liberally obeyed the divine call, and had no mercenary feelings in undergoing so many labors, dangers, and troubles; but having spontaneously performed his duty, he behooves not to repudiate a memorial of the favor of God. . . . Truly no ambition can be detected here, inasmuch as he desires nothing for himself, and does not rashly act from a feeling of covetousness but seeks in the popular consent a confirmation of the honor which God had already bestowed upon him.[26]

When Christian readers contemplate the humility of the human Joshua, they see the divinity of the eternal Son who became a second Joshua, counting not equality

22. Hawk, *Joshua*, 218–19.
23. Hawk, *Joshua*, 219.
24. Nelson, *Joshua*, 226.
25. Origen, *Homilies on Joshua*, 206.
26. Calvin, *Book of Joshua*, 215.

with God something to be coveted, but humbling himself and becoming obedient to death, even death on a cross. In contemplating this "mind" of Christ, as the apostle calls it in Phil. 2, Christians come to have the same mind in them so that their activism is that of the earthly body of the risen Christ. The imperative "Have this mind in you that was in Christ Jesus" instructively reminds those with faith of the indicative, who is the obedient and exalted Christ in whom faith ever rests.

SANCTUARY

20:1–9

How, then, is Israel to live between the already and the not yet? "With this chapter," Nelson writes, "the direction of the book of Joshua returns from land apportionment to issues of how life in the land is to be lived," forming a bridge to the book's final three chapters. The new life of the meek who inherit the earth ends the cycle of violence triggered by unrestrained blood vengeance. Justice is to be administered representatively by "the elders at the gate" for both Israelite and alien (20:9). "Such fairness is achieved by adherence to divinely instituted governing structures" (20:1–2)[1]—one of the aforementioned mandates of creation displacing the unjust structures of malice emblemized in walled cities shut up tight, threatening to unleash their chariots of iron.

A tacit answer is thereby given to the conditions of life on the land between what YHWH has already accomplished and what remains to be accomplished: criminal killing will still occur, although for Israel any killing is the usurpation of the lifeblood that belongs to YHWH alone, Lord and giver of life. It is utopian presumption lacking eschatological reserve to imagine that Israel has already fully arrived into life under the reign of YHWH, and accordingly to disown or disregard the difficult ambiguities attendant on living between what YHWH has already done and painful longing for what YHWH has yet to do. In the fog and friction of the abiding tension between the already and the not yet, therefore, the community must learn to discriminate between hateful killing and unintentional killing—roughly, between murder and manslaughter. Interestingly, premeditation does not seem to be an independent factor in this discrimination: a spontaneous

---

1. Nelson, *Joshua*, 230.

crime of passion can count as hateful, and an intentional act can have unintended consequences. Restraint of "blood vengeance" is, in any case, only half the story; envisioned also are safeguards against gaming the system. "However, equally, someone who had murdered another person should not be spared and allowed to give the excuse that the killing was unintentional. A trial would help distinguish real claims from fraudulent ones."[2]

The acknowledgment of moral ambiguity is not tantamount to moral relativism. Nor is moral ambiguity only a matter of difficult discernment of human motives. Rather, moral ambiguity also reflects the conundrum of law divided against itself, which we have witnessed throughout the narrative course of the book of Joshua. Moral ambiguity arises when the moral law becomes divided against itself in issuing contrary judgments in a concrete case. As we have seen paradigmatically throughout the book of Joshua, *herem* requires extermination of all Canaanites, but covenant fidelity requires that some Canaanites be spared in certain circumstances. This is not a trivial contradiction inasmuch as *herem* figures the righteous wrath of the God of love and *hesed* figures the spontaneous mercy of the God of love. On the highest theological plane, these two often appear to be in tension, if not contradiction—how much more so on the level of human justice on the earth! Israel must live its new life on the land in the unabated tension between these two and thus always with a healthy sense of the moral ambiguity of its life by virtue of the persistence of sin also in the life of the redeemed.

These chapters tell "the completion of the program which defines Israel's inheritance but further complicate the organization signified by it."[3] Justice, this side of the unambiguous reign of YHWH on the earth in its glory and fullness, which will be the triumph of *hesed* with its politics of reconciliation over *herem* as a politics of purity, must deal with a notable, for community-threatening, ambiguity of living between the already and the not yet—namely, with cases of unintentional killing. This difficult but necessary distinction between observable behavior and unobservable intention is introduced by the inauguration of the reign of God, who does not judge superficially but searches and judges the heart; this distinction, indeed, is finally only possible before YHWH, the true critical thinker, not deceived by appearances, who sees in secret and knows in secret. But the task of such discernment is laid on Israel here as the covenant-partner people of God. It is a distinction already present in the summons of the book

2. Pitkänen, *Joshua*, 338.
3. Hawk, *Joshua*, 220.

of Deuteronomy for the circumcision of the human heart, which Jesus, in the Sermon on the Mount, takes up to expose the secrets of the heart to the piercing sight of his heavenly Father. Paul the apostle also takes up the theme when he observes that not all who are called Israelites are true Israelites. One should not falsely impute this divine exposure of the heart, the seat of the human self, as some repressive superego, the "introspective conscience of the West"[4] attributable to scrupulous monks like Augustine and Luther and their corresponding misreading of scripture. Rather, these giants of scriptural theology in the West learned from scripture to search and judge the heart. The real problem is this: Who on earth can judge the heart? And how is one sinner to judge another sinner?

Society between the times will achieve only a rough justice, and even this is predicated on institutions that interrupt endlessly recycling vengeance. This interruption forces a time and place for urgent but ever-precarious discrimination by the community. Thus, 'are hamiqlat (cities of refuge or asylum) are established. "The Levitical towns are first 'properly' introduced in Numbers 35:1–8 in the canonical context (and order), and the passage here in the book of Joshua provides a fulfillment of the stipulations in Numbers."[5] The themes from the Priestly tradition reintroduced in the preceding chapters thus continue in chapter 20, devoted to establishing a judicial framework to check the recycling of violence by taking judgment out of the hands of immediately offended near and dear ones. No one is to be the judge of their own case.[6] As mentioned, there is a relationship here to Deut. 19:1–13 and Num. 35:25, although the notion of asylum can be traced back to Exod. 21:12–14, where the idea is more "sanctuary" than refuge—that is, that the holiness of the sanctuary covers and protects those who flee to it from blood vengeance. In any case, "the literary relationship in Joshua 22:2 to the other texts about asylum cities remains problematic."[7] Specifically, the term "city of refuge" does not occur in Deuteronomy, nor does the extension of asylum rights to the "alien," while the Numbers text seems to be dependent on Joshua![8] But we can leave these difficulties to the biblical scholars.

YHWH now commands Joshua to fulfill another of the instructions he gave through the hand of Moses—that is, in the texts from Numbers and Deuteronomy.

---

4. Krister Stendahl, "The Apostle Paul and the Introspective Conscience of the West," *Harvard Theological Review* 56 (1963): 199–215.

5. Pitkänen, *Joshua*, 341.

6. Piotr J. Małysz, "*Nemo iudex in causa sua* as the Basis of Law, Justice and Justification in Luther's Thought," *Harvard Theological Review* 100, no. 3 (2007): 363–86.

7. Nelson, *Joshua*, 229.

8. Nelson, *Joshua*, 229; Pitkänen, *Joshua*, 336.

The presupposition to the commandment is the existing, as it were, common-law ethos of blood redemption[9] reflecting a social situation lacking supervening judicial institutions that enjoy wide public legitimacy. The Christian temptation here is simply to dismiss the law of retribution, the *lex talionis*, even though it negatively bears witness to equality in the value of human lives. But the holy love of YHWH is against what is against love; the law of retaliation is a matter of enforcing the equal value of human life before its Creator, as in the notorious maxim "An eye for an eye, a tooth for a tooth." The taking of blood from one created in God's image is not only a crime against the victim but also a sin against the victim's Creator and Redeemer, who alone has the right to take back the life he has given. Invoking the dignity of the human creature made in the image of God, Gen. 9:6 sanctions this redemption of blood by blood, further elaborated in Lev. 24:17–22. Such equal justice restores the social equilibrium disrupted by hateful murder. Thus the law of retribution enforces the equality of value in human lives; it provides a negative moral sanction and practical deterrence in support of the equality of human worth by requiring the blood of one who has intentionally shed the blood of a fellow creature made in the image of God for likeness to God.

Massive inequities in the application of capital punishment in contemporary societies call into question secular criminal justice systems of today, but do not touch on the underlying moral point here of the equal value of human blood before God the Creator. Indeed, when we grasp that the law of retribution intends equality before the law, the equality in value of human lives because of the preciousness of human life as created by God, we see that the Levitical cities of refuge represent for the most part a ferocious divine rebuke to the racial injustice and cruel hypocrisy of criminal justice systems in America today, especially in regard to the unequal application of capital punishment. Reform is not a matter of repudiating the *lex talionis* but a matter of rigorously and self-critically observing its principles of equality and the preciousness of life.

In the absence of judicial institutions that enjoy social legitimacy, a common-law obligation to redeem a victim's shed blood falls to family members who have been thus deprived of one of their own. In this light Josh. 20 projects an innovative distinction between manslaughter and hateful murder: the lesser crime of manslaughter applies to one who kills inadvertently or ignorantly. But there is,

---

9. Pitkänen, *Joshua*, 333. The Hebrew word, frequently translated as "avenger," is *goel*. which is sometimes also translated as "redeemer." The meanings overlap. Pitkänen, *Joshua*, 234.

as mentioned, a danger created with this distinction of gaming the new system. Anyone who would defend himself against the grievous charge of hateful murder by pleading accident or ignorance may flee to one of the designated "cities of refuge." "The idea here is that the killer is to be protected so that he can be brought to a (fair) trial."[10] Reprieve is thus not automatic. Fleeing to a city of refuge, the fugitive meets the elders of the city at the gate, where customarily they gather. Only after a preliminary hearing may he be admitted into the city and given a place to dwell while awaiting the outcome of a trial. If the one who would redeem the blood of the victim pursues the fugitive to the gate of the city, the elders will not hand the killer over to him if there was no apparent hate in the deed, according to their preliminary judgment. The fugitive shall remain in the city of refuge until judgment has been rendered by the assembly or until the death of the high priest.[11]

This peculiar reference to the high priest seems to mean that his death as the "cultic leader of the nation nullifies the requirement to avenge,"[12] but it remains unclear whether a trial would still be necessary to clear the offender from criminal guilt. The church father Ambrose notices the difficulty, which causes him to reflect on the saving significance of the death of Jesus canceling the requirement to avenge by virtue of his appointment as heavenly high priest: "In this passage the literal interpretation causes difficulty. . . . Who is that high priest but the Son of God, the Word of God? We enjoy his advocacy in our behalf before the Father, for he is free from every offense, both willed and unintentional, and in him subsist all things which are on earth and which are in heaven. For all things have been bound by the bond of the Word and are held together by his power and subsist in him, because in him they have been created and in him all God's fullness dwells."[13] In principle and power, the death of Jesus as high priest fulfills and accordingly abrogates any obligation to avenge, for he is the righteous one who intercedes for those who crucify him.

In any case, the fugitive may then return home from whence he fled. Six geographically dispersed cities were thus appointed throughout the territory inherited by the tribes of Israel. Calvin sees a threefold benefit bestowed in the

---

10. Pitkänen, *Joshua*, 337.
11. Nelson, *Joshua*, 231.
12. Pitkänen, *Joshua*, 337.
13. Ambrose, *Flight from the World* 2.13, in *Joshua, Judges, Ruth, 1–2 Samuel*, ed. John R. Franke, Ancient Christian Commentary on Scripture: Old Testament 4 (Downers Grove, IL: InterVarsity, 2005), 88 (hereafter cited as ACCS).

institution of cities of refuge: safety for the innocent, preserving the land from a downward spiral of blood shedding; relief for the bereaved from the presence of a person who caused their sorrow; and a statute of limitations. Together the system shows clearly "how precious human blood is in the sight of God."[14] A final note in Josh. 20 states that these cities of refuge were available for all the people of Israel and also for travelers in their midst. While some scholars regard the cities of refuge in Josh. 20 as a utopian fiction projected back into history, perhaps the real utopianism is the one that grows impatient with the ongoing and indeed interminable struggle to make discriminant, albeit fallible, judgments in service of greater justice in a world beset with factual as well as moral ambiguities.

14. Calvin, *Book of Joshua*, 218.

CITIES ASSIGNED TO THE LEVITES

21:1–42

Calvin can begin our discussion of chapter 21 with his observation that "here we have at a later period a narrative that ought to have preceded."[1] The chapter in this awkward way signals an infusion of priestly themes wrapping up the book of Joshua as instruction for the postexilic remnant of Israel that has lost the land once given to its ancestors. Just so, another set of perplexities besetting life on the land between the already and the not yet is introduced—namely, those involving "the status of a tribe whose inheritance is YHWH rather than land."[2] How are priests, whose social role and authority consisted in a unique vocation of devotion to the worship of God on behalf of the other tribes, entailing the sacrifice of all other desires or loyalties (such as an allotment of land for their own tribe!), to make a living? Is it the case that in the postexilic situation all the remnant survives, no longer as a political sovereignty, but only as a priestly people?

No one—especially no priest of YHWH—can serve two masters; she will hate one and love the other. The Levites would have known what is written in Lev. 25:23 and addressed to all the tribes: "The land shall not be sold in perpetuity, for the land is mine; with me you are but aliens and tenants." Indeed, since the Levite inheritance is YHWH and his sacrifices, they are to embody this relationship by making a living, modest though it may be, from their share of the tithes and offerings brought by the tribes in support of the cult. Unlike the other tribes, they are to make a living not from the land but from the firstfruits of the land rendered back to YHWH by the rest of Israel in acknowledgment of blessings.

---

1. Calvin, *Book of Joshua*, 222.
2. Hawk, *Joshua*, 221.

The heads of the Levite families, however, approach Eleazar and Joshua, quoting Moses against Moses to the effect that Moses had commanded that they too be given cities to live in among the tribes of Israel along with access to pasture.

The deep ambiguity created by this request is that in granting city and pasture to the Levites within the other tribal inheritances, "the inheritance-land equivalency which undergirds the allotment of tribal territories" is broken. For example, we learn that "the town of Hebron is not to be considered Calebite (cf. 14:13–14; 15:13) nor Judahite (15:54) but Levite."[3] But for the apparent goodwill of Caleb in ceding his newly bequeathed place to the Levites, the implications of this seemingly slight modification within the overall organization of Israel are profoundly unsettling; combined with all the other exceptions and vagaries hitherto noted, "it reveals that *conquest* of the town does not necessarily lead to *inheritance* (cf. 19:47), nor does the fact that it is *given* by Joshua (14:13–14). *Allotment* does not necessarily stipulate *inheritance*, for the lot sometimes identifies property that is not an inheritance. And *inheritance* is not to be equated with *portion*, for one tribe will possess portions within the inheritances of others. *Inheritance* does not entail *occupation* or even communal endorsement of property."[4] In all this confusion about so-called land title, it is noteworthy that the book of Joshua brings its discussion of Israel's inheritance of the earth to conclusion by pointing one and all instead to the Levitical inheritance of YHWH.

What follows in any case is a lengthy list in this chapter of the various Levitical cities selected from the various tribal allotments. Genre-wise, this list is a "catalog" of cities, which, as just mentioned, "stands in some tension with the tenet that Levi possessed no inheritance." The catalog "intends to explain how . . . the tribe of Levi has its own special role and status, but is still integrated into the unity of Israel."[5] Yet, evidently, some priests are more equal than others. As presented, the Aaronic branch of Levi's family appears as "more prestigious and significant than the others. . . . Moreover the Aaronic cities all fall within the kingdom of Judah."[6] Moreover, close analysis reveals a "noticeable central gap left in the territory of Ephraim."[7] The evident tendency of the text is to establish a priesthood residing in Judah but claiming an all-Israel jurisdiction (cf. Ps. 78). Not only is

3. Hawk, *Joshua*, 222.
4. Hawk, *Joshua*, 223.
5. Nelson, *Joshua*, 236. See Pitkänen, *Joshua*, 341–45, for a treatment of the same problems that argues for the possible historicity of Levitical cities from the time of the settlement.
6. Nelson, *Joshua*, 237.
7. Nelson, *Joshua*, 238.

this yet further evidence for the postexilic audience of the first readers of the book of Joshua, it is also evidence of a shift away from land title and political unity centered on the now-failed monarchy toward cultic unity in the worship of YHWH through his institution of sacrifices in Zion. The priestly office thus assumes all the greater significance in the postexilic situation: as Calvin puts it, "the very high dignity of acting as stewards for God and preventing their countrymen from revolting from piety."[8]

8. Calvin, *Book of Joshua*, 225.

CONCLUSION TO ISRAEL'S INITIAL LAND REFORM

21:43–45

What are we to conclude? The "many gaps and geographical boundaries reveal a permeability in the social boundaries which configure Israelite society. Women join men in claiming and occupying land, while peoples of the land intermingle with the peoples of YHWH. Like the land itself, the nation of Israel does not display a thoroughgoing homogeneity, purity, or coherence."[1] The "not yet" mocks any pretensions of having achieved the "already." Israel is still on the way, a pilgrim people; it has not yet arrived. In fact, it has lost the land once given to it, and its population has been reduced to Zion and its Judahite surrounds. Yet the conclusion to these two chapters defiantly asserts in the face of evidence and experience the present victory of the already. All the land that YHWH had sworn to give to the fathers was now bestowed. Israel inherited it and settled down on it. In every direction YHWH gave Israel rest from conflict as he had promised the fathers. Not one enemy remained standing because YHWH had fought for Israel and delivered all enemies into their hands. None of the good that YHWH had spoken to the house of Israel failed. Everything came to pass.

"How then can these two things be reconciled, that God, as he had promised, gave possession of the land to the people, and yet they were excluded from some portion by the power or obstinate resistance of the enemy"[2]—not to mention, as Calvin is otherwise wont to do, hindered by their own sloth! The conclusion here "echoes other optimistic passages asserting total triumph such as 10:40–42;

1. Hawk, *Joshua*, 223.
2. Calvin, *Book of Joshua*, 226.

11:16–20, 23; 12:7–24; 23:1, rather than those notices of incompleteness and the continued presence of alien elements in the land such as 13:2–6; 15:63; 16:10; 17:12–18; 23:4, 7, 12–13."[3] Hawk's literary resolution of the contradiction is a theological one that distributes the already to YHWH and the not yet to Israel: the apportionment "puts Israel in the foreground and demonstrates repeatedly the nation's halting and incomplete response to YHWH's promises and commands. The concluding summary, however, emphasizes YHWH's actions."[4]

The conclusion of this entire part of the book of Joshua, in other words, maintains that in spite of human failure, "YHWH does not waver from commitments made to the nation."[5] Consequently, the already is not to be taken as a literal representation of what is the case on the earth; the already always refers to the announcement of the divine self-determination to redeem and fulfill the earth as the precious but grievously usurped creation for the sake of a new humanity, the Israel of God. The perception of the already breaks in with the fabulous events of water crossing and wall shattering; that is to say, it breaks in with the new creation of Israel, in whom the subjectivity of faith apprehending divine promise and divine promise realized in the new subjectivity of faith coincide as in the messianic figure of Joshua, the servant of YHWH in the making. It breaks in likewise with the usurping of the usurpers under the cruel figure of *ḥerem* warfare. This is not a cheap and easy grace that anesthetizes the consciences of the powers that be (or powers that would be) but a grace that rather afflicts such easy consciences, causing them to tremble for their thrones (or would-be thrones). It is a costly and militant grace, for YHWH bears with faltering, backsliding, erring Israel even as he bears down on his own sovereign agenda. Calvin similarly concludes, "The whole comes to this, that it was owing entirely to their own cowardice that they did not enjoy the divine goodness in all its fullness and integrity. This will be still clear from the following chapter."[6] But if humans fail, if even the elect fail, how is YHWH to fight for them?

---

3. Nelson, *Joshua*, 242.
4. Hawk, *Joshua*, 225.
5. Hawk, *Joshua*, 225.
6. Calvin, *Book of Joshua*, 227.

PART 3

✛ AN INCONCLUSIVE ✛
CONCLUSION

(JOSHUA 22–24)

THE TRUE UNITY OF THE
ISRAEL OF GOD

22:1–34

Modern scholars have debated whether the book of Joshua came into existence as the conclusion of a six-book Hexateuch, stretching from canonical Genesis through Joshua, or as the second book in a Deuteronomic history running from canonical Deuteronomy through 2 Kings. There is ample evidence for both positions. On the one hand, "when one reads Joshua in its final form, it is quite natural to see Joshua as the fulfillment of the Exodus/Sinai traditions as depicted in Exodus–Numbers. . . . At the same time, the overall theology of Joshua is clearly Deuteronomic"[1]—even if, as the commentary has shown, Joshua represents a dissent from within the Deuteronomic theology by showing how the law divides against the law, its indicative against its imperative. Elusive, however, is a clear articulation of the evident dependence of canonical Joshua on Priestly traditions, which, as we have seen, it most certainly contains in its canonical form and which indeed gather force by the end of the book.[2] *Ḥerem* warfare, as we have seen, represents a relentless politics of purity. The seat of the doctrine is in Deuteronomy, but the book of Leviticus also concludes with a sharp statement that anything devoted to the Lord for destruction is beyond redemption (27:28–29). Radical purification demands utter destruction of all that is alien to the rule of YHWH. Hence the dilemma that emerges in the narrative course of Joshua: the impossibility of carrying out either consistently or fully the destruction of the

---

1. Pekka M. A. Pitkänen, *Joshua*, Apollos Old Testament Commentary 6 (Nottingham, UK: Apollos; Downers Grove, IL: InterVarsity, 2010), 375–76.
2. See Pitkänen, *Joshua*, 363–80, for the argument for Shiloh traditions.

unredeemable, whether, on the one side, through Israel's sinful sloth or greed or, on the other side, by a collision of contrary Torah imperatives occasioned by the confused intermingling of the city of God and the earthly city in the temporal state between the already and the not yet of YHWH's saving action.

Augustine notices how, in the preceding chapters of Joshua, Jerusalem had not yet been taken from the Jebusites, an observation that gives occasion for a statement of his doctrine of these two cities—biblically, the symbolic cities of Jerusalem and Babylon.

> And see the names of those two cities, Babylon and Jerusalem. Babylon is interpreted confusion, Jerusalem vision of peace. Observe now the city of confusion, in order that you may perceive the vision of peace; that you may endure the one and long for the other. By what can these two cities be distinguished? Can we in any way now separate them from each other? They are mingled, and from the very beginning of humankind mingled they run on until the end of the world. Jerusalem began through Abel, Babylon through Cain: for the building of the cities were erected afterwards. Jerusalem in the land of the Jebusites was built: for at first it used to be called Jebus, from which the nation of the Jebusites was expelled, when the people of God was delivered from Egypt and led into the land of promise. But Babylon was built in the most interior regions of Persia, which for a long time raised its head above the rest of nations. These two cities then at particular times were built, so that there might be shown a figure of two cities begun of old, and to remain even until the end in this world, but at the end to be severed.[3]

So, for Augustine, purification begins by baptism into the city of God but is concluded only by the fabulous deed of God in the resurrection—that is, in the fullness of the new Jerusalem coming down from above. Therefore one cannot prosecute relentlessly a politics of purity until the revolution devours its own children; instead the politics of purity must be spiritualized into a lifelong policy of repentance, the ongoing circumcision of the desires of the heart until fixed on the love of God the common Creator above all and of all creatures in and under this loving God: *ordo caritatis*.

If we allow this Augustinian perspective—itself derived from his studious Christian reading of the canonical sweep of Israel's history with YHWH—to inform us now as we come to the conclusion of our reading of the book of Joshua, we discover that the Levitical-Deuteronomic diagnosis of the root sin

3. Augustine, *Explanations of the Psalms* 65 (ACCS 4:86).

of idolatry turns increasingly away from fixation on objects external to the self, which might be scapegoated as unredeemable objects damnable for their allure and thus meant only for destruction, to a new focus on the promiscuous desires of the human heart. This was the great biblical insight into the "religious affections" of "America's theologian,"[4] Jonathan Edwards: a "conviction of the unity of the human person.... Each person's love is the 'gravity' that determines whether a person rises or falls. [Edwards] interpreted affections in all their diversity as so many modifications of love arising from diverse circumstances in which love is expressed."[5]

It is not the external object, itself a good creature of God, then, that is idolatrous; rather, the promiscuous desire of the human heart turns the good object into an evil idol. All is good under God the Creator but becomes evil when put in the place of God as the object of ultimate desire. The politics of purity, it may be said, are thereby *radicalized* precisely by this "spiritualizing" turn inward to search and judge the heart. *Herem* as a verb becomes the gift and task of *self*-overcoming, which at the same time cancels *herem* as a noun tabooing tempting or seductive phenomena external to the self. The divine command to have no other gods is not thereby diminished, since it now reaches to the depths, to the heart of desire. The commandment de-divinizes all created things that they may be seen as gifts of finite goodness; just so it exposes unjust structures of malice that pretend to eternal fixity and sanctity as in fact usurpers of the earth. And while it narrows the scope of the policy of purification to the *root* of such idolatrous possessing in the desires of the heart, it generates there messianic longing for the gift of the Spirit creating new hearts. Less and less is it the literal idol that must be smashed and burned as if something in real opposition to YHWH's claim to be the one true God in heaven and on earth, and more and more is it the hardened heart even of elect Israel that must be circumcised. In turn this refocuses the good news of YHWH who fights for Israel as one who fights not merely or chiefly *against* Israel's real or perceived enemies but *for* the love of Israel. That divine pursuit of Israel's reciprocating love, alternating historically between anger and mercy, likewise hints messianically forward beyond canonical Joshua to a fulfillment that surpasses the politics of purity with the new politics of reconciliation.

4. Robert W. Jenson, *America's Theologian: A Recommendation of Jonathan Edwards* (New York: Oxford University Press, 1988).

5. Michael J. McClymond and Gerald R. McDermott, *The Theology of Jonathan Edwards* (New York: Oxford University Press, 2012), 314–15.

Two things are certain about canonical Joshua and have formed the basis for this theological commentary. First, the book of Joshua is certainly a bridge that can be read forward or backward in the canonical series that begins with Genesis and concludes with Ezra-Nehemiah. Second, in either case, the first readers of canonical Joshua were the postexilic faithful who read the book in the grim and ironic awareness that the promised land once given to their ancestors had been lost to them on account of covenant infidelity. Postexilic Judah was a client state of imperial powers, lacking anything resembling the king they used to have. Inevitably in this situation, leadership of the remnant community of Israel was contestable. Who was to lead? The priests? The scribes? The vicars of Persia or Egypt? Merchants, tribal chiefs, northerners or southerners? This canonical location in postexilic political chaos places our "epistemic access" in the perspective of the suffering dispossessed of Israel, and this is particularly important for the proper hermeneutical-literary reading of canonical Joshua and the rendering of its knowledge of God as YHWH who fights for us. The parallels between the postexilic situation and Israel's formative years when there was yet no king are intriguing.[6] Any surface reading of Joshua as a heroic war tale proceeding "from victory unto victory," rationalizing in the process ethnic cleansing on the way to Israelite monarchy-imperialism is thus deeply questionable. Readers of Joshua look back on a failed politics, probing what went wrong.

Indeed, we have seen that presentist ideological appropriations of *herem* warfare as crusade or holy war turn essentially *fabulous* warfare on its head by replacing the theologically integral element of YHWH's miraculous deliverances in the book of Joshua with strident summons to violent human activism utilizing religion as a sacralization of a politics of self-aggrandizement, rationalized with the claim to be pursuing purity. Already in the paradigmatic story of Achan's coveting, one Israelite makes this fatal mistake of secularization (which Israel's prophets later inveighed against when the monarchies sought to capture a *Gott mit uns*[7] from Israel's early traditions) and is punished for it in principled fashion. Likewise, the faithfulness of YHWH, holy and jealous for his sovereign purpose of the new creation of the Israel of God in land cleansed of Canaanite structures of malice and injustice, is attested in these concluding chapters—though not without narratively significant further inclusions of flesh-and-blood Canaanites intimating reconciliation in place of purge. This reiteration of the fidelity of

6. Thanks to Dave Delaney for this formulation.
7. Gerhard von Rad, *Holy War in Ancient Israel*, trans. Marva J. Dawn (Grand Rapids: Eerdmans, 1991), 94–114.

YHWH in spite of the infidelity of Israel pushes the book's theological inquiry a final, dramatic, and yet inconclusive step further: How is YHWH to fight for those who fail him? How is YHWH to continue fighting for Israel after the policy of purification fails? Joshua's final speech, as we will see, excludes the easy answer of cheap grace, which is simply to reject the policy of purification as a mistaken "picture of God." But YHWH who fights for us is and ever remains a holy and jealous God who will not ignore our sins! Merciful reconciliation cannot come forth except as the costly surpassing of a just reckoning with the ruin and guilt of sin—no more than a resurrection can come forth without first death and tomb.

The canonical book of Joshua draws to its close by tying together some dangling narrative threads by integrating Deuteronomic and priestly themes. It performs this weave through a series of extended farewells.[8] The first of these farewells concerns the relationship of the Transjordan tribes to the Cisjordan tribes and foreshadows the conflicts between the tribes in the book of Judges.[9] Joshua summons the Reubenites, the Gadites, and the half tribe of Manasseh, to whom Moses had bequeathed territories beyond the Jordan to the east. The reader will recall from Josh. 1:12–18 how warriors of these tribes had joined the others in the western campaign. Now, as they depart for home, Joshua begins his farewell speech by lifting up their obedience to the commandments of YHWH once mediated by his servant Moses and now again to YHWH's commandments as have been mediated by his own voice.

Despite Joshua's affirmation of their obedience to all the commandments, the reader may be troubled by several glaring anomalies. The first one concerns the very dismissal of the easterners from war in the west, as if the job were done. God's work is in our hands! This being so, the dismissal of the easterners troubles Calvin: How can Joshua consider them "to have performed their due measure of military service, while the enemy were still in possession of part of the land, of which the sole possession was to be the proper termination of the war?" Calvin reminds his readers that he has already untied this knot with his diagnosis of Israelite sloth. "Had the Israelites followed the invitation of God, and seconded his agency, nay, when he was stretching out his hand to them, had they not basely drawn back, the remaining part of the war would have been finished with no danger and little trouble. From their own sloth, therefore, they refused what God was ready to bestow."[10] And so the obligation of the easterners to the western

---

8. L. Daniel Hawk, *Joshua*, Berit Olam (Collegeville, MN: Liturgical Press, 2000), 277.

9. Richard D. Nelson, *Joshua: A Commentary* (Louisville: Westminster John Knox, 1997), 247.

10. John Calvin, *Book of Joshua* (North Charleston, SC: CreateSpace, n.d.), 229.

war was dissolved by the sinful sloth of the westerners and is now reciprocated by the easterners heading for home. The second anomaly that troubles Calvin is Joshua's exhortation that the booty-laden easterners share their spoil with their kin upon return home. It is not, however, the apparent violation of *ḥerem* warfare that troubles him here, but rather the sharing of the rewards with those on the home front who have not borne the burden of battle. In urging generosity, Joshua, Calvin says, "does not insist on the strictly legal view."[11] But that is precisely the problem in an address that insists to the contrary, not only on the strictly legal view, but on the full and factual fulfillment of all that Moses commanded by the easterners and westerners alike.

But perhaps by now in our narrative a "strictly legal view" has already collapsed on account of the accumulating conundrums that we have witnessed, as the law divides against itself in clashing rules face-to-face with confused reality. In fact the reference to the law here is quite specific and narrowly focused on a rule of rules—not the previously mentioned *ḥesed* but "one God, one Israel, one altar." The many rules of the Torah must themselves be ruled by Israel's rule of faith, the Shema, which practically and institutionally consolidates the worship of God to a single clergy at a single shrine. Calvin attends to how strictly the law prohibits two altars (Exod. 20:24), "for the Lord wishes to be worshiped in one place only."[12] This trinity of "one God, one Israel, one altar" indicates that "no more than one altar can be a place of lawful sacrifice. . . . [In Joshua that] is the altar of the tabernacle, implicitly at Shiloh."[13] As the story unfolds, neither Joshua nor Eleazar is involved but rather a representative of the new generation, Phineas, the son of Eleazar. Equally accented is "the idea of the unity of Israel in war ([22:]1–8)" as in worship.[14] As the easterners had been united with the westerners as a "band of brothers" in war, so they are to remain united in peace by common worship of the one true God at his one authorized altar administered by one clergy authorized for all Israel. Yet the ideal of unity here asserted begs the crucial question about the nature of unity. There are many doctrines of unity: uniformity or harmony, organic or artificial, identity or community, and so on. How does the trinity of the one God, the one altar, and the one priesthood cohere internally as a life—indeed, as a life of love? Ultimately, this is a question of the doctrine of God.

11. Calvin, *Book of Joshua*, 230.
12. Calvin, *Book of Joshua*, 232.
13. Nelson, *Joshua*, 248.
14. Pitkänen, *Joshua*, 361.

The contemporary Christian reader, in any case, cannot but at this juncture profoundly repent and lament the disgraceful disunity of the churches in doctrine of God, worship life, and ministry. So entrenched has the partisan spirit of denominationalism become that even with the great progress of the ecumenical dialogues in the time after the Second Vatican Council, the happy decline of overt hostility has now become a lazy pretext for complacency over against the positive will of the revealed God: "Now I appeal to you, brothers and sisters, by the name of our Lord Jesus Christ, that all of you be in agreement and that there be no divisions among you, but that you be united in the same mind and the same purpose" (1 Cor. 1:10). Unity in service, the diaconal works of charity and justice (such as it is), does not substitute for unity in doctrine of God, worship, and ministry. The reason is that service is ambiguous and as such subject to multiple and conflicting interpretations, just as the altar/memorial of the easterners is ambiguous. Requisite is the dialogue sponsored in theology and its work of clarification—in other words, the lively theological conversation that is the hard and continuing work for unity in doctrine of God, worship, and ministry.

Specifically, the book of Joshua continues, these eastern warriors have not deserted their western brothers-in-arms during all this time but have been on guard to keep the commandment of YHWH their God for all-Israel unity. Because the promise of rest from war has, at least in principle, been fulfilled in the west, the eastern warriors may now return to their tents in their land beyond the Jordan. Joshua tacitly provides a deep reason for the otherwise improbable claim that YHWH has given "rest from war" when the incompleteness of the conquest has also been frankly acknowledged. United in faith through the battles, the one Israel is, unlike the rebellious wilderness generation, at peace with the one God. Joshua exhorts them henceforth, as they will be physically separated by the Jordan River, to sustain this peace with God by faithfulness to the commandments in the instruction given by Moses, which Joshua now summarizes as follows: to love (*'ahav*) YHWH your God by walking in all his ways and keeping his commandments, to cling (*dabaq*) to him with all your heart and soul. Having finished this (Deuteronomic) exhortation, Joshua blesses the easterners and sends them on their way. The one YHWH is not divided by the river Jordan, for he is the living God in heaven and on earth; though the hearts of Israel be spread beyond the land of Canaan, all Israel may yet wholeheartedly love and cling to YHWH by persevering in his electing and promising word in the obedience of faith.

As the easterners depart, the reader is reminded that the inheritance of the tribe of Manasseh was divided into portions on either side of the Jordan. It is unclear precisely to whom Joshua speaks when he adds that they are to return to their tents in the east laden with booty from the western campaign: the lesser booty of cattle, precious metals, and clothing. If Jericho was de facto an exception, the narrator never actually states this or explains de jure how exceptions to or intensifications of the law of *herem* can be made, but leaves the reports of inconsistent application hanging. Reminiscent of the despoiling of the Egyptians in the exodus, the easterners in any case depart from Canaan with its earthly riches. Joshua tells them to share the goods taken from the slain of Canaan with their brothers at home. This instruction consequently sits uneasily with the rule of *herem* warfare as we have seen, yet in the command to generosity we may see the overruling rule of rules: the returning easterners are not to hoard in shame like Achan but openly to share in the spirit of *hesed*. Joshua 22:9 tells us that this addendum to the speech of Joshua was addressed to the two and a half tribes, which now depart from Shiloh in the land of Canaan to cross the Jordan back to Gilead, where the land for their possession was granted by Moses.

But when these tribes came to the Jordan River, they built a great *mizbeakh* (altar)—so the narrative bluntly specifies. Calvin observes that "nothing was further from their intention than to innovate in any respect in the worship of God. But they sinned not lightly in attempting a novelty, without paying any regard to the high priest, or consulting their brethren, and in a form which was very liable to be misconstrued."[15] Intricately, diverse notions of what unity itself is may be threatening divisions. Next, the narrator reports how the sons of Israel—that is, the westerners—heard about and reacted to the erection of this altar by the easterners; the report employs volatile language.[16] Characterized as the "sons of Israel" (what does that make the easterners?), the westerners now resemble the "kings of Canaan" in that they together constitute something distinctly other than, and at enmity with, the Reubenites, the Gadites, and the half tribe of Manasseh settling on the east of the Jordan.

The westerners hear of this altar built by the departing tribes. Its location is described vaguely as at the border but in the region belonging to them, the "sons of Israel," as opposed to land belonging to their erstwhile brothers, now "others." In fact the reader has trouble determining the exact location of this altar, with vision obscured by shifting perspectives in the narrative, mirroring the shifting

15. Calvin, *Book of Joshua*, 232.
16. Hawk, *Joshua*, 237.

perspectives of the two sides in dramatic confrontation about what constitutes the identity of the one people of God gathered around the one altar.[17] The implicit division is reinforced in the next verse, when we are told that the "whole assembly" of the sons of Israel (n.b., sans the eastern tribes) gathered at Shiloh where the one and only altar stood, and, "inflamed with holy wrath,"[18] prepared to make war against the other tribes, whose unforgivable sin had been to build a new and separate altar for themselves, thus making themselves into something other than the one Israel. The rhetoric here further insinuates that only "the land west of the Jordan truly comprises 'the Lord's land.'"[19]

Somehow—we are not told—cooler heads prevail and a delegation is sent across the Jordan to the land of Gilead. It is led by Phineas, the son of Eleazar the priest, who is accompanied by ten representatives from the leading families of the ten tribes of Israel settling in the Cisjordan. When they arrive, they speak in the name of "all the assembly of YHWH" (22:16 AT), asking what apostasy the departing tribes have committed by building for themselves a separate altar, thus rebelling against YHWH, the God of Israel. The delegation reminds the easterners of the apostasy at Peor—in the vicinity of the territory that they now occupy—a pollution from which even to this day Israel, they say, has not yet fully cleansed itself. They recall the purifying punishment that afflicted the assembly of all Israel at that time, when YHWH turned against all Israel on account of the sin of some.

Thus the social nature of sin with its radioactive guilt is reasserted: if the eastern tribes defect from YHWH, the anger (Hebrew *qetseph*, Greek *hē orgē*) of YHWH will fall on all Israel—which, of course, the delegation presumes to represent. The Achan-contagion threatens to recur. "Joshua 22:20 refers directly back to Joshua 7, the narrative of the Achan incident in association with the conquest of Ai. It is especially noteworthy that the priestly word *m'l* used to describe Achan in Joshua 7:1 occurs also in Joshua 22:20 (cf. also Joshua 22:31). Moreover, the concept of divine retribution based on *m'l* is similar in Joshua 22 and in Joshua 7. In both cases, the whole congregation of the Israelites would suffer because of the sin of an individual or a part of the community. . . . This concept of divine retribution is priestly."[20] Not all sin is lethal, but the guilt/pollution of lethal sin that breaks the covenant spreads like a contagion; it thus implicates/infects the

---

17. Hawk, *Joshua*, 237.
18. Calvin, *Book of Joshua*, 233.
19. Hawk, *Joshua*, 227.
20. Pitkänen, *Joshua*, 371.

whole community so far as it makes no effort to isolate the cancerous source and excise it. Yet, paradoxically, the inclusive understanding of sin expressed here is in some tension with the "othering" insinuation that the eastern tribes are not genuinely Israel at all. In recognition of this implicit contradiction, a remarkable offer by the westerners transpires, based on the curious premise that perhaps the easterners find their Transjordan land to be "unclean" (*teme'ah*): if so, they are urged to come over to the land that YHWH possesses and settle here. In effect, the westerners ask the easterners, like Joshua once asked the prince of the army of YHWH, "Are you on our side—or not?" That is, "Have you crossed back . . . *to stay*?"[21] But had not YHWH through his servant Moses settled the eastern tribes there in the Transjordan? How can that land be unclean? Why shouldn't they stay?

The narrative returns to the central question of the altar. In the eyes of the westerners, the altar erected by the easterners expresses an understanding of the unity of the people of God other than in the one authorized form of worship. To the westerners, the identity of the people of God is anchored in possession of the land of Canaan where the one altar is located; to the easterners, by contrast, the identity of the people of God cannot be marked by possession of territory west of the Jordan that they do not enjoy. The reader gets a mixed picture. "In terms of receiving gift and blessing, and responding with loyalty and obedience, [the easterners] are quintessential Israelites. But by settling across the Jordan, they have also separated themselves from 'the Israelites.'"[22]

The episode thus dramatizes the conundrum that runs throughout the book of Joshua's account of the possession of the land, even as it is colored by postexilic anxieties. "Could Yahwists who lived outside the holy land participate in Temple sacrifice or were they unclean (v. 17)? Were the offerings they brought products of an unclean land (v. 19)?"[23] Thus we have here a fresh and final iteration of the identity questions we have seen percolating throughout the book of Joshua, but now in concentrated and intense form concerning the true unity of the people of God: "Who was to be included in the people of God? Who will be excluded? On what basis?"[24] The answer here given by the easterners is that "what really matters is not one's place of residence, but one's confession that YHWH is God alone (v. 22). . . . The unity of YHWH's people is found . . . in shared faith and

21. Hawk, *Joshua*, 230.
22. Hawk, *Joshua*, 236.
23. Nelson, *Joshua*, 250.
24. Hawk, *Joshua*, 232.

fidelity and worship."[25] The easterners will concede that Shiloh in Canaan is the place in fact where the tabernacle sits; there YHWH has caused his name to dwell. The westerners therefore implore them—be it noted, rather generously—to take possession of land here "among us." Only do not rebel or make us rebels with you, they say, by erecting an altar other than YHWH's altar in the tabernacle established in Shiloh.

The easterners' response resounds, twice repeated: "YHWH God of gods!" This is an invocation of YHWH as witness; YHWH God of gods knows the truth, so let Israel also know! Calvin sees that there is "force and meaning in the reduplication . . . by which they with vehemence affirm, how faithfully they desire to persevere in the doctrine of the law, and how greatly they abhor all contrary superstitions."[26] The double invocation of YHWH as the one true God constitutes and seals their defense against the western accusation. "There is a strong creedal flavor to this."[27] The gospel of YHWH who fights for Israel is confessed by a creedal confession, akin to the Shema: "YHWH God of gods!" Unity for the easterners most fundamentally consists in this knowledge of God, whose saving action unifies without respect to geographical boundaries.

The credo of the easterners is brief, even truncated, but its meaning in context is clear and powerful: the point is the combination of the title, "God over all," and the particular proper name, YHWH, who has become the God of one people, Israel, and who has led them into Canaan to claim and sanctify this earth for their inheritance. YHWH's particular election of Israel and dowry gift of the land of Canaan to it, in other words, do not reduce YHWH to a local deity of one ethnicity residing in one territory alone. Rather, as God of gods, this particular YHWH is also present to bless those outside Canaan, for here too he has caused his name to dwell, not for sacrifices to be sure, but nevertheless truly in those who confess his name truly as God of gods. Indeed, the easterners invoke the *herem* curse (Greek *anathema*) upon themselves with YHWH as witness: "If we acted rebelliously or unfaithfully toward YHWH, do not save us this day! But may YHWH himself punish us if we built an altar intending to turn from YHWH who has chosen Israel and gathers Israel at Shiloh in the land of Canaan solely to offer sacrifices on the altar there" (22:22–23 paraphrased). The ecclesiastical anathema likewise invoked by Paul the apostle upon himself if he has deviated to

25. Nelson, *Joshua*, 250. Nelson regards the story as an allegory for the relationship between leavers and those who remained after the exile. But Pitkänen (*Joshua*, 367) makes a case to the contrary.

26. Calvin, *Book of Joshua*, 237.

27. Nelson, *Joshua*, 252.

the left or the right from the gospel revealed to him (Gal. 1:8–9) takes its origin here from the easterners, just as, when a Pharisee, it had been the anathema of the westerners that he had thought to execute on blasphemous Jewish Christians.

The same legal distinction reflected in the law of asylum from Josh. 20 reappears here, distinguishing between ambiguous behavior and hidden but true intention. Although the westerners' worry was understandable (the Hebrew word for altar, *mizbeakh*, derives from the verb for sacrifice, *zabakh*), the easterners say that their concern in building the altar was very different. The fear arose that in the future western children would say to eastern children, "What have you to do with YHWH, the God of Israel? YHWH made the Jordan River a boundary between us and thus you have no part of YHWH because you have *crossed back*! So we feared that your children might turn our children away from the worship of YHWH when they would come to Shiloh for sacrifices. That is why we erected this altar, not for sacrifices, but we made a copy of it to serve as a memorial witness between you and us and for our generations to come, so that we might offer sacrifices with you and your children would never say to ours that they have no portion in YHWH" (22:24–27 paraphrased).

"Although a non-sacrificial altar may seem to be an oxymoron, . . . sacrificial function was paradoxically but inevitably superseded by its narrative role as a witness to participation in sacrifice at the unique central altar"—at Shiloh.[28] Future generations would see the model of the altar of YHWH on the border as testimony to both sides of their unity in faith and worship. The attempt was to resolve a many-sided conundrum: losing recognition, including self-recognition, as belonging to the people of YHWH and maintaining unity in spite of diverse residences when the unity of faith includes specification of a particular land as the gift of YHWH to Israel, where the ark of the covenant sits, inquiries are made and oracles are received, and sacrifices are offered.

Phinehas the priest, with the family heads of Israel, is said to be pleased at the explanation and declares, "Now we—that is, all Israel who now dwells in Canaan—know that YHWH is in our midst, even here in the Transjordan visiting the easterners, because you have not betrayed YHWH by a treacherous deed. Indeed, by this explanation you have delivered (all) the people of Israel from the

---

28. Nelson, *Joshua*, 248–49. Calvin takes occasion here to warn against excessively literalistic iconoclasm: "No kind of statues are condemned except those which are intended to represent God. To erect a heap of stones as a trophy, or in testimony of a miracle, or a memorial of some favor of God, in the law is nowhere prohibited. . . . The only thing displeasing to God was to see the minds of men drawn hither and thither, so as to worship him in a gross and earthly manner." Calvin, *Book of Joshua*, 238.

anger of YHWH" (22:31 paraphrased). "There is now no danger of YHWH's departure as a result of cultic impropriety, a key concern of priestly theology."[29] So the western delegation returns from Gilead and brings the good report back with them. The good news pleased the sons of Israel who blessed God because there was no need to go to war against the eastern tribes and destroy their land. So the easterners name the altar "witness" because it attests that YHWH is God both east and west of the Jordan River. The easterners' explanation assuaged the doubt of the westerners in the moment. But doubts remain.[30] What will become of the unity of all Israel should the land be lost altogether and the authorized place of sacrifice destroyed and the people spread way beyond the Jordan into diaspora?

Calvin reflects darkly on the happy ending: "We never revolt from God, or fall off into impiety unless he abandon us, and give us up when thus abandoned to a reprobate mind. All idolatry, therefore, shows that God has previously been alienated, and is about to punish us by inflicting judicial blindness. Meanwhile, we must hold that we persevere in piety only in so far as God is present to sustain us by his hand, and confirm this perseverance by the agency of his Spirit."[31] Though the need of him is becoming manifest by this juncture, there has been no mention of the Spirit throughout the book of Joshua. Calvin's point can more precisely be stated: The idols as external objects of desire are but a symptom of the heart's false love. But to claim the heart's love truly, something more is needed than an imperative that sounds out impotently in face of sinful failure, only to threaten its own indicative. Somehow God must give what he commands.

---

29. Nelson, *Joshua*, 253.
30. Hawk, *Joshua*, 244–45.
31. Calvin, *Book of Joshua*, 239.

THE AGED JOSHUA BIDS ISRAEL
FAREWELL, NOT ONCE BUT TWICE

23:1–24:33

The book of Joshua has two conclusions back-to-back. The first is a "testamentary"[1] speech by Joshua in chapter 23. It is comparable to Moses's farewell in Deut. 31, exhorting Israel to loyalty to YHWH as Joshua prepares, like Moses did, to pass from the scene. One can note a progression through the course of Joshua's speech, "a clear escalation in the severity of the rhetoric" culminating in "the ultimate threat of YHWH's anger and personal divine involvement in [Israel's] destruction."[2] In this respect, there is little difference between this first farewell address and a second one in chapter 24.

The first speech, in chapter 23, exhorts hearers to demonstrate love for YHWH by obedience to everything written in the book of the law of Moses. When we call to mind the opening of the book of Joshua where Joshua, commissioned as YHWH's warrior, is told to conquer by way of obedience to the book of the law, the concluding paraenesis "recapitulates the main themes of the book and projects them into the future."[3]

By contrast, the second address concludes with a dialogue between Joshua and the people and then a "covenant" between Joshua and the people that puts the people on record. This "covenant" does not conform to the typical treaty pattern; indeed, it is little more than a "report about the making of a covenant,"[4]

---

1. Hawk, *Joshua*, 247n1.
2. Nelson, *Joshua*, 256.
3. Hawk, *Joshua*, 247.
4. Nelson, *Joshua*, 266.

yet not between the people and YHWH but between Joshua and the people. What it records, moreover, is the commitment of the people to do what Joshua deems impossible, and the record of this commitment is memorialized on stone witnesses to serve as an abiding testimony against Israel's future apostasy. Not surprisingly, then, "this chapter [24] has been a focus of a great deal of scholarly controversy."[5] Is it primarily a literary construction that brings the book of Joshua to—an exceedingly strange—conclusion (akin, say, to Mark 16:8 in strangeness)? Or is it history, reflecting more or less the liturgy of a covenant renewal ceremony deriving from the tradition of the shrine at Shechem? If such matters were not perplexing enough, Joshua's speech in chapter 24 contains a datum not found anywhere else concerning "the ancestors' worship of alien gods beyond the Euphrates and in Egypt."[6] In view of this datum, the divine threat assumes larger and larger place in Joshua's farewell until crescendoing in the classic choice of Deuteronomic theology: "Choose this day whom you will serve!" (24:15).

The speeches are introduced by mention of the passage of considerable time. This provides for two things of considerable importance in the speeches. The claim is made, first, that YHWH has given rest to Israel from all the surrounding enemies and, second, that Joshua's leadership has accordingly now come to an end. His legacy is that the Israel he leaves behind in death is at peace with YHWH by virtue of his generation's obedience of faith. Indeed, it is as if Joshua's inchoate messianic presence has enabled his generation's obedience of faith. Motivation for continued obedience is thus grounded in knowledge of YHWH who has fought for Israel by the mediation of Joshua, while the urgency of reiterating this grounding for a future of obedience is underscored by Joshua's impending demise. He will no longer be personally present to serve the word of YHWH to and for the sake of Israel. He will not be present to remind Israel of the grace of its election or to exhort Israel to the obedience of such faith. Only the memory of him abides. Thus, it is hinted, the book of Joshua is put into writing as memorialization, as scripture.

Joshua summons "all Israel," as represented by their heads, judges, and officials, and begins his speech with a statement of the obvious: "I am now old" (23:2). There follows in 23:6–8, in view of Joshua's departure from the scene, a "democratization of obedience" that makes "the people as a whole responsible for the

5. Nelson, *Joshua*, 265.
6. Nelson, *Joshua*, 266.

keeping of the covenant."[7] But the lifework of Joshua has yielded a legacy of truth that should be equally obvious to all Israel, if only they remember: You have seen what YHWH your God has done to the hostile powers on account of you! In all your battles, it is YHWH your God—it is he who fought for you!

Joshua next reminds the assembly not only of the "already"—namely, the nations already cut off to make place for Israel's inheritance—but also of the "not yet" of those remaining nations still to be dispossessed. Joshua's address thus "modifies the hyperbolic claims of possession in 21:43–45" and transforms "the glorious certainties of the past into the troubling openness and incompleteness of the future."[8] Joshua reminds them how he has allotted their lands, whether dispossessed already or yet to be dispossessed, to the tribes of Israel as their inheritance. Though Joshua is passing from the scene, YHWH their God remains and does not pass from the scene. He will thrust these remaining foes from Israel's sight, and they will possess the land according to the word of YHWH their God. Therefore Israel is firmly to keep and to do all that is written in the book of the law of Moses, deviating neither to the left nor to the right, since deviation from the bounded zone of YHWH's blessing leads fatally into the zone of curse— indeed, falls under the *herem* that befell the Canaanites. "Israel must now rely on Moses just as Joshua has done,"[9] but also Moses as clarified by Joshua's enactment of the word of Moses by his obedience of faith in the incipient messianic event of delivering on the promises of YHWH.

Thus a *new* understanding of Torah obedience is gained in the light of Joshua's work, and this in subtle but clear distinction from conquest and extermination. This new understanding is now lifted up and urgently exhorted in view of the persistence of Canaan foreseen in the life of Israel: the purpose of strict obedience to the law of Moses is to keep Israel pure and prevent pollution by mixing sexually and religiously with the remaining nations of Canaan, lest Israel begin to call on their gods, swear by them, serve them, or prostate themselves before them (in contrast to how Joshua had prostrated himself before the prince of the army of YHWH). Instead of falling into theological infidelity, they are to cling to YHWH their God as they have done all these days under Joshua's leadership. Why should Israel cling to YHWH alone? It is YHWH who fought for Israel, driving out great and numerous nations so that no one has been able to oppose Israel to this day. Just one of Israel chases away one thousand of the foe! The

---

7. Nelson, *Joshua*, 261.
8. Hawk, *Joshua*, 247–48. So also Nelson, *Joshua*, 259.
9. Hawk, *Joshua*, 248.

reason for Israel's victory is YHWH your God—it is he who fought for you, according to his word.

Therefore Joshua, in soaring rhetoric, summons Israel: "Take care to love YHWH your God!" (23:11 AT). Love qualifies the structure of master and vassal relationship that otherwise constitutes the covenant. What does "love" mean? To love YHWH is to hold fast or cling to YHWH according to his word; the two terms, "love" and "cling," mutually define each other and derive from Deut. 11:22; 13:3–4; and 30:20. "'Cling' (*dbq*) is thus defined by v. 12 in terms of marriage"[10]—that is, "to have and to hold." YHWH is available to Israel in his word of promise as spouse to spouse. Israel is to cling to YHWH as spouse clings to spouse; such clinging transacts in the perpetually renewed joyful exchange of nuptial vows: "I am yours and you are mine." One clings to YHWH by holding on to his word of promise in sickness and in health, for richer or for poorer, for better or worse as YHWH has first loved Israel in spite of murmurings, rebellions, and infidelities.

Love here is not, then, primarily an erotic feeling based on attraction; it is a choice, free and joyful to be sure, to fix desire on YHWH's promise alone and thus becomes a matter of policy for life that forms and reforms desire in the lived history of spouses bound together by promises. As Luther generalized the insight, "What your heart clings to in every time of trouble—that is really your God."[11] With respect to the commandments, love for YHWH is thus the rule of rules—"Hear, O Israel, YHWH your God, YHWH only!" (Deut. 6:5 AT)—as "clinging" is the reciprocation of YHWH's *ḥesed*. Love for YHWH is the "spirit" of the letter of the law—in Christian theological understanding, the Holy Spirit, not mentioned by name in the book of Joshua but here implied, bestows the Father's love on the Son and enables the Son's love of the Father, and also bestows upon believers the Father's love for the Son and the Son's love for the Father; so they are incorporated into this perichoresis of love by the Spirit-given union with Christ through faith. Love for YHWH that reciprocates his *ḥesed* is the authorial intention of the Spirit that informs understanding and application of all the varied regulations of the covenant through the changes and chances of life between the times.

Ḥerem, in this light, becomes the negative of this positive, the curse on penultimate loves whenever they displace the ultimate love owed solely to the living

---

10. Nelson, *Joshua*, 261.

11. Martin Luther, "The Large Catechism," in *The Book of Concord: The Confessions of the Evangelical Lutheran Church*, ed. Robert Kolb and Timothy J. Wengert (Minneapolis: Fortress, 2000), 388.

God, YHWH, God of gods in heaven and on earth, the one who truly is and promises to be God for us and for all. Calvin captures this "spiritual" retooling of literal *ḥerem* smartly when he comments that "God is defrauded of his honor whenever any particle, however small, of all the things which he claims for himself is transferred to idols."[12] In that case the root of idolatry lies in wayward desire, and not its varied external objectifications that change in history relative to a culture's time and place. Nor is desire as such to be extirpated—as if that were possible. It becomes theologically clear that all things are pure to the pure in heart, that no thing in all of God's creation lacks its specific goodness and value in the *ordo caritatis* if and when the heart of desire clings to YHWH's word of promise. Thus Joshua repeatedly exhorts the people, who value life and safety, to be careful in maintaining love of God, for such love is the source in human motive of all true obedience. True obedience is the obedience of faith in the God of *ḥesed* love who promises to be for those whom he chooses as his servants. "For if we do not cling to him with free and ardent affection, we shall study in vain to frame our lives in accordance with the external form of the law."[13] Indeed, Calvin, looking forward to the book of Judges, sees how Israel's presently attested "ardor proved evanescent, and they shortly after were initiated in nefarious Gentile rites. Hence, we perceive in the human mind an intemperate longing for perverse worship, a longing which no curbs are able to restrain."[14] Likewise Ps. 106:34–40 charges:

> They did not destroy the peoples,
>   as the LORD commanded them,
> but they mingled with the nations
>   and learned to do as they did.
> They served their idols,
>   which became a snare to them.
> They sacrificed their sons
>   and their daughters to the demons;
> they poured out innocent blood,
>   the blood of their sons and daughters,
> whom they sacrificed to the idols of Canaan;
>   and the land was polluted with blood.
> Thus they became unclean by their acts,
>   and prostituted themselves in their doings.

12. Calvin, *Book of Joshua*, 244.
13. Calvin, *Book of Joshua*, 244.
14. Calvin, *Book of Joshua*, 245.

> Then the anger of the LORD was kindled against his people,
>   and he abhorred his heritage.

Even the holy curbs of the law threatening just punishment do not avail when what is lacking is the ardor of love for YHWH, from which true understanding of his commandments and thus genuine obedience spring. Love for YHWH who shows *ḥesed* is the rule of rules, the "spirit" that informs understanding and application of the covenant regulations in the contested life between the already and the not yet. Love for YHWH rules out the idols; to cling to God in faith's love is to disbelieve the idols.[15] In spite of the substantive monotheism of the credo "YHWH God of gods," the practical context of contested life between the times remains henotheistic: there *are* other options on offer. There are many other things to which the heart can cling in times of trouble, but YHWH is loved when YHWH *alone* is held to his word—freely and joyfully but also sometimes painfully, as in psalms of lament and Job-like postures of protest in times of severe trial. While the analogy with marriage love qualifies the suzerain-vassal relationship as one initiated by love and sustained by love, it also articulates the divine intention for love's reciprocation by the beloved, which is not the basis of YHWH's love for Israel but surely is the fulfillment of it. Wyschogrod speaks here of the pathos of God, "a God whose glory is a self-imposed humanization, which preserves the independence of the world and of Israel. It is this that enables Israel to retain its being and not simply be absorbed into God, and it is the very same humanization of God that introduces into his love for Israel a need for Israel's response and leaves God deeply hurt when this response is not forthcoming. It is this divine vulnerability that makes real the relationship between God and man."[16] The fusion of the two metaphors of covenant—the relations between Lord and servant and between spouses—arises from the postexilic need in Israel for "internal boundaries" that exclude "exogamy as the quintessential act of 'joining' with the remaining nations. Marriage . . . becomes paradigmatic for the issue of communal boundaries"[17]—where adulterous desire on the part of the beloved Israel can deeply hurt, and thus anger for a passing moment, the God made vulnerable by *ḥesed*.

15. Christopher Morse, *Not Every Spirit: A Dogmatics of Christian Disbelief*, 2nd ed. (New York: Continuum, 2009).

16. Michael Wyschogrod, *The Body of Faith: God in the People Israel* (Lanham, MD: Rowman & Littlefield, 1996), 13.

17. Hawk, *Joshua*, 256.

YHWH's covenant with Israel, like a marriage, expects reciprocation and is thus daily renewed—or not! In this sense its vitality, though not its validity, is conditional on Israel's adherence to it. The unforgivable sin of covenant infidelity is to serve other gods and bow down to them. The righteous jealousy of YHWH will then erupt like a destroying flame (*khara 'aph-yhwh*), and it will burn polluted Israel off the good land given in Joshua's time. Thus warned, "Israel's sole charge is to remain loyal to YHWH in the face of remaining Canaanite difference."[18] *Herem* warfare has failed as a military strategy but survives—itself purified from a relentless politics demanding extermination of the polluting others—as a policy of theological-confessional purification of the self, a policy of daily turning to YHWH who turns to Israel in *hesed* love. But one wonders: If the threat of extermination against others has failed in application, how can it succeed when directed against the self? Isn't the self still in charge? How can anyone be a true judge in their own case?

What, then, if Israel's heart wanders and falls into adultery/idolatry, no longer hearing or knowing YHWH's unconditional election nor reciprocating this love? By the same token of YHWH's sovereign and unconditional love for Israel, which brought evil things upon the Canaanites for their evil ways, YHWH will also bring evil things upon an untrue Israel (cf. Num. 33:55–56). If, in other words, the marriage covenant fails, what remains is the Lord-servant covenant with dire consequences for fruitless and unfaithful servants (cf. Mark 11:12–14, 15–17, 20–21). In this way Joshua's speech "clarifies the tension between the unilateral and conditional character of YHWH's promises."[19] YHWH who has fought for Israel can fight against Israel if, unfaithful and fallen from grace and back under wrath (cf. Gal. 5:4), Israel reverts to the Canaanite structures of malice and injustice, the abiding object of holy love's wrath. This danger of failing at married love Israel must *know*, as delineated below.

Love, reverent and affectionate, for YHWH is formed by the knowledge of YHWH who shows *hesed* as the one true God. The Hebrew word for knowledge is famously used also for sexual intimacy, as in "Adam knew his wife Eve and she conceived." This is but an example of the biblical "unity of the human person," as described by Jonathan Edwards's rejection of faculty psychology: "Because both understanding and inclination are expressions of the total human self, the distinction between them is more analytical than actual. . . . The inclination's

18. Hawk, *Joshua*, 250.
19. Hawk, *Joshua*, 252.

affections include an intellectual dimension, while the mind's thoughts include an affective dimension."[20] It is in this sense of human love for YHWH that Israel must *know* in order to see through the falsity of the idols and resist their illusory seductions. Because YHWH is the living God in heaven and on earth, there is no escape from his knowledge of Israel, for he searches and judges hearts. Keep watch over yourselves, therefore, Joshua preaches, that you love YHWH your God. The alternative falls from grace and falls back into bondage that internalizes the oppression of Canaan, the dark Egypt of this world. This Israel must *know*.

If Israel falls back into the Canaanite bondage to the extent of intermarrying with them, they should *know* that YHWH will not again dispossess these nations for Israel. Instead, these nations will persist and become for Israel a baited trap, a lash on their backs, and a thorn in their eyes—metaphors signifying "political oppression and the loss of freedom and independence of action."[21] The same fate will befall an Israel reverting to Canaan: like the fate of Canaan, "YHWH will 'destroy' (*hašmîdô*) Israel . . . , a term used previously to signify the eradication of the peoples of the land."[22]

Joshua brings his exhortation to a close, reminding his audience again of the occasion of this peroration. Joshua is about to die like any other mortal on the earth. Everything on the earth is mortal. Nothing on the earth is permanent. His life is but a sign pointing elsewhere, a messianic sign to be sure, but not yet the thing signified. The viability of Israel's life through future time on the good land depends on its sustaining knowledge in faith of YHWH's faithfulness, for it is YHWH alone who connects the past to the future when otherwise the times fall apart into sound and fury signifying nothing. Joshua's dying wish is that all Israel will know in their hearts and souls the fulfillment of all the good things YHWH promised. This is Joshua's legacy to be preserved in memory from generation to generation. YHWH's word has never failed, but all his words have come true. The urgent repetition of this theme in Joshua's speech is because "as long as [Canaanites] stay within the land, Israel is in danger of becoming like them. . . . Israel's 'inheritance' is finally framed in social rather than geographical terms,"[23] let alone military ones, just as Israel's identity through time consists in ever choosing YHWH who has chosen Israel in *ḥesed* love.

20. McClymond and McDermott, *Theology of Jonathan Edwards*, 314.
21. Nelson, *Joshua*, 261.
22. Hawk, *Joshua*, 258.
23. Hawk, *Joshua*, 250.

So Joshua concludes this first farewell speech, tying together many loose ends of the narrative, "steadily dismantl[ing] notions of identity based on kinship, possession of territory, and strict obedience to the Mosaic commandments."[24] All such identity markers mean different things to different people, and so they do not prove capable of providing a single rule through changing time and circumstance for the unity of all Israel in its true identity as the elect people of God, whose covenant task on the earth through time is to reciprocate the love showered on Israel in forging the culture of a new humanity. Thus, in Hawk's literary reading, the book resolves on a single rule: Israel is the "people who chooses the God who has called them into being."[25] YHWH's relation to creation, says Wyschogrod, "now flows through his relation to Israel, and his relation to Israel is in the service of his relation to humanity." If we remember how the political gods of the ancient Near East were territorial, we perceive the theological singularity of YHWH's election of Israel for the blessing of the nations—namely, that if YHWH admits no territorial limitations but is confessed as God of gods, "the people of Israel were under his rule wherever they were, and it is for this reason that they could not worship the gods of other people when they found themselves in the territories for which those other gods had jurisdiction." Thus Israel's "peoplehood is not co-extensive with the land, as is the peoplehood of others [rooted in blood and soil], who cannot survive as a people once they are separated from their land. . . . But YHWH has taken up residence among this people and therefore in this people. The Jewish people is the dwelling place of [YHWH]."[26] The congregation of Israel is the body of faith. This is a rule of synergy, of theological compatibilism. The (messianic) question is, Who does this, who lives this way, who fulfills this theological compatibilism?

So this fulfillment of the law in the new human being who wills the will of God and does it on the earth is true also for Christianity in that Jesus Christ was born a Jew and remains a Jew forever. Just so, this is true also for Christianity in that the congregation of believers through all time and space is the earthly body of the crucified and risen Lord.

What matters for the future is loyalty to YHWH who fights for us, not racial purity, nor title to land, nor political sovereignty, nor uncomprehending adherence to the letter of the law of Moses absent the spirit of it, which is love for YHWH reciprocating throughout the culture of the new humanity being

24. Hawk, *Joshua*, 260.
25. Hawk, *Joshua*, 260.
26. Wyschogrod, *Body of Faith*, 102–3.

created by YHWH's love for Israel in the new synergism of theological compatibilism. According to this rule of rules, active and continuous choosing in the obedience of faith matters because YHWH shows himself capable of real and therefore diverse relationships with other creatures. Such real relationships of the Creator to the creature cannot be abstracted and systematized into a simple relation of timeless and spaceless divine self-sameness to all the diverse creatures on the earth, as if the differences in these real relationships with creatures were only in the creatures and not in the Creator. As YHWH reveals himself capable of particularity, the particular and earthly choice given to Israel to be the chosen people of YHWH matters ultimately. The abyss between loyal faith and disloyal unbelief thus divides true Israel from false Israel. And this line of demarcation is drawn in the book of Joshua beginning with Rahab's confession of YHWH as the true and living God in heaven and on earth whose will is a new humanity at peace on a liberated earth.

Having finished this speech by Joshua, the reader will be forgiven for thinking that the book has come to its natural conclusion. But the ending is extended for yet one more chapter containing yet one more final exhortation of Joshua. Now the setting is Shechem, where the tent of meeting and the ark of the covenant have come to rest. Here Joshua once more assembles all the tribes, as represented by their leaders who stand before YHWH. All Israel is standing "before God" (24:1), an expression that designates "the more sacred dignity and solemnity of the meeting. . . . So that each might consider for himself that God was presiding over all the things that were done, and that they were not engaged in a private business, but confirming a sacred and inviolable compact with God himself."[27] The scene foreshadows the future. After Joshua's death, the kind of individual leadership over the united twelve tribes that he has exercised in the train of Moses and in anticipation of Messiah will cease. Leadership of Israel will then fall on the assembled officials of the tribes. The testament-legacy of Joshua must be remembered if YHWH's leadership is to remain actual in Israel's heart of hearts and thus reciprocated in the obedience of faith.

In sum, Joshua's first farewell speech spells out the meaning and implications of the kingship of YHWH over the twelve tribes of Israel amid the "nations that remain"—these *nations* now strikingly designated as the "inheritance" of Israel in 23:4. In other words, these peoples, rather than their land, are suddenly and unexpectedly characterized as Israel's inheritance. From the canonical beginning,

27. Calvin, *Book of Joshua*, 250.

however, Israel was destined to be a blessing to the nations (Gen. 12:1–3), not at the expense of the nations, but as servant of YHWH under the reign of YHWH. Notably, nothing further is said now about destroying the alien nations; instead, as Hawk notes, "they remain. Israel may 'own' them or determine their place in the land, but there is no longer any command to exterminate them." An inclusion of the Gentiles into the Israel of God is thereby intimated (cf. Rom. 11:17–24). The congregation of believers amid the nations must remain the elect people of God and sustain this covenanted identity at peril of defection from the cause of YHWH. *Ḥerem* as warfare against flesh-and-blood others has thus been rendered passé and transposes into the self-purification of the people of God that spiritually (thus also in bodily behavior) separates them from the culture of Canaan. "Now at the end of the program the issue is no longer subjugation or occupation, but separation."[28] The book of the law of Moses, now as enacted and thus interpreted by the career of Joshua in the book named after him, comes forward in place of Joshua's charismatic ministry in person. Its words, as Joshua interprets them, set boundaries, and "to go outside these boundaries means becoming one of 'them'"[29] with whom Israel coexists on the earth, separately but more or less equally in right to life and property. Israel is to be *in* the world, therefore, but not *of* the world. Peaceful coexistence is the new and patient path forward between the times, and indeed the presupposition of a new politics of reconciliation (see further the epilogue).

Joshua's second farewell speech begins with a distinctive summation of YHWH's history with Israel beginning with the progenitor, Abraham, who long ago lived beyond the Euphrates and whose family there had served other gods. But YHWH took hold of Abraham the idolater and guided him through all the land of Canaan, multiplying his descendants and giving him Isaac, and to Isaac in turn Jacob and Esau. YHWH gave an inheritance to Esau in the hill country of Seir but sent the family of Jacob down to Egypt. Then YHWH sent Moses and Aaron to afflict Egypt with plagues, and thereby they brought Israel out. But when the Egyptians pursued the fleeing slaves in their fearsome chariots of iron to the cusp of the Red Sea, they cried out to YHWH and he put a cloud of darkness between the pursuers and the pursued. Subsequently, YHWH caused the sea to collapse on the pursuers. *Your* eyes saw what YHWH did to Egypt in all its vaunted military might!

28. Hawk, *Joshua*, 255.
29. Hawk, *Joshua*, 255.

Joshua, speaking for YHWH, uses the second person plural to contemporize the saving deeds of the past—for example, "And your eyes," he says to the present generation, "saw what I did to Egypt" long ago (24:7). Then *you* lived in the wilderness for a long time until YHWH brought *you* to the Transjordan inhabited by the Amorites. They fought with *you*, but YHWH gave them into Israel's hand, in the process giving over their land to Israel as its possession. The king of Moab rose up to make war and called on Balaam the soothsayer to curse Israel. But YHWH would not listen to Balaam and instead caused him to bless *you* and so *you* were delivered from this threat. Then *you* crossed the Jordan and came to Jericho, which resisted *you* as did all the other Canaanite nations. Nevertheless, YHWH delivered Jericho into Israel's hand. It was YHWH who did this for *you*. As with the darkness he sent to protect fleeing Israel from the pursuing chariots of Egypt, so also YHWH sent the "hornet"—a panic causing confusion—when Israel drove out the Amorites and their kings. Joshua comes to the peroration: YHWH fought *for you*! It was not by virtue of your sword or bow! Indeed, it is all fabulous gift from above. YHWH gives land that Israel did not labor to clear, cities to dwell in which Israel did not build, vineyards and olive groves from which to reap that Israel did not plant. Israel therefore is to fear YHWH by serving him completely and faithfully—YHWH who out of generous love violates even his own strict prohibition of booty, now that it has become clear that the root of all evil is covetous desire, not the cleared land nor the built cities nor the vineyards and olive groves.

When the reader reflects on Joshua's summary of YHWH's history with Israel, she may be struck by several items of new information—notably, that Abraham had been an idol worshiper and that Jericho resisted Israel. Most notable of all, however, is what is missing: the giving of the law at Sinai—especially notable after the previous farewell speech had made obedience to the Torah (revealed at Sinai) the very key to Israel's future on the land. We may see here, therefore, a subtle new iteration of *ḥesed* as the rule of rules—how it is that the knowledge of the indicative of grace, the electing claim of the saving God of *ḥesed*, clarifies and informs true obedience to the commandments. The omission of Sinai from the history of salvation indicates that the narrator wished to accentuate the sovereignty of YHWH's gracious election going back to the calling of Abraham, an unworthy idol worshiper and thus without any merit. Israel's success thus stems from faith in the promise, justification of the otherwise ungodly, election of the otherwise rejected. As we heard Luther earlier, so also Calvin holds forth vigorously to this effect:

[Joshua] begins his address by referring to their gratuitous adoption . . . so they could not boast of any peculiar excellence or merit. . . . They were no better than others. . . . Abraham, when he was plunged in idolatry, was raised up, as it were, from the lowest deep.

. . . Abraham was rescued . . . just to show how the free mercy of God was displayed in their very origin. . . . When he was lost, he was raised up from death to life.

. . . Abraham did not emerge from profound ignorance in the abyss of error by his own virtue, but was drawn out by the hand of God. For it is not said that he sought God of his own accord, but that he was taken by God and transported elsewhere.[30]

The grace of election provides the solid basis of the covenant relationship into which Israel has been called; indeed, sovereign grace creates Israel, as it were, out of nothing and sustains Israel in spite of its deviations to the left and the right. So it is clarified that obedience to the covenant is at its heart, the seat of desire, the obedience *of trusting faith*, never then a spiritless matter of keeping rules without understanding of the rule-giver's mind and purpose for the living of life between the times. The obedience of faith springs from a deeper, Spirit-effected affection of the human heart captured by unmerited grace; consequently, it is from love for YHWH that the understanding and keeping of rules springs. Joshua's career has demonstrated how the obedience that maintains and strengthens the covenant relationship develops spontaneously and creatively through the changes and chances of historical journey. Thus, in the end, "choosing YHWH is at the heart of what it means to be 'Israel,'"[31] if by "choice" here one means not consumer choice at the religious smorgasbord of Canaanite culture but what admittedly is lacking in the text of Joshua—namely, the Spirit's grace to trust in the promised grace spoken in the electing word of YHWH. Election is the condition for the possibility of true choice; just this is what makes this synergy of the obedience of faith to be *theological* compatibilism. Yet one may still ask, Who ever could choose YHWH apart from the Spirit of YHWH?

Otherwise, it can seem that, as trusting obedience to the word of promise, "the choice is no real choice at all. Yahweh will continue to be what Yahweh always has been, our God."[32] One recalls here Voltaire's cynical quip "Of course God forgives—that's his job!" This commentary has frequently alluded to Dietrich

30. Calvin, *Book of Joshua*, 250–51.
31. Hawk, *Joshua*, 263.
32. Nelson, *Joshua*, 270.

Bonhoeffer's famous but also frequently misunderstood critique of "cheap grace" in the name of "costly grace." Bonhoeffer's binary is frequently misunderstood along legalistic lines, as if his point was that disciples should prove themselves worthy of grace by their performance of rigorous discipleship—even though Bonhoeffer explicitly warns against this legalistic misunderstanding of his meaning. What he actually says in an opening salvo introducing the distinction takes square aim at what this commentary has described as the modern substitution of religious ideology for the knowledge of God:

> Cheap grace means grace as a doctrine, a principle, a system. It means forgiveness of sins proclaimed as a general truth, the love of God taught as the Christian "conception" of God. An intellectual assent to that idea is held to be of itself sufficient to secure remission of sins. The church which holds the correct doctrine of grace has, it is supposed, *ipso facto* part in that grace. In such a church the world finds a cheap covering for its sin; no contrition is required, still less any real desire to be delivered from sin. Cheap grace therefore amounts to a denial of the living Word of God, in fact a denial of the incarnation of the Word of God.[33]

Against this possibility of theological sloth indulging in cheap grace that would "sin in order that grace may abound" (Rom. 6:1), the imperative of the indicative returns with acute force: Israel surely ought to put away those other gods that their fathers served beyond the Euphrates in the time of Abraham or during their bondage in Egypt, for they are useless and dangerous distractions, passé before the reality of the sovereign grace of YHWH at work in Israel's history. Put vain idols away as useless things now that YHWH has shown himself the true and living God who will always be there for Israel, come what may. Similarly, the Pauline imperative of grace arises with acute force against slothful indulgence in cheap grace: "Therefore, do not let sin exercise dominion in your mortal bodies, to make you obey their passions. No longer present your members to sin as instruments of wickedness, but present yourselves to God as those who have been brought from death to life, and present your members to God as instruments of righteousness. For sin will have no dominion over you, since you are not under law but under grace" (Rom. 6:12–14). Here the imperative of grace is *analytic* to the indicative of grace urging full realization in all the life implications of merciful election. It is not *synthetic*, as if electing grace depended on performance, when in fact grace *is* YHWH who fights for us and as such

---

33. Dietrich Bonhoeffer, *The Cost of Discipleship* (New York: Touchstone, 1995), 43.

precedes and generates human performance. But neither is the imperative idle exhortation, since liberation is from the *power* of sin, not merely from its *guilt*; grace is for the living of liberated life in the new culture on the earth. The Pauline antithesis between life under the law and life under grace, however, is at most implicit in Joshua's concluding discourse. On its own terms, Joshua's discourse articulates a tension within the law between the saving intention of YHWH's electing grace for Israel's reciprocation and the catastrophic threat against Israel's defection from grace. The imperative of grace in Joshua *pleads* the promise: "How can you turn back again to the weak and beggarly elemental spirits? How can you want to be enslaved to them again?" (Gal. 4:9).

In passing, a stunning disclosure has slipped out in Joshua's exhortation against cheap grace. The book of Joshua has told the story of Israel's occupation of Canaan, "all the while carrying with them the gods of their ancestors ([24:]14) and even making room for the gods of Canaan (v. 23)."[34] With a glance ahead to Israel's history as it will unfold on the land, the double-minded thinking against which Joshua sharply warns seems to have been a kind of religious division of labor: YHWH is good for war and politics, but for rain and fertility when living off the land, a dash of Baalism provides crop insurance. Anticipating an Israel that limps along on either side (1 Kgs. 18:21–22), Joshua's rhetoric intensifies, requiring faith in YHWH's eternal favor to be reciprocated in love returned, realized concretely as the obedience of faith manifest in the culture of a new humanity and its social behavior on the earth given as a gift for human stewardship. Therefore serve the Lord! Does it seem bad to you to serve YHWH? Choose this day whom you will serve! I and my house, Joshua concludes dramatically, we will serve YHWH!

The honorary title given to Moses, servant of YHWH, now conferred on Joshua by the narrator, is thus extended to true Israel; true Israel as a unified whole is servant of YHWH. "Serving YHWH" signifies acceptance of the distinctive destiny, articulated in Joshua's version of Israel's story, of freedom from idols in new service to YHWH's reign of righteousness. Just this is the reciprocation intended. ""Serving other gods," by contrast, can only be a fall from grace. Serving YHWH means that Israel now understands that its true good consists not in a lazy presumption of unconditional favor—so all the nations think of their political gods—but in fearful acknowledgment of YHWH's sovereign purpose in electing Israel as the new and redeemed people who represent, *pars*

---

34. Hawk, *Joshua*, 276.

pro toto, the final victory of blessing for all the groaning creation, alien nations too, suffering still under the cruel regimes of the usurpers of the earth. Serving YHWH consists not only in fear of YHWH alone (and thus in fear of no others in heaven or on earth) and in love in the sense of clinging exclusively to YHWH (not unequally yoked to any others). At the root of proper fear and love is the inclination of the heart, the seat of the human person, captivated by YHWH as the sole object worthy of all desire. Action freely flows from disposition; if the disposition of the heart is right, the deeds of obedience flow freely and joyfully from *fides ex corde*.

Joshua's rhetoric crescendos until it lays down the Deuteronomic fork in the road. The circumcision of heart demands that Israel serve YHWH for YHWH's sake and to his glory and not for its own sake and would-be glory. Similarly, at the conclusion of his *Homilies on Joshua* (so far as we have them; they seem to break off prematurely), Origen comments on this redirection of the politics of purity from the elimination of other nations to spiritual purification of one's own community. He expresses the hope that

> the word of God that we speak to you may circumcise every uncleanness, cut back impurities, separate vices from those who hear and remove each thing by which the strength of the mind and natural efficiency is covered over. And thus through the word of God . . . you too will be circumcised by Jesus and you will hear, "Today I have taken away from you the reproach of Egypt."
>
> . . . What does it help us to have renounced this age in baptism but to retain the former filth of our behavior and the impurities of our carnal license? Thus it is fitting, after the parting of the Red Sea, that is, after the grace of baptism, for the carnal vices of our old habits to be removed from us by means of our Lord Jesus, so that we can be free from the Egyptian reproaches.
>
> . . . We display a sword called the word of God, by which word sins are separated and purged from the souls of the hearers.[35]

Thus the book of Joshua's final version of the politics of purity is retained by Origen, radicalized and at the same time deliteralized, though at the cost also in Origen of being depoliticized. How might a fresh Christian reading following in Origen's path retain the deliteralization but regain Joshua's this-worldly horizon, as John Howard Yoder sought?

35. Origen, *Homilies on Joshua*, ed. Cynthia White, trans. Barbara J. Bruce, Fathers of the Church (Washington, DC: Catholic University of America Press, 2002), 216–17.

The people protest against Joshua's peroration as if there were still any choice before them. They affirm that they have chosen and will never fall away from YHWH to serve other gods. "For YHWH our God—it was he who brought us and our fathers up from the land of Egypt, from the house of bondage, who before our eyes did these great signs, led and guarded us all the way we walked through all the peoples whom we passed. And it was YHWH who drove out the peoples who lived in the land before us; therefore we will serve YHWH, for he is our God. He is our God and we are his people—that is settled. That is just the way things are" (24:17–18 paraphrased).

The most dramatic and, literarily speaking, the most decisive enunciation of the knowledge of God in the canonical book of Joshua now occurs. "The rhetorical jolt is sharp and effective."[36] Joshua *contradicts* the ringing affirmation of the people who have just professed their undying loyalty to YHWH with their commitment to know and do his will according to the covenant.[37] "Because the people's response conveys genuine understanding and devotion, Joshua's rebuttal comes as a complete surprise."[38] It is as if the people's choice for YHWH, which had just been so urgently and forcefully demanded by Joshua, did not, indeed *could* not, suffice. Joshua's word of denial is an effective counsel of despair! "Here Joshua seems to act altogether absurdly in crushing the prompt and alert zeal of the people, by suggesting ground of alarm. For to what end does he insist that they cannot serve the Lord, unless it be to make them, from a sense of their utter powerlessness, to give themselves up to despair, and thus necessarily become estranged from the fear of God."[39] Calvin admits to being baffled by this absurdity and finally resolves it by arguing that Joshua's purpose was a rhetorical act of reverse psychology: "to make the obligation more sacred by their having of their own accord chosen YHWH's government, and taken themselves to his guidance, that they might live under his protection."[40]

But Calvin's resolution of the "absurdity" seems artificial. Calvin in fact sees in the end that "all that Joshua gained by his very great anxiety was to secure its rigorous observance for a few years."[41] In fact, more careful but all the more disturbing reading sees that Joshua bases his contradiction of the

36. Nelson, *Joshua*, 270.
37. Contra Pitkänen, *Joshua*, 396.
38. Hawk, *Joshua*, 274.
39. Calvin, *Book of Joshua*, 254.
40. Calvin, *Book of Joshua*, 255.
41. Calvin, *Book of Joshua*, 258.

people's will to obey on the impotence of the human will to do even what it wants in face of the infinite demand of the holy God in heaven and on earth, who is YHWH, requiring the purity of an exclusive fidelity: "You are not able to serve YHWH" (24:19 AT). Why? YHWH is the "holy" God, the one who is neither for nor against Israel taken as one nation among other nations with an autonomous will of its own, like other nations, then, dwelling in the dark Egypt of ignorance of God. YHWH has his own agenda corresponding to his own holiness. YHWH has fought for Israel according to this exclusive—that is, holy—agenda of a new humanity at peace on the earth, a blessing to all nations. Israel must know *this*.

Nelson opines that Joshua's prediction of Israel's human failure is not because of the weakness or wickedness of Israel but because jealousy is inherent in the nature of God: "YHWH is holy and jealous and does not forgive rebellion."[42] It is precisely and exclusively the one who is truly holy—that is to say, is other than all other possible objects of desire as creator of all that is not God—who has sole right and duty to be jealous for human love. This is the *theological* reason that obedience to the covenant has been persistently exhorted by Joshua throughout. All things work for good to them who *love God*—that is to say, to them who are called *according to his purpose* (Rom. 8:28). God is love, and so God's holy love is purely against what is against love, which includes the disordered love of creatures in place of the Creator. This militancy of divine and holy love for the same reason manifests in unmerited grace: the election of Abraham the idolater, the rescue of idol-keeping Israel in Egypt, and the gift of victory for idol-sneaking Israel in Canaan. Just so militant grace disallows all sentimentality in regard to divine love. It is precisely divine love that has the right to be *qano'* (jealous) and to insist, for human good, on holy love's sincere and wholehearted reciprocation so that all created things are loved in and under God but never in place of God. Divine jealousy richly and mercifully forgives transgressions within the covenant relationship, where this hierarchy of values is observed, but it cannot overlook transgression that subverts the covenant, the sin of disloyalty or infidelity that nullifies the very relationship and renders it void. Sin that destroys the covenanted relationship is literally intolerable: defilement, pollution, abomination, and thus beyond the reach of mere forgiveness. There is nothing left in its wake to redeem but only something utterly to destroy, since the something of the covenant is precisely Israel's adoption from a nobody among the nations to serve YHWH

42. Nelson, *Joshua*, 270.

as the one true God of all, thus solely for the holy purposes of YHWH for true blessing, not the false consolations of religious ideology.

The same resolute prosecution of the politics of purity to the bitter end—namely, the spiritual death of the sinner-idolater, culminating in the final purification of Peter, who weeps bitterly—attends the gospel narrative of the second Joshua. "And Jesus said to them, 'You will all become deserters; for it is written, "I will strike the shepherd, and the sheep will be scattered." But after I am raised up, I will go before you to Galilee.' Peter said to him, 'Even though all become deserters, I will not.' Jesus said to him, 'Truly I tell you, this day, this very night, before the cock crows twice, you will deny me three times.' But he said vehemently, 'Even though I must die with you, I will not deny you.' And all of them said the same" (Mark 14:27–31). In fact, Peter must die, though not in the way he imagined. Embedded in this prophecy of incapacity and spiritual death, however, is the novel indication that Jesus's unexpected Gethsemane satisfaction of the divine demand for purity will justly and powerfully reconcile deserter and denier, though not betrayer. With the resurrection of the crucified, whom the disciples proved unable to follow to literal death, the second Joshua rises to pursue and establish anew just those who had failed, working on them a veritable resurrection from spiritual death to a new and theological subjectivity. The politics of purity are thus fulfilled and transcended by a creative new politics of reconciliation as the God of love finds the holy way beyond the wrath of his love to the mercy of it. As the apostle summarizes, "God has imprisoned all in disobedience so that he may be merciful to all" (Rom. 11:32).

Wyschogrod similarly tackles the literary conundrum of Joshua's final judgment on Israel's incapacity when he writes that refusal to reciprocate divine love does not necessarily result "in the termination of concern or even love. It is possible to love—and here is the truth of *agape*—in spite of rebuff or absence of response. But such absence is never a matter of indifference and plays an important role in the relationship because response is always sought, needed, and hoped for."[43] This reference to agape love by Wyschogrod is an allusion to the much-discussed distinctiveness of Christian love as new-creative love that makes worthy by conferring worth, in Luther's words from the Heidelberg Disputation, "on a bad or needy person." YHWH's love is always partial (in the sense of favor or bias) in that it chooses, and thus he elects, a concrete object in distinction from others. As divine and partial love for Israel, the redeemed humanity, the beloved

43. Wyschogrod, *Body of Faith*, 63.

community, is God's concrete choice from all eternity, even so the temporal and temporary anger of this holy love is not some relapse from love but love's ferocious negation of its negation. That there is life beyond this spiritual death is the theological mystery of new-creative agape love surpassing righteous wrath to gain the mercy of reconciliation.

The wrath of the God of love is not, then, God's "proper" but rather God's "alien" work (Luther).[44] In wrath the God of love is hidden, discerned in the darkness by faith in God's properly creative and redeeming love, but not otherwise visible. God's re-creative love *is* creative just because it is not conditioned by the value of its lost and sinful object under God's wrath but rather bestows redeeming value on it. That is new creation from the old, *ex vetere*. Creative love is the proper, hence infinite expression of God's nature: *esse Deum dare*, "to be God is to give." That is creation out of nothing, *ex nihilo*. Redemption redeems and fulfills the sin-frustrated creation groaning in travail for its new birth. God wills properly to give good, supremely and eschatologically the good that he is himself. That is the goal of creation and new creation alike. But if this good that God would give is forsaken for other goods so that recipients of God's goodness turn from the self-giving God to other gods in pursuit of their human-all-too-human agendas of greed, exploitation, and domination, the holy and jealous God of love will crush these human usurpers of the earth, leaving their regimes of malice and injustice behind in the dustbin of history. Here God's properly creative love justly but improperly becomes destructive of what destroys the good earth in order to usurp the usurpers of it. Divine election is not, in this light, a privilege of immunity from wrath but a terrible burden of responsibility, all the more liable to wrath (cf. Amos 3:2) in the event of love's betrayal, as the fate of Judas in distinction from Peter shows.

It is above all crucial here to recall that the book of Joshua, and now especially its stunning conclusion, must be read in the perspective of the dispossessed, of those who have lost the land once promised to their ancestors long ago and given to them under Joshua; suffering Israel has felt this lash of God's wrath and cannot dispel it as some ideological illusion. "Joshua is a book about national victory and glory, but how is it to be read by those who had experienced national humiliation? For such readers there was little glory and much pain in being YHWH's people. . . . The readers are a people who have suffered at the

44. Oswald Bayer, *Martin Luther's Theology: A Contemporary Interpretation*, trans. Thomas H. Trapp (Grand Rapids: Eerdmans, 2007) 208–9.

hands of their God and from the vicissitudes of history." But such readers, upon finishing the book of Joshua, are nevertheless asked whether they will "serve the gods of history's victors who seem to have humiliated Yahweh and now dominate Yahweh's people."[45] Emil Fackenheim echoed this painful question of the book of Joshua's conclusion when he counseled fellow Jews for an additional 614th commandment (to the traditional number of 613 commandments in the Torah counted by the rabbis) after the Holocaust: "Thou shalt not give Nazism posthumous victories."[46] One shall choose the Israel of God; one shall choose life and not fall into Nazism's own nihilism, nor into a gnosticism that denies YHWH who fights for Israel.

So also, then, the people in response contradict Joshua's contradiction: they affirm that they will serve YHWH. We come now to a matter of utmost delicacy on account of the repugnant Christian history of the bloodguilt libel that makes of Jews in perpetuity the hated "Christ killers" of pogroms—as if Jews personified idols in their Christian midst. Against this shameful Christian tradition, however, let us attend closely to the text. Joshua does not rejoice at this reaffirmation of faith on the part of the covenant people. Instead he makes record of the terrible burden of responsibility undertaken in assuming the "yoke of the Torah" and inscribes it: "You are witnesses against yourselves, knowing now full well the holiness and jealousy of the God of love who has chosen you to serve him for the purpose of love. So today, in turn, your choice to serve this God exclusively is hereupon written in stone" (24:22, 27 paraphrased). And the people confirm the fact. Joshua reiterates the demand of exclusive henotheism in a world with many idols on offer, that the people do away with the foreign gods dwelling in their midst and instead turn their *lebab* (heart) to YHWH, the God of Israel. YHWH, the holy and jealous God of *hesed* love, is to be the *only* object of the heart's desire in Israel. Purity of the heart is to will one thing: "Hear, O Israel! YHWH our God, YHWH alone!" (Deut. 6:4 AT). The objective danger of the book of Joshua has thus reappeared for a final time in its course. But it should be clear by now that *herem* has ceased to be a noun and has become a verb, demanding not the extermination of polluting others but the purification of one's own desires. Thus it is that those Christians who have appealed to Joshua to exterminate "polluting Jews" in their midst have categorically missed the conclusive theological point and are themselves doubly liable to the wrath of God.

---

45. Nelson, *Joshua*, 272–73.
46. Fackenheim, *To Mend the World: Foundations of Future Jewish Thought* (New York: Schocken, 1982), 213.

It is more than startling at this conclusion of the speech to hear the demand to remove foreign idols from the midst of the people present, picking up on the hints dropped in the review of YHWH's history with Israel with which Joshua's speech began. This final surprise indicates that the idols have been kept secretly, concealed in the human hearts of visibly aniconic Israel. Is Israel in reality furtive Achan? Joshua's demand may be understood as the book of Joshua's last attempt at fine-tuning the doctrine of desire as the Deuteronomic heart, the seat and wellspring of motivation, and the true target of *herem* warfare. For an idol, one learns in the course of the Joshua narrative, is not in the first place an external object made with human hands to be worshiped as if real. Rather, idols have no real existence, for God is one (cf. 1 Cor. 8:4). Idols exist as external objectifications of theologically misplaced human desire. Misplaced desire gives way to captivation by demons (cf. 1 Cor. 10:20) who use alluring idols to ensnare and addict. These objectifications of misplaced desire can as easily be mental images or abstract concepts as they can be gilded statues or consumer toys. The commandment is not to smash the icons literally (which, being demythologized, can be kept—precisely—as works of art or other temporal goods and services, as things theologically *indifferent*), provided that Israel no longer sacrifices to them. Indeed, as we have seen, they can be transformed into memorials of YHWH who fights for us. The command to remove the idols is rather to extinguish, not satisfy, the idolatrous desires of the human heart. For "those who belong to Christ Jesus have crucified the flesh with its passions and desires" (Gal. 5:24). While it is doubtful that the people present at Shechem for this final farewell of Joshua fully realize this introspective depth of Joshua's command that they put away the idols they have secretly kept, not in their tents but in their hearts, they once again reaffirm their choice to serve YHWH alone, forsaking all others.

Equally startling is the next twist in the text, which does *not* tell of a new or renewed covenant between YHWH and Israel (as Calvin thought), but tells of one between Joshua and the people Israel that took place in Shechem and issued in statutes and ordinances.[47] Given the preceding dialogue between Joshua and the people, however, this is fitting. Joshua wishes the choice of the people for YHWH, who has chosen them to be his Israel, to be publicly ratified, together with an explicit acknowledgment of its obligations and implications that were made clear by Joshua's prophecy of the impotence of Israel's will vis-à-vis the persistently wayward desires of Israel's heart. So this addendum is recorded "in the book of the

47. Nelson, *Joshua*, 276–77.

law of God" (24:26)—perhaps the very canonical addition of this book of Joshua to the book of Deuteronomy. In any case, Joshua makes a memorial, setting up a great stone under an oak tree in the sanctuary of YHWH. He calls the great stone a "witness," for it has heard all these words spoken back and forth on this fateful occasion, above all the words of YHWH spoken to the people by the mouth of Joshua. Therefore the stone, having immutably recorded the witness of Israel that it will serve YHWH alone, will stand as an immovable deposition against Israel when the people deviate from the path to which they have committed themselves. On that note Joshua dismisses the people to their inheritances.

The death of Joshua occurs "after these words" (24:29 AT). His mission is fulfilled; his time has come to an end. Now at last is he awarded the title that was reserved for Moses at the beginning of the book: *'ebed yhwh*—"servant of YHWH." His age is given as one hundred and ten. He is buried by his people at the border of his inheritance in Timnath-serah. Israel served YHWH during his lifetime, and thereafter continues faithful all the days of the elders who remain after Joshua—those who under Joshua knew "all the deeds that YHWH did for Israel" (24:31 AT). Service to YHWH waxes and wanes, however, on the knowledge of YHWH's saving deeds, because the faith that obeys is the faith from the heart of desire that knows YHWH alone as savior and learns in the weal and woe of lived history with him to cling to him alone. Joshua's last speech about the fulfillment of YHWH's promises to the fathers is now accentuated with the notice of the burial of the bones of Joseph, carried from Egypt to the land promised to Jacob, Joseph's father. Indeed, they are interred in the very parcel Jacob had bought in Shechem from the Canaanite Hamor, which became the inheritance of the sons of Joseph. The promise of God has come full circle. Also buried in Ephraim is Joshua's coworker, the priest Eleazar, on the inheritance of his son Phinehas. Thus all that YHWH promised to do for Israel is fulfilled. "This well-constructed ending, however, does not succeed in closing the story, which overflows the narrative's discrete boundaries."[48]

The spiritual power of the book of Joshua does not consist in the pat answers and platitudinous assurances of triumphalist theologies of glory, the religious-ideological bromides easily produced, but falsely, by superficial reading looking for quotable quotes. The book's prophetic punch instead lands squarely on such misreaders in the new and messianic questions framed by careful reading. These questions cause us to look for the God who fights *against* us who imagine ourselves his friends in order to fight *for* us as for enemies (cf. Rom. 5:1–12).

48. Hawk, *Joshua*, 279.

EPILOGUE

On Jewish-Christian Coexistence
before YHWH Who Fights for Us

Jewish reading of the book of Joshua abides, and it has accompanied Christian reading such as has been presented in this commentary. This commentary has sought to reflect post-Christendom reality by the accompaniment throughout of salient remarks from theologian Michael Wyschogrod's *The Body of Faith: God in the People Israel*, the thrust of which may now be summarized. "Judaism is not an ideology that insists on purity and excludes all impure versions. Judaism is the election of the Jewish people, which remains tied in an eternal covenant with God no matter what fallacious or partly fallacious views or sinful actions this or that segment of the people develops. In this respect Christian identity is quite different. Being a Christian is a matter of faith. The church is a spiritual community of those elected in faith."[1] This differentiation entails for Wyschogrod a further one regarding the "this-worldliness" of the messianic future for which Judaism hopes as opposed to Christianity's "otherworldliness." "Judaism is the religion of the land of Israel. It is a religion that is inconceivable without the land of Israel. . . . It is an essential component of the faith because it is the location of God's preeminent dwelling both past and present. . . . And because this is so, if the Jewish return to the land is to be taken seriously, then the cultic dimension of Judaism, which is so closely tied to the land of Israel, must gradually reappear

---

1. Michael Wyschogrod, *The Body of Faith: God in the People Israel* (Lanham, MD: Rowman & Littlefield, 1996), 243.

in Jewish consciousness."[2] This statement represents a theologically more consistent Zionism than earlier—that is, "secular"—iterations. Wyschogrod is speaking about the sacrificial worship at the temple according to the Bible and suggesting that somehow Israel's ancient "cultic holiness" must reappear in post-Holocaust Judaism, which finds its cultic home in the land of Israel.

Classical Christian theological tradition, however, has rejected as "chiliasm" such belief about the restoration of temple worship in the land once given to the tribes of Israel. For example, in the words of the Augsburg Confession XVII: "Likewise rejected are some Jewish teachings, which have also appeared in the present, that before the resurrection of the dead saints and righteous people alone will possess a secular kingdom and will annihilate all the ungodly."[3] Without doubt, that was the correct judgment against the Christian Müntzer's sixteenth-century reading of Joshua and indeed directly aimed at him. By the same token, it does not directly contradict Wyschogrod's claim. We should note immediately, therefore, that what is being rejected here as a "Jewish teaching" is in fact a rival Christian theology. All the same, an abiding divergence between Christian and Jewish theologies of Joshua is indicated in this confusion, one that can be made fruitful for Christian theological self-examination. In rejecting the "otherworldliness" of Christian eschatology predicated on its new Joshua, Jewish theology asks in the name of the old Joshua, How can your best of news be proclaimed in a world that remains in sorrow and pain? It is a *good* question. Would that Christians were perplexed all the more with such "Jewish" perplexity about their own supposedly "good" news![4] For it is precisely from this Jewish perplexity regarding "Christ crucified," an apparent contradiction in terms, that Christianity also, albeit as a spiritual community drawn from the nations and united by faith in this most peculiar belief, meets the politics of purity with an alternative politics of reconciliation, so far, that is, as it rightly understands the Pauline interpretation of "Christ crucified": "He made him to be sin who knew no sin, so that in him we might become the righteousness of God" (2 Cor. 5:21).

The reader will have quickly noticed that this commentary employs neither the substitution of the title "Lord" for the Hebrew Tetragrammaton, transliterated

---

2. Wyschogrod, *Body of Faith*, 245.

3. *The Book of Concord: The Confessions of the Evangelical Lutheran Church*, ed. Robert Kolb and T. J. Wengert (Minneapolis: Fortress, 2000), 50–51.

4. J. Louis Martyn, "Epistemology at the Turn of the Ages: 2 Corinthians 5:16," in *Christian History and Interpretation: Studies Presented to John Knox*, ed. W. R. Farmer et al. (Cambridge: Cambridge University Press, 1967), 269–87.

YHWH (ancient Hebrew has no vowels, only consonants), nor the common scholarly reconstruction of the divine name thought to be pronounced "Yahweh." Previously the English-language rendering of this proper name, widely disseminated from the King James translation in the seventeenth century, was "Jehovah." Canonically, however, the opaque term "YHWH" was provided to Moses as a proper name at the burning bush in Exod. 3:15. The Hebrew name is some kind of construction of the Hebrew verb *to be*, meaning perhaps "I am," or "I am that I am," or "I will be who I will be." With Wyschogrod this author prefers the third rendering as the one that makes the most contextual sense of the name's introduction in Exod. 3, in effect saying to Moses, "Do not presume already to know who or what I am, but learn to know me from my named deeds."

The decision of this commentary to use the transliterated name, however, does not depend on this interpretation of its etymology. Certainly this third interpretation would tend against a long-standing alternative understanding of the revealed divine name as enunciating the ontology of perfect being, God as *esse ipsum subsistens*. The alternatives here have far-reaching implications for the doctrine of God, which can hardly be settled on the exegetical basis of Exod. 3, given what R. Kendall Soulen has rightly tagged the "opacity" of the divine name.[5] Names can have original meanings, in other words, which may be etymologically reconstructed, but in their usage through time have become opaque to long-forgotten genealogies and now simply function conventionally to point out someone or something as sign points to thing signified. No one in contemporary English, for example, who meets a Mr. Nelson wonders who the "Nel" is who fathered the new friend. In deference to Jewish tradition, and in reverence to this opacity, the Christian theologian Soulen abstains from pronouncing or even spelling in written language the (reconstructed) divine name; instead he adopts the Jewish custom of substituting (in English) the word "Lord" (*adonai* in Hebrew, *kyrios* in Greek) and referring impersonally to the divine name as the Tetragrammaton.

Soulen's reasoning is that, as sign to thing signified, the Tetragrammaton refers to (not represents)[6] a transcendent divine subject who bears this opaque name in historical relation to Israel; as such it is the same sign above all other signs given to Jesus in Phil. 2:9. It is a pure proper name, opaque but for its function of pointing away from itself to a particular subject, with no intrinsic meaning as

---

5. R. Kendall Soulen, *The Divine Name(s) and the Holy Trinity*, vol. 1, *Distinguishing the Voices* (Louisville: Westminster John Knox, 2011), 10.
6. Soulen, *Divine Name(s)*, 79.

some kind of representation;[7] it works properly to point away from itself to the signified divine transcendence of a unique subject who cannot be captured by any definition or in any representation. Soulen acknowledges that the divine name acquired in its reception history a cloud of connotations, such as God's eternity, the distinction of Creator from creature, gracious condescension, and irrevocable faithfulness. These accretions are not as such mistaken, if taken as connotations, for they may have acquired a certain validity in the history of usage as believers learn to know YHWH by the biblical narrative that identifies him.

Nevertheless, the root theological function of the divine name is purely to refer to the divine Who in an oblique way, generating a *theological* apophatism *by virtue of* this revealed name[8]—*not* a philosophical apophatism *in spite of* names.[9] Philosophical apophatism, associated with the negative theology of the Platonic tradition, points to an unknowable yet metaphysically real divine "nature" or "substance" beyond all named gods/idols in human cultures, which are in turn depicted by multiple forms in the violent contention saturating human history. By contrast, theological apophatism refers to the divine "person," a subjectivity that on gracious invitation can be addressed by name but never captured and instrumentalized in the name provided (yet recall the messianic witness of Josh. 10:14). In other words, for Soulen the opacity of the revealed name guarantees Karl Barth's brief against Feuerbach concerning the irreversibility of subject and predicate in theological statements (e.g., love is not God; rather God is love).[10] The opacity of the divine name, YHWH, has this singular and crucial function to denote the ungraspable, incomprehensible divine subject. In view of this, the divine name may further be protected from profanation by the Christian adoption of the Jewish tradition of abstaining from its pronunciation, as if to say that you cannot misuse God's name if you never actually pronounce it.

Whether Soulen has correctly captured the thinking of the Jewish tradition in this regard we must leave for Jewish scholars to judge. Certainly respect for living Judaism requires Christians to defer to their customary circumlocution in shared public space and thus to refrain from voicing the divine name within Jewish earshot. But in an explicitly Christian-theological commentary on the book of Joshua one may not so defer, taking the book then as Old Testament scripture that anticipates the coming of Christ from the wilderness of testing into Galilee

7. Soulen, *Divine Name(s)*, 13.
8. Soulen, *Divine Name(s)*, 48–49.
9. Soulen, *Divine Name(s)*, 21.
10. Soulen, *Divine Name(s)*, 54.

to inaugurate the reign of God by driving out the demons, and thence his procession to Jerusalem, where he will be installed as a king of a kingdom *coming to* this world, just so precisely not *of* this world. YHWH of the Hebrew scriptures is the very one whom Jesus addresses as "Abba, Father," the nearness of whose kingdom he proclaims and enacts in his new iteration of the Joshua campaign of old. This identification of Israel's YHWH with Jesus's Father, such that in anticipation of Nicaea's *homoousios* the Johannine Jesus can reveal himself in a series of "I Am" statements, is crucial to Christian knowledge of God. For this identification of YHWH with the eternal Father who eternally generates his own Son on whom he eternally breathes his Spirit, and in this way comes messianically to the earth to redeem creation, constitutes the biblical and Christian theological approach to divine unity in distinction from the philosophical approach of protological simplicity.[11]

Supremely, as we have seen in the commentary, the unity of creator and redeemer in YHWH's history with creatures consists in the event of the God of love surpassing the wrath of his love to find the mercy of it for Israel and through Israel for all nations. This mediation of Israel, as servant of YHWH in the event of reconciliation, is the root and font of messianic hope. This is true both of Judaism and Christianity so far as they are true to the biblical sources. They diverge in the spiritual-theological interpretation of Joshua's gospel of YHWH who fights for us over the need for, and the truth of, Christianity's crucified Messiah. To the ears of Judaism this iteration of their own messianic tradition grates on the ears. It sounds all too painfully, in view of Jewish experience, like proclaiming as good news Joshua defeated, humiliated, his corpse hung like the Canaanite kings on a tree to die in disgrace and be buried in a cave whose entrance has been heaped with stones to memorialize defeat forever. For Christianity, of course, this ignominy is both true and yet, decisively, not the end of the story. In the apocalyptic light of Easter morn, the paradox of "Christ crucified" resolves into what Philip Ziegler calls a "radical redefinition."

> The existence of every believer is to be conformed to the life of the Crucified, to own him. It does so inasmuch as it takes shape in lives of service, lives of humble self-giving for others, and as such lives marked by suffering. For in the service of the Master who is the servant of all, and whose life is given over for all, the epitome of faithful following can only take the shape of self-dispossession for the sake of

11. Paul R. Hinlicky, *Divine Simplicity: Christ the Crisis of Metaphysics* (Grand Rapids: Baker Academic, 2016).

others (Mark 10:42–45). As concepts of kingship and captaincy are here subjected to radical redefinition in view of the actuality of the Messiah's cross, so too is the meaning of the martial struggle into which the Christian is drawn.[12]

For Christians, YHWH fights for us by the grant of his Spirit who prevails in the believer's "self-dispossession": "If any want to become my followers, let them deny themselves and take up their cross and follow me" (Mark 8:34). This is the Christian-spiritual retrieval and repurposing of the politics of purity: the lifelong repentance of self-dispossession (see 1 Cor. 6:20).

Believers can do that as children of God just because and only because their heavenly Father, YHWH who fights for us, has surpassed the wrath of his love in the self-donating Son and self-communicating Spirit. This dramatic event of God surpassing God to achieve mercy beyond wrath, enacted between Gethsemane and the empty tomb, transacts in the believer's corresponding "self-dispossession" by Spirit-wrought repentance and faith every time the gospel of YHWH who fights for us is proclaimed, when and where the Spirit pleases to bestow. But, in the first place, this occurs as the internal turning point in the life of God in his history with his creation, as Walter Brueggemann has explained: "At the moment of ominous deciding, Yahweh refused to act in self-regard, because Yahweh found in Yahweh's own internal life a depth of devotion to the well-being of Israel that was not, until that moment of crisis, available to Yahweh."[13] As an event in the life of God, it is as new for God as it is for us. As proclamation of the good news of YHWH's self-overcoming to triumph for lost and sinful Israel, this event is obscured, however, when the divine name YHWH is replaced by generic terminology such as *adonai* or *kyrios*. These are titles or abstractions that, if they do not strictly designate the creator of all that is not God, incline otherwise toward unbaptized philosophical monotheism.[14]

Moreover, if the purpose of avoiding pronunciation of the divine name is to guard against its profanation by verbal misuse, silence is a strategy that fails the Christian interpreter. Because it is Israel's YHWH who fights for us, one can profane the divine name not only by prophesying falsely in his name but also by refraining from enunciating the prophetic "Thus says YHWH . . ." when

12. Philip G. Ziegler, *Militant Grace: The Apocalyptic Turn and the Future of Christian Theology* (Grand Rapids: Baker Academic, 2018), 196.

13. Walter Brueggemann, *Theology of the Old Testament: Testimony, Dispute, Advocacy* (Minneapolis: Fortress, 1997), 299.

14. Robert W. Jenson, *Unbaptized God: The Basic Flaw in Ecumenical Theology* (Minneapolis: Augsburg Fortress, 1992).

such proclamation is given and required by the Spirit. It is by using the divinely given name properly that Christian theology tests to see who and what God is by singling out his named and saving deeds for human recognition, a test that turns on Jesus's identification of YHWH who fights for us as his Abba, Father, who does battle for us precisely by the sending of his Son and Spirit. This commentary has thus followed the usage of L. Daniel Hawk, who transliterates the divine name as YHWH—that is, without any vowels. Since this transliteration is literally unpronounceable in English, it serves both to give an indication of the holy strangeness of the divine name and yet provides, as does the Hebrew text of Joshua, a proper name by which believers can reciprocate divine love in the personal and communal address of prayer, praise, and thanksgiving. Readers may provide a pronunciation for YHWH, or refrain from pronouncing, as they see fit.

This discussion raises the larger question of Christian appropriation of the Hebrew scriptures. It is the case today that conscientious Christian theology rightly recoils from the historic crime of the Nazis against the Jews popularly (and ambiguously) named the Holocaust (from Greek for "whole burnt offering" and thus a conceptual cognate of *ḥerem*). They rightly wish to root out any sources in traditional Christian anti-Judaism that have contributed to the Nazi crime. Consequently, some have gone so far as to regard Christian appropriation of the Hebrew scriptures as its own "Old Testament" as an act of hermeneutical violence: as if robbing the Jews of their own Bible. There is a grain of truth in this, as David Nirenberg has documented in his wide-ranging but subtle analysis of the way foundational binaries, like old-new, literal-spiritual, law-gospel, and so on, may be put to work to make Judaism the ugly trope for *whatever* one wishes to supersede and leave behind in the dustbin of history. The binary in its formality has no intrinsic meaning and thus is suitable for *whatever* purposes contempt imagines. What Nirenberg's scholarship shows us is that this highly variable "teaching of contempt" evolved in the absence of human dialogue with living Judaism because it was an exercise *entirely internal* to Christian identity dynamics,[15] as noted above with respect to the Augsburg Confession's rejection of chiliasm. In other words, to call a Christian a Jew or a Judaizer or a Pharisee was a ready-to-hand smear tactic within Christendom; in the course of time when this nasty habit detached from its intra-Christian ecclesiastical domain, it was culturally available in post-Christendom cultures for new deployment in various forms of modern race-theory anti-Semitism. The irony of ironies: Nazis

15. David Nirenberg, *Anti-Judaism: The Western Tradition* (New York: Norton, 2013).

disowned even the pro-Nazi German Christians by 1937, saying in effect that as Christianity had superseded Judaism, so today National Socialism is superseding also the highly compromised "German Christianity."

One of the great benefits today after a generation of post-Christendom/post-Holocaust theological dialogue between Christians and Jews is better historical knowledge of what some have called the original schism, when ecclesia and synagogue separated in the aftermath of the Jewish wars of the first and second centuries of the Common Era.[16] In this light, well-meaning contemporary repudiation of Christian use of Hebrew scripture as its own Old Testament, unwittingly reproducing the heresy of Marcion, is based on colossal historical ignorance of the origins of rabbinic Judaism as well as early Catholic Christianity—including, to begin with, early Christianity's own struggle to retain the Hebrew Bible as canonical scripture over against a rival gnostic alternative animated by hostility to the Hebrew scriptures.

But such critique is equally ignorant of the rise of normative Judaism. The hermeneutical equivalent in Judaism to the New Testament, which construes the Hebrew scripture as its "Old Testament," is rabbinic commentary in Mishnah. Normative or rabbinic Judaism emerged simultaneously with early Catholic Christianity, both reacting to the catastrophe of the destruction of the temple in Jerusalem and both searching the scriptures of Israel to comprehend the event. For Judaism as it had hitherto existed, the deep trauma in this was the cessation of sacrifice there, the cultic center that held theologically fractured and fractious Second Temple Judaism together. Each community subsequently interpreted the disaster as divine punishment for sin (which they could have found prophesied in Josh. 24 as elsewhere), but the knowledge of the sin that elicited this divine judgment diverged between them. For the first-century scribes and Pharisees of the time of Jesus and Paul who gradually became the rabbis of the diaspora synagogues, the sin was Israel's inadequate obedience to the whole law, all 613 commandments found in the Torah. For the first-century Jewish Christians, as may be seen in the Gospels of Matthew and John in particular, the sin was disobedience to the gospel of the new Joshua, Jesus—disbelief in him as Israel's crucified and risen Messiah. Consequently, both communities laid claim, but in correspondingly different ways, to the legacy of the scriptures of Israel, each employing their own proper hermeneutical lens as they became discrete religions mutually delimited.

16. I have given an account of this dialogue and research in my systematic theology; see "On Jewish Perplexity as a Principle Internal to Christology," in *Beloved Community: Critical Dogmatics after Christendom* (Grand Rapids: Eerdmans), 416–28.

In historical fact, moreover, Christian claim to the scriptures of Israel originated very early on when the predominance of believers was still among the Jewish people, undoubtedly beginning with Jesus himself. Thus the divergent appropriations of scripture originate in and as an intra-Jewish controversy still in the Second Temple period. Consequently, classical Christianity and classical Judaism emerge historically as alike eisegetical variations on the Hebrew Bible; neither repristinates purely what was once written, but rather each appropriates from it for purposes of encouragement and hope for the present-day faithful. The apostle Paul laid down the Jewish-Christian hermeneutic of the Hebrew Bible when he wrote, "For whatever was written in former days was written for our instruction, so that by steadfastness and by the encouragement of the scriptures we might have hope" (Rom. 15:4)—provided that we identify penitently with the dispossessed of the earth. The present Christian theological commentary on the canonical book of Joshua, as we have seen, has read the book from this perspective.

Only when the two communities mutually anathematized each other, however, refusing to live together in spiritually conflicted but politically peaceful coexistence by way of face-to-face human dialogue, did their paths separate behind walls of uncomprehending hostility. Within centuries, the political establishment and numerical superiority of increasingly Gentile Christianity in the new political formation of Christendom, however, made the ghettoization of Judaism unequally injurious. Addressing this failure in understanding between scriptural communities, Jewish theologian Peter Ochs has developed a reparative program of common "scriptural reasoning." He draws attention to four salient characteristics of postliberal theology's principled rejection of supersessionism: (1) ecumenism, undertaking reparative unity among the divided churches and beyond; (2) reformation by return to the sources in scripture study and scriptural reasoning; (3) an ecclesial hermeneutic of scripture as the ecumenical church's book; and (4) narrative reading of the Gospels as themselves rereadings of the Old Testament in the light of the Spirit made known in Christ. Readers may detect all of these characteristics of scriptural reasoning in the commentary they have just finished.[17]

Reference to the Holocaust and consequently to post-Holocaust theology, however, does serve to illuminate a new set of dilemmas confronting both

17. See my review essay: Paul R. Hinlicky, review of *Another Reformation: Postliberal Christianity and the Jews*, by Peter Ochs, *Journal of Scriptural Reasoning* 13, no. 2 (November 2014), http://jsr.shanti .virginia.edu/back-issues/volume-13-number-2-november-2014-navigating-john-howard-yoders-the -jewish-christian-schism-revisited/a-review-essay-on-peter-ochs-another-reformation-2.

Christian and Jewish theological thought, especially bringing into question the use of the biblical legacy to bring hope for us today. The title of this epilogue, containing the word "coexistence," borrows political terminology from the twentieth-century Cold War, when the mutually assured destruction of nuclear arsenals pointed in each other's direction required both sides to recognize the need for and the desirability of sharing the earth despite ideological rivalry. Something similar to this sober recognition of political reality requires Jews and Christians to realize that in the post-Holocaust world, perpetuating their respective polemical traditions of mutual hostility, in distinction from authentic disagreement about the messianic future promised by the scriptures of Israel as a whole, threatens each and both together with mutually assured suffocation in the "dark Egypt of this world," an "iron cage" increasingly hostile to messianic hope. Let us in conclusion review this situation from both the Jewish and Christian sides.

In the penetrating study mentioned in the chapter on preliminary considerations, Zachary Braiterman analyzes the dilemma for "post-Holocaust Jewish thought," beginning with a careful rereading of Richard Rubenstein's notorious attack on the biblical "God of history."[18] Fundamentally, by "the God of history" Rubenstein meant the theology of Deuteronomy with its promises of YHWH's protection in exchange for obedience and with its threats of YHWH's retribution for disobedience. Rubenstein regarded this theology as utterly discredited by the catastrophic event of the Nazi mass murder. He pointed to the "ultra-Orthodox" Jews who, already in their nineteenth-century rejection of Zionism as unfaithful disobedience to the covenant and continuing along the same lines after the Nazi crime, taught that victims had brought this catastrophe upon themselves by their abandonment of covenantal life. Rubenstein dialectically concurred with these ultra-Orthodox adherents of Deuteronomic theology that such was the only possible scriptural interpretation of the Nazi massacre of European Jews, if one held theologically that blessing is the result of obedience and catastrophe the result of covenant disloyalty. And thus, he argued, Deuteronomic theology had to be jettisoned along with the historical God of the covenant who, Rubenstein accused, had failed to keep his end of the covenant bargain in the promise of protection. YHWH had *not* intervened in history to protect Jews and stop the Nazi mass murder. So much for the God of history.

18. Zachary Braiterman, *(God) after Auschwitz: Tradition and Change in Post-Holocaust Jewish Thought* (Princeton: Princeton University Press, 1998).

Well known thus far, yet that is but half a reading of Rubenstein, according to Braiterman. For Braiterman there is a further, far more penetrating problem, as mentioned in our preliminary chapter. Yet further clarity has emerged on this problem in the time since Rubenstein's seminal book, helping make the Holocaust trauma the focal point today of Jewish identity. This is the very problem of the book of Joshua: honest reading of the "genocidal" legacy of Israel's radical and exclusive monotheism on display in this canonical book inclines post-Holocaust Jews to reject it not merely for failed promises but for its ethically repugnant promises and threats, which result in creating victims and then blaming the victims for the victimization. In other words, it would be too cruel an irony for contemporary Jews in the post-Holocaust world if the world had learned holy wars of extermination from the Hebrew Bible. Better to abandon YHWH, the God of history and covenant as depicted in the scriptures, than to continue to believe that he fights for us (and thus against others) in total war.

Braiterman's analysis of the deeper problem is reinforced by contemporary Israeli scholars Yonina Dor and Naomi De-Malach, who explore the treatment of the book of Joshua in contemporary Israeli schools. "Zionism turned the [Bible] into a secular and cultural text with historical, literary, humanistic, and national dimensions. But after the (political) religious movements had begun to appropriate it to suit their own views, its status in Israeli society declined. . . . Archaeological digs at biblical sites, which used to be at the center of young people's search for their roots, have been replaced by trips to Poland. . . . The book of Joshua is a conspicuous case of a constitutive narrative that was once perceived as relevant to the fulfillment of Zionism, but whose plain meaning is now hard to accept."[19] In other words, modern Israelis at first took the book of Joshua as a representation of what had really happened and as such a resource for contemporary Israeli identity with its claims on the land of Palestine up to and including dispossession of the Palestinians. But archaeological evidence, partisan political appropriations by modern Israel's religious right, and the overriding trauma of the Holocaust took their revenge on this politicized biblical literalism. What was once an asset became the unbearable embarrassment of genocide taught in the Bible, specifically in the book of Joshua.[20] And the only defense

19. Yonina Dor and Naomi De-Malach, "Teaching Bible Stories Critically: 'They Did Not Spare a Soul'—The Book of Joshua in an Israeli Secular Education Environment," in *Joshua and Judges*, ed. Athalya Brenner and Gale A. Yee (Minneapolis: Fortress 2013), 40–41.

20. A similar disillusionment among American evangelicals who have supported Zionism by way of a "premillennialist" reading of the book of Joshua can be found in an essay by Bruce K. Waltke. He

available against this crushing realization was the usual historical-critical gambit of debunking Joshua's historicity.

Christian theology can hardly resolve this dilemma for Jewish thought, but it can certainly learn from it. One thing that can be learned from it is Braiterman's account of how Rubenstein in his journey instantiates a classic slide in ancient Jewish theology, concurrent with but rival to the rise of normative Judaism, following the collapse of apocalyptic faith in the wake of the defeats of the Jewish rebellions in the first and second centuries: the slide into gnosticism. Here too the failure of the so-called God of history led to Jewish renunciation of YHWH, sinister creator of this dark world, a demon in disguise, cruelly oppressing his people with impossible expectations but also deluding them into undertaking unlikely rebellion revisited back upon them in catastrophic defeat. Rubenstein's own post-Holocaust turn to forms of radical feminism, the Kabbalah, and the mysticism of ritual untethered from biblical narrative and from the dogma of the Shema repeats this classical early Jewish disillusionment with the God of the Bible in the genesis of gnosticism.

Christian thinkers will recognize this pattern of disillusionment from early Catholicism's battle within its own ranks against the gnostic temptation, preeminently in the thought of the late second-century church father Irenaeus, who contended for the unity of the Testaments—theologically, for the unity of God as creator and redeemer.[21] Of course, the question of such Christian canonical unity could not frame the problem for rabbinic Jews in these early centuries inasmuch as the question was particular to the Christian community, which knew both its reliance on the scriptures of Israel and its new key to their understanding in the gospel proclamation of the crucified Messiah. Their access to the Old Testament text was provided by the knowledge of Christ crucified as the Logos of God, whom they therefore looked to appear also in his antecedent history with Israel. This very narrow bridge of epistemic access creates for the Christian simultaneously the necessity *both* of receiving the Hebrew scriptures as authoritative prophecy of the Logos incarnate *and* of the spiritual-literary reading of it as their Old Testament. Such an approach to the unity of the Testaments manifestly had to deliteralize the Old Testament, as the church father Origen, several centuries

---

argues that "premillennialism, by its insistence on a literalistic interpretation of the Old Testament, adds to church doctrine what the Spirit did not clearly tell the church." Bruce K. Waltke, "The Doctrine of the Land in the New Testament," *Crux* 53, no. 2 (Summer 2017): 2–9.

21. Paul R. Hinlicky, *Divine Complexity: The Rise of Creedal Christianity* (Minneapolis: Fortress, 2011), 133–58.

after Irenaeus, has illustrated for us in the present commentary—even as Origen must be criticized and in places corrected for insufficient attention to the literary sense of canonical Joshua and too careless employment of the invidious binaries identified by Nirenberg. The abiding problem here is that of the continuity and discontinuity between the old Joshua with his sword of bronze and the new Joshua equipped with a two-edged sword of the Word by the Spirit of God.

We are not there yet. Christians and Jews have in common the "already/not yet" template of Second Temple apocalyptic, which frames their existence on the earth as journeys in the obedience of faith that is not yet sight. Because the story of God's ways with Israel is not yet finished, the rival plotlines of this unfolding story in Judaism and Christianity cannot in principle be forcibly decided one against the other, least of all by bad-faith resort to the coercive power of the state. But neither can rival plotlines for the same canonical story be ignored. As ancient Israel was taught to coexist in spite of every tension with Rahab and the Gibeonites, so today we realize that coexistence is the peaceful political alternative to the mutually assured destruction entailed by an unchastened politics of purity. Much more needs to be said and could be said, but thus far the knowledge of God derived from literary-theological reading of the book of Joshua can bring us: in the end YHWH fights for Jew and Christian together or fights against each separately.

SCRIPTURE INDEX

Old Testament

Genesis

1:28 215
4:13–15 106
9:6 106, 226
12:1–3 260
12:1–7 13n21
13:14–18 13n21
15:17–21 13n21
17:1–27 94
32 55
34 93
49:8–12 204

Exodus

1:12 143
3 275
3:15 275
4:24–26 94n17
4:25 93n11
7–14 180
12:1–32 74
12:2 89
12:3 89
12:44 94
12:48–49 94
13:8–9 83
14–15 140
14:14 22
14:24 161
15:3 22

15:15–16 68
15:17 42
16:35 97
17:9–16 13n21
17:11 134
20:24 242
20:25 93n11
21:12–14 225
22:21–24 40
23 30, 32
23:22 29
23:23 22
23:27 22, 29, 161
23:28 22
23:29–30 22
24:4 89
24:13 13n21
24:17 19
26:34 216
29:43–45 215
32:17 13n21
33:2 29
33:3 96
34 70
34:11 29
40:21 76n5

Leviticus

10 80
10:1–3 19
18:24–25 73, 108
18:27–28 73

18:28 108
23:23–24 108
23:25–29 108
24:17–22 226
25:23 108, 168, 229
27:28–29 237

Numbers

3:31 76n5
4:5 76n5
7:89 76n5
10:33–36 76n5
10:35–36 78
11 13n21
11:1 19
11:18 80
13 13n21
13–14 22
13:22 182
13:28 182
13:32–33 182
14 134n3
14:2–3 125
14:8 96
14:28–30 13n21
14:36–38 13n21
14:44 76n5, 78, 109
14:44–45 125
16:13–14 96
16:35 19
21:21–35 183
22–24 198

25:1–5 65
26:65 13n21
27:1–11 213
27:8 213
27:18–23 13n21
31 114, 198
32:1–42 60
32:38 13n21
33:55–56 256
34:1–12 191
34:17 13n21
35:1–8 225
35:25 225

Deuteronomy

1:7 91n1
1:28 182
1:38 54n2
2:10–11 182
2:21 182
2:24–3:11 170
2:26–3:22 183
3:12–22 60
3:21 54n2
3:28 54n2
4:21 43
4:39 69
5:22 19
6:3 96
6:4 270
6:5 253
6:8 83
6:10–11 178
7 5n1, 30, 34–36, 38
7:1–5 138
7:2–4 65
7:5 72, 85
7:23 161
7:24 72
7:25 72
7:25–26 128
9:2 182
9:4–5 73
10:16 38
10:18 38
11 145

11:9 96
11:18 83
11:22 253
11:29–30 89
12 216
12:3 85
12:29–32 138
13:3–4 253
13:17 132
15:4 43
15:8 146
15:63 146
16:22 85
18:10 94n18
19:1–13 225
20:1 177
20:10–15 137
20:10–18 152
20:10–20 71
20:17 151
20:18 137
21:22–23 141
24:15 251
27 145
27:2–13 87
27:5–6 146
27:35 145
28:46 83
28:52 104n8
29:4–6 154
29:10–12 152
29:15 152
29:17–29 138–39
30:20 253
31 250
31:1–29 59
31:6–8 13n21
31:23 13n21
34 13n21

Joshua

1–11 183
1:1–9 53–59
1:3 101
1:4 56
1:6 57

1:7 57
1:7–8 146
1:9 57
1:10–18 60–63
1:12–18 241
1:13 57
1:15 57
1:17–18 61
2:1–24 64–75
2:8 66
2:9 68
2:11 69, 92
2:25 124
3 83
3:1–17 87
3:1–4:24 76–90
3:10 81
3:11 82
3:13 89
4 84
4:3–5 87
4:7 86
4:8 87
4:8–9 87
4:9 87
4:10–11 87n52
4:10–19 87
4:14 88
4:15 88
4:18 89
4:19 89
4:20 89
4:20–5:1 87
4:21–24 89
4:24 76
5 94
5:1 124
5:1–15 91–101
5:2 93
5:2–9 86
5:4 94n18
5:6 96
5:10 89
5:10–12 95
5:12 76
5:13 42, 99

5:13–14 119
5:13–15 92
5:14 99
5:15 42
6:1–27 102–19
6:9 115
6:17 112, 115
6:17–21 112
6:18 112, 114
6:21 112
6:23 121
6:24 129
7 64, 139, 245
7:1 121, 128, 245
7:1–26 120–33
7:4–5 57
7:7 91n1
7:11 128
7:20 128, 130
8:1–2 114, 139
8:1–29 134–43
8:8 129
8:19 129
8:20 140
8:26 140
8:29 135, 141
8:30–35 87, 144–48
8:33 144–45
8:34 145, 149
8:34–35 146
8:35 144
9 65, 113, 150–51
9:1–2 149
9:1–27 149–57
9:6 89, 144
9:6–7 149
9:9 151
9:23 156
9:24–25 151
10 150, 159, 170, 178
10–12 149–50
10:1–15 158–65
10:6–7 89
10:12–15 57
10:14 50, 276
10:16–43 166–71

10:26 163
10:27 163
10:40–42 232
10:42 50, 170
11 172, 174, 178
11:1–15 172–78
11:4 175
11:6 129
11:6–9 177n18
11:9 129
11:11 129
11:12–14 114
11:16–20 179–81,
    233
11:18 174
11:19 175
11:21–23 182
11:22 182
11:23 43, 233
12 183, 185, 187
12–19 6n2
12:1 184
12:1–24 183–88
12:2–5 183
12:4–5 183
12:7 184–85
12:7–24 185, 233
12:16–18 185
13 185, 195
13–19 204
13–21 183
13:1–7 191–95
13:2–6 233
13:8–33 196–98
13:14 194
13:32 198
13:33 194, 197
14:1 199, 221
14:1–5 199–201
14:2 205
14:3–4 194
14:6 89
14:6–15 202–3
14:13–14 230
15 204, 212
15:1–12 206

15:1–17:18 204–14
15:13 205, 230
15:16 206
15:19 206–7
15:20–62 206
15:54 230
15:60–62 207
15:63 150, 158, 207,
    233
16:1 205
16:1–10 210
16:10 150, 212, 233
17:1 205
17:1–13 212
17:3 206
17:4 205
17:6 43
17:12–13 150
17:12–18 233
17:13 212
17:14 214
17:14–18 206, 213
17:17–18 214
17:18 206, 212
18:1 114, 205, 215
18:1–19:51 215–22
18:7 194
18:10 205
18:11 205
18:11–28 219
18:21–24 219
19:1 205
19:1–9 220
19:10 205
19:10–48 220
19:17 205
19:24 205
19:32 205
19:40 205
19:47 220, 230
19:49–50 202
19:49–51 221
19:51 215, 218
20 225–26, 228, 248
20:1–2 223
20:1–9 223–28

20:9 223
21 196, 229
21:1–40 194
21:1–42 229–31
21:43–45 232–33,
    252
22 47, 61, 200, 216,
    245
22:1–8 242
22:1–34 237–49
22:2 225
22:5 146
22:9 244
22:9–34 216
22:16 245
22:17 246
22:19 101, 246
22:20 245
22:22 246
22:22–23 247
22:24–27 248
22:31 245, 249
23 61, 250
23:1 233
23:1–24:33 250–72
23:2 251
23:3 50
23:4 86, 150, 233,
    259
23:6 146
23:6–8 251
23:7 150, 233
23:10 50
23:11 253
23:12 253
23:12–13 150, 233
24 250–51
24:1 259
24:7 261
24:12 29
24:13 178
24:14 264
24:17–18 266
24:19 56, 62, 267
24:22 270
24:23 264

24:26 89, 114, 146,
    272
24:27 270
24:28 43
24:29 53, 272
24:31 93n11, 272

Judges

1:1 13n21
1:10–15 206
1:21 158, 209
2:3 29
2:6 43
2:6–10 13n21
2:21–23 13n21
3:3 191
4:15 161
5:2 99
6:9 29
17–18 220
20 134
21:25 42

1 Samuel

4 109, 216
7:10 161
8 49
14–15 134n3
15 113n36
15:23–24 130
17:26 81
26:19–20 101

2 Samuel

2:12 149
5:24 99
12:13 130
19:21 130
21 155
22:15 161
24:17 130

1 Kings

9:15–16 211n30
16:34 118
18:21–22 264

18:31–32 89
20:28–30 110
20:42 113n36
21:3 43
22:19 99

2 Kings

1:10 19
1:12 19
5:15–19 101
23:21–23 97

2 Chronicles

20:1–34 102

Nehemiah

9:23–25 14
9:36–37 14

Psalms

20:7 176
37 44
37:9 44
37:11 44
42:3 81
42:9 81
44:3 29
78 230
78:55 29
80:9 29
84:3 81
103:21 99
106:34–40 254–55
110:1 166n1

Isaiah

41:8–9 30
42:2 30
43:10 30
44:1–2 30
45:4 30
49:6–7 30

Jeremiah

7:12 215
31:33 xv

Hosea

2:1 81
11:8 112
11:8–9 70

Amos

2:9 29
3:2 269
5:15 71

New Testament

Matthew

1:21 13n21
5:5 44
6:24 36
6:33 105
17:20 162
25:41 174
27:25 8
27:65–66 166–67

Mark

1:23–24 92
1:24 91
3:14–19 92
3:27 173
4:41 163
8:34 278
10:42–44 168
10:42–45 278
10:45 49, 168
11:12–14 256
11:15–17 256
11:20–21 256
14:27–31 268
16:8 251

Luke

1:50–53 44–45
1:51–55 175
1:72–75 118
3:8–9 20
3:17 123
13:35 8
17:6 162

John

5:46 62
6:15 171
12:28 19

Acts

1:6 212
7:45 13n21
13:19 13n21

Romans

1:5 50
1:17 136
2:15 37
2:29 38
5:1–12 272
6:1 263
6:12–14 263
8:19–23 45
8:28 267
11 47
11:1–2 210
11:17–24 260
11:26 210
11:32 48, 268
12:9 71
12:19 186
12:21 187
15:4 48, 281
16:20 57
16:26 50

1 Corinthians

1:10 243
5:4–6 122
5:7–8 95
6:11 95
6:20 278
8:4 271
10:20 271
11:18 95
11:18–22 95
11:27–31 95
15 166n1
15:24–25 167

2 Corinthians

5:21 274

Galatians

1:8–9 248
3:13 141
3:26–28 18, 47
4:9 264
5:4 256
5:24 271
6:15 34
6:15–16 18, 48
6:16 34

Ephesians

6:12 77, 169
6:17 36

Philippians

2 222
2:8–9 88
2:9 275

Colossians

2:14–15 135

1 Thessalonians

1:9–10 186
4:17 78

Hebrews

4:8 13n21
11:30–31 13n21

James

1:22 208

Revelation

13:21–22 198
20 186
21:3–4 197

AUTHOR INDEX

Adkins, Brent, 117n47

Agamben, Giorgio, 11n14, 29n64, 116

Ambrose, 227

Armstrong, Karen, 5n1

Athanasius, 113, 157

Augustine, xiii, xv, 100n43, 123n14, 238

Barth, Karl, 127n29, 193, 276

Bayer, Oswald, 269n44

Benne, Robert, 6n2

Berry, Wendell, 185, 216n5

Bonhoeffer, Dietrich, 1–2, 68, 116, 218–19, 263

Boone, Catherine, 44n104

Boyd, Gregory A., 24–25

Braiterman, Zachary, 31, 282–84

Brueggemann, Walter, 70–71, 84, 278

Burke, Edmund, 43

Butler, Trent C., 7n6, 10, 13–14

Calvin, John, 37, 49–50, 55, 58–59, 64–65,
    66–67, 69, 72, 79–80, 81n27, 82n32, 83n34,
    86–87, 91, 92, 93–94, 97–98, 100, 105n15,
    106–7, 112, 117, 122, 123–24, 125–26,
    126n25, 130, 131–32, 141, 149–50,
    152, 154n30, 156, 161n13, 162, 166–67,
    176–77, 180–81, 200–201, 204n2, 205–8,
    211, 215, 217, 219–20, 222, 227–28, 229,
    231, 232–33, 241–42, 244, 245n18, 247,
    248n28, 249, 254, 259n27, 261–62, 266

Davis, Ellen F., 42–44

Dawkins, Richard, 12

Delaney, Dave, 21n40, 240n6

De-Malach, Naomi, 283

Dor, Yonina, 283

Douglas, Ann, 103n7

Dozeman, Thomas B., 29n63, 32–33, 54n1,
    64nn1–2, 67n11, 69n17, 70, 73n29, 75n31,
    76nn3–4, 78n11, 78n14, 79n18, 80n25, 81,
    82n30, 86nn44–45, 87nn47–48, 89n60,
    93n11, 94n17, 97n25, 98n30, 99–100,
    104nn8–9, 109–10, 115nn41–42, 120n2,
    121, 126n27, 128n30, 129n32, 131n40,
    131n42, 135n4, 135n6, 137, 139n19,
    140n25, 140n27, 141n31, 146n9, 151nn9–
    10, 152n18, 156n36, 159n5, 163, 166n1,
    174n8, 175n11, 178n21, 180n4, 182n1,
    183n2, 184n5, 184n7, 187n12

Earl, Douglas S., 11–12

Edwards, Jonathan, 239, 256–57

Fackenheim, Emil, 270

Francis, Pope, 168

Haleem, Harfiyah, 30n68

Hawk, L. Daniel, 5, 11n15, 25, 56n9, 58n13, 59,
    61n3, 62, 64n3, 65n5, 76n5, 83nn35–36,
    84n39, 87nn50–51, 88n55, 89n57, 90n61,

92nn7–9, 94nn14–15, 96n23, 97n26,
98n33, 99n35, 99n38, 102n1, 107n18,
108n22, 110n27, 113n35, 113n37, 118–19,
120nn1–2, 121n4, 122n10, 124n16, 125,
126n26, 129nn34–35, 130n38, 132n43,
136n12, 138, 139n18, 139n21, 140n28,
144n1, 144n4, 145n7, 147n17, 152n14,
152n20, 153n22, 154n29, 155n33,
156nn37–38, 160n9, 162n15, 162n17,
163n25, 165n31, 168n5, 170n11, 175n12,
176n13, 177nn17–18, 178n20, 179n1,
182n2, 184n6, 191n1, 194, 196n2, 200n3,
202n2, 202n4, 203n5, 207nn11–12,
210nn24–25, 211n27, 211n29, 212, 213n37,
220n19, 221nn22–23, 224n3, 229n2,
230nn3–4, 232n1, 233, 241n8, 244n16,
245n17, 245n19, 246n24, 246nn21–22,
249n30, 250n1, 250n3, 252nn8–9, 255n17,
256nn18–19, 257nn22–23, 258, 260,
262n31, 264n34, 266n38, 272n48, 279
Heschel, Abraham Joshua, 40
Hütter, Reinhard, 208n16

Irenaeus, xi–xii, 284–85

Jenson, Robert W., 2n3, 6–8, 9, 239n4, 278n14
Jobes, Karen H., 16n29
John of Damascus, 86
Jowett, Benjamin, xii–xiii

Kelsey, David, 17
King, Martin Luther, Jr., 118–19
Kirk-Duggan, Cheryl, 16n30

Lactantius, 54
Levine, Baruch A., 54n2
Lilla, Mark, 28n61
Lindbeck, George A., 17
Lubac, Henri de, 7n5
Luther, Martin, xiii, 36–40, 84n37, 116, 173,
253, 268–69

Malysz, Piotr J., 225n6
Marcus, Joel, 92n3

Martyn, J. Louis, 14n23, 182n3, 274n4
McClymond, Michael J., 239n5, 257n20
McDermott, Gerald R., 5n2, 239n5, 257n20
McIntyre, Alasdair, 26
Milgrom, Jacob, 19
Morse, Christopher, 6n3, 143n37, 255n15
Mouw, Richard J., 25n52
Müntzer, Thomas, 22, 32, 37, 173, 274

Nelson, Richard D., 16, 18, 28, 33n75, 42,
49–50, 54n1, 56n7, 57n11, 59n15, 70n18,
76nn1–2, 78n13, 81n29, 82n31, 82n33,
84n38, 85n40, 87n52, 88n56, 90n62, 92n5,
97n27, 98, 99n40, 101n46, 105n14, 109n23,
112n30, 113n36, 115n44, 116n45, 118n49,
121n3, 121nn7–8, 130n36, 134nn1–2,
139n20, 139n23, 141n29, 144n2, 145,
146n11, 149n2, 150n8, 151nn11–12,
152n17, 152n19, 152n21, 155n32, 158n1,
159, 162n16, 163nn26–27, 167, 171n13,
172n1, 176n15, 178n23, 183n1, 184n4,
185n9, 187n11, 192nn2–3, 195n9, 196n1,
199–200, 200n2, 202n3, 203n6, 206nn7–8,
207n10, 210n21, 210n23, 210n26, 211n28,
211n31, 212, 213–14, 215n2, 215n4,
216n8, 218n11, 219nn15–16, 220n18,
220n21, 222n24, 223, 225nn7–8, 227n11,
230nn5–7, 233n3, 241n9, 242n13, 246n23,
247n25, 247n27, 248n28, 249n29, 250n2,
250n4, 251nn5–7, 252n8, 253n10, 257n21,
262n32, 266n36, 267, 270n45, 271n47
Nemesius of Emesa, 164
Niebuhr, H. Richard, 158–59
Nirenberg, David, 279, 285
Noth, Martin, 162n19

Ochs, Peter, 193n7, 281
Origen, xi, 8, 48–49, 54, 55, 57, 62, 66, 68, 74,
77–78, 80, 95–96, 99, 102–5, 127, 135–36,
142–43, 147n14, 153–54, 161, 169–70,
173–74, 181, 192, 197–98, 203, 209, 212,
217–18, 221, 265, 284–85

Pitkänen, Pekka M. A., 27, 33n76, 60n1,
61n2, 70n20, 77n6, 80n26, 85n42, 88n54,

89nn58–59, 92, 97n27, 102n2, 108nn20–
21, 109n25, 114n40, 122n9, 124n17,
129n33, 134n3, 141n32, 141n33, 147n16,
147n18, 151n11, 154n28, 163n21, 170n12,
174n9, 178n22, 179, 185n10, 193n6,
199n1, 200n4, 202n1, 204n1, 204n3,
205n5, 209n20, 212n34, 215n3, 216nn6–7,
219n17, 224n2, 225n5, 226n9, 227n10,
227n12, 230n5, 237nn1–2, 242n14,
245n20, 247n25, 266n37
Prudentius, 131

Rad, Gerhard von. See von Rad, Gerhard
Rösel, Harmut N., 15nn27–28, 16n29, 49–50,
56n10, 71n23, 79n19, 85n41, 88n53, 91n1,
97n25, 98n32, 99n39, 99nn36–37, 101n45,
105nnn13–14, 108n20, 109n24, 110,
114n39, 115n42, 120n2, 122n11, 124nn18–
19, 126n24, 128n31, 134n3, 135n5, 137,
139n17, 139n22, 139n24, 140n26, 144n3,
145n8, 146n10, 147n15, 147nn12–13, 149,
150n7, 151n13, 152n16, 152n18, 153n23,
154n27, 155n31, 156n35, 157n39, 158n2,
160n8, 160n10, 161n11, 161n14, 163n23,
165n30
Royce, Josiah, 131n39
Rubenstein, Richard, 32n72, 282–84

Seevers, Boyd, 93n12
Seibert, Eric A., 25–26
Silva, Moisés, 16n29
Simons, Menno, 22–24, 143

Smith, Ted A., 40n93
Soulen, R. Kendall, 275–76
Stahl, Titus, 25n54
Steigmann-Gall, Richard, 142
Stendahl, Krister, 225n4
Strawn, Brent A., 1n2, 26–27, 40–41
Stubbs, David L., 78, 96n22, 208

Thiemann, Ronald, 6n3
Thiessen, Gerd, 164
Thompson, Deanna A., 34
Tillich, Paul, 103

Voltaire, 262
von Rad, Gerhard, 21–22, 27, 30n69, 240n7

Waltke, Bruce K., 283n20
Walton, J. Harvey, 29n63, 72–73, 113
Walton, John H., 29n63, 72–73, 113, 159,
183n3
Weinfeld, Moshe, 29–30
Wilkie, Christina, 168n6
Work, Telford, 35–36
Wyschogrod, Michael, 4, 9, 15, 17–18, 26,
31n71, 39–40, 43, 45–46, 56, 61, 69,
71nn24–25, 106, 123n13, 136, 147–48,
174, 210, 255, 258, 268, 273–75

Yoder, John Howard, 22, 24, 265

Zegler, Philip G., 142n36, 277–7

SUBJECT INDEX

Abihu and Nadab (sons of Aaron), 19
Abraham, election of, 261–62
abuse, sexual, 123–24
access, epistemology of, 13–15
accommodation, cultural, 110–12
Achan, 65, 114, 120–33, 245
Achsah, 206–7
activism, faith and, 208, 240–41
Adonizedek, 160
affections, religious, 239, 256–57
agape, 268–69. *See also* love
agency, Joshua's, 57–59
agriculture, land and, 42–44
Ai, city of, 124–33, 134–43
alien work, God's, 269
already, the. *See* promise
altars, rules concerning, 146–47, 242, 244–49
ambiguity, moral, 224
ambush, deception and, 137–40
Anakim, the, 182, 202–3
anger, love and, 71
"Anti-Leviathan," Joshua as, 195
antinomianism, 9
apocalyptic, 4, 46, 176
apophatism, 276
apportionment, land. *See* distribution, land
ark of the covenant, the, 76–88, 109–11, 216
Armageddon, Merom and, 175–76

Asher, inheritance of, 220
asylum, cities of, 225, 227–28
attributes, exchange of, 161–63

ban, the. See *ḥerem*
baptism, circumcision and, 95–96
Barmen Declaration, 142
becoming, double, 203
benefits, faith with, 126–27
Benjamin, inheritance of, 219–20
blitzkrieg, Joshua and, 170–71
blood, redemption of, 226–28
bloodguilt libel, the, 270
booty, 33, 113–14, 131–32, 136–37, 242
boundaries, inclusion and, 168–69

Caleb the Kenite, 202–3, 206–7
Canaan, possession of, 41–46
canon, the, 13–16
capital punishment, modern, 226
catechesis, 86–87
cattle, *ḥerem* and, 137
causality, double. *See* compatibilism, theological
character, God's, 16–18, 21–29, 33–41, 255
cheap grace, 263–64
chiliasm, 212, 274
choice, election and, 262–63

Christ. *See* Jesus Christ
Christianity, Judaism and, 273–85
Christus victor, 48–49, 135–36
church, unity of, 243
circumcision, election and, 92–98
Cisjordan, 199–200, 241–46
cities, Levitical, 225, 227–31
claim, territorial, 56
clergy sexual abuse, 123–24
clinging, love as, 253
coexistence, religious, 273–85
coherence, dramatic, 6
collective, guilt as, 245–46
collective, Israel as, 60–61, 121–24
colonialism, Israel and, 185–86
commissioning, Joshua's, 53–59
communication of idioms, 161–63
community, 18–19, 127–28, 130–31, 209, 245–46
compatibilism, theological, 138–39, 160–61, 258–59
confession, creedal, 247–48
consumerism, religious, 126–27
consummation, eschatological, 174
contradictions, biblical, 10–16
coram Deo, 124–25
counting, literary use of, 184
courage, fear and, 88
covenant, 56, 144–48, 154–57, 250–52, 271–72
covetousness, 131–32, 238–39
creation, 78, 81–82, 268–69
creed, confession and, 247–48
criminal justice, modern, 226
cross, the, 24–25, 277–78
cult, identity and, 72–73
culture, accommodation and, 110–12
cutting off, imagery of, 86

Dan, inheritance of, 220–21
darkness, metaphor of, 23
daughters, inheritance and, 212–13
deception, warfare and, 106–7, 137–40, 152
deliteralization, 4
desire, idolatry and, 239, 254, 271

despair, sin of, 208, 266
devoted things. See *ḥerem*
Dinah, Shechem and, 93
dispossessed, the, 192–93, 269–70, 278
disputes, land, 206–7
distribution, land, 199–200, 206–22, 232–33
divisions, church, xvi
doctrine, interpretation and, xii–xvii
double becoming, 203
double causality. *See* compatibilism, theological
dramatic coherence, 6

eastern tribes, Israelite, 60–63
Ebal, Mount, 144–45
ecumenism, interpretation and, xvi
Egypt, 97, 186
elasticity, borders and, 168–69
Eleazar the priest, 199–200
election, 92–96, 261–69, 273
engraving, idolatry and, 85, 146–47
Ephraim, inheritance of, 210–11
epistemology. *See* knowledge
eschatology, realized, 136. *See also* promise
Eucharist, 95
example, punishment as, 123–24, 132–33
exchange, attribute, 161–63
exile, the, 14–16, 204
exodus, the, 80–83, 186

fabulous, the, 3–4, 110–11, 163–65, 175
faith
    obedience and, 55–56, 117–19, 208, 261–69
    power of, 161–62
    rule of, xii–xvii, 18–19, 47–50
falsehood, law and, 67
farewells, Joshua's, 250–72
fear, 88, 91–92, 104
feet, symbolism of, 89
fiat, divine, 136–37
figural reading, 26–28. *See also* literary reading
foreskins, hill of, 93

genocide, scripture and, 25–26
Gentiles. *See* nations, the

Gerizim, Mount, 144–45
German Christian party, 18, 141, 219, 280
giants, Anakim as, 182
Gibeath-haaraloth, 93
Gibeonites, 149–57, 160–62
Gilead, 213
Gilgal, 89, 97
gnosticism, 284–85
God. *See* YHWH
gospel (message), 68
grace, 103–4, 261–69. See also *ḥesed*
gratitude, obedience and, 56
grave-memorial, Canaanite royalty, 167–69
graven images, 85–86
guilt, collective, 121–24, 245–46

hands, symbolism of, 140
hanging, execution by, 141
hardened, hearts as, 179–81
Hazor, 173, 175, 177–78, 220
hearts, hardening of, 179–81
Hebron, 203
ḥerem
   ambiguity and, 224
   booty and, 33, 121, 137
   identity and, 72–73, 113–18, 239, 260
   judgment and, 19–20, 112–13, 253–56
   messianism and, 172–78, 186–88
   monotheism and, 69–70
   nature of, 3, 29–41
   Rahab and, 64–66, 113–16
   variability of, 121, 136–37, 178
hermeneutics. *See* literary reading
ḥesed
   ambiguity and, 224
   law and, 97–98, 261–69
   Rahab and, 67–68, 70–72, 116
high priest, 227
history, 9–10, 15–16, 172–74, 178–81, 282–83
holiness, 19, 80, 267–69
Holocaust, 31–32, 141–43, 270, 279–85
Holy Spirit, 12–13
holy war, 21–22, 27–28
hospitality, Eucharistic, 95

humanization, God's, 255
hyperbole, 57, 175

iconic, ark as, 109–11
iconoclasm, 180, 248n28
identity
   coexistence and, 273–85
   ḥerem and, 72–73, 113–18, 141–43, 187–88
   unity and, 237–49, 258–60
ideology, religious, 33–41, 263
idioms, communication of, 161–63
idolatry, 85–86, 238–39, 249, 254, 270–71
images, graven, 85–86
inclusion, boundaries and, 168–69
indicative, imperative and, 57, 59, 117
individualism, guilt and, 121–24
inheritance, land and, 41–46, 108, 194–98, 199
   daughters and, 212–13
injustice, racial, 226
intermarriage, *ḥerem* and, 137
interpretation. *See* literary reading
Israel, wholeness of, 55–56, 60–61, 121–24,
   237–49
Issachar, inheritance of, 220

Jabin, king, 173, 175, 177–78
Jashar, Book of, 162–63
jealousy, God's, 267–69
Jebusites, 146, 207–10
Jericho, 68, 98–99, 102–19
Jerusalem, 146, 160, 207–10, 219
Jesus Christ
   the law and, 54–55, 62–63
   messianism and, 7–9, 21–29, 45–50
   prefiguring of, 167, 276–77
   warfare and, 36–41, 135–36
Jordan River, crossing of, 68, 76–90
Joseph, inheritance of, 210–14
Joshua, inheritance of, 221–22
Josiah, King, 5n1
Jubilee, Year of, 107–8
Judah, inheritance of, 204–14
Judaism, 7–9, 17–18, 273–85
judgment, 19–20, 41, 174
justice, sanctuary and, 223–28

killing, unintentional, 223–28
kings
    herem and, 140–41, 159, 166–81
    land and, 194
    YHWH and, 66–68, 91–92, 183–88
knowledge, 13–15, 16–21, 33–41, 104–5,
    256–57

land, the
    claim to, 56–57, 108, 167–68, 183–88, 273–74
    distribution of, 199–200, 206–22, 232–33
    loss of, 14–16, 41–46, 191–95, 204, 269–70
    subdued, 215–16
land grant narrative, 199
law, the
    ambiguity and, 17–18, 224, 242
    Christianity and, 9, 36–41
    hesed and, 116–17, 261–68
    ritual and, 144–48
    succession and, 54–55, 58–59
    warfare and, 58–59, 88, 94–95
lazy, Israel as. *See* sloth, sin of
leadership, Joshua's, 259
Levites, the, 194–201, 225, 227–31
lex talionis, 226–28
libel, bloodguilt, 270
literalism, biblical, 3–4, 6, 9–16, 172–74
literary reading, 2–16, 26–28, 193–94
liturgy, 76–90, 102–19
livestock, *herem* and, 137
lot, distribution by, 200, 205–6, 215–22
love, 253–57, 267–69
lying, law and, 67

Makkedah, 169
malice, conquest of, 77
Manasseh, inheritance of, 210–14, 243–44
man of Israel, the, 152–53
manslaughter, sanctuary and, 223–28
Marcion, 41
marriage, 137, 253, 255–57
Masoretic Text, 16n29
meeting, tent of, 215
memory, identity and, 83–90

Merom, waters of, 175–77
messianism, 45–50, 158–65, 172–74, 273–74,
    277–78. *See also* Jesus Christ; servant of
    YHWH, title of
metals, precious, 114
ministry, Levitical, 196–98
miracles. *See* fabulous, the
modernity, xii–xiii, xv–xvii, 28–29
monotheism, 5n1, 28–29, 69–70, 81–82
monuments, memorial, 85–87
moral ambiguity, 224
Moses, 53–59
murder, sanctuary and, 223–28
myth. *See* fabulous, the

Naboth, 43
Nadab and Abihu (sons of Aaron), 19
nakhalah. *See* inheritance, land and
name, God's, 274–79
Naphtali, inheritance of, 220
narrative, 2–4, 6–7
nations, the, 84, 259–60
Nazis, the, 141–43, 279–80
Nicene tradition, xiv–xvii
noncombatants, slaughter of, 112–13
normative Judaism, 280–81
northern kings, Canaanite, 172–78
not yet, the. *See* promise
noun, *herem* as, 121

obedience
    compatibilism and, 161
    faith and, 55–56, 117–19, 251–55, 261–69
    reciprocity and, 61–62
occupation, land and, 184–85. *See also* land, the
"one," repetition of, 184
Othniel, 206–7
ought, moral, 117
ownership, land, 184–85, 194–95, 199. *See also*
    land, the

paraphrase, biblical, 2
Passover, 74, 89, 94–95, 97–98
pathos, God's, 255

patriarchy, inheritance and, 213

people, Israel as, 84

person, God as, 16–18, 21–29, 33–41, 255

Peter (apostle), 268

pharisaic Judaism, 7–8, 17–18, 280–81

Phineas, 245, 248–49

pollution, sin as, 128

poor, the, 71–72

possession, land and, 184–85, 191–95, 199, 269–70. *See also* land, the

postliberal theology, 193–94

postmodernity, xiii, xv–xvii

prayer, petitionary, 126–27

precious metals, 114

predicates, exchange of, 161–63

premillennialism, 283n20

presence, God's, 57

presentism, theological, 111–12, 240–41

prince of the army of YHWH, 99–101

procreation, circumcision and, 94

profanation, YHWH and, 278–79

progressive revelation, 111–12

promise, 2, 6–7, 174, 176, 232–33

property. *See* ownership, land

prostitution, 65–66, 71–72

P source, 54n2

punishment, exemplary, 123–24, 132–33

purity, politics of. See *ḥerem*; identity

rabbinic Judaism, 7–8, 17–18, 280–81

race, injustice and, 226

Rahab, 64–75, 95, 113–18, 120–21

realized eschatology, 135–36

reasoning, scriptural, 281

reciprocity, obedience and, 61–62

reconciliation, politics of. *See* Jesus Christ; messianism

refuge, cities of, 225, 227–28

repetition, literary, 176, 184

rest, 57, 60–61, 172–78, 243

retribution, law of, 226–28

revelation, progressive, 111–12

revulsion, theological, 112–13

robe of Shinar, 132

rule of faith, xii–xvii, 18–19, 47–50

sacrifice, altar and, 248

sacrilege, 121

salvation, history of, 111–12

sanctification, 92–93, 129–30

sanctuary, judgment and, 223–28

scripture, appropriation of, 279–85

second circumcision, 96

secrecy, obedience and, 64–65, 123–24

self, human, 124–25

self-dispossession, Christian, 278

separation, ritual, 129–30

Septuagint, 16n29

servant of YHWH, title of, 53–54, 100, 264–65, 272. *See also* messianism

settled, land as, 216

seven, symbolism of, 107, 110

sex, obedience and, 65–66

sexual abuse, clergy, 123–24

Shechem, 93, 146, 271–72

Shema, 242

Shiloh, 215–22, 242

Shinar, robe of, 132

shofar. *See* trumpets, symbolism of

Simeon, inheritance of, 220

sin

    community and, 127–28, 130–31, 209, 245–46

    covetousness and, 131–32, 238–39

    grace and, 263–64

    warfare and, 106–7, 208

slavery, 113–15, 153–57, 211–12

sloth, sin of, 208, 217, 241–42

sons of Israel, 244–45

southern kings, 166–71

sovereignty, God's, 41–46, 80–83, 180–81, 183–88, 261–69

spear, Joshua's, 140

speeches, Joshua's, 250–72

spies, Israelite, 64–75, 115, 124

Spirit, Holy, 12–13

spiritual meaning. *See* literary reading

stones, memorial, 85–87

striving, Israel's, 55–56

subdued, land as, 215–16

subjectivity, interpretation and, 46–47

succession, Joshua's, 53–59

sun and moon, command of, 161–65
supersessionism, 8
synergy, compatibilism and, 161–63

temple, the, 274, 280
tensions, narrative, 10–16
tent of meeting, 215
territory. *See* land, the
tests, epistemological, 16–21
Tetragrammaton, 274–79
theology, task of, 197–98
theophany, 80–83, 98–101
Torah. *See* law, the
tradition, doctrinal, xii–xvii
transcendence, theophany and, 81–82
Transjordan, 196–98, 241–46
treasury, YHWH's, 114
trickster, Rahab as, 67–68, 70
triumphalism, Christian, 7–9
trumpets, symbolism of, 104, 107–9
typology. *See* figural reading

unconquered, Canaan as, 191–95, 200
unity, Israelite, 237–49, 258–60. *See also*
    identity
Ur-Joshua, 13n21
usurpation, land and, 41–46. *See also* sovereignty,
    God's

value, human, 226–28
vassalage, 100, 153–57
vengeance, sanctuary from, 223–28
vineyard, Naboth's, 43
violence. *See* warfare
vulnerability, divine, 255

warfare, 7, 21–29, 57–59, 172–78. See also
    ḥerem
wilderness, the, 96
works, faith and, 208
worship, 196–98, 242–46
wrath, God's, 40–41, 186–87, 269, 278. See also
    ḥerem; judgment

YHWH
    character of, 16–18, 21–29, 33–41, 255
    the fabulous and, 163–65
    ḥesed and, 70–71
    identity and, 246–49, 258–60
    name of, 274–79
    sovereignty of, 66–68, 80–83, 91–92, 261–69
    warfare and, 98–101, 106–7

Zebulun, inheritance of, 220
Zelophehad, daughters of, 212–13
Zionism, 5n2, 210, 212, 283–84